Advanced Praise for Global Information Technology Outsourcing

'Lacity and Willcocks have shown us again why they are the world's leading IT outsourcing gurus. They continue to give us comprehensive research and perceptive observations that are required reading for anyone managing IT, irrespective of outsourcing. Their use of the narrative to provide us with the outsourcing experiences of early adopters is done with flair, delivering complex concepts with clarity and insight . . . the most comprehensive work on IT outsourcing to date.' *Sara Cullen, National Partner, Australia Business Process Management, Deloitte Touche, Tohmatsu*

'Mary Lacity and Leslie Willcocks have delivered a valuable collection of relevant facts to anyone who is deliberating whether to subcontract part or all of a firm's information technology to an "outsourcing" services organization. The readers will find here most of the advice that premier consultants would deliver for a very large multiple of the price of this book. The scope of this work and the actionable recommendations are as comprehensive and as complete as anything presently available from any public source.' *Paul A. Strassmann, former CIO of General Foods, Kraft, Xerox and the US Department of Defense*

'A book that fits the often used phrase of "must read" for anyone that is in search of a clear understanding of what information technology outsourcing is all about. Anyone, particularly executive managers beginning at the CEO level who are searching for the most efficient methods of exploiting the advantages of information technology, should read this book and make it mandatory reading for their subordinates.

Absolutely no one should jump into outsourcing prior to taking advantage of the outstanding case studies outlined in this book.' *Emmett Paige, President, OAO Corporation*

'I once asked the CEO of a leading Australian company how he rated the information technology capability of his firm both before and after (what was at that time) a landmark outsourcing deal. He gave it a 5 out of 10 rating before the deal and exactly the same rating five years on. His response plays to one of the consistent themes of this book – outsourcing IT is not a quick fix panacea. It should be undertaken intelligently and selectively with realistic objectives, clearly articulated expectations of performance by both parties and

ideally some sharing of risk and rewards. Leslie Willcocks and Mary Lacity have produced an excellent guide to sensible and successful outsourcing, the best I have read on the topic. It should be mandatory reading for any senior executive who is a consumer or provider of IT services.'
Gail Burke, Executive Director & CIO, Macquarie Bank, Australia

'Provides a comprehensive treatment of what has become a huge subject. Yet the style is crisp and concise ... with lots of illuminating anecdotes and examples underlying the deeply thought general principles and taxonomy. The studies selected for detailed presentation are excellent and the analysis points up the problems as well as the successes in a way that rings with credibility.' *Rob Westcott, Vice President and CIO, General Motors Acceptance Corporation International Operations, UK*

'The IT revolution is still very young ... the start of its journey from aggressive "box and software" marketing to customer-responsive service delivery has been a significant feature of the last decade and much of the learning ... has been developed in ... IT outsourcing.
Lacity and Willcocks have ... unrivalled access to a diverse array of outsourcing deals across the globe, and ... have established themselves as serious and critical observers of evolving practice ... their new book ... is a powerful synthesis of their learning (and) is presented with a clear emphasis on the practical ... A book that business leaders should read. Their chapter on risk management is a groundbreaking contribution to a ... neglected aspect of sourcing practice (and) their central chapters provide a rich analysis of best practice in melding the management of IT into the fabric of modern enterprise ... A vitally important business guide as IT "outsourcing" decisions become IT "sourcing" decisions, and as the "e-economy" brings the rapid growth of virtual corporations and integrated supply chains assembled with purchased services.' *Richard Sykes, Chairman Morgan Chambers plc. − Europe's largest independent consultancy in IT services & business process sourcing*

'Lacity and Willcocks tell it like it is and pull no punches. A "must read" for any organization contemplating outsourcing or trying to fix a broken outsourcing relationship. The reader learns what has and hasn't worked through case studies of several high profile outsourcing deals around the globe − from Australia to the UK to the US. Planning for outsourcing, negotiating the deal, making the relationship work − it's all here.' *Bob Young, Executive Director, South Australian Government Account, EDS (Electronic Data Systems)*

'For those of us with a deep knowledge and experience of outsourcing, this book is required reading. For those who are just starting out on the journey, it is essential reading − it has the potential to save you much time, grief and money (in that order)!'
Robert White, CEO, Lucidus Management Technologies

Global Information Technology Outsourcing

Global Information Technology Outsourcing

In Search of Business Advantage

Dr. Mary C. Lacity
University of Missouri, USA

and

Dr. Leslie P. Willcocks
University of Oxford, UK

JOHN WILEY & SONS, LTD
Chichester • New York • Weinheim • Brisbane • Singapore • Toronto

Reprinted May 2001

Other Wiley Editorial Offices

John Wiley & Sons, Inc., 605 Third Avenue,
New York, NY 10158-0012, USA

WILEY-VCH GmbH, Pappelallee 3
D-69469 Weinheim, Germany

John Wiley & Sons Ltd, 33 Park Road, Milton,
Queensland 4064, Australia

John Wiley & Sons (Asia) Pte Ltd, 2 Clementi Loop #02-01,
Jin Xing Distripark, Singapore 129809

John Wiley & Sons (Canada) Ltd, 22 Worcester Road,
Rexdale, Ontario M9W 1L1, Canada

British Library Cataloguing in Publication Data

A catalogue record for this book is available from the British Library

ISBN 0-471-89959-3

Typeset in 11/12pt Palatino by C.K.M. Typesetting, Salisbury, Wiltshire
Printed and bound in Great Britain by Biddles Ltd, Guildford and King's Lynn
This book is printed on acid-free paper responsibly manufactured from sustainable forestry, in which at least two trees are planted for each one used for paper production.

Contents

Acknowledgments

Two colleagues were invaluable co-authors on chapters of this book:

David Feeny, Director of the Oxford Institute of Information Management Templeton College, Oxford University, made major contributions to Chapters 7 and 8. In particular, David Feeny and Leslie Willcocks were the creators of the nine core IT capabilities model, which has been successfully adopted by several international organizations. David is a widely-sought-after internationally known speaker and consultant on information strategy and management. His research on CEO and CIO relationships has won international awards. He has published widely, including the book *Managing IT as a Strategic Resource* (McGraw-Hill, 1997), and articles in the *Harvard Business Review, Sloan Management Review, MIS Quarterly,* and *McKinsey Quarterly.*

Thomas Kern is Assistant Professor in Information Management at Erasmus Universiteit, Rotterdam, and completed his doctorate at Christchurch, Oxford University. He is co-author of two of the in-depth case studies presented in Chapter 4—British Aerospace and Inland Revenue. Thomas Kern's major work has been into relationships in IT outsourcing, the subject of his doctorate. He has published widely on this theme in journals such as *Information Systems Journal, Journal of Strategic Information Systems,* and *Journal of Global Information Management.* He is co-authoring a forthcoming book with Leslie Willcocks entitled *The Relationship Advantage* (OUP, 2001).

A number of people are sincerely thanked for enabling us to focus our time on this project. Bud Banis, David Ronen, and Marius Janson from the University of Missouri—St. Louis kindly resumed an extra burden of service on our behalf. Mark Kuban, Michael McDevitt, and Antonina Kelly provided a quiet and supportive writing environment. Special thanks to all at Oxford Institute of Information Management—Pam, Jenny, Chris, David, Sue, Gerd—for making so much possible, and for being such great colleagues, and to all at Templeton for making it the great working place it is. Stephanie has always been superb for morale, and Michael Christopher Kuban delayed the book somewhat but has forever enriched Mary's life, and all those who come in contact with him.

We also wish to acknowledge Wendy Currie and Guy Fitzgerald, Professors at Brunel University, London, and Rudy Hirschheim, Professor at University of Houston, for their participation and contribution to the early phases of this research. This collected body of research was sponsored over many years by many organizations, including the University of Missouri—St. Louis, the Oxford Institute of Information Management, Origin, and Business Intelligence, based in London. Also thanks to all at Wiley, especially Diane Taylor, for seeing the book through to its final form.

Finally, a huge debt is owed to the more than eight hundred participants we interviewed and surveyed, and the many students and executives who listened patiently to our views and evidence, and commented so constructively over the years. In particular, interview participants patiently endured our stream of questions and follow-up phone calls. We would like to thank them individually, but most participants requested anonymity. For those participants who did not wish anonymity, your names are acknowledged in the appropriate places throughout the book. Without you this work would not have been possible. Our heartfelt thanks.

Introduction

Despite the rapid growth in Information Technology (IT) outsourcing—a market predicted to grow to over $US120 billion by the year 2002, and even $US150 billion by 2004—most companies are still seeking the elusive 'added-value' they anticipated. While early deals focused on cost reduction, many organizations in their second or third generation of IT outsourcing are seeking significant business advantage. Customers expect IT outsourcing to dismantle bureaucratic IT organizations, to refinance fixed costs into variable costs, to meet global IT skill shortages, to access industry-specific applications, and even to generate revenue with their IT suppliers. In short, IT outsourcing promises to transform IT functions into lean, dynamic groups that respond quickly to business needs and opportunities. But do customers actually achieve these business advantages? And if so, how?

For the past 10 years, we have conducted in-depth case studies in over 75 organizations by interviewing nearly 300 executives (see Appendix B at www.umsl.edu/~lacity/cases.htm for case study profiles) and throughout the 1990s (1994, 1998, 1999) regularly surveyed outsourcing participants in the United States, the United Kingdom, Australia, Europe, and Japan. In addition, at Oxford Institute of Information Management we have assembled a database of more than 250 organizations and their outsourcing details and experiences. We found that most organizations still achieve modest goals of reducing costs and improving service for a targeted set of discrete IT activities. Such a selective strategy proves to be low risk, and is generally successful. Organizations seeking more radical transformation through mega-outsourcing face greater risks and challenges, but success stories have been found and documented in this book. We document and discuss strategic uses of IT outsourcing, but also the dangers of strategic disadvantage to the business that can result from poorly thought through IT sourcing strategy. Once organizations exhaled safely after their Year 2000 projects proved successful, they have been found experimenting widely with emerging sourcing options available in the e-Economy (see Chapter 9).

While the global economy has changed rapidly with open trade, a more mobile work-force, and most importantly the Internet, certain customer IT goals and objectives have remained astonishingly the same during the past 40 years. Customers want flexible, low-cost, well supported IT products and services to enable business objectives. IT sourcing trends to meet these goals have mirrored underlying shifts in IT cost drivers. During the 1960s, many customers could not afford expensive mainframes and thus sought IT sourcing through time-sharing. During the 1970s and 1980s, the advent of minicomputers and microcomputers drove hardware costs low enough to justify customer ownership and control of IT assets. During the 1990s, the increasing costs of IT software, the global IT skills shortage, and the pressing need for bandwidth, again shifted the economics of IT in favor of packed solutions and outsourced infrastructure.

ERP (enterprise resource planning) software illustrates how shifts in IT cost drivers led to innovations in sourcing. During the early 1990s, companies around the globe were seeking redesigning business processes to radically slash costs and improve service. But this model led to massive and expensive IT projects to enable the redesign. Enter ERP. Rather than redesign business processes first, then build IT to implement the new designs, the ERP model promises that best practices and processes are built into the software—implement the package and change your business processes to fit within ERP's parameters. The latter model promises the benefits of redesign without incurring excessive IT costs.

Most recently, the explosion of the Internet and application service providers (ASP) has again shifted the underlying economics of IT. Why house your own software when an ASP can provide it to you over the Internet for a variable price? We are witnessing the dawn of a new era in the way business-to-business transactions are conducted. Consider procurement. In the past, customers sought strategic sourcing through a set of preferred suppliers, often enabled by fixed network connections for electronic data interchange (EDI) purchasing, invoicing, and payment. With the Internet and ASPs, connections are virtual, allowing customers to bid for nearly every purchase. Besides the revolution in business-to-business transactions, the same drivers are radically changing business-to-customer transactions. Only five years ago we thought consumers would only buy low-cost products and services such as books and clothes over the Internet. Today, consumers are purchasing their most expensive assets online—cars, home mortgages, and insurance.

How can companies use their IT assets—hardware, software, and people—to leverage business performance, or even deliver new business directions, and new business models? And how can the burgeoning external IT services market be leveraged to achieve such business advantage, and harness the opportunities of the rapidly evolving e-Economy? In this book we outline proven, emerging, and innovative practices on IT sourcing. Beginning with the formulation of a strategic sourcing framework, readers are given tools to identify their core IT capabilities, to evaluate emerging market options, to negotiate sound deals to mediate risk, and to ensure that those deals meet expectations through appropriate relationship management.

Readers will learn about the following practices in-depth. We describe proven practices, which are effective practices uncovered by our extensive body of research as differentiating successful sourcing decisions from failures. Proven practices (emerging particularly from Chapters 1, 4, and 8) include:

- the use of a selective sourcing strategy rather than all-or-none outsourcing strategies,
- identifying core IT capabilities to keep in-house,
- identifying non-core IT capabilities for potential outsourcing,
- conducting a rigorous evaluation of market options and supplier offerings,
- clearly defining IT outsourcing expectations and mitigating risk in a contract, and
- implementing post-contract management processes and structures to enable supplier success.

Such practices serve as a foundation for sound sourcing decisions, despite pleas to abandon them. For example, some experts argue that detailed contracts are obsolete within a year or two and thus should be abandoned for a 'partnership' approach. This research has consistently found that detailed contracts are a critical success factor to successful deals. Detailed contracts serve to solidify, document, and disseminate IT outsourcing expectations among stakeholders. Customers and suppliers also learn to resolve conflicts during contract negotiations—activities that are best rehearsed before the deal goes 'live'. Suppliers have repeatedly reported that they can predict how relationships will unfold based on the customer's ability to articulate, negotiate, and resolve issues during contract negotiations—no supplier wants a naive customer.

Emerging practices are practices that are gaining increasing media attention, but for which only preliminary or anecdotal evidence of success and failure currently exists. Emerging practices include business process outsourcing, value-added deals based on business performance, e-sourcing, and application service providers. In several examples, allegedly new practices are really variations on older business models. We noted, for example, that ASPs have been identified as a major emerging trend for the new millenium. But is it new? ASPs use a business model in which a supplier owns and maintains IS assets and disseminates software over the Internet for a variable fee. This business model is identical to the time-sharing model in the 1960s. The difference is that in the 1960s, hardware was the cost driver; today it is software and skills.

Innovative practices are practices successfully used by a few organizations which may or may not be replicated by others. Chapters 2, 3, and 6 document case studies in which customers and suppliers found new ways of partnering and/or implementing innovations to resolve evolving limitations with their exchange-based contracts. For example, the government of South Australia used outsourcing to stimulate the local economy. South Australia (SA) government's $AU600 million, nine-year contract with EDS is distinctive from more traditional outsourcing because one contract is used to govern two distinctive components: one component for the development of South Australia's economy, and one component for IT service provision for 150 South Australian agencies. The economic development package has been a success. EDS has exceeded its yearly targets to meet the overall goal of pumping more than $AU200 million into the South Australian economy during the nine-year relationship. Though there are question marks about other aspects of this arrangement, in 1999/2000 the deal won an international award for best government outsourcing relationship sponsored by the *Outsourcing Journal*.

The book progresses from descriptions of participants' IT sourcing practices and experiences to a set of prescriptive frameworks. Our goal is to clearly demonstrate that frameworks are objectively and empirically derived from participants' successes, failures, and overall lessons. It is our aim to help other practitioners make sound sourcing decisions to enable their businesses to prosper in the new millenium.

1
Global Trends and Practices: An Assessment

'Rather than jumping into outsourcing everything, many companies prefer to start slow'—Tony Macina, Managed Operations, IBM Global Services.

'The belief is, if you give the problem away, the third party will be able to magically make it disappear. This tactic doesn't succeed because the client hasn't invested the time to address the underlying business processes'—Jerry Cooperman, VP of Gartner Group.

Yes, [the supplier] can achieve all the things that were proposed—but where is this famous 'added-value' service? We are not getting anything over-and-above what any old outsourcer could provide—BAe IT Services manager

INTRODUCTION

Many high-profile, IT outsourcing multi-million/multi-billion 'mega-deals' are by now familiar. Companies that have outsourced significant portions of their IT functions by transferring their IT assets, leases, licences, and staff to outsourcing suppliers include British Aerospace, Chase Manhattan Bank, Continental Airlines, Continental Bank, Enron, First City, General Dynamics, Kodak, and McDonnell Douglas (now Boeing). Since these first mega-deals were signed, the outsourcing market has grown in size and scope of services (see Table 1.1). In 1999 there was some slowdown after very rapid growth in 1998, but if there were fewer mega-contracts in 1999, there was an increase in medium-sized deals. Moreover, many we talked to were planning outsourcing, but

Table 1.1   *Size of IT outsourcing market*

Sources	Findings
Caldwell (1995)[1]	The studies performed by Dataquest note that the IT outsourcing market grew from $US9 billion in 1990 to $US28 billion in 1994 representing a growth rate in excess of 25% per annum. Other figures produced by Dataquest suggest even greater growth. According to their research, in 1995 companies spent $US22 billion in the network management and desktop services outsourcing market. They predicted this market to grow to $US37 billion by 1998.
www.infoserver.com	Outsourcing Institute's survey of 1200 companies indicates that 50% of all companies with IT budgets of $US5 million or more are either outsourcing or evaluating the option. They also report that one-twelfth of IT dollars spent in 1995 flowed through an outsourcing contract.
www.infoserver.com	The Yankee Group estimated global revenues for IT outsourcing to be $US50 billion in 1994.
www.infoserver.com	International Data Corporation estimated the global outsourcing market for 1995 at $US76 billion, $US100 billion in 1998, and will exceed $US151 billion by the year 2003.
www.ft.com/ftit/August (1999)	Gartner Group projected a 16.3% growth rate worldwide, and a $US120 billion market by 2002.
www.input.com October (1999)	Input predicted the US market alone would grow to $US110 billion by 2003, reflecting a 22% annual growth rate. 24% of the total represents business process outsourcing, growing at 29% annually.
Lacity and Willcocks (2000b)	Based on prior research and a survey of the US and UK, the report predicts the global IT outsourcing market to exceed $US150 billion in 2004 to include application service provision, business process outsourcing, internet development outsourcing, enterprise resource planning (ERP) sourcing. On average, 30%–35% of organizational IT budgets will be outsourced by that date.

postponing implementation until the Year 2000 (Y2K) threat and other issues had passed.

IT outsourcing not only shows growth across sectors, but also across global regions. The market has been taking off in South America, parts of South East Asia, and Western Europe, all of which have previously resisted the trend. Thus across the 1997–2002 period IDC has predicted annual growth rates of 16% for Asia/Pacific, 20% for Latin America, 8% for Western Europe, 5% for Japan, 14% for Canada, and 26% for the rest of the world.

Most notably, the increased competition in the outsourcing market, and a mounting customer experience base, have afforded customers the leverage to negotiate more favorable/flexible deals. Small suppliers are entering the market by focusing on niches. An example has been Convergent Communications, which targets companies with 25 to 500 desktops. Large suppliers are even differentiating their services to focus on niche markets. For example, in 1997, AT&T Solutions separated its outsourcing unit into three divisions for network building, network management, and consulting. Indeed, there has been some further diversification of the market away from a one-size-fits-all model to 'best of breed' in which specialist suppliers in such areas as desktops, networking, call centers, datacenters and applications management take on their parcels of the IT operations. Sometimes, in big deals, the use of such suppliers is increasingly taking the form of sub-contracting. On our estimates, in such deals, as much as 30%–50% of the work might be sub-contracted in this way. At the same time, e-commerce developments—the need to act speedily and with little expertise to do so, combined with the expanding third party services available—have been pushing the boat out further in terms of what firms are willing to contemplate outsourcing. Thus we will see the rapid development in 2001 of, for example, Web application hosting/application service providers, and business process outsourcing.

This variety and expansion of choice is the good news. But with the environment becoming more muddled with new trends, options, and terms, practitioners are constantly challenged to make sense of the evolving marketplace and IT sourcing practices. Moreover, this is invariably against a background of IT skills shortages. Thus Meta Group estimated that in the United States up to 30% of the 1999 IT workforce comprised outsourced staff, and that the trend was expected to continue to 2003 at least. On their figures for the United States 400 000 IT positions were unfilled in 1999, and this labor gap could increase to 1.2 million by 2003. With IT outsourcing in myriad forms as an option, managers wrestle with difficult questions. What operational efficiencies can we achieve by outsourcing? Are they significant? Does IT outsourcing help us to focus on the business strategy and core capabilities of the firm? Are there proactive, strategic dimensions to IT outsourcing itself, for example gaining access to world class IT or revenue generation from a business alliance with a large supplier? Or can outsourcing result in operational inflexibilities that can actually harm the pursuit of today's market, and strategic inflexibilities and lost opportunities that can actually damage corporate direction and ability to shape the future? In the course of this book we will see examples of all these possibilities. In this chapter, we survey findings on current IT outsourcing practices focusing on the period 1992–2001. (In Chapter 9, 'Future Sourcing', we will also survey further developing trends.) Some of these practices are well-established, and for those we assess the validity of these practices based on prior research and experience. The newer practices are documented, but only time will prove their viability.

In general, survey research indicates that the vast majority of companies are still pursuing a *selective sourcing* strategy by only outsourcing a subset of their IT activities. In particular, *transitional outsourcing*–the temporary handing-over of an IT function to a supplier—has become a viable way to manage the migration from legacy systems to client/server applications. Selective outsourcing has proved generally successful, although the size of these deals warrants less public attention than mega-deals.

In contrast, *total outsourcing* (defined here as outsourcing greater than 80% of the IT operating budget) continues to gain media attention, primarily due to the dollar value of these deals. These early deals were fixed-price, exchange-based, long-term contracts for a baseline set of services. Specifically, suppliers offered to do 'whatever the customer was doing in the baseline year' at 10%–30% less than the customer's baseline budget. Many of these fixed-price, exchange-based, total IT outsourcing deals, however, ran into trouble. Companies often renegotiated their contracts mid-stream or—in extreme cases—terminated them prematurely. Some companies are reconfiguring total outsourcing deals by overcoming the pitfalls of fixed-fee, exchange-based contracts through new types of contracting, including:

1. *Value-added outsourcing*: 'combine customer and supplier strengths to market IT products and services, which creates shared risks and rewards, or to achieve mutually beneficial internal business improvements'.
2. *Equity-holdings*: 'create common goals through joint ownership'.
3. *Multi-sourcing*: 'using multiple suppliers to eliminate monopoly supplier power and achieve advantages of "best-of-breed"'.
4. *Offshore outsourcing: 'cheaper, quicker, better'*: 'sourcing IT abroad, tapping into favourable price differentials, and skill/performance developments'.
5. *Co-sourcing*: 'performance-based contracts, tying supplier payments to business performance'.

6. *Business process outsourcing*: 'outsourcing a process and its IT, identified as "non-core", that a third-party can do at least as well, at competitive price'.
7. *Spin-offs*: 'internal IT departments go solo, empowering IT staff to behave like suppliers'.
8. *Creative contracting*: 'tougher shoppers'—attempts to improve exchange-based contracts'.

Has this added up, by 2001, to what Rita Terdiman, VP of Gartner Group, predicted in 1996?:[2]

> What you are really seeing in the outsourcing world is a major trend towards all sorts of creative alliances. It may or may not always take the form of an equity stake, but certainly there's more skin in the game for both partners.

As we shall see, not quite. Although in many cases it is too soon to assess the viability of these contracting trends, we can comment on levels of success so far, and also present anecdotal evidence from many of the adopters.

SELECTIVE OUTSOURCING

Practice: Selective IT sourcing is the most common practice

Although the large multi-million/billion dollar, long-term deals make headlines, research has systematically unveiled that selective IT out-sourcing is the more common practice. With selective outsourcing, IT is viewed as a portfolio of activities, some of which are owned and managed internally, some of which are outsourced. The following surveys found selective outsourcing as the most common practice:[3]

- In a survey of 300 IT managers in the United States, on average less than 10% of the IT budget was outsourced.
- A survey of 110 *Fortune* 500 companies found that 76% spent less than 20% of the IT budget on outsourcing, and 96% spent less than 40%.
- A survey of 365 US companies found that 65% outsourced one or more IT activities, but only 12 outsourced IT completely.
- A survey by IDC found that 'in the United States, outsourcing takes around 17% share of the IT services market'.
- A survey of 48 US companies identified domestic and global IT sourcing practices of America's most effective IT users, as deter-

mined by *Computerworld's* Premier 100 list.[4] Seventy-seven percent of the respondents outsourced at least one domestic IT function, but outsourcing was generally targeted at select activities such as support operations, training and education, disaster recovery, etc.

Sears, Roebuck, and Co. provides an example of selective outsourcing. Sears formed two contracts, one with ISSC for distributed systems and the helpdesk and one with Advantis (a joint venture between Sears and IBM) for mainframes. Sears focused the new internal IT staff on development of new applications while the IT suppliers managed the 'old world'. In 1996, Don Zimmerman, Senior Systems Director, Sears, said 'The more mundane IS functions we outsource, the better we can leverage our resources.'

Digital Equipment Corporation (DEC) (now owned by Compaq) has signed many selective outsourcing deals with customers. DEC often wins deals against major competitors because of their willingness to support modular outsourcing. Examples of DEC deals include: a five-year contract with Perkin Elmer, a scientific instrument manufacturer, to run the datacenter; a three-year contract with Dow Chemical for help desk operations; and a contract with GE Aircraft for midrange computers. DEC sees such selective outsourcing contracts as entrées to more business once they prove themselves on smaller deals. For example, in 1997 GE aircraft expanded the scope of the DEC contract to include management and support of Oracle operations. DEC-Japan is hoping to emulate this strategy to capture market share in Japan. During 1998 the Japanese financial crises put Japanese corporations in a severe cost-cutting and outsourcing mode.[5] Senior supplier managers have also pointed to this selective trend:

> Piecemeal outsourcing is a trend that's been evolving over the last couple of years. Now, it's the majority of the outsourcing deals you see—Chuck Jarrow, Director of Marketing at CSC, 1997.

> Rather than jumping into outsourcing everything, many companies prefer to start slow—Tony Macina, Managed Operations, IBM Global Services, 1997.

Assessment: Most companies are successful with their selective outsourcing strategies

Sourcing success is defined as meeting expected sourcing objectives. Only a few studies assessed expected outcomes against actual outcomes, but these indicate that selective outsourcing generally meets customer expectations:

- In a 1994 survey of 110 *Fortune* 500 companies, Collins and Millen[6] found that 95% realized increased flexibility, 95% focused in-house staff on IT core competencies, 86% realized personnel cost savings, and 88% improved service.
- Our survey of 1000 US and UK CIOs found that selective outsourcing was successful. In particular, respondents rated overall supplier performance as 'good', respondents mostly realized the benefits they expected from IT outsourcing, and respondents characterized the majority of problems/issues as only 'minor' in nature (see Appendix A for details).
- Lacity and Willcocks (1998) studied 61 sourcing decisions, including total outsourcing, total insourcing, and selective outsourcing. Although there were 15 reasons given for sourcing decisions, cost reduction was the most prevalent (80%), followed by service improvements (59%). We found that 85% of selective outsourcing decisions met customers' expected cost savings, whereas only 29% of total outsourcing decisions and 67% of total insourcing decisions met expected cost savings.

Other surveys did not include a measure of success, but instead asked respondents for expected outcomes. For example, in a survey of 48 US companies on *Computerworld's* Premier 100 list, 90% expected to save money with their sourcing decisions.[7] Other important expectations, in order of rank, included reduced need to hire IT professionals, improved cost predictability, and improved focus on strategic use of IT.

Why is selective outsourcing successful? Information technology spans a variety of activities in terms of business contribution, integration with existing processes, and level of technical maturity. Such diversity demands tailored solutions. Typically, no one supplier or internal IT department possesses the experience and economies of scale to perform all IT activities most effectively. While some activities, especially stable IT activities with known requirements, may be easily outsourced, other IT activities require much management attention, protection, and nurturing to ensure business success.

Practice: The types of IT services most commonly outsourced are infrastructure and support IT activities.

Surveys indicate that the types of services most commonly outsourced are programming, mainframe operations, education and training, PC maintenance, disaster recovery, and data entry. Although surveys rank-order the most commonly outsourced IT activities differently (see Table 1.2), these same activities surface again and again. No surveys

Table 1.2   *Global surveys on IT outsourcing*

Author(s)	Survey	The most commonly outsourced IT functions were:	
Arnett and Jones (1994)[9]	Survey of 40 US CIOs	Contract programming (67%) Mini/mainframe maintenance (67%) Software support and training (56%) Workstation/PC maintenance (39%) Systems integration (28%).	
Collins and Millen (1995)	Survey of 110 US companies	Education and training (50%) PC support (49%) Network services (33%) Applications development (33%) Application maintenance (26%) Datacenters (24%)	
Dekleva (1994)	Survey of 365 CIOs and CFOs	Software maintenance (39%) User training (37%) Applications development (35%) Microcomputer support (35%) Disaster recovery (22%) Datacenters (7%)	
Grover, Cheon and Teng (1994, 1996)	Survey of 63 US companies; Survey 188 companies	% Growth over 3 years: • Systems operations (36%) • Applications development and maintenance (30%) • Telecommunications management (17%) • End-user support (16%)	
Lacity and Willcocks (2000b, see Appendix A)	Survey of 101 and UK CIOS	US outsourcing: Client/server & PCs (66%) Help desk (63%) Disaster recovery (60%) Mainframe (60%) End-user/PC support (54%) Networks (46%)	UK outsourcing: Disaster recovery (75%) Midrange (73%) Client/server & PCs (68%) Networks (66%) Mainframe (61%) End-user/PC support (45%)
Willcocks and Fitzgerald (1994a)	162 UK CIOs	UK outsourcing: Hardware maintenance (68%) User training and education (42%) Datacenters (38%) PC support (34%)	
Sobel and Apte (1995); Apte et al. (1997)	Survey of 48 US companies, 141 Finnish companies, and 86 Japanese companies	US outsourcing: Support operations (48%) Training and education (48%)	Finnish outsourcing: Software development (48%) Support operations (46%)

Disaster recovery (40%)	Software maintenance (42%)
Software development (33%)	Data network (39%) Training & education (38%)
Data entry (22.9%)	

Japanese outsourcing:
Software development (61.6%)
Datacenter operations (44.2%)
Software maintenance (38.4%)
Support operations (33.7%)

found that companies systematically outsource strategic planning, IT management, or customer liaisons. US and UK surveys generally indicate that 60% of applications are still developed and maintained in-house, although Finland and Japan outsource applications more frequently.

Assessment: Several studies found that outsourcing infrastructure IT activities is generally successful.

Grover, Cheon and Teng[8] (1996) conducted two surveys ($n = 68$ and $n = 188$) and correlated the types of IT functions outsourced with perceived success. They found a high rate of perceived success associated with outsourcing systems operations and telecommunications, but outsourcing applications development, end-user support, and systems management 'did not lead to increased satisfaction' (p. 103).

Willcocks and Fitzgerald (1994a) found that it was easier for participants to outsource 'technically mature' activities. Customers understood how to cost and evaluate such activities and therefore could negotiate a sound contract. IT infrastructure, such as mainframe operations, networks, and telecommunications are often technically mature, and may be successfully outsourced.

General Dynamics (GD) serves as an example of successfully outsourcing almost the entire IT infrastructure. The key to success here appears to be cleaning-up in-house prior to outsourcing the IT infrastructure. (A similar lesson emerges from the DuPont case in Chapter 2.) At GD, the motivation for IT outsourcing was the sagging defense industry, which prompted a corporate-wide cost reduction and return to core-competency strategy. Prior to outsourcing, GD went through a rationalization of IT, including datacenter consolidation. In 1992, General Dynamics signed a 10-year, $US3 billion IT outsourcing contract with CSC. GD transferred almost 2500 people to CSC. The infrastructure was already managed by a centralized organization, which facilitated the transfer to CSC:

> General Dynamics had already been through the rationalization process. They'd rationalized down the three data centers and various other things. They picked this up and handed it over to CSC, they retained a total of 5 people to manage the whole operation, and that was a Vice President who looked after the strategy and some assistants who checked the monthly invoices and things like that—Account Executive, CSC.

Practice: Companies use transitional outsourcing to build the new world.

Transitional outsourcing is the practice of temporarily outsourcing during a major transition to a new technology. Transitional outsourcing is gaining momentum as a solution to the resource shortage caused, for example, by the advent of client/server computing. Companies do not have the staff to simultaneously run legacy systems while building new client/server applications.

Companies often outsource legacy systems while the in-house IT staff focus on new development. One of the first highly advertised cases of transitional outsourcing was Sun Microsystems. In 1993, Sun Microsystems signed a three-year, $US27 million outsourcing contract with Computer Sciences Corporation (CSC). CSC ran Sun's legacy systems while Sun's staff built client/server systems. Similar deals include:

- In 1995 Elf Alochem signed a four-year, $US4.3 million contract with Keane, a Boston company. Keane maintained Elf Alochem's accounting systems (which run on a range of platforms) while Alochem's internal staff migrated applications to client/server.
- In 1995 Owens−Corning Fiberglass signed a five-year, $US50 million contract with Hewlett−Packard. HP maintained the legacy systems while the Owens−Corning IT staff implemented SAP (which runs on a client/server platform) in 75 sites worldwide.
- In 1996 NASDAQ stock exchange outsourced legacy systems to Tate Consulting Services (Bombay, India) while the NASDAQ IT staff developed client/server systems.
- Rich Products Corporation, a Buffalo-based food manufacturer, outsourced applications maintenance to CTG in a three-year, $US3 million deal while the internal IT staff developed new systems. According to the CIO, speaking in 1997:

It was more important to have these people work on new developments, such as those involving the internet, than to have them supporting legacy systems—CIO Mike Crowley, Rich Products.

Assessment: Transitional outsourcing is generally successful.

Legacy systems are technically mature, and thus customers can negotiate a sound support contract for a short period of time. In addition, customers who focus in-house staff on the development of new technologies often 'buy-in' supplier resources to supplement in-house skills. This strategy worked well in cases Willcocks and Fitzgerald (1994a) studied because the in-house staff provided the needed business perspective, while the supplier transferred technical skills during the project. By the time the new systems were complete, significant organizational learning had occurred. Customers could therefore support the new technology themselves or, in some cases, negotiate a sound maintenance contract. Subramanian and Lacity (1997) studied first-time implementations of client/server systems. In the three companies studied, the systems were developed in-house, but outside expertise was hired in to evaluate technical plans, to train the IT staff, and/or to help with the conversion.

Selective Sourcing Summary

Selective sourcing continues to be the practice most companies pursue, and the success rate for this strategy appears to be high. Given the diversity of assets, skills, and capabilities required to provide the diversity of IT activities, selective sourcing enables organizations to seek the best sourcing option for given IT activities. Selective sourcing creates an environment of competition which overcomes organizational impediments to improvement and motivates performance. Selective sourcing also provides flexibility to adapt to changes, allows companies to capitalize on organizational learning, and is less risky than total outsourcing.

Selective sourcing, however, does have one major limitation: the transaction costs associated with multiple evaluations, multiple contract negotiations, and multiple suppliers to manage and coordinate. Some organizations have rejected selective sourcing for this reason, and instead seek total outsourcing solutions, with fewer evaluations, fewer contracts (although the remaining contracts are wider in scope and longer in duration), and fewer suppliers to manage and coordinate.

In the next section we document the problems associated with many, largely earlier fixed-price, exchange-based, total contracts and discuss organizations that have tried to reduce the risks of total outsourcing through creative contracts and alliances. Time and again the importance of risk mitigation practices in IT outsourcing surfaces, and so we have devoted Chapter 6 to this topic.

TOTAL OUTSOURCING: NO LONGER 'A GAME FOR LOSERS?'

Early mega-contracts were primarily fixed-price, long-term, exchange-based relationships. The contracting model had a number of false assumptions, such as the ability of a customer to predict needs over the long-term, and the misconception that suppliers were 'partners' despite the lack of shared risks and rewards. These early contracts encountered one or more of the following problems (see Lacity and Hirschheim 1995a; Willcocks and Fitzgerald 1994a):

- excess fees for services beyond the contract, or excess fees for services customers assumed were in the contract;
- fixed prices that exceeded market value over the long term;
- failure to improve service levels or declining service levels, primarily due to poor contractual definition of service levels, or a lack of user understanding of the contract;
- inability to adapt the contract to changing business and technology needs;
- loss of power due to a monopoly supplier condition;
- inability of the customer to manage the user/supplier interface.

Many customers found that they must re-negotiate or even terminate these deals mid-stream. In other cases, customers of mega-deals have banded together to tackle common supplier issues.

Newly signed mega-deals are rarely based on fixed-price, long-term, exchanged-based relationships with a single supplier. Instead, customers are seeking to avoid these pitfalls through value-added outsourcing, equity deals, multi-sourcing, co-sourcing, and creative contracting.

Practice: Companies often re-negotiate (or terminate) fixed-price, exchange-based, long-term contracts.

The press is increasingly reporting that major fixed-price, exchange-based, long-term, total IT outsourcing deals are being renegotiated. Few total IT outsourcing mega-deals reach maturity without a major stumbling block. Conflicts are increasingly being resolved through contract re-negotiations or, in some cases, through early termination. In 1997 the Gartner Group, based on a survey of 250 CIOs, estimated that

75% of all IT outsourcing customers would renegotiate their deals before the year 2000. Of this 75%, Gartner expected 10% of customers to terminate their contracts early, and 20% to switch suppliers. Other sources have produced similar findings.

- At Millbank, Tweed, Hadley, and McCloy, 40% of their IT outsourcing legal work entails contract renegotiations. John Halvey, a lawyer for Millbank Tweed, estimated in 1997 that only a small portion of renegotiations will lead to switching suppliers because the incumbent supplier has a 5% to 10% cost advantage over new bidders.[10]
- Twenty percent of the IT outsourcing work at Shaw, Pittman, Potts and Trowbridge involves renegotiations. Robert Zahler, a partner, concurs that most contracts do not lead to switching suppliers, but rather in finding a common ground with the original supplier.
- Coopers and Lybrand surveyed 428 high-growth companies with revenues less than $US50 million. Eighty-three percent outsourced some IT, accounting, or manufacturing. In 1997 24% of survey respondents planned to terminate their agreements.[11]
- In a survey of 1000 US and UK CIOs, we found that 32% of respondents have cancelled at least one IT outsourcing contract. When respondents prematurely cancel IT outsourcing contracts, 51% switched suppliers and 34% brought the IT activity back in-house (see Appendix A).

Experts generally agree that renegotiation is preferred over termination:

> When the contract no longer fits the users' needs, both sides will sit down and renegotiate the contract. Very few users exercise the termination of the contract; they're too dependent on the outsourcer—Harry Glasspiegal, Partner at Shaw, Pittman, Potts and Trowbridge, 1995.

Examples of contract renegotiations include:

- Enron renegotiated its seven-year, $US2 billion contract (signed in 1989) with EDS after three years—the original contract improperly defined baseline services and service levels.
- When First Union acquired First Fidelity in 1996, it renegotiated a 10-year contract between First Fidelity and EDS because the contract did not meet the needs caused by the change in business.
- TransAlta almost terminated their $US75 million outsourcing deal to DEC in 1996 due to poor customer service, but the newly appointed VP decided to renegotiate because he feared terminating the service during a software roll-out.

- Xerox and EDS renegotiated their $US3.2 billion, 10-year contract only two years into the contract (see Kern and Willcocks 2001).
- Chase Manhattan Bank was reported to have renegotiated its $US90 million per year contract with AT&T (signed in 1994) after the contract impeded the success of an acquisition.

There are also examples of contract termination:

- In 1997 LSI Logic terminated a five-year deal with IBM Global Services and re-hired transferred staff.
- Zale Corp signed a 10-year deal with ISSC in 1989. After Zale recovered from bankruptcy in 1994, they decided to terminate the ISSC contract early and find another supplier.
- Chase Manhattan Bank terminated its contract with Fiserv for check processing when it got in the way of their merger with Chemical. Chase paid Fiserv $US15 million to terminate the contract (in 1996).
- Mony, a New York-based insurance company, terminated a $US210 million contract with CSC halfway through the deal (in 1997).
- Lacity and Hirschheim (1993a) studied one chemical company that terminated a seven-year contract prematurely due to unexpected excess fees and poor service. The company re-built an IT department by purchasing mid-range technology and 'buying back' 40 former IT employees from the supplier. In another instance, a manufacturing company terminated an outsourcing contract in one of their subsidiaries when IT costs rose to 4% of sales in that subsidiary. The company migrated the subsidiary's systems to the parent company's data center.

The rate of renegotiation is so prevalent that some customers are including renegotiation stages in the original contract. For example, California Federal Bank's long-term contract with Alltel Information Services was designed as a 'Protocol of Change'. The Executive Vice President for the bank stated: 'Our contract is written so that we can easily add to or reduce the scope without going through arduous negotiations.'

Other companies are *avoiding* contract renegotiations by beginning long-term relationships with short-term contracts. For example, Cigna began what they hoped to be a long-term relationship with Entex Information Systems with a one-year contract (this case is further explored in the section, 'Creative Contracting'). In a 1995 statement that successfully predicted a telling point for the next decade, Clara Martin, partner at Klein and Martin, said:

> You're dealing with an industry that's undergoing radical change monthly. You don't want to have tied yourself into a deal three years ago that will

hamper you three years from now in a way you could never have possibly anticipated.

Practice: Large IT outsourcing customers are banding together to tackle supplier issues.

The International Information Technology Users Group (IITUG), formed in August 1996, is comprised of information technology leaders of several major organizations who are significant consumers of purchased information technology services (see website on http://www.iitug.org). Termed 'The Billionaire Boy's Club' by the press, members are customers with billion dollar IT outsourcing contracts including American Express Bank, Bethlehem Steel, Blue Cross and Blue Shield, Boeing, British Aerospace, British Petroleum, General Motors, Hughes Electronics, JP Morgan, Kodak, Rolls-Royce, SNET, South Australian Government, Textron, United Healthcare, and Xerox. The main aims of IITUG are to:

- disseminate non-proprietary technical information;
- discuss information management and information technology issues;
- promote information-sharing and leveraging of best practices, processes, and quality programmes;
- identify and pursue joint initiatives aimed at improving the application of information technology; and
- provide a common view to suppliers on strategic information technology drivers.

Assessment: Members continue to find IITUG a valuable tool for addressing common outsourcing problems and improving service and relationships.

We asked participants from our major case studies how IITUG works in practice. In essence, customers work with three major suppliers—EDS, IBM, and CSC—to improve services and relationships. The following quotes attest to the effectiveness:

> To help the company gather more information about IT outsourcing, it formed a major outsourcing users group of 15 companies to include Xerox, McDonnell Douglas, American Express, and Kodak, among others. Notwithstanding the sectoral differentiation between these businesses, it is a useful exercise to pool information about managing outsourcing relationships. Indeed, the same problems tend to arise in each participating company irrespective of sector, market, and technology factors—Quote from BAe Outsourcing Report.

It's extremely valuable. What we are really trying to do is shake the industry. That's the best way to talk about it. This industry is very immature. When you think about the amount of dollars being pumped through there now, and the secrecy around benchmarks. I can benchmark my telephones but not my computers. So we are trying to shake the industry. And in the room, there are $\frac{2}{3}$ of the value of all contracts in the room at one time in terms of deals done to date—Principal Contract Administrator, South Australian Government.

We sit down and say, gee, I'm sitting down with my supplier and working out this problem in the LAN segment. Often you find they have the same problem, and you talk about, 'hey I'm thinking of doing this.' And they may say, 'We tried that and it didn't work.' I find it very valuable because I couldn't talk to anyone in Australia with the same experience. I can sit down and talk to these guys, and find out that experiences are commonly spread among all the deals. You find that everyone has had bad days and good days. And so it's good for that sharing of experience—Principal Contract Administrator, South Australian Government.

In discussions with the outsourcing user group, the particular problem [of desktop computing] affected all of these organizations. An essential question was: How effectively can we do upgrades, moves, changes, etc.? Irrespective of whether this service was offered internally or externally, managers concluded that the whole operating model of managing DCE is changing and that will mean getting the business to agree to a more standardized environment—Quote from BAe Outsourcing Report.

Finding: Companies most likely to outsource on a large scale were in poor financial situations, had poor IT functions, or had IT functions with little status within their organizations.

Why have so many total outsourcing contracts run into problems? Studies generally have found that total outsourcing was done by weak companies in terms of financial performance, IT performance, or IT status:

- In a provocative and well researched article 'Outsourcing: A Game for Losers', Paul Strassmann conducted an analysis of financial statements for *Fortune* 1000 corporations.[12] He reasoned that if total outsourcing was done for strategic reasons, then the phenomenon would be equally distributed among *Fortune* 1000 companies. His statistical analysis found that companies that outsourced most of the IT budget were in poor financial situations. His findings strongly complement our own for early large-scale total outsourcing contracts, discussed in Chapter 4.
- In a sample of 55 major US corporations, Loh and Venkatraman[13] found that outsourcing was negatively related to IT performance and positively related to IT costs. Interestingly, in related work they

found in the early 1990s that press announcements of large-scale IT outsourcing deals were positively correlated with improvements in the customer company's share price. A parallel, not least in rationale for the announcement, can perhaps be observed in the frequent company announcements of Internet strategies during 1999 and 2000.

- Arnett and Jones (1994) surveyed 40 CIOs to determine the structural features that distinguish companies that outsource IT from companies that insource. They found that companies that outsourced were characterized by: lower CEO involvement in IT, CEOs who do not personally use a computer, and Heads of IT who are several reporting levels from the CEO.[14]

Customers, however, may be using IT outsourcing as a financial savior less frequently. In Appendix A we discuss a finding based on a survey of 1000 UK and US CIOs which indicates that only 15% of 101 respondents expected IT outsourcing to alleviate cash-flow problems.

Assessment: Research has shown that alliances between weak and strong companies do not work.

Some companies used IT outsourcing as a way to salvage a bad situation, be it poor financial performance or an IT function wrought with problems. For example, some senior executives at large companies signed long-term IT outsourcing contracts to receive a large cash infusion for IT assets—up to $US300 million in one case we studied. But such cash infusions might be looked at as a loan—one with a potentially high interest rate to be paid during the course of the contract. (Note: Banks do not accept IT assets as collateral because of the rapid depreciation rate.) And outsourcing a problem function rarely seems to work— the problems are often just transferred to and blamed on the supplier instead of the internal IT staff:

> The belief is, if you give the problem away, the third party will be able to magically make it disappear. This tactic doesn't succeed because the client hasn't invested the time to address the underlying business processes—Jerry Cooperman, VP of Gartner Group, 1995.

Outsourcing cannot typically transform a weak company into a strong one. In a 1995 study of over 200 alliances, Bleeke and Ernst found that alliances fail when weak companies partner with strong companies. In another study of 37 companies comprising over 500 interviews, Kanter found that both partners must be strong in order for the alliance to work.[15] Alliances work when each 'partner' brings something to the table—something we are seeing more companies try to achieve in 'value-added' outsourcing.

EMERGING TRENDS

From 1996 we have seen a range of practices—new and not so new—gaining ground, in addition to the underlying patterns discussed so far in this chapter. In the final chapter we will also point to and discuss trends emerging in the new millennium, and assess the likelihood of further development, and conditions for success. In the rest of this chapter we describe and assess eight practice trends that developed some momentum in the 1996–2001 period. These have been alluded to already and are presented in Figure 1.1.

These trends would seem to be a product of a number of factors. In some respects some are reactions against previous practices in other organizations that seemed to have had a high disappointment rate. In some cases they are the result of a long learning period with IT outsourcing and act as a corrective to (sometimes an over-reaction against) previous practices that did not work. In these respects the practices adopted can be seen partly as risk mitigation approaches. In some cases the practices have been experimental—'let's find new ways of doing this'—even if they are relatively untried. Many of the practices we will detail are also attempts to develop a more strategic approach to IT outsourcing, with ostensibly more strategic objectives beyond 'running the IT service well', and also represent attempts to look for the elusive 'business value-added' from relationships with suppliers. We begin with one attempt at the latter: value-added outsourcing.

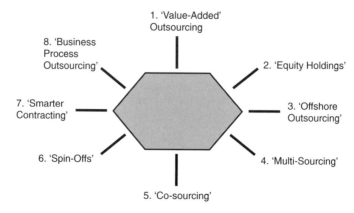

Figure 1.1   *Eight trends in IT outsourcing 1996–2001*

Practice 1: Value-added outsourcing: combining strengths to market IT products and services, or develop mutually beneficial internal business improvements.

Customers are looking for 'value-added' from their IT outsourcing suppliers. With value-added outsourcing, the 'partners' combine strengths to add value, such as using the supplier's marketing capabilities to sell customer-developed applications to external customers. Because each partner shares in the revenue generated from external sales, the partnership is not based on an exchange, but rather on shared risks and rewards.

One of the biggest deals touted as a 'value-added' deal was the Xerox–EDS contract (see Kern and Willcocks 2001). Unlike many other large total outsourcing deals, Xerox was not in a position of financial weakness when they negotiated the contract. At the time of the contract signing, the President of EDS and CEO of Xerox announced:

> We realized that each of our companies brought to the table specific best-in-class capabilities that enabled a level of performance that neither could achieve independently. This is a case of two technology companies enabling one another to achieve a shared vision for adding value for their customers (reported on October 10, 1996, at http://www.xerox.com/PR/NR950321-EDS.html)

In this case, value-added took the form of future shared revenues for the development and sale of a global electronic document distribution service.

Other examples of value-added contracts include:

- Kodak and IBM formed Technology Service Solutions to provide multivendor PC maintenance and support services to the manufacturing industry.
- Mutual Life Insurance of New York and CSC planned to market software and services to the insurance industry.
- Andersen Consulting and Dow Chemical formed a strategic alliance in which the partners planned to sell any systems developed for Dow to external customers. In 1996 the services were being offered through three alliance centers—two in the United States and one in Belgium—which encompassed Dow Chemical's $US100 million per year investment in IT consulting, projects, and applications support.

Assessment: Value-added deals promise to overcome many of the limitations of fixed-fee, exchange-based contracts, but the

partners must truly add value by offering products and services demanded by customers in the market.

Plans to sell customer assets to the general market place are often overly optimistic. Home-grown systems were built to meet idiosyncratic business needs. To transform such a system to a commercial product, a significant investment is required to modularize and generalize the software. According to discussions with Phil Yetton, Director of the Fujitsu Center for Managing Information Technology in Sydney, Australia, companies must spend up to nine times the initial development cost to transform a home-grown application into a commercial application. Few customers are willing to invest in such an enterprise because it is not the core of their business. Moreover, as in the case of British Home Stores—CSC 10-year deal in 1993, the 'value-added' by commercially exploiting home-grown software together is too small a part of the overall contract to influence its direction, the motivations of the parties, and their priorities, which tend to be focused on dealing with today's pressures and where the largest returns are likely to be.

In some cases, customers use the term 'value-added' to describe their 'exchange-based' contracts when they hope to gain something extra by outsourcing with a particular supplier. In reality, several value-added deals had to be re-thought after implementation. For example, the Xerox–EDS deal was renegotiated away from a value-added deal to an exchange-based deal:

> We went into it I think with the partnership idea in mind, I don't mean a financial or legal partnership, but a cooperative, collaborative approach in mind. The problem is unless you write your contract that way, it isn't going to work that way. It probably isn't going to work that way anyway because at the end of the day, the two corporations had different objectives... The route we are going down now is moving towards a supplier relationship. I think we've pretty much given up any ideas we had that this was going to be a partnership—Senior Executive, Xerox (quoted in Kern and Willcocks 2000).

In another example, Dow Chemical's relationship with Andersen Consulting is largely exchange-based despite the 'value-added' label. The focus of the contract centers around IT services provision, not external sales. Andersen Consulting was responsible for increasing Dow's IT system development and support productivity by 30% and for decreasing the time of development by at least 40% during 1997–1999. Measures focused on *internal* applications development and support. For example, productivity was measured in terms of function points compared with 1995 Dow baseline measures.[16]

'Value-added' has been understood in this way in several deals, as referring to internal improvements in the two companies' business performance. In the British Aerospace (BAe) case study to be discussed in Chapter 3, we show how the initial notion of 'value-added' has evolved during the contract. In 1994 BAe selected CSC because CSC had major contracts with other aerospace companies. BAe believed CSC would 'add value' because of access to software and services in the aerospace industry. But the deal is an exchange-based one, and no such transfer of applications and services was specified in the contract. The supplier is not free to share products and services from other clients. A year into the contract, the IT Services Director claimed:

> Yes, [the supplier] can achieve all the things that were proposed—but where is this famous 'added-value' service? We are not getting anything over-and-above what any old outsourcer could provide.

Four years into the contract, BAe and CSC agreed that the disappointment over the value-added notion was attributable to different definitions and perceptions of the term. The parties agreed on a three-tiered definition of value-added (utility value-added, capacity value-added, and business value-added), of which CSC is clearly delivering added-value on the first two tiers today. Plans for achieving the third tier were underway by 1999 (see Chapter 3).

Practice 2: Some customers and suppliers have been signing equity-holding deals by taking ownership in each other's companies.

One of the major limitations of traditional exchange-based contracts is that the customer and supplier had no shared risk and reward. The supplier's profits were based on maximizing their profit, given the fixed fee, and by charging excess fees for services beyond the contract. The customer's profits were based on trying to get as many services as possible for the fixed fee, hoping for free upgrades and access to new technology. To tie their futures together more closely, some companies are buying each other's stocks. These include suppliers buying the client's stock, clients buying the supplier's stock, or both parties taking a stake in the formation of a new entity (Willcocks and Lacity 1998).

For example, in 1996 Swiss Bank signed a 25-year outsourcing deal with Perot Systems worth $US6.25 billion. The partners planned to sell client/server solutions to the banking industry. The bank was to acquire 25% shares in Perot Systems and Perot Systems was to acquire a share of a European software company—Systor AG—owned by the bank. Five hundred and twenty Swiss Bank employees joined forces with 200 Perot

System employees. Swiss Bank retained sole control of any security-related functions, proprietary applications, and hardware, while the alliance covered global operations, management, and system engineering functions. Other examples of equity holding deals include:

- Delta Airlines and AT&T(NCR) formed TransQuest to provide IT solutions to the airline/travel industry. Under the $US2.8 billion, 10-year agreement, Delta transferred 1100 employees and 3000 applications to TransQuest while NCR contributed 30 employees, software, and cash. Their goal was to generate $US1 million a year for the 50–50 partnership.

- In Australia, when Lend Lease outsourced all its information systems to ISSC, it took a 35% holding in ISSC Australia.

- Telstra (Australia's telecommunications company) signed a $US2.9 billion contract with IBM Global Services. Telstra took a 26% stake in a new joint venture with IBM, Advantra, for network services. Advantra in turn provided Telstra with network operations and management.

- Japan's Daiwa Bank and IBM Japan created a joint venture in 1998. Daiwa Bank, one of the largest banks with over $US130 billion in assets, owns 65% of the venture. Daiwa expects to save about $US38 million over a 10-year period. The bank also expects improved customer service and new business initiatives based on the Internet and deregulation.

- Commonwealth Bank of Australia and EDS signed a 10-year contract worth $US3.8 billion in 1997. Commonwealth Bank paid $US130 million for a 35% stake in EDS Australia. John Mulcahy, Head of IT at the bank, said that the deal concentrates more on generating revenues than on cost reduction.

Assessment: The viability of these jointly-owned entities is questionable.

While the mechanism of truly shared risks and rewards overcomes the previous conflict of exchange-based contracts, these new entities must have a core competence so that they can attract external customers. In essence, equity deals are 'value-added' deals with the additional incentive of shared ownership. In most cases these new entities still earn the lion's share of revenues from the original customer.

Bob Fawthrop of supplier Logica argues that because the venture's primary customer is also an owner, there is an inherent conflict of interest in joint-equity deals. The customer has two competing goals: to maximize cost-efficient service delivery from the joint venture and to maximize the revenue of the joint venture. How can they do both? Furthermore, he argues, the same executives sit on the Boards of the customer company and the joint-venture company. Which hat should they wear? Should they be pushing for more services at a reduced cost, thereby squeezing revenues from the venture, or should they push for generating joint-venture revenues, which will essentially come from the customer company in service fees? Clearly, equity deals are not substitutes for exchange-based contracts if the prime customer is also a joint owner.

Updates on Delta Airlines, Swiss Bank, and Lend Lease also indicate a general failure in the equity model. The Telstra–IBM arrangement was also in the process of being radically revised in early 2000. In 1996, the Delta–AT&T joint venture was terminated. Delta brought everything back in-house. NCR's inexperience with large-scale professional service deals was a major contributing factor to the early termination.

In 1997, the Swiss Bank–Perot Systems partnership was whittled down from 25 years to 10 years, from $US6.25 billion to $US2.5 billion. And Swiss Bank's investment dropped from 26% to 15% in Perot Systems. The high hopes for external sales and joint profits were replaced with the realities of fire-fighting and under-staffing. One former Perot Systems executive we interviewed describes what happened:

> [The deal] was a complete blue bird. Nobody had planned it. It went into contract very quickly, I would say in three to four months. And the plan was we would take over their entire infrastructure and have a joint software house for financial services which this company would sell in the German-speaking market . . . The contract has been subsequently renegotiated downwards into a supplier contract. There is still the equity share, but it's more of a service contract.

In fact in January 2000 UBS signalled the end of the four-year IT 'strategic alliance' when it bought back Perot System's 40% stake in Systor, UBS's information technology company. UBS remained Perot's biggest customer, accounting for more than 25% of its annual revenues, but the focus was to be only on the management of computer operations.

We spoke with a consultant hired to re-vamp the Lend Lease–ISSC contract. He believed that the equity deal served as a poor substitute for a sound contract:

> You structure the deal that says I've got all the resources, thank you very much, you haven't got any resources now I've got your complete football club, pitch, players, everything. So we'll tell you what we can and cannot do for you. So [the supplier] doesn't have to get out of bed in the morning and

they still get paid. What that says is that you've got to have some mechanisms that say I will pay you more money if you deliver.

It has also been observable in some equity deals that the supplier is made complacent rather than energized. This may be exacerbated by poor contracting—not enough detail, poor service baselines and measurement. A split may also occur in perceptions between the customer's senior managers and those responsible for operations. Strategically the supplier argues that it is in both companies' interests that they focus on generating new business and profits; operationally the adverse impact of this finds customer users and contract managers complaining of poor service and loss of good supplier staff to new contracts.

Practice 3: Multi-sourcing: one contract, multiple suppliers.

In the May–June 1995 issue of the *Harvard Business Review*, John Cross described the multi-supplier outsourcing strategy of BP Exploration (BPX). Rather than totally outsource to one supplier, BP hired three suppliers under an umbrella contract which obligated the suppliers to work together:

> We decided against receiving all our IT needs from a single supplier as some companies have done, because we believed such an approach could make us vulnerable to escalating fees and inflexible services. Instead, we sought a solution that would allow us both to buy IT services from multiple suppliers and to have pieces delivered as if they came from a single supplier.

BPX reported that this sourcing strategy helped to reduce the IT staff by 80%, and reduced IT operating costs from $US360 million in 1989 to $US132 million in 1995 (see Chapter 6).

In July 1996, JP Morgan announced a similar multi-supplier strategy. JP Morgan signed a seven-year, $US2.1 billion contract with four major suppliers. Computer Sciences Corporation (Pinnacle Alliance) continues, as at 2000, to be responsible for the coordination of CSC and three other suppliers: Andersen Consulting, AT&T Solutions, and Bell Atlantic Network Integration. JP Morgan transferred 45% of its IT staff—over 900 people—to the alliance firms. These 900 people joined the 600-plus staff of the alliance firms devoted to the contract. The alliance is responsible for datacenters, midrange computers, distributed computing, and voice and data services in New York, London, and Paris. Interestingly, despite the size of the deal, the contract is worth only about 30% of JP Morgan's $US1 billion annual IT budget, and may be considered an example of selective IT sourcing. JP Morgan is keeping IT strategy, application development and support, and supplier management in-house. The contract is expected to save JP Morgan $US50 million annually. Although cost savings were a driving factor, JP Morgan executives claim the real impetus was to help retain its leading edge in technology, better service to end-users, and an internal focus on new applications. According to an internal interviewee, the contract is based on 'a flexible team approach in which JP Morgan sets the strategic direction'.

In 1997, DuPont signed a series of 10-year contracts worth $US4 billion with Computer Sciences Corporation (CSC) and Andersen Consulting (AC), making this the second largest IT outsourcing alliance as at that date. Unlike JP Morgan, DuPont decided against a prime contractor. Instead, DuPont relies on mutual dependencies to ensure supplier coordination, cooperation, and collaboration (see Chapter 2).

In 1998, Chevron outsourced mainframe computer operations to EDS, voice and data networks to GTE, and helpdesk support to Sprint. Chevron expected to reduce IT costs by 10% during the five-year, $US450 million deal. Chevron transferred 400 employees to the alliance, while retaining 700 IT employees for applications and desktops.

Assessment: With multi-sourcing, the risks of going with a single supplier are mitigated but replaced to a degree by additional time and resources required to manage multiple suppliers.

The key to multi-sourcing is supplier coordination and management. This can be expensive. Using a 260 organization database assembled at Oxford Institute of Information Management, we investigated post-contract management costs in IT outsourcing deals. These fell between 4% and 8% of total IT outsourcing costs across the lifetime of contracts, even without considering the effectiveness of those IT management arrangements and practices (see Chapter 7). Multi-supplier deals were invariably in the upper section of this cost spread. Some reasons can be read into the following.

In the BPX case, there were initial difficulties in getting the suppliers to work together (see the BP case study in Chapter 6 for more details). BPX hit upon a plan to provide seamless service whereby one of its three suppliers served as a primary contractor at each of its eight business sites. Its job was to coordinate the services provided by the three suppliers to the businesses supported by that site. Framework agreements allow business managers at each of the eight major sites to negotiate with the IT suppliers for customized services. BPX notes that the suppliers worked well together to deliver day-to-day service, in part because they were so interdependent. However:

They are also rivals competing for our future business. As a result they are reluctant to share, for example, best practices with one another—John Cross, BPX IT Director, 1995.

The JP Morgan case also shows a multiple supplier approach, but in this case one contractor is made the principal contractor throughout, whereas in BPX each contractor had a principal role in at least some part of BPX. While the JP Morgan approach simplifies the administrative pattern, the BPX practice, in principle, develops greater interdependence among suppliers.

DuPont does not use a prime contractor. Rather than a legal arrangement, DuPont's deals successfully rely on mutual dependencies to ensure CSC and AC cooperate where functions overlap. Because AC-led projects require CSC infrastructure, and CSC projects require AC support, each supplier is motivated to cooperate with each other:

> And because of the integration of our supply chains, you are always going to have a situation where there's going to be some Andersen interfaces with CSC, and CSC interfacing with Andersen. So they are both going to be, if you will, in the same predicament. So they both need each other to be successful and if they try to [hurt] each other, it just won't work, because the [hurt] guy will just get even on the next transaction—DuPont, Global Alliance Manager.

JP Morgan and DuPont retained many more staff internally than BPX. It is fairly clear that all three companies, however, would find it difficult to recreate its original IT function if this were required. But in BPX's case, total outsourcing is almost irrevocable. This makes risk mitigation on supplier management even more critical than in the JP Morgan and DuPont cases.

Practice 4: Offshore outsourcing: 'cheaper, quicker, better'. Leveraging price advantages, and skill and performance resources, abroad.

Offshore programming and software development industries have rapidly emerged worldwide in countries such as Ireland, Israel, Malaysia, Hungary, Mexico, the Philippines, and Egypt. By 1998 over a quarter of the top 500 US companies were outsourcing software development projects overseas. In 1990–1998 India's software export industry grew from $US240 million to over $US2 billion, a compound growth rate of over 50% a year. Typically, companies have asked for a greater cost saving (30% compared with 20%) to outsource offshore rather than domestically. Increasingly, however, competition for skills and rising costs of doing business in sites like India have driven up the price. But continuing IT skills shortages in the developed economies have served to increase the attractiveness of offshore outsourcing, and services on offer are no longer mainly just programming skills provision. With its proximity to the US market, a country like Mexico can deliver 'nearshore programming' and compete successfully against a country like India—the market leader, but thousands of miles away.

One company, UK retailer Sainsbury, budgeted £30 million to deal with the Year 2000 (Y2K) problem. The conversion work was done entirely, and very successfully, offshore in India through satellite links using Sainsbury's mainframes during off-peak hours.

Another phenomenon is the use of offshore skills by major IT suppliers. There is a long list of global companies tapping into offshore resources. Just looking at India, BT, IBM, AT&T, Novell, Microsoft, Oracle, Unisys, and Hewlett Packard all have development centers there. Some suppliers are following the lead of Origin and setting up software factories to develop ERP solutions for global clients like Fuji, Shell, and Phillips Morris. This is a response to the severe skill shortages for big ERP projects in Europe and the United States.

Assessment: Rising capability abroad, and skills shortages in the United States and Europe, mean that offshore cheapness might be less important than quality, speed, and range of tasks that can be covered. Detailed specifications, control, and clear lines of responsibility are paramount.

Many companies have followed up good experiences with offshore outsourcing Y2K work by letting further contracts. As just one example, UK's largest vehicle leasing company, Lex Vehicles, signed further contracts with Indian-based Mastek for a CTI integrated call center.

Our own studies of Holiday Inns and Ford reveal the need for detailed contracts and specifications, and strong controls for long-distance work (Kumar and Willcocks 1999). Having key vendor managers on the customer site is advantageous; however US labor/immigration laws, for example, historically have restricted this practice. Looking just at the sometimes notoriously difficult ERP projects, in a standard on-site project design requirements are frequently revised as the development process progresses. For the cross-border structure to work, we found that there needs to be more solidity to the initial design, and less tinkering along the way (Willcocks and Sykes 2000). This in turn means that the client and ERP provider need to work much more closely at the initial design phase, with the help of forecasting tools. When planning to go offshore, there is considerable interaction but this is restricted to the design and specifications 'front office'. Development is then standardized and can be done offshore, using standardized methodologies and a highly transparent, controlled approach to the development process, so that clients can monitor progress and quality at all times.

Practice 5: Co-sourcing: performance-based contracts.

The largest IT outsourcing supplier, EDS, pioneered a new term in the customer/supplier relationship: 'co-sourcing'. With co-sourcing, EDS does not simply manage IT resources, it aligns them with business objectives. 'Co-sourcing goes beyond marginal reductions in IT costs to the effective alignment of IT assets and expenditures with business objectives. The result is the enhancement for the entire enterprise', said Gary Fernades, Vice-Chairman of EDS in 1996. Or as its news media chief put it: 'Outsourcing is done to you, co-sourcing is done with you.' The change in EDS's focus was supported by an internal retraining effort. In the same year *Fortune* magazine reported that EDS employees were taught to focus more on customer service, a program referred to by insiders as the 'Charm School'. Ted Shaw, VP of EDS's banking services division, noted 'EDS is still primarily a fee-based outsourcing business.' Even in 2000, however, co-sourcing, is still a relatively new concept, and accounted for only a small percentage of revenues.

One of the first examples of co-sourcing was EDS's contract with the City of Chicago for a parking ticket processing system. Instead of paying for the application, the City of Chicago agreed to pay EDS a share of the revenues generated from the system. In Chicago, known as the windy city, people often complained that they never received a ticket or that the ticket must have blown off the car. EDS added glue to the back of the tickets, and this simple change increased revenues significantly. Sources told us that this project was financially beneficial to both parties, and that EDS gained a very high return on investment (ROI):

> At first, it was making money but returns were marginal. EDS put glue on the back of the tickets. Seriously. What happened in Chicago, because this is the windy city, everyone was saying 'my ticket blew away'. And that one change they made in business process, they created a kind of ticket that had this small amount of glue. It was written up as a joke—we are a high-tech company and how do you make more money: put glue on things.

EDS provided a similar service in London. Each borough in London had its own ticket processing system, which made it very difficult to track offenders across boroughs. London set up a centralized agency, but it had no IT infrastructure. EDS came in and established the IT infrastructure and applications. One informant we spoke to said:

It works well. The customer is delighted because they didn't have an infra-structure. EDS run everything down to sending tickets out and collecting cash.

Another example of co-sourcing is EDS's contract with an unnamed US pharmaceuticals company in which the rate of payment is based on EDS's ability to reduce the development and registration process for new drugs.

Other outsourcing companies also offer performance-based contracts because customer demand has been growing. For example, in the mid-1990s Perot Systems announced a deal with Citibank in which Perot Systems would share in the revenues of Citibank's Travel Agency Commission Settlement system. Perot Systems' 'performance-based' contracts, like EDS, continued into 2000 to account for a small percent of total business.

Assessment: Co-sourcing works well when supplier capabilities are contractually structured to complement customer needs.

Co-sourcing successes have worked well in several areas. In the City of Chicago and London parking ticket systems, EDS' core capabilities in re-engineering and application development served to generate revenue. In these cases, win/win situations for customers and suppliers were created.

Other co-sourcing deals have been less successful because of a poor fit of supplier capabilities with customer needs or a poor contractual frame-work. For example, an informant told us that EDS's co-sourcing contract with a London-based book club did not work well because the manage-ment of a blue-collar workforce was not one of EDS's core capabilities. The deal was a revenue-sharing one in which EDS would improve book sales through innovative IT. Apparently, the staff required only low-level, low-paid skills for catalogue shipping, warehousing, etc. High turnover rates plagued delivery. In addition, the warehouse was situated in a remote area of London, making it difficult for the workers to com-mute. And as one informant told us, 'We had people in jeans and tee-shirts who were very scruffy and it horrified EDS.' EDS is a company that knows how to manage highly motivated, highly educated, white-collar professionals. Clearly, this situation was not a cultural fit.

Another example of a co-sourcing deal facing structural challenges was the Rolls Royce–EDS–AT Kearney (owned by EDS) deal. In essence, EDS's contract provided Rolls Royce with IT operations at a baseline cost, while the AT Kearney contract was priced on the ability to re-engineer business processes. In practice, AT Kearney carried a high level of risk that was not entirely within their domain of control.

Successful re-engineering requires cooperation and acceptance from all three parties, but only Kearney's rewards were based on delivery. Parties were committed, however, to making the deal work. (When innovations in outsourcing are first implemented, it is not uncommon for initially faulty courses to be re-charted.) For more information on the EDS–Kearney CoSourcing Service, see http://www.eds.com/ industries/manufacturing/offerings/mfg_cosourcing.shtml.

Practice 6: Business process outsourcing—'Outsourcing a process and its IT, identified as 'non-core', that a third-party can do at least as well, at competitive price'.

Rather than just outsource the information technology associated with a business process, business process outsourcing (BPO) outsources the entire delivery of a business process to a supplier. Eric Blantz, an analyst at Dataquest, an IT research company, defined BPO as outsourcing an entire business process for an extended period of time:

> The key term is ongoing responsibility. So these are long-term contracts. If it is project-based then we don't consider it BPO. If however they were to take over a company function, such that the company maintains little or none of that competency in house, then that would be considered BPO. (Reported on www.infoserver.com on January 20, 2000).

BPO has become one of the fastest growing segments of the outsourcing market. Input, Inc. estimated that BPO would assume one-quarter of the outsourcing market by 2003. According to a research report on 304 multinational companies sponsored by PriceWaterhouseCoopers in 1998, the most common processes outsourced included payroll (37%), benefits management (33%), real estate management (32%), tax compliance (26%), claims administration (24%), applications processing (21%), human resources (19%), internal auditing (19%), sourcing/procurement (15%), and finance/accounting (12%). The most important strategic benefits derived from BPO included cost reduction (79%), focus on core business (75%), and improved service quality (70%). However, participants from the study also identified several barriers to success, including organizational resistance (56%), unclear performance measures (56%), loss of control of the process (48%), lack of prior outsourcing experience (43%), and lack of planning (42%).

Assessment: While BPO is a logical extension of IT outsourcing, customers must incorporate the planning and learning acquired through prior IT outsourcing experiences.

At British Petroleum for example, BPO of the accounting function occurred only after IT outsourcing in the late 1980s. In 1991, BP outsourced all its accounting operations in the North Sea area, then accounting operations in South America, North America, and the rest of Europe. Overall, Colin Goodall, CFO for British Petroleum (BP) affiliate Sidanco and formerly CFO for BP/Europe, reports that BPO led to better service and cheaper costs. However, he reports that some of the outsourcing deals have not worked. Goodall states:

> Some things we've taken back because the deal didn't work or because the organization that it went to wasn't up to it or didn't share our values. But it's more likely the problem was that we may not have paid sufficient attention to making it work. Outsourcing is not an easy option. You don't just throw it over the fence and let the other guy get on with it. It can require more effort up front than doing it in-house (reported on www.infoserver.com in January 2000).

Thus, BPO requires at least the same—and likely more—attention to decision-making, supplier selection, contract negotiation, and relationship management as IT outsourcing. In early 2000 BP Amoco (BPA) further announced the outsourcing of its human resource function, including IT components, on a $US600 million five-year deal with Exult, based in Irvine, California. BPA outsourced the administrative and IT burden, reserving for itself only 'the things that require judgement and policy'. The risks of such a big IT project—to standardize globally on and make accessible real-time human resource systems—were obvious, but difficulties would not harm business directly, an experienced specialist was being used to take the initial financial risks, and there was a potential $US2 billion reduction in operational costs associated with the venture (see also Chapter 6).

Practice 7: Spin-off successful IT functions into independent companies.

The idea of tranforming an internal IT department into an external entity is certainly not new, but the practice still continues. The spin-offs allegedly empower the IT entity to behave like suppliers. Freed from the bureaucratic restraints associated with being a support function, spin-off companies can focus on a marketing mentality, one that delivers good customer service at competitive prices. In the past, spin-offs generally have not been successful. For example, Mellon Bank, Sears Roebuck, Kimberly-Clark, and Boeing had only limited success with their spin-off IT companies.

NV Philips, the electronics multinational, was more successful, though over a long period of time. By the early 1990s it had spun off its 183 software development and support staff to a new company, Origin, at that time part-owned with Dutch software house BSO. In 1991, NV Philips also transferred all its communications and processing staff into a wholly owned company, Philips C&P Services, with an open mandate to seek third-party business. In practice this proved difficult. New commercial and marketing skills were needed; the external services market was highly competitive, and populated by existing suppliers with track records, eager to keep out potential threats. Ninety-five percent of its active business turned out to be with NV Philips. Subsequently, new Origin was formed combining Origin and Philips C&P Services. Over the years Origin has developed into a competitive IT services company, with some major corporations as customers dotted around the world.

Assessment: Experiences from the past suggest that spin-offs are only successful if they have a core competency to attract external customers.

Like equity deals, the success of spin-offs depends on the ability to attract a critical percentage of sales from third-party customers (rather than sales primarily from the original founding customer). Two notable examples of successful spin-offs have been American Airline's Sabre unit and EDS. American Airlines already had a great product with many external customers—their famous airline reservation system. The spin-off has continued to attract large numbers of external customers. In 1997, for example, they signed a multi-billion dollar deal to provide all US Airways' strategic and support IT functions, including data center operations, network management, and application development and support. Another successful spin-off is EDS. Initially sold to General Motors in 1984, EDS became its own company in 1996. Clearly, EDS has been able to attract many external customers besides General Motors. The viability of other spin-offs will also depend on whether they have a viable product to attract external customers, and the ability to develop the new commercial and marketing skills needed to run a spin-off.

Practice 8: Creative contracting: 'tougher shoppers' attempt to improve on the limitations of traditional contracts.

John Halvey, partner in Millbank, Tweed, Hadley, and McCloy, noted in the mid-1990s that contracts were changing, but that it was the customers who were pushing for tougher deals and better contracts:

The user community is much more sophisticated. They've learned through experiences where trigger events are that can cause trouble . . . understanding the legal changes in outsourcing deals means the difference between a happy relationship and an unqualified disaster.

Harry Glasspiegal, partner at Shaw, Pittman, Potts, and Trowbridge, also noted at that time that, 'Vendors are in a bigger rush than ever to close. They don't want clients shopping around, getting outside legal advice.' But shop they do. For example, Ameritech studied outsourcing for 15 months before awarding a 10-year, multi-billion dollar contract to IBM in 1996. In addition to longer evaluations, some of the 'creative contracting' practices are documented below.

Practice 8a: Include a customer-written contract with the Request For Proposal (RFP).

When Elf Alochem, a Philadelphia chemical company, searched the market in 1995 for an IT outsourcing supplier, they took a novel approach by sending out a completed contract along with the Request For Proposal (RFP). The contract enabled the company to exactly specify what they wanted from an outsourcing supplier, as well as provide all suppliers with precise information to make an informed bid. The four-year, $US4.3 million contract was awarded to Keane, a Boston company. From 1995 through to 1999 Keane maintained Elf Alochem's accounting systems that run on a range of platforms while Alochem's internal staff planned and developed a migration to client/server.

The IT director at chemicals multinational ICI, Richard Sykes, had a detailed contract written up and issued with the RFP to four potential suppliers in 1995 for the outsourcing of datacenter operations. The five-year deal was signed with Origin in February 1996. It involved the vendor paying £4.5 million for the computing facility and taking responsibility for transferring 400 datacenter staff to its own payroll. As at early 2000 the deal had proved successful, and renegotiation was being considered. At DuPont (see Chapter 2 for more details), the Global Alliance Manager felt that the major task of translating a technical-based RFP into legal requirements was frustrating. In essence, parties start negotiations from scratch once bids are awarded based on the RFP. Perhaps Elf Alochem's approach may serve as a model to minimize such transformations.

Practice 8b: Provide for competitive bidding for services beyond the contract.

Customers are increasingly aware of the threat of giving monopoly power to their outsourcing supplier. Customers are protecting themselves by including contract clauses that specify that the customer will competitively bid any service beyond the contract. Specifically, customers hope to ensure supplier motivation and competitive pricing. All four of our mega-deal case studies—British Aerospace, Inland Revenue, South Australia, and DuPont—include competitive sourcing for services beyond the contract.

But: Competition does not always protect the customer.

In practice, some services beyond the baseline must be awarded to the original supplier because the services are too integrated to bring in another party. At Inland Revenue, for example, the customer finds that this competitive bidding option is a bit naive. EDS's presence is so all-encompassing that it is virtually impossible to carve out areas for another supplier. Instead of formal market-testing, Inland Revenue uses 'informal' market-testing on a limited basis to help negotiate better prices:

> Generally we wouldn't go into a formal market test. Because the way we would invoke market test is that we informally test the market against the EDS price and provided that was reasonable, we wouldn't go to a formal market test at all—Account Manager, IR.

We have seen two cases in which the decision to outsource additional work to another supplier created significant maintenance problems. The first time a US aerospace company went outside of their multi-billion dollar outsourcing contract, the supplier refused to support the entire function:

> Our contract says we can go elsewhere. When [the supplier] wanted to charge us $2500 to upgrade each of our HP workstations to 2 gigabyte hard drives, we went elsewhere and bought them for $1000. Now [the supplier] won't support our machines because we put somebody else's hardware in them—User, Aerospace Company (year two into a 10-year contract).

From the supplier's perspective, they cannot assure the quality of products or services delivered outside the original contract.

In a similar circumstance, one petroleum company awarded a large-scale development effort to a company other than their primary contractor. After the system was developed, the supplier refused to run the application on their mainframes unless they were awarded the support contract.

Practice 8c: Flexible pricing.

The term 'flexible pricing' has been used to cover a variety of pricing mechanisms, including supplier-cost-plus pricing, market pricing, fixed-fee-adjustments-based-on-volume-fluctuation pricing, or preferred-customer pricing. Customers are increasingly using multiple mechanisms to alter prices within one contract.

Some customers are negotiating for a share in the supplier's savings. Customers are well aware that unit costs drop 20%–30% annually, and they want this reflected in their price. Some customers are tracking supplier costs with 'open-book accounting' clauses and demanding a percentage of supplier savings. The BAe and CSC contract provides an example of open-book accounting:

> It's open book accounting. So [BAe] get to look at our costs and they get to measure us independently on productivity benchmarking—CSC Account Executive, Division C.

On the whole, there is a limit on the margin the supplier is allowed to charge for the entire basket of services. Although the margin is not applicable to individual services, BAe felt open-book accounting would serve to increase their negotiating position. (It should be noted that most practitioners involved in IT outsourcing that we talk to do remark that 'open-book' accounting is rarely totally open-book accounting.)

Other customers are relying on annual third-party benchmarks to assess current market prices. However, several customers we spoke to felt that benchmarking is only mature for mainframe and midrange operations. Customers complain that the benchmarking industry is still immature in the areas of distributed computing and IT applications development and support. As one informant notes:

> Our experience being honest is that I haven't been terribly happy with the benchmarking process. This is not happy for CSC nor BAe. It's just the process seems to be a little bit naive—BAe Contract Manager, Division B.

Many customers have clauses to adjust their fixed-price fee based on volume fluctuations. In essence, customers are seeking variable IT costs rather than fixed costs. This rather standard clause works well for customers as evidenced by the 65% of UK and US survey respondents that realized this benefit of outsourcing (see Appendix A—expected vs. actual benefits of IT outsourcing).

Overall, most pricing adjustments appear to occur bi-annually rather than monthly or yearly due to the costs associated with measuring and agreeing upon such adjustments.

Practice 8d: Begin long-term relationships with a short-term contract.

Executives at Cigna Healthcare of Atlanta, Georgia, wanted a long-term relationship with their IT outsourcer, Entex Information Services. Cigna, however, pushed for a one-year contract even though Entex would be required to make significant investments in Cigna, without any guarantee for the future. But the short-term contract served to motivate both sides—Entex wanted the renewal to reap their investment, Cigna wanted renewal rather than incurring the costs of switching to a new outsourcer. The strategy worked well for both companies, as the contract and relationship were subsequently extended.

Summary

Companies are still signing large, total outsourcing deals, but the flavor of these deals is very different from the early exchange-based contracts. Customers are much smarter owing to the mounting experience base with IT outsourcing. Customers, on the whole, better understand the strengths and limitations, and are constructing deals to maximize the likelihood of success. Companies are trying to avoid the trap of a sole supplier through multi-sourcing, or looking for ways to share revenues or cost savings with suppliers. These contracting options must be closely monitored to determine the critical success factors.

If the user community is becoming more sophisticated, and is learning through experience where trigger events are that can cause trouble, there are still all too many that do not contract sufficiently, and flexibly enough to ensure they get what they think they have been promised and expect (see Appendix A on Contract Completeness). Therefore we give two short war stories to sound warning bells.

In 2000 a fast-growing, hi-tech supplier sought to exit a total out-sourcing arrangement it had made some four years earlier. It had contracted poorly for the deal, but was now unhappy at the suppliers' performance and wanted to switch suppliers at the end of the five-year contract. Over the years many of the people involved in managing the contract were themselves (independent) contractors, and the firm had not been focused on the IT service and its management precisely for the reason why it outsourced—to intensify management attention on business expansion. All this made the development of an exit strategy exceedingly difficult, especially as the termination clauses in the contract were also poorly drawn up and incomplete on important issues.

In 1996 the UK-based retail conglomerate Sears signed a 10-year £344 million total outsourcing deal—for finance, logistics, and computer operations—with Andersen Consulting without an open competitive bid. At the time Sears were in considerable financial difficulties, and the deal was signed in the boardroom, with little IT input. Some 900 staff were to be transferred to Andersen Consulting and large cost savings were anticipated (£25 million a year by 2000). Within 17 months, following the resignation of the CEO who signed it, the deal was terminated. Five hundred staff went back to Sears. Sears spent £35 million implementing the deal, and some £70 million in fees over 1996–1997. Contracting for the deal was not particularly good, nor were the evaluation procedures and measurement systems that were eventually put in place. Strategically and operationally the deal made little sense, as was subsequently recognized by senior management. Sears then went down a more selective, multi-supplier route. Termination clauses were poor and there had been no pre-agreed strategy for exit management included for buy-back of assets or their transfer to another provider, software licensing, third-party consents, and staff transfers. Exit management probably cost Sears in excess of £15 million.

CONCLUSIONS

The sourcing market for information technology continues to grow and evolve. The more pervasive (but less audible or visible) trend continues to be the selective outsourcing of IT for a specified sub-set of IT activities. In particular, customers are using transitional outsourcing with increasing frequency—outsource the old, stable, well-understood world while insourcing the development of the new world. Selective sourcing has proved to be a successful sourcing strategy, especially where it has developed additional informed sophistication based on experience and strategic concerns. The benefits include:

- maintaining flexibility and control,
- motivating in-house and supplier performance by creating a competitive environment (anything may be up for grabs),
- maximizing individual strengths of in-house staff and suppliers,
- reducing risk associated with total sourcing solutions because mistakes are smaller, and
- learning can be incorporated more quickly.

In this regard the future-gazing model put forward in 1995 in our *Harvard Business Review* article would seem to have stood the test of time (Lacity, Willcocks and Feeny 1995). However, selective sourcing does have some downsides, as we recognized at the time. These include:

- increased transaction costs associated with multiple evaluations, multiple-contract management,
- potential lack of integration, cooperation, and coordination among multiple sources, and
- over-focus on detailed operational advantages at the expense of strategic concerns.

As we emphasized in 1995, and many times subsequently, selective sourcing works most effectively within the context of business-strategic concerns and an overall IT sourcing strategy that retains both flexibility and control.

To mediate these risks, companies are trying new sourcing options, including different forms of supplier management, to reduce transaction and coordination costs (see Chapter 6 for a detailed treatment of mediating risk).

Other emerging contracting models include co-sourcing, value-added sourcing, joint-equity sourcing, and flexible-pricing contracts. Although we have treated these options as independent, there is obviously much overlap and confounding of terms. Value-added deals may refer to sharing revenues from selling a jointly developed product, or contracting with a supplier that brings industry-specific expertise to the table. Joint-equity deals may be thought of as 'value-added' deals with an additional incentive of joint ownership. Performance-based contracts can refer to the supplier's fees being tied to a *customer's corporate performance* (such as sales revenue), or based on the *supplier's performance* (such as productivity and quality improvements). Flexible pricing deals may refer to reducing fixed fees based on a supplier's internal costs, or based on best-of-breed benchmarks. Some of these newer options will not reach maturity for years to come, and thus notions of success often rely on expectations rather than outcomes. Although time is needed to assess the validity of many of these new contracts, the best practices for ensuring value from IT will likely be the same: proper diagnosis of problems, rigorous evaluation of sourcing options, sound contract negotiation, and active post-contract management, all identified and treated as core capabilities of the client organization.

NOTES

1. Caldwell, B. (1995). Outsourcing Megadeals—More than 60 Huge Contracts Signed Since 1989 Prove They Work. *Information Week*, Issue 552, November 6.

2. Schmerken, I. and Goldman, K. (1996). Outsourcing Megadeals: Drive the New IT Economy. *Wall Street & Technology*, **14**, no. 4, April, 36–41.
3. For details of these surveys and pieces of research see: Caldwell, B. (1996). The New Outsourcing Partnership. *Information Week*, **585**, June 24, 50–64; Collins, J. and Millen, R. (1995). Information Systems Outsourcing by Large American Industrial Firms: Choices and Impacts. *Information Resources Management Journal*, **8**, no. 1, Winter, 5–13; Dekleva, S. (1994). CFOs, CIOs, and Outsourcing. *Computer World*, **28**, no. 20, May 16, 96; Foley, A. (1993). Hong Kong Bucks Asia Services Trend. *Computer World*, Hong Kong, May 13, 1, 56; Apte, U., Sobol, M., Hanaoka, S., Shimada, T., Saarinen, T., Salmela, T. and Vepsalainen, A. (1997). IS Outsourcing Practices in the USA, Japan, and Finland: A Comparative Study. *Journal of Information Technology*, **12**, no. 4, December, 289–304.
4. Apte et al. (1997) *op. cit.*
5. Personal discussion by Mary Lacity with Kuniaki Watanabe, President of Digital Equipment Corporation Japan in Tokyo, Japan, January 20, 1998.
6. Collins and Millen (1995) *op. cit.*
7. Sobol, M. and Apte, U. (1995). Domestic and Global Outsourcing Practices of America's Most Effective IS users. The *Journal of Information Technology*, **10**, no. 4, 269–280.
8. Grover, V., Cheon, M. and Teng, J. (1996). The Effect of Service Quality and Partnership on the Outsourcing of Information Systems Functions. *Journal of Management Information Systems*, **12**, no. 4, Spring, 89–116.
9. Arnett, K. and Jones, M. (1994). Firms that Choose Outsourcing: A Profile. *Information & Management*, **26**, 179–188; Collins and Millen (1995) *op. cit.*; Sobol and Apte (1995) *op. cit.*; Grover et al. (1996) *op. cit.*; Apte et al. (1997) *op. cit*; Dekleva (1994).
10. Quoted in Caldwell, B. (1997). Outsourcing Deals Often Renegotiated. *Information Week*, Issue 628, April 28, TechWeb News.
11. See Caldwell, B. and McGee, M. (1997). No Big Savings—Too Many Outsourcing Deals Don't Pay Off as Expected. *Information Week*, Issue 621, March 10, TechWeb News. Also Caldwell, B. and McGee, M. (1997). 'Outsource or Not? *Information Week*, Issue 657, November 17, TechWeb News.
12. Strassmann, P. (1995). Outsourcing, A Game for Losers. *Computer World*, **29**, no. 34, August 21, 75. See also Strassmann, P. (1997) *The Squandered Computer*. Information Economics Press, New Canaan.
13. Loh, L. and Venkatraman, N. (1992). Determinants of Information Technology Outsourcing: A Cross Sectional Analysis. *Journal of Management Information Systems*, **9**, no. 1, 7–24.
14. Arnett and Jones (1994) *op. cit.*
15. Bleeke, J. and Ernst, D. (1995). Is Your Strategic Alliance Really a Sale? *Harvard Business Review*, January–February, 97–105; Kanter, R. (1994). Collaborative Advantage, the Art of Alliances. *Harvard Business Review*, July–August, 96–108.
16. Described in Klepper, R. and Jones, C. (1998). *Outsourcing Information Technology, Systems and Services*. Prentice-Hall, New Jersey.

2
Inside Mega-Contracts: South Australia and Dupont

There is generally an expectation of management on the user side that here is this knight in shining armour, I'll get three times better service at half the price ... so you have this large gap in expectations from the start—Contract Administrator, South Australian Government.

The principal reason we separately sourced applications is quite simple. There is no single supplier who could cover the range of applications to cover hospitals, utilities, government ... . There are best-of-breed suppliers in those areas and it's not sensible to outsource to one—Contract Administrator, South Australian Government.

In terms of a positive outcome [on economic development], EDS has exceeded our expectations—Contract Administrator, South Australian Government.

We didn't do it because it was broken—Dupont Global Alliance manager, 1999.

This is a commercial business transaction, not a partnership. Suppliers have to keep earning the business everyday—Dupont Executive, 2000.

INTRODUCTION

In the previous chapter we found that the most common practice continues to be selective outsourcing of targeted IT activities. So why does press coverage of mega-deals significantly over-shadow the more common practice of piecemeal outsourcing? Simply this: mega-deals fascinate. The magnitude of billion dollar contracts amaze most organizations still struggling for incremental IT budget increases. The 10-year deals perplex most organizations that have difficulty planning for IT past a three-year time horizon. The scope of mega-deals astonishes organizations reticent to hand over even minor responsibilities to outsiders. But most of all, mega-deals fascinate us because they are potential bellwethers to the future of internal IT functions.

In this chapter and the next we present four in-depth, mega-deal case studies of South Australian Government, DuPont, British Aerospace, and Inland Revenue. These cases provide a rich context for understanding because they embrace nearly every conceivable aspect of IT outsourcing. Each case covers the business context driving the decision, the decision process and, most importantly, the post-decision experiences and management practices. As such, there are many lessons to be learned from what these organizations did right, as well as the practices they would have done differently in hindsight.

Although the cases cover three continents (Australia, the United States, and the United Kingdom), two public sector and two private sector organizations, and span four years of start-dates, the similarities of experience among cases far out-number the idiosyncratic differences (see Table 2.1). The reader will immediately begin to see patterns of experiences in the following stories. Throughout Chapters 4 through 8, the cases will be used as contextual examples of general lessons, practices, and experiences. In particular, Chapter 8 will draw heavily from these cases to explain relationship management across the different phases of any IT outsourcing arrangement.

Table 2.1   *Overview of case studies*

Customer	Supplier	Contract signed	Contract duration	Value of contract	Scope of contract
South Australian government	EDS	1995	9 years	$AU600 million	• IT infrastructure • Economic development of South Australia
DuPont	CSC & Andersen Consulting	1997	10 years	$US4 billion	• IT infrastructure • Applications
British Aerospace	CSC	1994	10 years	£900 million	• IT infrastructure • Applications
Inland Revenue	EDS	1993	10 years	£1 billion	• IT infrastructure • Applications

The cases were selected for study because they were visibly debated in the trade press. The South Australia Government contract with EDS was under severe attack from public officials as well as decentralized government agency users who claimed that IT costs increased as a consequence of outsourcing. Despite the controversy over the internal operations of IT, the economic development portion of the South Australia–EDS contract won an award for best government outsourcing relationship sponsored by the *Outsourcing Journal* (see http://www.outsourcing-journal.com/issues/feb2000/html/government.html). DuPont's $US4 billion deal with CSC and Andersen Consulting warranted media attention due to the sheer size of the deal. British Aerospace gained media attention when the IT out-sourcing decision prompted a strike by BAe IT employees belonging to a trade union. The UK Inland Revenue's IT outsourcing contract brought fears of breeches of confidentiality because an American Company would have access to citizens' tax data. But headlines are newsworthy for short periods of time. What was actually happening to these organizations during their 10-year outsourcing deals?

The cases presented in this chapter are based on interviews with senior executives, business unit managers, senior IT managers, consul-tants, and supplier managers from the four organizations. These stake-holders invariably stated that the media failed to disclose all sides of the issues and failed to take a larger view of the outsourcing deals. Our resulting cases may be less dramatic (or traumatic) than the press cover-age surrounding these deals, but the accounts seek to illuminate all sides to sourcing issues.

CASE 1: SOUTH AUSTRALIAN GOVERNMENT

In 1997, the Australian federal government announced a decision to outsource all federal government information technology (IT) within one year. To attract better prices and to simplify the decision process, government IT was bundled into four large clusters to be outsourced via four, large-scale, long-term contracts (later reduced to three clusters/three contracts). Facing such short deadlines, government servants need to quickly learn how to create requests-for-proposals, analyze supplier bids, and successfully implement and manage IT outsourcing contracts. Although government IT outsourcing has been done on a piecemeal basis, the only large Australian IT outsourcing contract that has been active for a substantial period of time is South Australia (SA) govern-ment's $AU600 million, nine-year contract with EDS, signed in 1995.

Subsequently, SA's contract has gained the attention of government and the media as a learning vehicle.

SA's IT outsourcing contract is distinctive from more traditional outsourcing. One contract is used to govern *two distinctive components*: one component for the development of SA's economy, and one component for IT service provision for 150 SA agencies.

> Our strategy for outsourcing, if you distill it all down, had two thrusts. One was to improve the effectiveness of the use of our computing infrastructure, lower cost, higher quality, and shift management focus to the business and end-use. On the other side, we wanted to build a critical mass of IT industry leaders by attracting global players. So we needed a deal big enough to attract them—Contract Administrator, SA Government.

The economic development package has been a success. EDS has exceeded their yearly targets to meet the overall goal of pumping more than $AU200 million into the SA economy during the nine-year relationship. EDS established a large base in Adelaide, South Australia, that increases employment, provides international marketing channels for local software firms, generates housing starts, plus many other multiplier effects. This one-off opportunity provides an exemplar of thinking about IT outsourcing in a strategic way. However, generally speaking, such an advantage is non-replicable for other government agencies because large IT suppliers have already established their worldwide homes.

Five years into the contract, the IT service provision contract has been more controversial. Opponents argue that agency costs have increased significantly. Proponents argue that across the whole of government, total costs of IT have been reduced. In addition, proponents credit EDS with almost doubling the local area network (LAN) capacity, facilitating a government restructuring, and improving service in a number of areas. Such controversy was expected because IT outsourcing was a top-down decision by the centralized government of SA.

A key lesson that emerges from the case is the need to foster realistic stakeholder expectations about the cost/service trade-offs of IT delivery (a point also emerging from our survey—see Appendix A). With so many stakeholders involved—government officials, centralized contract management teams, agency delivery teams, end-users, IT personnel, and suppliers—quite naturally different groups have had different objectives and expectations of the cost and service to be delivered via the IT outsourcing contract. Contract managers for both the SA government and EDS had to work together to temper expectations and perceptions of the contract. Once transition tasks were complete, the partners then looked to focus on more strategic issues, in the mature phase of the contract (see Chapter 8). The outsourcing contract continued to be controversial in its performance aspects into 2000.

South Australia: Background

As at 2000, the Commonwealth of Australia had a population exceeding 19 million (see Table 2.2). The democratic, federal government comprises six states and two territories. In 1996, of the 1.5 million people in the State of South Australia, 1.1 million lived in Adelaide. As the Contract Administrator for the SA Government notes: 'So we are really a city state.'

Prior to outsourcing, the SA government comprised 150 agencies, providing many services that are often privately owned in other state governments, such as in the United States:

> Our government agencies cover a broad spectrum: all health systems, the hospitals, public schools, water utility, power utility, justice, corrections, policy, courts, standard government administration, forestry management, community welfare, public housing, and more. Compared to the US, for example, water is usually privately run. Electric is usually privately run. So it covers in all, about 150 agencies. So we are dealing with heterogeneous agencies here, like every hospital has its own Board. The power authority and water authority have their own Boards. The courts have to be separate from government so they have a Justice Council. So you talk about managing all these different agencies, they are all separate government agencies under the administration of the Crown—Contract Administrator, SA Government.

In 1994, the Premier of SA wanted to stimulate economic growth. Manufacturing was not seen as a growth business, with plant automation actually decreasing employment. The Premier envisioned IT as a basis for long-term economic growth. His cabinet created the Information Technology Development Task Force, which subsequently created the IT 2000 Vision. The Vision declared that by the year 2000,

Table 2.2   *1996 Australian population*

State (capital)	Population
News South Wales (Sydney)	6 190 000
Victoria (Melbourne)	4 541 000
Queensland (Brisbane)	3 335 000
Western Australia (Perth)	1 763 000
South Australia (Adelaide)	*1 479 000*
Tasmania (Hobart)	473 000
Capital Territory (Canberra)	308 000
Northern Territory, (Darwin)	178 000

SA would be recognized as an international center of excellence in IT, particularly as a source of software and IT services for the Asia/Pacific region. But how can such an industry base be bootstrapped? The strategic implementation of this vision was to contract out the *whole of government* IT to attract a sufficiently sized international IT leader to SA:

> In order to do that they needed to attract a world-class, multinational company to town to serve as the anchor department store in a shopping mall. And so in looking to do that, they would outsource the entire infrastructure of IT for the whole state. It had to be big enough to attract a big company—VP of Operations, EDS.

SA Government's IT Department Prior to Outsourcing

Prior to outsourcing, 60% of the 90 000 people employed by the SA government had desktop computing. The government owned/leased and operated 12 datacenters, 11 mainframes, 376 midrange computers, 1102 LAN servers, and 3193 wide area network (WAN) devices. At the time, IT decisions were completely decentralized, causing inefficiencies from lack of economies of scale and duplicate functions. For example, the government operated 24 different accounts payable systems. Government IT managers had tried to consolidate and standardize, but such cost reduction tactics were continually thwarted by the agencies. Services were substandard in many agencies—only three agencies had service-level agreements. And most of IT was used for back-office operations, not for services visible to citizens:

> There was a major benchmark done in 1993 on IT computing and management done by Deloittes. What it showed, the public sector with a $6 billion turnover, we had 24 accounts payable systems, 5 general ledgers, for basically the same activities. And so, to be best-of-breed, we needed more resources, because most of our IT was back office. So most resources were managing the infrastructure rather than the business. We wanted to shift our resources to managing the business, not the infrastructure—Contract Administrator, SA Government.

IT costs were not controlled well owing to job categorizations and the different cost-based accounting system used by most agencies. During the Request For Proposal (RFP) process, it was estimated that 1000 people were doing some IT work in the agencies, but their job classifications did not capture this as an IT cost. The different accounting systems also hid IT costs. For example, the Treasury paid for IT assets on behalf of a significant number of agencies, but agencies were not charged back a depreciation expense on these assets, which masks anywhere from 8% to 25% of total costs of IT ownership:

> We found asset accounting in IT is not good. It doesn't matter whether you are in government or in a commercial organization. An upgrade here, an upgrade there, it's hard to control. If anyone tells you they can get at 100% of IT costs, it's just not true because it's spread throughout the business. It's much more pervasive and it's not managed as a cost center. We added 25% for additional hidden costs we knew we would never find. A lot of that is how you give personnel support from your peers next to you—Contract Administrator, SA Government

SA Government's Outsourcing Decision Process

By February 1994, the overall sourcing strategy to implement the IT 2000 Vision was established:

- convert the IT infrastructure to an outsourced utility;
- standardize in-house desktops and common applications;
- redirect agency personnel to mission critical/customer systems.

Initially, the SA Premier wanted to implement the IT 2000 Vision by signing a contract within two months. But the IT managers, along with the support of hired consultants, convinced the Premier that the contract must be detailed to be successful. In the end, the entire decision process took over two years (a similar length of time for the Inland Revenue deal—see Chapter 3).

Table 2.3 provides a view of the sourcing strategy that was ultimately implemented. The SA government included most of the infrastructure in

Table 2.3 *SA Government's IT sourcing strategy*

Standard desktops			Public interface
Standard desktop application packages: e.g. *MS Office*			
Common applications: Human resource management; Financials; Records management			
Agency sector applications	Agency sector applications	Agency sector applications	Agency sector applications
EDS provides: LAN/WAN network management	AATP provides: Telecommunications services management	Telco provides: Mobile network	Voice network
EDS provides: Local processing; File servers and midrange			
EDS provides: Large-scale processing; Mainframes			

the scope of the RFP, including mainframes, midranges, file services, and network management. Although telecommunications, voice, and mobile networks are normally considered part of the infrastructure, they were excluded from the scope of the contract. The SA government felt these growing areas could be used to attract another economic development partner in the future.

Desktops were excluded from the scope of outsourcing because SA could obtain better prices than a third party could offer:

> Our view is that suppliers cannot add value there. Price competition is such that prices change every 3 months, that's how fast the life cycle is. When the price drops, you don't want to lock yourself into a long-term contract. You have to pay that negotiated price, unless somehow you have some complicated flexible pricing system. That would also make us have a monopoly supplier which would be a considerable risk—Contract Administrator, SA Government.

Application development and support were also excluded from the scope of outsourcing:

> The principal reason we separately sourced applications is quite simple. There is no single supplier who could cover the range of applications to cover hospitals, utilities, government. It's just a pipe dream to think you can do that. There are best-of-breed suppliers in those areas and it's not sensible to outsource to one—Contract Administrator, SA Government.

The RFP requested two proposals, one for economic development and one for IT service provision for the in-scope infrastructure. The former requested a supplier to stimulate the development of an IT industry in SA. The latter requested a supplier to provide the same level of IT service at a reduced cost.

At the end of March 1994, two suppliers were selected as potential IT partners: EDS and IBM. The SA government felt these suppliers could build an IT-based industry in Adelaide because of their size and global competitiveness. Both companies responded to the RFP. Two SA teams independently evaluated the suppliers, one team evaluated the economic development proposal, the other team evaluated the IT services provision proposal. In September 1994, both teams selected EDS's proposal as the best and final offer.

After the RFP process, it was readily apparent to both SA and EDS that they were very far from a final agreement. Because SA's RFP for the IT service provision was loosely defined, EDS could not rely on the government's data to make a specific bid. For the next seven months, the partners went through due diligence to gather and verify the cost, volume, and quality of current IT services in the agencies. Because the outsourcing decision was forced on the agencies, many agencies resisted the due diligence process, claiming it was expensive and unwarranted. The SA government outsourcing team spent much time convincing agency heads that the effort was required because their payments after outsourcing would be based on baseline figures. The following agency data was collected:

- complete list of hardware and software;
- software licenses;
- hardware leases;
- maintenance agreements;
- IT costs included in user budgets;
- IT costs of internally developed software, some of which was expensed, others capitalized;
- each IT person's salary and benefits;
- information on people who spent less than 50% of their time doing IT work.

Besides the agency resistance, the next biggest challenge was normalizing the cost and service data across 150 agencies. Costs were difficult to normalize because of the different accounting systems:

> Some people put their costs against the IT group. Some agencies put IT in the cost of corporate overhead. Others left it on the side in a swamp. The depreciation costs and financing costs had to be standardized. In the different agencies, you find a mainframe, exactly the same box, we could have an IBM mainframe. One agency would have a three-year life, another a five-year life, you'd have another with a seven-year life. The same technology with different lives of technical obsolescence. So we had to standardize—Contract Administrator, SA Government.

Services were difficult to normalize because of the erratic definition of service levels:

> If you think of it in simplest form, we contracted current service levels at reducing existing costs. So in order to try to track current service levels, a few agencies if you asked them what the service levels were for a LAN or an application, they haven't a clue. Generally, they didn't. A lot of agencies, and I can't remember the exact percentage because it's been so long, but I'd guess more than half have actually taken three or four attempts to establish service-level agreements—Contract Administrator, SA Government.

Like many other organizations that go through such a process, immediate benefits arise from a departmental assessment of IT costs and services. For the first time, agency managers began to understand that IT is not a free resource; IT requires business unit managers to assess cost/service trade-offs:

But that had a lot of benefits. We got management's attention that you pay for what you get. What do you think you are getting? What do you get? What are you capable of getting?—Contract Administrator, SA Government.

In April 1995, a long contract negotiation process commenced. SA hired a number of experts to assist in these efforts, including Technology Partners and Nolan Norton to help define the contract and to benchmark services, Thomsons and Shaw Pittman for legal assistance, and Peat Marwick for financial modeling. Although these experts were expensive, SA IT managers claim that most of the experts served to temper long-term risks and to negotiate a better deal. In the area of distributed computing, however, SA found that the consulting industry was still immature:

My experience with them is mixed. The area that has the weakness in experts is in the LAN environment. We sought help from three consulting groups. The advice is quite varied. But over time it will mature—Contract Administrator, SA Government.

SA's IT employees were fully informed of the decision process. SA established newsletters, group briefings, workshops, and a telephone hotline to disseminate information and to field employee questions. The open communication served to foster employee and union buy-in, even if the answer to a query was: 'we don't know yet'. Only one agency had a half a day strike over the impending decision.

Well there were points in time where the union was opposed. But when it came down to it in the end, the union was behind it—VP of Operations, EDS.

Early on, SA identified key people they wanted to retain, and identified 200 people for transfer to EDS. SA IT managers and EDS representatives met with identified individuals to assure them that their salaries, benefits, and employment conditions would be equivalent or better with EDS. In the end, 95% of the identified people agreed to transfer.

The contractor also had a key role in building the confidence of individuals that they were going to be a good employer that was offering an exciting future for their career prospects—Contract Administrator, SA Government.

During contract negotiations, the duties and responsibilities of SA and EDS had to be clearly delineated. Because IT infrastructure is a highly integrated service, the parties needed to ensure that activities would not fall between the cracks. For each service segment, including mainframe, midrange, LAN, WAN, and workstations, the activities comprising that service segment were identified. For each activity, responsibilities were then assigned to the SA government, EDS, or both (see Table 2.4). Like many other IT outsourcing contracts, the responsibility matrix is very detailed, defining at one point in time 831 IT infrastructure activities. (The responsibility matrix serves as a working document, and exact figures in Table 2.4 were valid as of August 1998.)

To ensure that shared responsibilities were executed smoothly, the responsibility matrix describes each party's primary and secondary duties. For example, 'mainframe application tests' are a joint responsibility. The SA government has the *primary* responsibility of running the application test while EDS has the *secondary* responsibility of providing infrastructure resources for the test.

While the responsibility matrix defines each party's duties, service-level agreements define the quality of service. In total, as of 2000, there were still hundreds of service-level agreements. Service-level agreements are defined by application, by agency, and by platform. For example, the payroll system for government departments in 1998 ran on a Sun midrange computer. This payroll system has a service-level agreement for when the application must be up, response time for the system, and a time schedule for when the 30 000 government employees must be paid. Failure to meet the payroll on time would generate a cash penalty. Other agency applications, such as the hospital patient records system, continue, into 2000, to have service levels requiring 24-hours-a-day, seven-days-a-week availability.

During the contract negotiations, EDS was able virtually to work around the clock because they could delegate some tasks to the office in Plano, Texas, during the Australian nights. Thus, EDS would arrive with much accomplished at the start of each workday. This ability served to speed up negotiations, but it exhausted the SA team who

Table 2.4   *Number of infrastructure activities performed by EDS and SA*

Service	Number of EDS responsibilities	Number of SA responsibilities	Number of shared responsibilities	Total activities defined by service
Mainframe	109	46	23	178
Midrange	112	46	24	182
LAN	86	32	21	139
WAN	35	14	7	56
Workstations	83	33	21	137
Infrastructure elements	77	44	18	139
Total				831

did not have the same advantage. The SA team often worked past midnight and on weekends during this six-month period. After the six-month negotiation process, the contract was signed on October 30, 1995.

SA Government's Contract Overview

The SA government–EDS contract is a confidential document, and only a handful of SA civil servants are privy to its contents. The Contract Administrator explains why secrecy serves both parties' interests:

> Because this was leading edge and because of the interesting things we have packaged, governments do things like foster industries with handouts. There are incentives built in on the industry development side in the contract, which if we put commercially in the marketplace, could be used by EDS's competitors. We actually want EDS to grow, so we had as much interest in not letting EDS's competitors understand our deal. Also, setting benchmarks in terms of what other industries could do with us in other areas because we have a general strategy of outsourcing. If you made the contracts publicly available, then they would want to lead you—Contract Administrator, SA Government.

The anonymity of the contract frustrated agency managers, who viewed the contract as forced upon them. Only a 20-page summary document was distributed to agencies, but this found its way into the public domain.

According to the summary document and interviews with participants, the economic development component obligated EDS to generate $AU200 million worth of economic benefit to SA during the nine-year contract. In addition to building an EDS base in Adelaide, the contract requires EDS to help local software firms to market their products to Asia/Pacific. The IT service provision component requires EDS to provide the baseline level of service at a reduced cost. This component of the contract was expected to save the SA government $AU100 million over the nine-year contract:

> Estimated cost savings are not based purely on the contract price. When we say $100 million in savings over 9 years, that includes the shift in policy from us to outsourcing. The other chunk is from our agencies cleaning out their houses. So when we talk about the savings, it's not just the outsourcing policy attributable to the supplier. That's consistent with all the major contracts. All the anecdotal evidence suggests, the moment you announce contracting out, managements sorts themselves out—Contract Administrator, SA Government.

Contract prices were set only for the first few years of the contract. In principle, SA and EDS would renegotiate prices based on external benchmarking.

In principle, SA's Principal Contract Administrator (PCA) can contractually exempt users from purchasing infrastructure services from EDS. This clause is designed to temper the power of a monopoly supplier condition. In practice, this option has not been exercised:

> It is a non-exclusive contract. We can exempt someone from buying from EDS, but that is not our desire. So it is a non-exclusive contract, because we want to protect our negotiating position. But we are generally trying to build a relationship with this key supplier—Contract Administrator, SA Government.

SA Government's Transition Period

A nine-month transition period of assets and people was planned, with the first wave of agency transfer completed by April 1996, the second wave in June 1996, and the last wave in September 1996. Like all large-scale outsourcing contracts, the first year or so focused attention on translating a legal contract into a daily work practices. Challenges included:

- establishing the post-contract management infrastructure and processes;
- implementing consolidation, standardization, and rationalization;
- validating services, costs, service levels, and responsibilities for baseline services;
- managing additional service requests; and
- fostering realistic expectations of supplier performance.

Post-Contract Management Infrastructure and Processes

The SA government and EDS both have had a PCA to serve as the primary manager of the relationship. The PCAs meet monthly to review performance. The SA PCA has a core team of seven people, initially titled 'contract administrators':

> They are contract administrators. But every time they go into the agencies, the agencies go, 'Oh, what's the problem?' It's amazing. There is an immediate negative, 'there's a problem'. So we changed their name to service advisors— Contract Administrator, SA Government.

Each agency has an account manager. Larger agencies have full-time people while smaller agencies have part-time people. Account managers are responsible for the day-to-day purchasing of services and the management of delivery. During the transition, some SA contract agency managers had difficulty adjusting to their new roles as procurers rather than providers of IT:

> We are forcing our people to think business not technology. But for some of the agencies, that's been a difficult transition. For example, the engineering organizations were a well established IT group, those managers who managed the datacenters, managed by kicking the tires. They still want to focus on inputs. The newer agencies, the ones not as skilled, they had a fresh start without all the baggage—Contract Administrator, SA Government.

On the EDS side, customer service managers directly interact with agency IT managers and users. Their job is to determine specific user requirements, particularly for change requests:

> The customer service manager talks to the customer to understand the change they really want. To get it all detailed out. Once a change request is formalized, we have an internal process that goes through it to see how extensive the change is. Do we need systems engineers? Is it an off-the-shelf solution? Based on that, we determine price. We respond back to the customer with an impact statement. It says, this is what it means, this is what it will do, this it what it will cost, this is when it can be implemented. Then the customer decides if they want to go ahead or not—VP of Operations, EDS.

Looking at daily work practices, SA and EDS have attempted to establish seamless services for users. For example, users call one helpdesk, which is operated by SA employees. The first-line helpdesk determines if the user has an application (SA domain) or an infrastructure (EDS domain) problem. Problems are routed to the appropriate support staff.

In the area of distributed computing, one might expect coordination problems because the SA government owns and operates the client machines, and EDS owns and runs the server machines. In practice, however, the SA government uses the EDS server machines as file servers for standard applications like MS Office, which actually run on the desktop. From the SA government perspective, there have been no major problems with the division:

> PCs are a commodity. We set the standards for the LAN servers. There are no problems here. EDS is required to manage the end-to-end service, but they don't have the applications. So, I mean it's a bit like mainframe computing, you can run the datacenter and not control the applications. People say there is a lot of integration, and there is in respect to something like a help desk, but not with applications. Today, more and more of the applications run on the

desktop. The server is just a server. Really this is about buying a box ... We don't see any value in paying a third party a margin on buying toasters—Contract Administrator, SA Government.

From EDS's perspective, they would have preferred to manage both the client and server machines:

We have responsibility all the way up to the connection to the PC on the desktop. We don't have responsibilities for the applications or the equipment on the desktop. It would make our lives easier and our customer's lives easier if that was folded in—VP of Operations, EDS.

The post-contract management infrastructure and processes continued to evolve as lessons were learned and as the relationship progressed beyond the (18-month) transition period. For example, by 1998 the SA PCA was working on two major issues. First, the SA PCA wanted to integrate the IT planning function with contract monitoring:

The thing I noticed, all contract management used to be about monitoring the t's and i's of the contract. And planning was separate. I think they are all progressively changing. They now realize, you can't have the contract monitors separate from the planning people. One of the things I'm trying to do is bring them closer together. That's one thing I'm trying to do—shift from a contract focus to a service focus. You need to have a close integration with the standards, the technology trends, and planning. In a lot of other organizations, it's too far apart—Contract Administrator, SA Government.

Second, he wanted to foster the generalist skills of his in-house management team. As the contract progressed, these people's detailed technical skills eroded because they were no longer involved in daily work. Instead, they needed to learn how to access this expertise on the marketplace on an as-needed basis:

Over time, some of the skills you want in, no one is an expert in everything. So what we want are good generalists who can tap into bought-in expertise, you buy-in your specialists. You have a core group of people here because you want them to have ownership and pride and care. So they are generalists. When you need expertise, they know where to go to get it, and how to get it—Contract Administrator, SA Government.

Implementing Consolidation, Standardization, and Rationalization

To realize the cost savings, both parties implemented cost reduction tactics.[1] A major effort to standardize was facilitated by a restructuring of the government agencies from over 140 to 10 superagencies. This helped EDS to standardize certain software and to reduce administrative overhead. The new organizational structure was also coupled with a consolidation of datacenters. EDS successfully consolidated 12 mainframe datacenters into one Information Processing Centre (IPC).

> There was a big effort, we call it CRS. Consolidation, rationalization, and standardization that would be undertaken. Through that, for example, we consolidated all the mainframe processing. Several mainframes were scattered around and now they are consolidated to one site. We are in the process of putting in standardized systems. Over the life of the contract, we will be reducing headcounts by doing things like remote management of local area networks—VP of Operations, EDS.

From the SA government's perspective, EDS's consolidation was very successful:

> EDS did in 12 months what we couldn't do in four years—Contract Administrator, SA Government.

The SA government and EDS then established hardware and software standards to reduce redundancy, facilitate roll-outs, and reduce management overhead. On the desktop, there are only four approved desktop machines. Midrange computing was standardized to four platforms: UNIX, HP, DEC, and Sun.

> So we dictate the standards there, but they are mutually agreed upon with our supplier. But we have total control of standards and strategic direction—Contract Administrator, SA Government.

The SA government has also tried to standardize service levels. By late 1997 they were finding it impossible to monitor the hundreds of service levels defined in the contract:

> Part of the standardization process is I have the same set of functions in Agency A as B. We had to contract at the platform level for major applications in each agency. We had a service-level agreement at the agency level. And that's one of the things we are trying to do is shrink that down because it's just not manageable. We are hoping to standardize more—Contract Administrator, SA Government.

Validating Services, Costs, Service Levels, and Responsibilities for Baseline Services

Although most contracts define in detail the baseline set of services, all customers find they must adjust the baseline after outsourcing commences.[2] Many customers overlook IT activities not captured in formal budgets, over-state baseline service levels, under estimate actual volumes, and fail to fully cost IT.[3] This reality is attributable to the integrated and disseminated nature of IT (see Chapter 5). The SA government's experiences were no different from other large-scale contracts:

> In the early part of the relationship, ... you spend a lot of time defining the scope of services of what you are going to get, and what you are going to pay for. Unfortunately, your supplier in the early part says, 'that's not listed there, you have to pay for that'. Where you think you should get added value, the customer sees it as 'We didn't have to pay for it before, it was part of the service.' We had early on, a lot of demarcation as far as who does what. It gets in the way—Contract Administrator, SA Government.

> We still have three major issues that should have been put to bed a long time ago. The agreement on what the baseline was, agreement on the purchase price of the assets, and unit pricing in the LAN segment. Those are the three things right now that are obstacles to a very positive relationship. We all understand that there are different opinions and we are trying to resolve them—VP of Operations, EDS, 1998.

Managing Additional Service Requests

One of the greatest surprises for both parties was the deluge of user demand for additional services. During the two-year decision process, the SA government stopped buying IT. This created a massive backlog of demand:

> The whole process until we had a contract in place was about two and a half years. During that period of time, the government pretty much put a freeze on buying the equipment, things like that. So there was a pent-up demand that we all under-estimated. The number of change requests overwhelmed us. The number of change requests so far has been something like 2000. And this is new servers, new LANs, those kind of things. We went, for example, and these are approximate numbers, at the time of taking over the baseline, they had about 1000 LAN servers out there. And there are now about 1800. So that's an example—VP of Operations, EDS, 1998.

EDS also had to reconfigure the infrastructure to accommodate a massive change in government structure:

> The government just went through another election in October, and the same party retained control, but they have made significant changes in the structure of the government. They have organized and consolidated the entire government into 10 large departments. There has been a lot of need on a very fast turnaround to reshuffle and to reorganize the infrastructure to support the reorganized government. The fact that we can do it is a tremendous benefit to the customer as a result of having this contract in place. Without us, and the government has acknowledged this, it would have been very difficult for them to achieve—VP of Operations, EDS.

Additional services beyond the baseline cost EDS money, which has been recovered through excess fees. According to two participants, in total, the excess fees for additional services only amounted to about $AU2 million per year (approximately 3% of the average yearly value of the contract) for the first three years, and rose above this subsequently. The formal change request process ensures that SA agencies understand the value they receive from additional services. For each requested change, EDS provides an impact statement which details the value and cost to the user. However, sometimes agencies have used the formal change request process for exploratory purposes:

> One of the frustrating things to us is the change request process. Right now (1998) it's being used as tire kicking. We are trying to work with the customer and say, 'Hey look if all you are trying to get is a rough estimate for budgetary purposes, let us know. We can give you that kind of information and it's a lot faster and a lot easier for us. If you are serious about the change, fine, let's go through the whole process, doing the detail.' Other than that, the departments are not creating wish lists. The governments are under budgetary constraints and they don't have excess money to spend. I think they are pretty good about that—VP of Operations, EDS.

Fostering Realistic Expectations of Supplier Performance

Both the SA and EDS contract managers realize the need to temper agency expectations, particularly because the agencies had little influence over the decision:

> So [the former Premier of South Australia] was, if you will, the architect, the motivating force behind that whole thing, the godfather of it. He basically drove it. In the end, it was a very difficult process to get through the government and the bureaucracy. Without his commitment, the political push he exerted, it never would have happened. It would have died along the way a number of different times—VP of Operations, EDS.

In order for the relationship to work, SA and EDS contract managers have worked hard to create realistic agency expectations:

> I've actually been an outsourcer before. I've been on a bidding side. I understand the challenges a supplier faces. There is generally an expectation of management on the user side that here is this knight in shining armour, I'll get three times better service at half the price. And also what happens, that expectation grows as you get closer to contract, so you have this large gap in expectations from the start—Contract Administrator, South Australian Government.

> I would say the challenge is service delivery. Because it's the expectation of the end user. Are the expectations realistic? In this environment it is very

difficult because the concept was originated and implemented from a central government standpoint. All the departments and agencies had no say in whether they were going to be outsourced, number one, and what the nature of that arrangement would be. To this day, they have not been given very good access to the terms of the contract. So this has been a challenge for us in trying to meet their expectations. Frankly, it's been difficult at times. But by and large, it's a matter of expectations. The contract is based around existing levels of service at a reduced cost. The existing levels of service were quite poor in some cases, but the users expected that once outsourced, everything would be wonderful—VP of Operations, EDS.

The discussion section explores the issue of cost savings and expectation management in more detail.

Discussion and Analysis of the South Australian/EDS contract

The success of any decision is usually measured against the initial objectives of that decision. A number of qualitative objectives were achieved. For example, SA has been able, over the first five years of the contract, to focus in-house IT attention away from infrastructure towards more value-added agency applications:

Before outsourcing, 55% of our resources went towards tweaking boxes. But you can have the best tweaked boxes in the world doing nothing for your business—Contract Administrator, SA Government.

In addition, SA was able to achieve the benefits of EDS's consolidation without incurring initial investment costs:

Our average datacenter was between 20 and 40 MIPS. You can run 400 to 1000 MIPs and not even blink. But a 20 to 40 MIP datacenter, the actual utilization is around 60% if it's really run well. So you have 40% slack on your hardware; you generally have 50% slack. If we were going to do it ourselves, if we were to consolidate ourselves, we would have cost increases at first for investment. But day one of the contract, we have cost savings. Where we get the benefit, we have a variable cost and pay for what we use. We also don't own the infrastructure so we get better cash flow—Contract Administrator, SA Government.

South Australia also articulated two main financial objectives:

- realize $AU200 million in economic development over the nine year contract; and
- realize $AU100 million in cost savings on baseline services over the nine year contract

Although the contract had just passed the half-way mark at the time of our analysis (mid-2000), a preliminary assessment of success on these two objectives is possible.

Results of the Economic Development Contract

By all accounts, EDS have exceeded their yearly targets on economic development.

> In terms of a positive outcome [on economic development], EDS has exceeded our expectations—Contract Administrator, SA Government.

Before the contract, EDS only had 30 people working on the GM–Holden contract. By 1998, EDS employed over 600 people and established in Adelaide:

- an IPC, one of only 16 EDS mega-datacenters world-wide;
- an Information Management Center (IMC), one of only 3 EDS global network management centers world-wide;
- a Systems Engineering Center (SEC), one of 40 EDS centers world-wide; the SEC has 110 people developing applications, including a year 2000 center;
- an Asia/Pacific Education Resource Center, which has provided training courses for over 6000 EDS employees throughout the region, on site and remotely.

In addition, EDS was able to help a number of small Adelaide software companies access international marketing channels:

> Our IT industry [in Adelaide] is really a cottage industry in software development. The small companies have some really good products, but it's not a Silicon Valley. EDS helps those companies get to places where they couldn't. So what they do, they take our local software and sell it through their Asian channels. They help with marketing and training—Contract Administrator, SA Government.

EDS has also attracted other global players to Adelaide. For example, EDS and Microsoft announced a deal in which EDS would establish one of Microsoft's four major global internet datacenters in Adelaide.

The multiplier effect of EDS's base in Adelaide includes housing starts, hotel bookings, meals, and rental of government/university property. Thus, the initial vision of Premier Dean Brown has been realized—SA attracted a major IT supplier to develop the economy:

> So we are building all of those new jobs, that account for our economic development contract, worth hundreds of millions of dollars over the nine-

year life of the contract. We are well ahead of schedule on delivering on that—VP of Operations, EDS, 1998.

Results of the Information Services Provision Document: Is SA saving money on Government IT?

The initial vision of the information services (IS) provision contract was to save the SA government $AU100 million over the nine-year contract *over baseline IT services*. Both EDS and the SA government implemented a number of practices that reduce IT cost drivers, such as consolidating datacenters and standardizing infrastructure platforms. But has SA been saving money on its IT baseline? The trade press and Australian public radio still debate this issue. Opponents have regularly argued that agencies spend much more on IT. For example:

> The opposition in South Australia said that the costs of the EDS contract were already blowing out to the tune of $AU20 million. The claims were based on information supplied to a Select Committee of the State Parliament by more than 20 government departments whose computers are now being run by EDS—Tom Morten, Australian Broadcasting Company, National Radio, Background Briefing Transcript, July 13, 1997.

Proponents argued that 20% of hidden IT costs had just become visible by that date. IT costs, such as depreciation on IT assets, were previously hidden by the cost accounting system. IT personnel costs were hidden by the previous job categories, such as civil servants spending part of their time backing up LANs or analyzing infrastructure requirements.

> We are operating there in a politically hotly-contested environment. The opposition take every opportunity to take a crack at the guys in power. For a long time, our contract was the biggest thing going on in town, it was fair game as a football to kick back and forth. So, it came up. But there's not so much anymore. People realize it was a story and not fact that instead of saving people money it was costing the government more. Where that came from, some of the departments and agencies are experiencing higher costs than they did before. But that's because they are now seeing the full cost. Before, the cost of capital was carried by the Treasury, the initial purchase cost by central government. All the agencies saw was the support costs. Now, they are being charged back at a full cost. It was a great story that made headlines. If you look at the whole of government, the savings are there—VP of Operations, EDS.

The SA contract administrator agreed that savings on the baseline had been realized:

We monitor the baseline services, and we have every change request that affects the baseline. There is a price and a cost. We model that data. So we check each year down to the last dollar change in baseline versus additional services and we measure the price. Ours can be measured because it's just the infrastructure. We know what our costs were, we track price/performance. Gartner tells us every year what the historic stuff is and the current costs. So it is easier—there is less risk in managing infrastructure than applications. There is no doubt about that. So we track this curve right down to the number of boxes. And I have to report on this annually, on the savings. So I can tell you how much we spent each year of the contract, how much of that was for baseline, and how much of that was for additional business and what percentage of savings we achieved—Contract Administrator, South Australian Government, 1998.

As agencies began to understand the full costs of IT baseline services, they subsequently asked: 'Are we getting a fair market price?' But even this question has been difficult to answer because of price bundling. The agencies, for example, argued that they were paying too much for a LAN server. In mid-1997 the contract price was $AU1797 to run a Pentium 90[4] chip LAN server with 25 users for one month (Australian Broadcasting Company, National Radio, Background Briefing Transcript, July 13, 1997). Agencies went to market and found lower prices, but these prices did not include cost of ownership, service, and maintenance. The situation was analogous to the average cost of a desktop; benchmarking firms vary estimates from $AU5000 to $AU20 000, depending on the services included (Lacity and Hirschheim 1995b):

It's an interesting challenge. In moving from providers to purchasers, our minds shift in thinking. That gets in the way, that shift gets in the way of the relationship. In 9 times out of 10, the real costs are confined and buried in corporate accounts—they are invisible. So when people say, 'Why is this costing so much? It used to only cost me this', you have to mediate expectations which is why we adopted a central contract management model—Contract Administrator, SA Government.

Partnering in Practice

Another major indicator of success for many contracts is the quality of the relationship between a customer and a supplier (Kern and Willcocks 2001; see also Chapter 8). All customer/supplier contracts involve relationships with many stakeholders. In the case of SA, the supplier has relationships with centralized government officials, SA contract administrators, agency IT managers, and agency users.

Perceived winners, such as the centralized government (who realized the cost savings) and the Treasury department (who received the cash payment for the IT assets), have been strong advocates of the relationship. EDS has enjoyed the full support of the previous and current Premiers. If any future election changed the party in power, then the supplier would have to foster new relationships:

> During the nine-year term of this contract it is very possible that the party holding office will change. We, of course, are not aligned politically, but must remain focused on the thrust of the agreement and partnership with the government. Should the government adopt a different view toward outsourcing and the strategic direction of IT within government, we have to be flexible. This would not be a new experience for us as we work with governments all over the world and governments do change—VP of Operations, EDS.

At the contract administration level, both parties have been committed to fostering a good relationship from the start of the contract. For example, after the six-month contract negotiation process, the parties recognized the need to shift from adversaries defending the interests of their perspective organizations to cooperators. An outside consultant was brought in to facilitate a 'love-in' session attended by 30 SA and EDS employees. Each party was asked to articulate their perceptions of each other, resulting in much needed laughter and a new found lightheartedness.

But the dynamics of the relationship at the contract administration level can vary with the tasks at hand. If the task involves discussions over general contract terms, then the parties are sometimes adversarial because they must protect and represent their own organization's interests. If the task involves mediating agency expectations, then the parties at the contract administration level are often cooperative. If the task involves publicly discussing the economic development impacts of the contract, then the parties are collaborative. The following quotes provide examples of how the relationship adapts for specific tasks:

> So really our challenge, and I know from talking to other people it is a real challenge, is relationship management. We are trying different things. We have these consultative boards, we have one-on-ones, we work with them on public speeches, we promote together the Asia/Pacific resource center. In part it helps them, in part it helps us. So withstanding all the parts where there is positive synergy, when it comes to the straight contract, it's tough. So we are still working through ways to try to deal with that. I know that I certainly haven't found the answer yet, but not too many other people have found the answer either—Contract Administrator, SA Government.

> The requirement is that every decision that the government makes is open for public scrutiny, and you can't always achieve an agreement that makes good

business sense. It has to be something that the auditors can come in and follow a well-documented process on how you got from A to B to ensure that the public's interests have been served. This is not to mean that you ignore process. You can't have two business people sit across the table and agree on a good business decision. In the public sector, you can't do that. It makes it more difficult to manage a relationship like this without it becoming an adversarial relationship. It takes an extra amount of understanding on the part of the supplier to really understand what motivates the team on the other side of the negotiating table—VP of Operations, EDS.

We have to sit with the agencies and EDS to make expectations reasonable. It's a balancing act. We get accused by the agencies, 'Why are you siding with the supplier, you are supposed to be on our side?' But you need to be even-handed. Suppliers have to make a reasonable margin to stay in business. You don't want them to lose money because the worse their business gets, the worse your business gets. At the same time you don't want them to make outrageous profits at your expense—Contract Administrator, SA Government.

At the agency level, several issues had to be addressed as impediments to a good relationship. First, the decision was forced on the agencies. Second, agency costs increased because they are being charged full IT costs instead of partial costs. Third, agencies did not (and still do not) understand the details of the confidential contract, so they have made assumptions about what duties the supplier is supposed to perform at what cost.

That's the other side, they don't understand the cost side of the equation. They think we are here to give them everything they need. And by and large, over time, they are learning what they can expect and what they should be measuring our performance against … I find that we are getting to a point, where, yes it's still an issue, but it is becoming less of an issue—VP of Operations, EDS.

During the first few years of the contract, the customer/supplier relationship focused on transition tasks. Subsequently, the parties worked to focus the relationship on more strategic issues:

Within the contract there are a couple of areas that have not received a lot of focus up to this time (1998). Up until now, the main focus has been on the transition and getting everything settled and organized. There is a provision for a strategic planning committee on which we are represented. Together we will look forward to the direction that the government wants to go to add value to the partnership. And we can advise them on the best ways that we can work together to achieve changes. Help them look at additional whole of government initiatives. That's an area we believe we will really start to add value to the partnership—VP of Operations, EDS.

SA Government: Conclusion

The SA government–EDS contract is unique because of the economic development aspect of the contract. In this capacity, the customer and supplier truly have been strategic partners because each party benefits from EDS's growth and presence in the Adelaide economy. Such a relationship is not only rare, the competitive advantage is generally non-replicable. However, the case serves as testimony to the use of IT outsourcing for strategic purposes (see also Willcocks and Lacity 2000 for other examples). Other private sector and public sector organizations can use this exemplar for thinking beyond mere exchange-based relationships.

The issues arising from the IT service provision component of the relationship are not unique. The financial restructuring resulting from IT outsourcing contracts typically creates realistic and full cost chargeback of IT for the first time in most organizations. Financial redistribution creates perceived winners and losers, resulting in predisposed allies and opponents of outsourcing. The real challenge to any large-scale contract is the continual fostering of realistic expectations of IT delivery among varied stakeholders.[5]

In addition, assessing actual cost savings is confounded by the fact that *the baseline moves.* The SA government, like every large IT outsourcing customer, has significantly altered the volume and composition of the baseline service. After the contract was signed, the SA government grew from 1100 LAN servers in 1996 to over 1800 LAN servers in January 1998, and more subsequently. In addition, baseline services were unacceptable in some areas. For example, at the beginning some of the datacenters were dangerously wired and EDS had to spend money to ensure safety. In other areas, agencies wanted to improve baseline service levels and they regularly worked with EDS to determine the cost/service trade-offs of proposed improvements.

One of the occurrences not planned for was the fact that the SA government contract was one of the first for EDS in Australia. What happened when they secured additional large-scale contracts? In September 1997, EDS signed a $AU5 billion 10-year deal with Commonwealth Bank. One consequence was that many EDS staff on the SA contract were moved over to facilitate the transition of and staff the new contract. Even large global suppliers often have much more restricted access to their own staff than is realized—in EDS's case a potential 100 000 labor pool world-wide at the time. This may be for reasons of geography or prior commitments, and even large suppliers can get hit by IT skills shortages in specific areas. All this means that the supplier will need to prioritize demands for labor. Once a deal is won, and transition has taken place, there is always the temptation to move good staff on to the next deal, not least to ensure the best possible start for each deal.

Finally, the biggest worry articulated by the citizens of SA was, 'What happens at the end of this contract?' Phil Eastick, IT ministerial liaison for the SA government, reported that even though the contract expires after nine years, the government had no intention of bringing IT back in-house. Instead, the government would continue to keep policy and strategy internal while outsourcing non-core activities (reported on www.outsourcing-journal.com/issues/feb2000/html/eds_1.html).

CASE 2: DUPONT

In 1997, DuPont signed a series of 10-year contracts worth $US4 billion with Computer Sciences Corporation (CSC) and Andersen Consulting (AC), making this the second largest IT outsourcing alliance as at that date. The decision process, from the creation of the RFP to the signing of the contracts, took 18 months. By 2000, CSC had 2600 people providing global infrastructure and applications and AC has 400 people providing chemical applications for DuPont. DuPont retained 60 centralized people (initially 100) to manage the contracts and over 1000 distributed business and technical people to provide business IT leadership, process control computing in manufacturing, and research and development (R&D) computing (including a Cray supercomputer). At the time of the initial interviews, only eight months had elapsed since the alliances began. Partners were focusing on translating the 30 000 lines of contract into daily work practices. Transition management lasted for another year. In a follow-up interview in early 2000, it was clear that DuPont's business and technology needs had evolved since the signing of the contracts. DuPont has worked successfully with both suppliers to adapt the relationship to meet those needs.

The DuPont deals have no primary contractor; DuPont signed completely separate contracts with the suppliers. In other mega-outsourcing deals involving multiple suppliers, a prime contractor ensures integration, coordination, and cooperation among suppliers. (See JP Morgan's deal as an example in Chapter 1, but also BPX in Chapter 6.) Rather than a legal arrangement, DuPont's deals successfully rely on mutual dependencies to ensure CSC and AC cooperate where functions overlap. Because AC-led projects often require CSC infrastructure, and CSC projects often require AC support, each supplier is motivated to cooperate with each other:

And because of the integration of our supply chains, you are always going to have a situation where there's going to be some Andersen interfaces with CSC, and CSC interfacing with Andersen. So they are both going to be, if you will, in the same predicament. So they both need each other to be successful and if they try to [hurt] each other, it just won't work, because the [hurt] guy will just get even on the next transaction—Global Alliance Manager, DuPont.

In addition to cooperating on existing projects, CSC and AC compete with each other (and outside suppliers) for new projects. A 'gentleman's agreement' among the account managers ensures that people in the trenches are not placed in conflict-of-interest situations. The parties agree that individuals working closely with the other supplier will not participate on competitive bid teams for additional work.

Thus far (2000), DuPont views the decision not to employ a prime contractor as sound business practice:

We've figured out how they both simultaneously work day-to-day, shoulder-by-shoulder, and for new work, like major projects, compete with one another ... It's actually worked better than we thought it might. We were worried about the situation. Did we make a mistake?—Global Alliance Manager, DuPont.

Despite the distinctive features to DuPont's deals, we will also see that DuPont's post-contract management practices to date are very similar to the other three cases (see also Chapter 8).

DuPont: Background

DuPont was founded in 1802 and incorporated in 1915 in Wilmington, Delaware. DuPont strives to be the global leader in energy, chemicals, and specialty products. The CEO's 1996 letter to shareholders states DuPont's mission: 'We want to be the most successful energy and chemical-based company in the world, dedicated to creating materials that make people's lives better and easier—John Krol, President and CEO of DuPont since 1987.

DuPont's 20 strategic business units operate in 70 countries. Annual revenues for 1997 were $US45 billion (see Table 2.5), approximately half from their petroleum business (via Conoco), and half from chemicals, fibres (such as Nylon®, Lycra®, Dacron®), polymers, life sciences, and diversified businesses such as agriculture, imaging, and electronics. Other notable products include Corian®, Teflon®, and Stainmaster®. In 1997, 53% of sales occurred outside the United States. World-wide, DuPont has 120 joint ventures and 30 new joint ventures currently underway.

Table 2.5 *1997 company statistics*

Revenues	$US45 billion
Earnings	$US3.6 billion
Number of employees	100 000

In 1996, DuPont strove to focus on their core competencies. The CEO describes DuPont's competitive advantage: 'We have a unique set of businesses that derive their superior competitive advantage from strong core technology platforms, product brand franchises, and engineering capability.' The company does research in over 75 sites world-wide. Forty research sites are US based, leading to a significant number of US patents (over 2500 in 1996). For the past four years, DuPont has focused on their core capabilities and divested non-core businesses. In 1996, for example, DuPont sold their medical products businesses and divested 30% of their photomasks business. They also plan to exit from electronic imaging, caustic chlorine, and advanced composites. They acquired Polyester and other businesses from ICI for $US3 billion.

For the past few years, DuPont has gone through a major reorganization, with focus on cost reduction and increased capital efficiency. The goal continues to be the reduction of overhead costs, either by distributing functions to strategic business units (SBUs) where costs are directly billable, or possibly by outsourcing business processes, such as financial accounting.

DuPont's IT Department Prior to Outsourcing

Prior to outsourcing, DuPont's IT department was headed by the Vice President and CIO. The CIO was advised by a Business Information Board, comprised of a select group of senior VPs. The official role of the Board was to help set IT strategy, but in reality the Board served more as a vehicle for status reporting. The centralized IT groups, comprised of approximately 3000 people, provided data and applications, planning and security, datacenter operations, and telecommunications to the 20 SBUs (see Tables 2.6 and 2.7). Regional IT centers provided support in Asia, Canada, Europe, Mexico, South America, and the United States. Within the SBUs, approximately 1000 distributed IT staff worked on SBU specific systems and reported to the VP of IS within the SBU.

The cost of this world-wide support totaled over $US1.2 billion. In 1989, DuPont's Information technology budget was perceived by senior management as too high. 'He didn't ask what value, only that the number was too big'—Alliance Planning manager, DuPont.

Table 2.6   *Twenty strategic business units (SBUs) supported by IT*

1. Advanced fiber and materials	11. Films
2. Agricultural products	12. Fluoroproducts
3. Automotive	13. Lycra[R]
4. Conoco Downstream	14. Non-wovens
5. Conoco upstream	15. Nylon[R]
6. Corian[R]	16. Packaging and industrial polymers
7. Dacron[R]	17. Pharmaceuticals
8. Elastomers	18. Printing and publishing
9. Electronic materials	19. Specialty chemicals
10. Engineering polymers	20. White pigments

In 1990, a process of continuous IT improvement sought to significantly reduce IT costs. In 1991 and 1992, the elimination of work and redundancy reduction cut the IT budget to $US1 billion. Rather than 100 datacenters distributed throughout the SBUs, three mega-centers were created in Delaware, Oklahoma, and Germany. From 1993 to 1996, the IT budget was further reduced to $US650 million through re-engineering, value-added refocusing, and renewal. For example, each plant maintained idiosyncratic maintenance systems that were subsequently standardized. Other cost saving practices included buying more packaged software rather than building software, selecting packages that ran on the current architecture (to avoid further IT investments), and reusing existing code. In total, DuPont reduced the IT budget by 45% ($US550 million) within six years.

The cost cuts were accomplished with no disruption in service. The users in the SBUs accepted these cost reduction measures because they had significant pressure from their senior management within the SBUs. These SBU managers consistently applauded the IT group on their continuous cost reduction performance:

> While the people who use systems day to day don't feel the same, nobody ever complained at the senior VP level, they loved it—Alliance Planning Manager, DuPont.

Table 2.7   *Scope of DuPont's information systems*

Mainframe and midrange computers	800
Personal computers	65 000
Local area networks (LANs)	>500
Telephones	120 000
Data exchange customer links	>2500
Internet access per day	1 700 000
Business information systems	>3000
Customer invoices per year	5 000 000
E-mail messages per month	17 000 000

However, IT costs cannot be cut by 45% without consequences. IT assets and skills were not being renewed, and the IT infrastructure needed several hundred million dollars worth of investments. In the datacenters, for examples, DuPont needed dual power supplies and back-up generators, disaster recovery, and contingency plans for data-center redundancies. The IT group was operating on borrowed time, and any datacenter disasters would potentially cripple DuPont. But when SBU managers were asked to invest in disaster recovery, the response was negative:

> The datacenters were band-aided together, but Dupont is self-insured, so they don't think in terms of insurance—Alliance Planning Manager, DuPont.

Rather than fund capital investments in IT, outsourcing became a serious option. In addition to avoiding the cost of renewal, DuPont cites five reasons for considering outsourcing:

1. *Variable costs.* Prior to outsourcing, 90% of DuPont's IT budget was fixed. DuPont wanted to transform the fixed operating budget to a 'pay-for-use' variable budget.
2. *Service speed and flexibility.* DuPont wanted greater flexibility and speed in responding to business needs.
3. *Skill renewal.* DuPont also wanted access to supplier IT skills, including state-of-the-art business solutions, methods, and technologies. They had already adopted a number of practices from Andersen Consulting that improved legacy system maintenance, including Method I, tool kits, and service control standards. What other areas could be improved by supplier know-how?
4. *Cost reduction.* DuPont's IT department delivered cost savings six years in a row. This precedent created senior management expectations for continuous cost improvement. But where else could IT costs be reduced? Perhaps suppliers can leverage their resources to provide additional cost reductions and productivity improvements.
5. *Career development.* Greater professional development and career advancement opportunities for the IT workforce was a major evaluation criterion. DuPont wanted their IT employees to be fully employed at equivalent or better benefits.

DuPont's Outsourcing Decision Process

The entire decision process took 14 months and required the involvement of 100 people at various times. In February 1996, DuPont selected a core group of IT people to prepare a comprehensive 'three foot' Request For Proposal (RFP). The RFP contained no cost data, but provided details on every IT job and the services provided. In April 1996, 12 companies were invited to respond—only four did: IBM, Phillips, CSC, and AC. Phillips dropped out almost immediately. In June 1996, DuPont evaluated the proposals using an extensive list of criteria (see Table 2.8).

Table 2.8   *Outsourcing evaluation criteria*

Minimal requirements	Deliver variable cost Lower cost via SLA Lower cost via productivity improvement Fair treatment of people Access to skills Operational competence
Differentiators	DuPont ability to influence Cultural fit, values, ongoing trust in relationship People opportunity Ongoing ability to invest/renew Integrated leading edge solutions capability Deliver value to DuPont businesses
Judgment calls	Ability to execute globally Speed of execution Commitment to deliver Gap fit with DuPont capabilities
Economic	Price versus in-house case Variability Potential gain share
Change driver	Source and implementation of idea Competitive value-added Business process improvements
Deliver capability in the near term	Transition plan Implementation methodologies Project management capability Global integration Tower integration SLA experience
Deliver capability in the near term	Technology planning Industry leadership Continuous improvement approach
Technical solution viability	Distributed computing Cross functional Mainframe Applications Midrange Telecom

	Impact on personnel Ability to address variability Ability to build relationships Quality of people—professionalism, innovation, thought leadership
People opportunity	Near term and long term
People treatment	Comparability of compensation and benefits Culture—respect for individual
Cultural compatibility	Flexibility, partnership potential Source of rigor and discipline
Contract management	SLA compliance management Billing and invoicing Retained organization to interface
Viability	Financial health Ability to invest IS services industry success Chemical and process industry success Management and professional strength

DuPont considered five main alternatives prior to selecting the two-supplier alliance:

1. keep in-house
2. pilot approach
3. multi-supplier selective outsourcing
4. single-supplier approach
5. two-supplier alliance approach

1. *Keep in-house.* DuPont did not invite an internal bid team, because they were confident that they had already extracted as much value as possible from their current resources. In addition, an in-house bid would not be able to compete on two of the driving forces—the desire for variable costs and the avoidance of a renewal investment. DuPont was also concerned about their ability to attract top IT talent.

2. *Pilot approach.* In the past, DuPont had used some piecemeal outsourcing. The main arguments against this approach were economies of scale. Large deals get better prices and transaction costs are lower.

3. *Multi-supplier selective outsourcing.* The main argument against this alternative was that transaction costs were too high because there would be too many points of contact. Also, it was argued that it was harder to negotiate better prices with multiple suppliers.

4. *Single-supplier approach.* The main arguments for this alternative were a single point of contact, easier to administer, and easier to

integrate. However, DuPont did not believe that any one supplier was strong enough in all requirements at all locations.

5. *Two-supplier alliance approach.* The two supplier alliance approach was finally selected because it required only a small increase in administration and coordination and required only a small loss of scale over the single-supplier approach. In addition, DuPont can leverage the best strengths of two suppliers and maintain some ongoing competition in strategic areas. CSC and AC were selected as partners.

From August 1996 until December 1996, DuPont conducted due diligence with selected partners. One hundred percent of the infrastructure would be given to CSC, but applications would be divided based on competency.

From December 1996 until the second quarter of 1997, negotiations occurred. As the Global Alliance Manager describes, the major task was the translation of technical RFP requirements into legal requirements. A legal firm specializing in IT outsourcing contracts was hired for this task. Early on, it was determined that a contract should be signed for each country, 22 in all. Local employee regulation, tax laws, and currency issues warranted the need for country agreements. DuPont spent much time gathering exhibits of all the services provided in the different countries.

During the negotiation process, DuPont spent a lot of time negotiating equivalent benefits, including equivalent salaries, equivalent health care, and dental care for the 3000 employees targeted for transition. In particular, DuPont and AC spent time explaining to the IT staff the differences between Andersen's consulting practice and Andersen's BPM practice (its outsourcing business). These divisions have different career paths, career expectations, benefits, etc. In situations that were not equivalent, cash was distributed to employees to equate the benefits.

The contracts were signed in the second quarter of 1997.

DuPont's Contract Overview

DuPont outsourced almost all the IT infrastructure to CSC, including telecommunications, datacenters, midrange computing (VAX, UNIX), and desktops. CSC also maintains a number of existing applications, including US C&S Generic and Plant Applications, European, and Canadian Applications. AC has 400 people responsible for chemical-specific applications.

The CSC contract, which is a much larger deal than the AC contract, is based on flexible pricing and world-wide service-level agreements.

Although the relationship has been described as a strategic partnership, the contract primarily treats the relationship as an exchange.

Price

There is an overall master service agreement, but no billing occurs at this level. Instead, each country has a pricing schedule that reflects the cost of living and is defined in the local currency. All monthly billing is based on the source country. Thus, if an English subsidiary buys datacenter services from Germany, the bill is originated in Deutsche Marks and translated to Pounds Sterling at the current exchange rate.

The contract encompasses 20 different billing units, including stand-alone desktops, desktops connected to a LAN, mainframe MIPs, gigabytes of storage, tape mounts, UNIX boxes, and IT staff charges by job category. The pricing schedules anticipate price reductions in some areas (such as MIPs), and price increases in other areas (such as IT staff). In all, the whole basket of services is expected to cost 7% less during the contract.

The contract includes benchmarking and market-testing provisions to alter prices during the relationship:

> We want an appropriate price, one that is either negotiated or we have benchmarking and market provision that would enable us to go back and renegotiate pricing should we find that something in the future becomes, in our view, not competitive. Then we have retained the right to insource or outsource any component of what we have collectively given to Andersen and CSC. So there are certain minimums that are a factor, but we feel that we've negotiated a fair degree of flexibility that will keep the suppliers fair in their price to us—Global Alliance Manager, DuPont.

Service Levels

A consulting firm helped to define service levels. The objective was to document current service levels as the baseline, with a goal of long-term service improvement, especially in the area of desktop computing. There are over 600 services defined at different locations world-wide. DuPont determined for each location whether each service would be 'standard', 'differentiated', or 'not provided'. Each service is also ranked by criticality, and escalation procedures (and even cash penalties for non-performance) are specified. Procedures are defined for root cause analysis to determine why non-performance occurred and how it could be prevented in the future. In the spirit of a partnership, DuPont agreed that no cash penalties would occur in the first year to allow the partners a fair chance to transition and to verify service levels.

Volumes

DuPont has a 10-year forecast demand for baseline services, which they know is highly inaccurate. Although DuPont wanted complete variable costing of IT, the partners are guaranteed a certain volume of service. DuPont is obligated to pay at least 50% of baseline volumes ('take or pay'). This clause ensures that the suppliers will earn a fair return on their investments. The contract, however, does include a 'significant events' clause which would trigger a renegotiation if volumes significantly declined. In actuality, volumes are expected to increase over the course of the contract.

In the contract, neither CSC nor AC can enter into any local contracts with DuPont SBUs. All CSC–AC contracts must go through the centralized Global Alliance Manager. This provision was designed to prevent cost creep and to maintain control world-wide.

The contracts also intend for the relationships to become more strategic in the future. Both CSC and AC plan to explore marketing of specific solutions in the chemical, oil, and gas industries to external customers outside of the alliance. DuPont would share in a fraction of the generated revenue.

DuPont's Transition Period

In total, 3100 people transferred from DuPont to CSC and AC (about 40% of these people are outside the United States). But the transfer of staff is only one of the activities parties go through during a transition period. Like the previous case, DuPont anticipated an 18-month period to conduct the following transition activities:

- distribute and interpret the contract for the user population;
- establish the post-contract management infrastructure;
- establish the post-contract management processes;
- implement consolidation, rationalization, and standardization;
- validate services, costs, and service levels for baseline services; and
- manage additional service requests.

Distribute and Interpret the Contract for the User Population

DuPont's Global Alliance Manager said, 'the lawyers delivered 10 boxes to my office and said, "that's the contract" '. The contract is 30 000 lines long. Because it is impossible to execute the relationships from this contract, a two-inch summary document was distributed. However, DuPont found that even a summary document is open to interpretation. People world-wide needed to translate the document into daily work practices, a process that halted work and impeded the relationship in the early days:

> We find that anything you write down and distribute to a group of people, those people interpret it differently and they try to execute against their interpretation—Global Alliance Manager, DuPont.

For example, work on 150 major projects was halted due to lack of project pricing. Lower level employees were not sure how to behave— how can we do this work when it has not been properly priced and approved? Once the general account managers were aware of the problem, they sent clear messages to lower level employees: do the work and we'll worry about the price.

To help people around the world understand their roles, DuPont and the suppliers are developing a responsibilities matrix. Like a similar document developed at South Australia—EDS (see above), the DuPont document defines exactly which party is responsible for a given activity, and whether that activity is within scope or subject to excess fees. The document is constantly refined as precedents are set and as learning accumulates. These documents are being developed by the centralized alliance managers, then rolled out to county CIOs:

> So we are going to roll this out to the CIOs of each of our businesses and functions and regions because they need to understand how things work if they are considering projects and doing what–if scenarios. 'If I do this or that, what might it cost me?' They'll get help from the demand management team and program management team, but they need to understand the complexity of this. So you can see that just in these documents, it's not simple, but relative to all these words [in the official contract], it's something people can use— Global Alliance Manager, DuPont.

Establishing the Post-Contract Management Infrastructure

DuPont retained 1200 IT people, 100 people (down to 60) in a centralized business center, and 1100 people in the SBUs with business and technical responsibilities.

DuPont's Centralized IS Business Center Staff   One hundred IT employees initially worked in the IT Business Center. They are responsible for start-up of the deal, alliance management, finance management, productivity improvement, value–delivery integration, and human resource management. Staff were selected prior to the decision, and represent the best of the DuPont IT talent. Some of the duties of each group include:

- The *Alliance Management* people are responsible for contract management, business demand management, and service and quality management.
- The *Finance* team reviews bills and monitors chargeback, creates budgets, determines affordability, and determines pricing and life-cycle management.
- The *Productivity Improvement* team is responsible for architecture, standards, IT best practices, infrastructure review, security and crises management, and leveraging opportunities.
- The *Value Delivery Integration* team creates IT strategy and IT business plans, manages processes, provides IT foresight and insight, and explores commercial possibilities.
- The *Human Resource* team provides hiring, placement, and career development of people retained by DuPont.

DuPont's Decentralized Business and Technical IT Staff   Initially, DuPont retained 1100 people who were distributed in the business divisions and R&D organization. (This number was later reduced during the middle years of the contract.) These IT people understand the business needs and are responsible for planning and communicating IT requirements to CSC and AC.

> Once they scope out business requirements, we put CSC and AC at the table—Alliance Planning Manager, DuPont.

It is within these 20 plus business units that interaction occurs with CSC and AC, not at the board level. The Business and Technical IT staff also provide IT services for activities not included in the alliance, such as R&D computing, and Asia/Pacific, Mexico, and South America applications.

Establish the Post-Contract Management Processes

During the transition, local interpretations on project pricing temporarily halted work. The project pricing issue prompted a new problem management process. Lotus Notes is now used to document all issues. The problem is assigned a number and a one-page problem summary is attached. Joint DuPont–supplier teams are assigned responsibility for the issue. Each issue has three ratings—green (acceptable), yellow (some problems), and red (significant problems). If the problem escalates to red, the problem is transferred to the general account managers. For issues with a red status, the general account managers hold bi-weekly status meetings on these issues, expecting some progress from the teams for each issue. The goal is to have all problems resolved before reaching this level. The operating principle of each team is to be fair, not to exploit any contract inefficiencies. During the transition period, 120 of the project issues were successfully resolved in this manner.

Implement Consolidation, Rationalization, and Standardization

Because DuPont consolidated, rationalized, and standardized before out-sourcing IT, there are not many opportunities for the suppliers to implement cost-reduction tactics to meet their projected margins.[6] In particular, the IT infrastructure was operating at best-of-breed costs and services:

> First of all, it has been difficult for them to [rationalize] in the infrastructure area because our infrastructure area was well planned. We knew that from the benchmarking activity. So as we went through the whole RFP process, there were some suppliers, even though they would like to have the DuPont account, dropped out because they didn't see enough margin in it for them—Global Alliance Manager, DuPont.

The suppliers, however, have an opportunity to deploy cost-saving tactics in the area of applications development and support:

> The applications area did not have as much attention in terms of working on the efficiency and the effectiveness, so there is an opportunity for improvement there—Global Alliance Manager, DuPont.

In addition, CSC has been able to meet their margins in part by selling excess capacity on ex-DuPont assets:

> But beyond [margins generated from rationalization], they have opportunities for further economies of scale and leveraging with other clients. So for example in our datacenter, they have decided to expand that datacenter as a major East Coast datacenter. And there are already customers' work that's being run from that datacenter. So there's an opportunity for economies of scale with other customers—Global Alliance Manager, DuPont.

But as one DuPont informant indicated, '[the datacenter sales] are small change'.

Validate Services, Costs, and Service Levels for Baseline Services

A major transition challenge for all relationships is validating the baseline and continuing to refine the contract. DuPont's Global Alliance Manager was somewhat frustrated that after all the negotiations, there was still about 18 months' work to translate the contract into daily work practices. He even called the IT outsourcing consulting firm he hired to ask them, 'Why didn't you tell us we weren't even close to done?'

For example, the monthly bills were incorrect by millions of dollars, primarily because services had not been fully defined. For example, what should be included in mainframe billable units? If the supplier makes an error that causes more consumption of mainframe MIPS, shouldn't the supplier pay for that? To resolve this issue, joint owners from DuPont and the supplier negotiated billable units with the assistance of an outside expert. Another example is full time equivalents: should DuPont be charged for meeting times and training hours?

Defining and interpreting services can be quite complex. Consider, for example, a standard PBX upgrade. What should be included in the fixed price of a PBX upgrade? Is analyst time spent identifying requirements billable or included in the fixed price? Are installation, wiring, and shipping and handling costs included or billable?

DuPont, like other customers, realizes that more staff should have been retained to address these issues:

> We didn't realize that part of the transition would include continuing to negotiate the deal. Had we known that was coming, we would have saved more resources, or kept more resources to help with both the continuing negotiation, definition of the deal, as well as I would say it has taken more resources than anticipated to put in place all these managing processes that are required as part of the transition or start-up of the deal—Global Alliance Manager, DuPont.

As far as validating baseline service levels around the world, joint teams are verifying services locally:

> First of all, there are service-level verification teams around the world that are jointly staffed with DuPont people and CSC people and Andersen people. They are agreeing on the benchmark for service levels. Then there is required reporting and there is similar work being done to operationalize the service-level agreement part of the deal—Global Alliance Manager, DuPont.

DuPont and suppliers agree that it was fair to suspend cash penalties for non-performance during the transition year. As one DuPont employee noted, '90% of the service lapses were inherited from us'.

Parties are working together to improve service lapses, rather than merely trying to blame one another.

Managing Additional Service Requests

Services beyond baseline (and thus subject to excess fees), can be triggered by exceeding projected volumes on existing services or by demand for entirely new projects.

At DuPont (and all other mega-contracts we have studied), user demand has exceeded projected demand. Prior to outsourcing, demand was constrained by the centralized IT group:

> In old times, each SBU bought from global leverage (i.e. the centralized IT group). There was lots of negotiating pressure to keep costs down—Global Planning Manager, DuPont.

Now, the alliance partners are motivated to meet all IT demands, which could lead to excess fees beyond baseline. There are three DuPont people in the business center that are trying to track actual demand and to forecast demand:

> What we found is that everyone is using more IT than baseline—Global Planning Manager, DuPont.

For new projects, DuPont retained the right to insource additional work, or bid additional work between CSC and AC or among other outsourcing suppliers. Even 4.5 months into the deal, DuPont had already bid out some extra work to ensure fair market pricing.

Overall, the transition period has required more energy than anticipated:

> We didn't realize that the transition at start-up was going to be as involved and difficult as it has been. Not that things haven't worked, because they have, but it's just that we didn't realize there would be all these loose ends to tie up—Global Alliance Manager, DuPont.

DuPont's Post Transition: The Middle Years

During the middle years, DuPont's relationship with suppliers has matured as DuPont faced a number of business and technical changes. Overall, DuPont has been extremely pleased with the suppliers' ability to access scarce IT skills to staff new projects. However, DuPont executives continue to stress that the success of the contracts requires 'a massive effort of hands-on management everyday'. Below are some highlights from the middle years.

Adjusting the Relationship to Changes in Business and Technology

In August 1999, DuPont divested Conoco, which represented nearly 50% of DuPont's revenues in 1996. What immediately springs to mind is DuPont's 50% take-or-pay clause: Did the sale of Conoco require DuPont to pay for baseline IT volumes no longer required because of Conoco's exit? On the basis of discussions in 1999 with a DuPont executive, it became evident that the sale of Conoco was a recognized possibility back in 1997, and thus contingencies were foreseen in the contracts for divestitures as well as mergers and acquisitions. And although Conoco generated 50% of revenues, it only consumed 15% of DuPont's overall IT volumes. In actuality new IT projects have continued to exceed baseline IT volumes.

Since the contracts were first signed, DuPont identified a new, $US400 million world-wide SAP/Y2K project. DuPont decided that merely making systems Y2K compliant did not enhance the business value of the systems. Therefore, DuPont refreshed the technology in order to improve processes while becoming Y2K compliant. DuPont realized that both suppliers needed to be a part of the SAP project. One supplier was able to bring in nearly 400 SAP specialists from around the world. To supplement the other supplier's SAP skills, DuPont transferred 300 people from the divisions over to the supplier. The supplier then bore the costs associated with SAP training. In addition to the success of the project from a Y2K perspective, the SAP project significantly improved process control and supply chain management.

Despite the success of most of the IT projects, desktop management was still a troublesome area during the middle years. DuPont had initially retained a number of suppliers for different desktop functions. User satisfaction was very low because they had to call multiple suppliers for procurement, adds, changes, moves, and help. DuPont launched a three-month desktop improvement task-force, which resulted in a redesign of the desktop services. Users now have 'one-stop shopping', which has served to improve satisfaction levels. This situation serves as an example of the trade-off between getting best suppliers through multi-sourcing versus the additional transaction costs required to coordinate multiple suppliers. By having one user interface, DuPont's IT department assumes the burden of the coordination roles.

Benchmarking Performance to Theorectically Reset Prices

DuPont's contracts require that service levels and costs be periodically benchmarked. Although DuPont still manages 600 service levels, the benchmarking effort organizes IT services into 'towers' including telecommunications, desktop, midrange, and applications. DuPont adopted a balanced score card approach which uses a number of measures to determine an overall bill of health for each tower. Three outside consulting firms have been hired to assist in the benchmarks. Since the benchmarking effort was still underway during the last quarter of 1999, no prices have been reset.

In general, service levels have been good as assessed by the fact that no service lapses have resulted in cash penalties. DuPont feels that the cash penalty clauses (which are only triggered by two successive service lapses) have served to motivate the suppliers to attend quickly and effectively to service issues.

Discussion and Analysis of DuPont–CSC–AC Contracts

In 2000 DuPont was only starting the third year of the deals, and it is difficult to assess whether the decision will ultimately be successful. We can, however, assess how the contracts have progressed so far against the five initial objects:

1. *Variable costs.* Prior to outsourcing, 90% of DuPont's IT budget was fixed owing to depreciation on assets, salaries, wages, etc. After outsourcing, DuPont has significantly reduced their capital investment in IT by selling assets to their suppliers (thus reducing depreciation expense). The IT operating budget is now only 50% fixed, owing to the requirement of guaranteeing the suppliers at least 50% of baseline volumes.

2. *Service speed and flexibility.* Prior to outsourcing, DuPont wanted greater flexibility and speed in responding to business needs. DuPont executives stated that they never could have hired 400 people to man the SAP/Y2K project on their own. Their suppliers were able to quickly provide people from around the globe to staff the short-term project.

3. *Skill renewal.* DuPont also wanted access to supplier IT skills, including state-of-the-art business solutions, methods, and technologies. After outsourcing, DuPont credits suppliers with a quick injection of new skills, such as a 'Team Red' for desktops, and an SAP RII team, and more rigorous development methodologies. DuPont credits this training with the improvement in function point productivity. (Function points are a measure used to assess application development and maintenance productivity and quality.) Overall, DuPont views employee training as a core competence of both suppliers.

4. *Cost reduction.* DuPont expected a modest 7% cost savings during the 10-year relationships. Like all mega-contracts, determining cost savings will be very difficult for DuPont because the volume and composition of baseline services will change dramatically Overall, the

budget has increased because of the increase in demand for more IT resources. Normally customers abandon the question, 'Did we achieve savings?' in favor of 'Are we getting a fair market price?' DuPont is no exception.

5. *Career development.* Greater professional development and career advancement opportunities for the IT workforce was a major evaluation criterion. After outsourcing, the ex-DuPont staff had successfully transitioned, but now DuPont wonders if they gave away too much expertise:

> The other key learning that we've had I would say was that we were a little behind in our expectation about how much technical resource we would need on an ongoing basis. And we thought that we could pretty much deplete ourselves of a lot of that and our partners would handle all that kind of stuff for us. And what we are finding is that DuPont has to make technical decisions on behalf of DuPont and the partners aren't going to have the same degree of intensity of DuPont's interests at heart—Global Alliance Manager, DuPont.

We also note that several years into the contracts, DuPont swapped employees by giving 300 decentralized IS analysts to one supplier in exchange for bringing some contract facilitor/managers back in-house. It is not uncommon for customers to face serious difficulties in accessing a priori which staff should be retained and which staff should be transferred (see Chapter 6 for a discussion).

Partnering in Practice

Many people also characterize the success of a contract by the quality of the customer/supplier relationship. DuPont's relationships with their suppliers display similar dynamics as the previous case study. Parties are often adversarial when negotiating contract interpretations, cooperative when scoping out new requirements, and even collaborative when facing the public eye (see Chapter 8).

What is also interesting is the relationship between the suppliers, CSC and AC. The supplier/supplier dynamics are nearly identical to the customer/supplier dynamics. The suppliers cooperate on IT delivery where functions overlap. Suppliers are competitors (and thus adversaries) when bidding for work beyond the baseline contract. The dynamics are even more interesting because CSC and AC have no formal contractual relationship. Instead, cooperation is facilitated by inherent mutual dependencies and competition is governed by gentlemen's agreements among account managers.

Because IT functions are highly integrated, both CSC and AC are motivated to cooperate:

So we have several major projects that are going on. Andersen has won a couple of these fairly large projects. There's no way that an SAP project can be implemented without using infrastructure. So they have to run on computers. They have to use networks. PCs are involved. And, moreover, the applications interface with a number of applications, a lot of which CSC has responsibility for. So on these new projects, CSC has to provide a supporting infrastructure and applications interface with Andersen. They have to work together as a joint project team. In fact they are doing that—Global Alliance Manager, DuPont.

During contract negotiations, the suppliers were initially concerned about confidentiality of their business practices. In reality, the protection of proprietary practices has not been an issue:

> They had a concern [about confidentiality], but they've had more concern at the beginning than what I would call playing out in practice. So as time goes on, they have less and less concern about it. And the reason for that is that while there is no formal contract between Andersen and CSC, there's a gentleman's agreement between the two account executives in terms of what is prudent business practice that they can both live with that would be considered fair—Global Alliance Manager, DuPont.

The gentleman's agreements also extend to competition practices on new projects. The suppliers agree that joint CSC–AC project team members will not serve as competitors on future project work for a period of one year:

> They would be sensitive that you wouldn't take a team of individuals that have been intimately involved in working with one another's methodologies to serve as a proposal team on another endeavor, certainly outside of DuPont, but even within DuPont in a short period of time. After 12 or 18 months, things change quickly enough that they don't seem too concerned about it— Global Alliance Manager, DuPont.

In order for such gentleman's agreements to work, it is vital that general account managers have continuity of experience. Because parties act on the intent and spirit of the relationship, rather than on a contractual agreement, the key DuPont, CSC, and AC players must remain the same, at least during and until precedents are institutionalized.

DuPont Conclusion

Although the DuPont deals are too recent to declare definitive outcomes, the case does provide preliminary lessons.

First, customers should try to reap the rewards of consolidating, rationalizing, and standardizing IT prior to outsourcing. By implementing such practices themselves, DuPont received the full financial reward of cost-reduction tactics. Indeed, DuPont reduced IT costs by 45% prior to the decision. In other cases, however, customers outsourced because they could not politically implement cost reduction programs due to organizational resistance.

Second, outsourcing can be used for reasons other than reducing IT costs. As DuPont Global Alliance Manager notes, 'We didn't do it because it was broken.' Instead, DuPont sought to avoid capital expenditures in IT and to move from a fixed to a variable operating budget. Indeed, DuPont is extremely pleased with the infrastructure investment made by CSC, including major improvements to three mega-datacenters as well as in telecommunications. CSC was able to finance the investment by using the datacenters to attract over 20 non-DuPont clients. DuPont encourages this initiative because they receive the benefits of technology renewal without bearing the investment costs.

Third, global outsourcing decisions have the advantage of lower transaction costs and better prices, but greater risks in getting the contract defined. In hindsight, the Global Alliance Manager believes that it might have been easier to have negotiated the US component first, then expanded the relationship globally:

> Trying to do the whole thing at once has it advantages because of the leverage of, 'you guys get the whole enchilada'. But it has the disadvantage of it's a tremendous amount of work to worry about all these details. And in fact, what we have discovered is we did not get all the details worked out. We've had to continue the negotiations, but we've been fortunate in that we don't have to start over. But overall, we would [in hindsight] probably have broken it up. We wouldn't have done the transaction all at once—Global Alliance Manager, DuPont.

Fourth, multiple supplier relationships can both cooperate (and compete) without a primary contractor. While such dynamic roles are found on other accounts, the roles are not governed by legal contracts at DuPont. As such, the absence of legal arrangements requires the retention of key individuals to ensure continuity and trust. These individuals serve as organizational memory until precedents, processes, and structures are institutionalized. The account managers seek to 'honour the intent' of the contracts. They try to avoid the use of lawyers to 'pore over the contract' and instead agree on precedents without official contract amendments. They also seek to be fair. In the beginning, each party tried to win every issue, but that led to unproductive animosity. Now each party agrees to be financially neutral, to give and take more, and to accept 'yes we can live with this'. (In the next two cases, presented in Chapter 3, trust was slowly built on a track record of supplier performance.)

Although DuPont was initially worried about the decision not to have a prime contractor, they are very pleased with the cooperation between CSC and AC—so far:

> We don't have a prime contractor, but in fact we have two suppliers who have to work together with one another every day but have no contract with each other. So we've established this process architecture and ways of operating that both CSC and AC have participated with DuPont in that joint definition...Our alliance management in DuPont has had to facilitate the understanding of how that would all work. What makes it work is they both have the same opportunities and the same issues and problems with one another ... I believe we are the first transaction of this magnitude where we didn't have a problem—Global Alliance Manager, DuPont.

Finally, we note that DuPont's alliances are exchange-based, despite the initial 'strategic partnership' label.[7] The term partnership referred to the hopes that CSC and AC may market DuPont systems to external customers. As of year three, this aspect of the contract is 'small potatoes'. DuPont's hope is similar to other cases initially described as 'strategic partnerships' in the trade press. In practice, we have never found a supplier who could market idiosyncratic client software. In reality, to transform a customer's home-grown software to a viable commercial package typically requires 10 times the initial development costs. Customers are simply not interested in such investments. And suppliers are preoccupied with operationalizing the contract, at least for the first few years. We end this case with a recent quote from a DuPont executive, 'this is a commercial business transaction, not a partnership. Suppliers have to keep earning the business everyday!'

NOTES

1. A thorough account of cost reduction tactics in IT can be found in Lacity and Hirschheim (1995a), and Hirschheim and Lacity (2000). Both sources include detailed case examples. In Chapter 6 there is a discussion of the economics of IT and of IT outsourcing. The general finding is that advantages come from both economies of scale effects and improvements in IT management practices, but that economies of scale often start lower than is often credited, and many improvements in management practices are replicable by an in-house team.
2. See Willcocks and Lacity (1999) and Willcocks, Lacity and Fitzgerald (1996).
3. See Willcocks and Lester (1999a). A decade of research on IT evaluation metrics and procedures shows a patchy performance overall. This becomes most obvious and problematic when outsourcing occurs because most suppliers will be very detailed about what level of service and resources are secured at what prices. One beneficial effect of IT outsourcing, and its threat, is a resulting tightening in IT evaluation procedures. Graeser, Willcocks and Pisanias (1998) found that there are all too few occasions when IT evaluation processes

improve. The main ones are: the appointment of a new senior manager who needs to understand the organization; a real or perceived organizational crisis; serious question marks raised about the business value of the IT being delivered; and where senior management buy into, and support, a new measurement system, for example the balanced business scorecard. However, IT outsourcing has usually been the most serious single catalyst for improvements in IT evaluation practice.

4. SA and EDS no longer deploy this older technology; as technologies advance, prices are renegotiated.

5. Our survey found this to be a weak part of supplier practice into 2000—see the Appendix.

6. The same happened in the case of BP Exploration—see Chapter 6.

7. Lacity and Willcocks (1998) observe that this was a typical finding in their research into 61 IT sourcing decisions in the 1991–1996 period.

3
Inside Mega-Contracts: British Aerospace and UK Inland Revenue

Here's what we can get costs down to ourselves, so don't bother bidding if you can't beat this—General Account Manager, BAe.

What may be only £6000 today might set a precedent worth £10 million—IT Services Manager, Division B.

Trust can only come through people fulfilling their commitments that they've made—CSC Account Executive, Division A.

If you went into our business streams . . . They've never seen it. They've only seen an extract from the contract—Account Manager, IR.

I see ourselves as in competition for resources and attention with all the other customers of the supplier—IT manager, IR.

INTRODUCTION

In the early 1990s, British Aerospace (BAe), like other major defence companies, experienced major financial losses due to the end of the Cold War and the economic recession. BAe's CEO instigated two major strategies to save the company: focus on core competencies in aerospace and refinance the entire balance sheet. During the financial crisis, information technology (IT) spending came under scrutiny. BAe decided to outsource most of the £120 million IT operating budget and sell most of the IT assets, worth about £250 million on the balance sheet. After a year and a half long decision process, BAe selected Computer Sciences Corporation (CSC) as a sole IT supplier. In April 1994, BAe and CSC signed a fixed-price, £900 million, 10-year contract for IT infrastructure and applications.

Given the legacy of BAe's hard-nosed approach to third-party contracts, BAe negotiated a highly favorable deal. CSC was obligated to provide all baseline services for the fixed fee, regardless of volumes. During contract negotiations, CSC assumed that BAe's volumes would likely decrease as the company downsized. (Thus, CSC's margins would likely increase over the life of the contract.) In reality, BAe bounced back with a vengeance, and by 1999 became the most profitable aerospace company in Europe. Consequently, CSC came to earn very low margins on the account:

> BAe got an exceptional deal when it signed its agreement with CSC. It was also an agreement signed at a time when the business prospects of BAe looked very different. Since the signing of the agreement, BAe has spent considerably more on IT than it is today, and it is doing much more, particularly in, say, desktop computing. Most of the contract bid was fixed price rather than variable price. That would have offered CSC protection if BAe's business had perhaps been in decline. But in reality, BAe's business has been in growth and as a result BAe has had phenomenal value out of the fixed-price contract because what they'd got is far more work content and for the CSC cost at a fixed price . . . But this contract is very important for CSC's growth in Europe. We are prepared to operate it at a low margin. And CSC this year (1997), despite the fact that we've not been making significant returns, continues to invest heavily in this account. We view BAe as a very important client, we will continue to invest in them—CSC Executive.

Overall, CSC has delivered the cost savings and is meeting contractual service level agreements. However, both parties had to realign the contract (in mid-1997) to meet changes in business and technical requirements.

Like all mega-contracts, the BAe–CSC relationship has continued to be an evolving and dynamic one. At first, the BAe IT managers and CSC managers fought hard over contractual issues. But as time progressed, the IT teams for both parties have galvanized. Together, they have worked with business units to temper realistic expectations of CSC's contractual obligations and to focus on more strategic issues such as exploiting IT for business advantage:

> So typically, in the first couple of years of a contract of this nature, I think it's all about cost reduction, service provision, meeting standards that have been committed to. And then following that, increasingly it's about the re-tooling of the IT department and the IT capability in the business –CSC Executive.

The characteristic of the relationship is that it was very antagonistic 12 months ago (1997). There were a lot of major problems. And working through now, there is much more goodwill in the relationship and I use the word goodwill because that seems to be the key to actually making a relationship work—BAe Contract Manager, Division B.

Two key lessons emerge from the case.

First, trust is based on a track record of contractual performance. Thus, contracts are initially important because they define performance requirements and, as such, serve as the foundation of relationships. After the supplier builds a track record of delivering on the contract, the relationship can involve more strategic and intimate roles. After a few years, BAe invited CSC to participate in strategic planning, and CSC has been an integral team player on a number of business change programs. Both parties have worked hard to deliver added-value from the relationship.

Second, IT managers for both parties must work together to foster realistic user expectations about an outsourcer's contractual obligations versus additional fee-for-service capabilities.[1] Many issues that arise during an outsourcing relationship are about the nature of IT itself, rather than supplier-specific. For example, cost/service trade-offs—such as standardization vs. customization or centralization vs. decentralization—affect IT costs and service levels *independent of the provider of those services*. Users must understand: exceptional IT products and services beyond the baseline cost CSC money that must be recovered. BAe and CSC have created a number of innovative processes to assess and to mediate realistic user expectations.

Our second case in this chapter provides a range of insights into IT outsourcing. In the early 1990s, the United Kingdom's (UK) central government sought to market test the cost-efficiency of 25% of all its activities against external suppliers. In line with government policy, the Inland Revenue (IR), which is responsible for administration of all UK taxes, decided in 1992 to outsource most of information technology (IT). In November 1993, a £1 billion, 10-year contract was awarded to US computer supplier, EDS. At the time, this represented the biggest outsourcing contract ever awarded in Europe. In 1993, the estimated cost savings from handing over IT assets, staff, and management of activities were £225 million over the life of the contract.

Currently in the eighth year of the relationship, EDS has delivered the promised cost savings according to a 'constant volume' model maintained by the IR. In reality, such cost assessments become increasingly ridiculous because the volume, composition, and services have radically changed during the eight years. Perhaps more importantly than the cost savings, the IR and EDS have used IT to enable a number of tax reforms, most notably the Self Assessment initiative, announced in 1995 and delivered in April 1997. A more thorough, and generally positive, assessment of the 'value-for-money' aspect of the relationship was made several times by the National Audit Office between 1998 and 2000.

Like all mega-contracts, the IR–EDS relationship is an evolving and dynamic one. At first, the IR IT managers and EDS managers fought hard over contractual issues. But as time progressed the IT managers for both parties worked more as a team. Together, they worked with business streams to temper realistic expectations of EDS's contractual obligations and to focus on more strategic issues such as budgeting and setting priorities. That did not mean that service issues went away, and, indeed, by late 1999 there were several press reports of many internal complaints of delays and downtime affecting the service being offered to the general public. It also seemed that the cost of the contract had risen from £1 billion to an expected £2 billion over the 10-year contract, largely due to the extra work given to the supplier.

Below we detail how the outsourcing deals originated and unfolded over time. We also analyze each case to pull out the major lessons that can be learned from them. Neither case makes outsourcing appear as anything less than hard work and constant adaptation to change. Both reveal that in order to really understand IT outsourcing there is no substitute for tracking outsourcing arrangements as they develop over time.

CASE 3: BRITISH AEROSPACE

Background

British Aerospace (BAe) was formed in 1978 from a series of independent companies in the UK aerospace industry, including Military Aircraft, Airbus (commercial aircraft), Jetstream (commuter aircraft), Dynamics (weapons), and Royal Ordnance (weapons). Since its inception, BAe Holding continued to foster the independence of its operating divisions. Business units are in charge of their own profitability and support services, including IT. The decentralized culture was required because each strategic business unit (SBU) operated under drastically different production, marketing, and legal environments. For example, the Airbus division may produce two to three products (aircraft) per year, whereas another division, like Royal Ordnance, may produce 90 000 products (weapons) per year.

The use of third-party suppliers has been another key cultural attribute of BAe. As at 2000, BAe generally continues to follow a supplier/customer relationship model in which hard bargaining and clearly defined contracts serve as the basis of the relationship. One ex-BAe employee quipped, 'In fact their whole ethos was to write adversarial contracts.' Their suppliers agree:

> Looking at BAe and its Military Aircraft business, for example, 70% of the cost of that Eurofighter is brought in from somewhere else. So they are used to, and their whole culture is around one of deal-making and negotiating and hard bargaining. And they are brought up in that and they play hard ball extremely well—CSC Account Executive.

BAe contracts almost always involve a Prime Contractor. The supplier may sub-contract, so long as they deliver on the contract.

> The advantage of this approach is to organize the coordination, control, and accountability around a single supplier rather than have multiple suppliers— quote from a BAe Outsourcing Report.

In 1992, BAe suffered a net profit loss of £66 million on sales of almost £10 billion. Stock prices plummeted from £7 per share to £1 per share. BAe was under-capitalized, with too many liabilities on the balance sheet. In addition, the economic recession and cuts in the UK government Defence budget significantly affected sales. Dick Evans, CEO, sought to improve profitability by focusing on core competencies in aircraft, divesting non-core divisions, and refinancing the company. BAe subsequently sold Rover, Corporate Jets, and Ballast Nedam. BAe reduced headcount by 21 000 employees. As a result, profitability increased to £230 million on £11 billion in sales in 1994:

> British Aerospace has, as a result of these changes, been refocused back on its roots at aerospace and defence. Within these roots lie the core engineering and technological strengths upon which the management of our business can build British Aerospace as Europe's leading aerospace company—Dick Evans, CEO, 1994, Letter to Shareholders.

The IT outsourcing decision was made in this business context—one of financial trouble and the subsequent strategy to divest non-core businesses. The divisions were under immense pressure to operate more efficiently. Although the decentralized culture was not organized to achieve economies of scale, financial troubles were pointing towards a centralized IT solution. During this period, BAe established, for the first time, a Corporate IT Director. His major task was to determine whether IT should be organized differently. He was not given an outsourcing mandate, but this seasoned BAe employee knew it was a viable option.

BAe's IT Department Prior to Outsourcing

Consistent with BAe's decentralized culture, each division operated their own autonomous IT function. In 1992, BAe's total IT budget across divisions was approximately £120 million. In total, there were about 1800 IT employees, about one-third of whom belonged to the Manufacturing, Science, and Finance (MSF) union. Because of the decentralization, it was difficult to identify the exact number of IT assets, but the 1993 IT infrastructure amounted to an estimated £250 million in assets and included approximately:

- 20 000 PCs
- 1400 workstations
- 350 DEC machines in the Military Aircraft Division (MAD) (no numbers available for other divisions)
- 8 IBM mainframe datacenters, a total of 850 MIPs
- 1 Cray supercomputer
- a corporate-run WAN

There were many home-grown and packaged software applications dispersed throughout the divisions. For packaged software, there were approximately 350–400 different software license agreements. But even packaged software was modified within each division. Material Requirements Planning (MRP), for example, required substantial customization because some divisions process batches of one, others process batches of 100 000. Owing to the idiosyncratic nature of the businesses, there was little cooperation among the business units concerning IT.

There was a central IT group created, primarily to evaluate telecommunications and to create a standard, mainframe-based operating business architecture (OBA) model. The divisions, however, resisted standardization:

> The business units turned around and said, 'why should I change to this? It's going to cost me nothing but grief, I'm quite happy doing things the way I want to do them.' And even the ones that took the OBA insisted on having it modified to their specific requirements—BAe Contract Manager, Division B.

The IT community possessed advanced IT skills and capabilities. In some divisions, like MAD, IT skills were widely recognized by hardware suppliers, who often called MAD IT employees for technical advice. One MAD employee notes:

> MAD [IT employees] had a reputation for being arrogant, but it was based on legitimate expertise—IT Contract Manager, MAD.

The user community is also extremely computer literate. Almost half of BAe's employees continue to be qualified engineers. In some divisions, users actually designed their own systems:

> Some end-users specify requirements better than service providers … the Automated Airborne System, [the users] specified their own workbenches and code generators. They design at the chip level and don't even rely on a packaged operating system. Their main concern: the system better keep the aircraft up—IT Contract Administrator, Division B.

Thus, BAe's IT needs prior to outsourcing were met by highly qualified IT experts who delivered decentralized and customized IT solutions. Such IT practices are costly by nature, and the IT cost came under scrutiny when the company was suffering financial losses.

BAe's Outsourcing Decision Process

During BAe's financial crises in 1992, EDS approached the Corporate Finance Director with an unsolicited bid to take IT assets off the balance sheet. Although the EDS offer was attractive, BAe felt they needed more data:

> We were very ignorant of outsourcers' capabilities and track records—BAe General Account Manager.

A full-scale investigation of IT outsourcing commenced. The entire decision process lasted a year and a half and involved the services of outside expertise including lawyers, financial modelers, auditors of the Request For Proposal (RFP), auditors of the in-house proposal, and technical experts.

In late 1992, the Corporate IT Director created two independent teams, a six-person outsourcing evaluation team and an insourcing team to develop an in-house proposal. Regarding the latter:

> The in-house proposal was not intended to be a bid to compete with other suppliers. But rather it was to inform the company what might be possible internally, and also to provide useful benchmarking information to use in the discussions with the other outsourcing parties—Quote from a BAe Outsourcing Report.

In December 1992, the outsourcing team sent a request for information to 20 potential suppliers. In March 1993, 10 suppliers were invited to a bidders meeting. Two weeks later, five suppliers responded with a short proposal and a three-hour presentation. By April, the outsourcing team short-listed three suppliers: IBM–DEC (co-bidders), CSC, and EDS.

In June 1993, BAe sent out a complete RFP to the short-listed suppliers. The scope of the RFP included most of the infrastructure, applications development, and applications support. The RFP contained cost estimates for in-scope resources, including almost 1500 IT people. The cost estimates were based on the insourcing proposal. Suppliers were told:

> Here's what we can get costs down to ourselves, so don't bother bidding if you can't beat this—BAe General Account Manager.

Although BAe planned to outsource the majority of applications, BAe felt that a supplier could not provide software cheaper because BAe would have to pay their mark-up. Instead, they were looking for 'value-added', such as getting free software from other clients:

> We were looking for a multiplier effect—BAe General Account Manager.

BAe planned to retain about 300 people for core IT capabilities, including IT strategy, contract administration, relationship management, and strategic IT systems:

> The company has within its mainstream engineering organization, genuine leading edge capability in some IT related areas, e.g. product embedded software within the airplanes and missile systems. Such capabilities and skills would not be outsourced under any circumstances. Indeed, they were considered to be a core competence. The company boasts a software development capability which goes far beyond anything that external suppliers are able to provide. In this capacity, IT is seen as part of the business—Quote from a BAe Outsourcing Report.

After distribution of the RFP, the outsourcing team invited the bidders for on-site tours. Kevin Howley of CSC actually hired a bus, nicknamed the 'Battle Bus' to enable his team of 40 people to travel in comfort.[2]

In return, the bidders invited BAe to visit a number of supplier reference sites. These reference sites highlighted the need for BAe to define a comprehensive and detailed contract. In particular, the outsourcing team needed consistent cost data, consistent service data, including standard service-level agreements for 500 services. BAe also rejected the idea of a 'partnership', as IT suppliers and customers do not share revenue nor are they responsible for each other's debts:

> Suppliers are not partners. Business is expected to be done in a business manner ... this is based on [BAe's] strong tradition of dealing with suppliers —BAe General Account Manager.

In July 1993, the three short-listed suppliers submitted their final bids. BAe felt that all three suppliers were committed to winning the bid because they spent a significant amount of time and resources on the bidding process. A BAe manager estimates that each supplier had 30 employees working on each bid, and spent approximately £2.5 million during the process.

In August, one supplier was eliminated because its bid was 20% higher than the other two suppliers. Ironically, this supplier knew BAe the best because of past business interactions. The supplier admitted their bid was high because they simply did not believe some of the claims in the RFP.

The remaining two external bids and the in-house proposal were very similar in price (only a 1% difference). The in-house proposal showed that BAe could compete with external suppliers on price. But the suppliers were able to do a number of things that BAe could not achieve on their own. Suppliers would bear the initial investment costs required to implement cost reduction tactics such as datacenter consolidation. Outside auditors noted that initially BAe would need to hire 50 people to deliver the savings. But in the end, the insourcing proposal served its purpose of increasing BAe's negotiating power. At this stage, the main objective of outsourcing shifted from cost reduction to value-added:

> The focus had shifted to one which is described as 'value-added'. In looking at a comparison of the cost model between internal and external performance, it became clear that either option could be equally cost effective. However, the key question for the company was: Is there something which a third party (whose capability lay within exploiting IT) could bring to the business that we could not otherwise acquire? This question was considered for a period of two to three months—Quote from a BAe Outsourcing Report

From August 1993 to November 1993 the divisions became involved in the evaluation of the two remaining bidders. Some of the divisions would not benefit financially from outsourcing, and argued against the bids. The Corporate IT Director forcefully argued that the entire IT functionality across all business units had to be placed on the auction block to attract an external supplier.

CSC also marketed IT outsourcing very hard to the divisions. CSC answered many tough questions about value-added outsourcing, such as, 'What did CSC bring to General Dynamics that they couldn't have done otherwise?' This decentralized marketing strategy finally sold divisions on CSC:

> At this stage BAe said, 'now we need to involve the business units and make presentations on the basis of what it's going to be like for you.' And allow the managers, not the IT managers, the managers running manufacturing and design and things like that, to ask us questions. Some of these managers were very hostile to begin with. They couldn't imagine how anybody

could do a better job than they'd been doing for years. Some of them were very open. Many of them were quite happy for this process to happen—CSC Quality Manager (transferred from BAe).

Several BAe and CSC informants indicated that CSC was successful in winning the bid, in large part, because of their expertise in aerospace and their ability to talk business language:

> The senior managers within BAe, and even more the managers within the business units, by and large didn't want to hear people talking pure IT. What they wanted was to hear people talking their language, the language of making airplanes. And we were able to do that, we were able to produce these people who talked their language—CSC Quality Manager (transferred from BAe).

In November 1993, the final report was made and approved at the Board level. The next four months were spent in due diligence to verify RFP data. CSC could alter their bid during this time if they found any major missing items from the RFP. Also during this time, service-level agreements (SLAs) were defined for the corporate IT and 14 divisions. CSC resisted cash penalties for non-performance on SLAs, but a BAe informant notes, 'They confused partnership with non-performance.'

Employee Relations

As of June, the employees (and the MSF union) were not informed of the evaluation process because management did not want to de-motivate employees, particularly if they decided to insource. In July 1993, however, a trade publication announced BAe's impending outsourcing decision, which panicked the employees. BAe quickly responded by conducting bi-weekly status meetings with employees, even if there was nothing to report. BAe also established a hotline:

> We opened a helpline, an 0800 number anybody could ring up. It was staffed by HR people who very quickly built up a list of standard answers to the standard questions. And if you could answer the question, answer it. If not, you say, 'I will get somebody to either give me the answer or ring you back.' And surprising to me, at the time but perhaps less so now, a very high proportion of the questions related to pension rights. And the pension area is hugely complex. We had to have a specialist team on it—BAe Contract Manager, Division B.

During the decision process, the MSF union, however, continued to protest publicly against outsourcing:

> The Manufacturing Science and Finance white-collar union said yesterday that BAe wants to outsource up to £250 million of information technology

work. The union claimed this would remove the company's ability to control its own information technology systems and pose a threat to national security—Ian Fazey, 'BAe Computer Staff to Strike over Jobs Fear', *Financial Times*, Wednesday, August 25, 1993, p. 7.

In addition, union employees feared that outsourcing was being used to eliminate IT positions. In August, the union IT employees had a one-day strike over the impending contract:

> Outsourcing is simply a means of enforcing redundancies. We've met with the three shortlisted bidders and it was clear two of them were not interested in our terms and conditions—BAe IT Analyst, quoted in 'BAe Strike Gives Vent to FM Fears', *Computer Weekly*, September 2, 1993.

Eventually, almost all IT employees identified for transition agreed to transfer to CSC.

BAe's Contract Overview

In April 1994, BAe and CSC signed a 10-year, £900 million contract. CSC paid BAe £75 million for their IT assets and transferred 1450 BAe employees.[3] The contract comprises four infrastructure packages:

- datacenters (35% of annual cost)
- networks (14% of annual cost)
- distributed computing (26% of annual cost)
- applications (25% of annual cost)

Pricing

The contract obligates CSC to provide all baseline services at a fixed price. Because BAe was in financial trouble during the contract negotiation, both parties assumed volumes would likely decrease as non-profitable businesses were sold. From CSC's perspective, a decline in volumes would mean an increase in their margin.

However, BAe wanted the fixed fee to reflect market prices over the 10-year period. BAe was fully aware of the rapid price/performance curve in IT, and provided a number of mechanisms for altering the fixed price. The contract stipulates that the four infrastructure areas will be benchmarked every year by a named third party. CSC is obligated to match the top 10% best-of-breed performance and cost standards. However, both parties realized that benchmarking was very immature in the areas of distributed computing and applications, so open-book accounting of CSC's costs was added to cap CSC's margin:

It's open-book accounting. So [BAe] get to look at our costs and they get to measure us independently on productivity benchmarking—CSC Account Executive, Division C.

On the whole, there is a limit on the margin the supplier is allowed to charge for the entire basket of services. Although the margin is not applicable to individual services, BAe felt open-book accounting would serve to increase their negotiating position.

BAe also included non-exclusivity clauses to promote fair market pricing for services beyond baseline:

This enables the company to periodically ask other suppliers to compete with the other major supplier for a specific project—Quote from a BAe Outsourcing Report.

Service-Level Agreements

As at 2000, over 500 service level agreements (SLAs) are provided in the master SLA. But the contract is essentially executed at the division level. There are 11 operating division contracts that specify additions, changes, or deletions from the master SLA. If CSC fails to meet SLAs for critical services, they must pay a cash penalty. (However, CSC was not successful in negotiating a clause that rewarded CSC for over-performance.)

Risk Mediation

To temper BAe's risks of a long-term, single-supplier agreement, the Corporate IT Director hired Arthur Andersen to help identify and negotiate contract amendments. In total, 140 technical, human resource, and commercial risks were addressed.

On the human resource side, BAe committed CSC to retain all transferred staff for the first year to ensure a smooth transition. (Afterwards, CSC would have to reduce headcounts to deliver the cost savings.) Another example: BAe was concerned about CSC staffing of key functions, so they implemented a veto clause in the contract. (This clause has already been exercised when one potential CSC manager was asked, 'How will you judge your performance?' When he answered, 'By my profit margins', BAe rejected him.)

On the commercial side, confidentiality of data was a concern. In the BAe–CSC contract, the issue was not just confidentiality from external competitors, but among BAe divisions:

What that meant was CSC is going to protect BAe's information because it's commercially sensitive. It was latched onto by the business units who said, 'yes and you are going to protect our information not only from the world at large, but from all other parts of BAe because we are independent businesses'—CSC Quality Manager (transferred from BAe).

BAe's Transition Period

Because mega-contracts are negotiated by a team of 20–50 people, a transition period of one to two years is typically required to translate a massive legal contract into a working relationship serving tens of thousands of users. Like all large IT outsourcing deals, BAe spent a couple of years facing the following transition challenges:

- distributing and interpreting the contract for the user population;
- establishing the post-contract management infrastructure;
- establishing the post-contract management processes;
- implementing consolidation, rationalization, and standardization;
- validating services, costs, service levels, and responsibilities for baseline services;
- managing additional service requests; and
- fostering realistic expectations of supplier performance.

Distributing and Interpreting the Contract for the User Population

Actual IT outsourcing contracts in mega-deals are impossible to execute from because they are typically massive documents written in obscure legal terminology. In the early days of a mega-contract, one of the major tasks of the centralized contract management team is to develop user guides to the contract. The guides are designed to describe what the supplier is obligated to provide under the fixed-fee structure in user terms. But at BAe (and all companies we have studied), the contract and user guides are always open for interpretation, no matter how well the negotiating teams believe they nailed down the details.

Some examples serve to illustrate the ambiguity typically found in contracts. For example, CSC is obligated to provide network *enhancements* under the fixed fee, but BAe is required to pay for network *extensions*. How do users know the difference between an enhancement and an extension?

Now the difference between an extension and an enhancement. Say next door didn't have the network. Is that an extension or an enhancement because it's giving it to my secretary and it's the same network in theory—CSC Account Executive, Division A.

Another example: If BAe needs system maintenance that requires CSC to bring the datacenter down over the weekend, who pays CSC overtime?

Both parties initially took a tough stand on contract interpretations because they set precedents for the entire 10-year relationship:

> What may be only £6000 today might set a precedent worth £10 million—IT Services Manager, Division B.

As precedents were established, the centralized BAe Contract Manager published a newsletter that was distributed to all business units:

> Unfortunately in my view, it wasn't possible for the central document to take account of all the nuances that the business-level agreements required. So that no sooner was the services agreement in operation, than there were meetings of people about interpretations of the contract. What did it actually mean? And that was built up so there is one supporting body of agreed interpretations—CSC Quality Manager (transferred from BAe).

Eventually, contractual disputes subsided:

> 'There was a rash of work building contract resolutions over the first 12 months and then slowly it dissipated away and I haven't seen a contract resolution put in [for a while]. So 12 months, probably from April 1994 to the summer of 1995, contract resolutions were coming through and being published, but since that time, few to none at all, I've not seen any for the last year—BAe Contract Manager, Division B.

Establishing the Post-Contract Management Infrastructure

In the area of contract administration, BAe's Corporate IT Director manages the master service agreement, interprets the contract, mediates disputes, resolves issues, and identifies opportunities. According to a BAe public presentation, the duties of the Contract Manager and his team include:

- assisting user organizations in reviewing business processes and identification of IT needs;
- defining the overall IT architecture across the business;
- providing training to business users and awareness of potential benefits;
- ensuring the IT strategy is consistent with partners', customers', and suppliers' needs;
- ensuring that quality, security, and health and safety requirements are met; and
- managing outsourcing.

Each division has their own BAe contract manager and support staff. The size of the support staff depends on the size of the division. MAD's contract management team, for example, had 16 people: six IT commercial managers, seven IT service managers, and one strategic manager.[4] IT commercial managers focus on financial management. IT service managers focus on demand management and service levels, including annual benchmarks.

As with all outsourcing arrangements, residual IT staff must learn new skills and capabilities to carry out contract administration roles. BAe recognized that the staff needed to develop two key skills:

> These skills fell into two broad categories ... [Retained IT] people were largely responsible for managing the relationship with the supplier. The competencies and skills were managerial and technical in nature. Firstly, people were needed with the skills of negotiating, influencing, and coordinating. It was necessary to articulate business requirements to a supplier on a continuing basis. Secondly, people were needed with good technical skills who could also undertake an internal consulting role. These people were needed to articulate the IT-related solutions within a business context to the supplier—Quote from a BAe Outsourcing Report.

Several divisions actually provide training in the areas of negotiating and managing supplier relationships. In areas where training would not suffice, BAe moves IT staff around the organization to seed expertise. They also consider recruiting these skills from the marketplace.

On the CSC side, there is a general account team that oversees the entire relationship. In each BAe division, CSC has an Account Executive, Account Manager(s), and Account Analyst(s). Distributed throughout the division, CSC Professional Service groups handle application development, application support, helpdesks, desktop services, network services, and other infrastructure items.

The structure of the management teams, however, can vary by division. In two large divisions, for example, the roles of the BAe Contract Manager and CSC Account Manager are embodied by one CSC person who is 'seconded' back to BAe. The reason for keeping this person as an official CSC employee is to allow access to CSC world-wide resources:

> If you ask me to go join BAe, I'm cut off from CSC. I can't call Index [an IT research subsidiary of CSC]. I can't call the States. I can't call other people consulting in the UK and say, 'Listen, I'm working on this, can you do this and that?' ... And we had a chat openly between CSC Vice President and BAe Executive. And I said, 'It's going to be very difficult, we can't write a terms of reference.' It's very difficult to do that here. It's basically the shake of a hand and we've got to trust that this will work—CSC Account Manager, Division C.

While this dual role works well for the two divisions, other divisions rejected this structure as politically infeasible:

> I don't think anyone can serve two masters with competing environments—BAe Contract Manager, Division B.

Establishing the Post-Contract Management Processes

Service levels are tracked within the division. Most business units, however, focus on only a few of the 500 defined service levels:

> I think our conclusion is that we seek no more than a dozen key performance indicators. Otherwise, yes the relationship is more complex than that. But unless you pick the 12 maximum most important keys, you again will have something which is unmanageable because you are trying to manage too many points—BAe General Contract Manager.

In general, CSC has delivered on the SLAs, but in the transition period the BAe and CSC IT managers found that user expectations/needs were not being met:

> So what you can do firstly, you can see if CSC are making the contract or not and sort that as an issue. But, secondly, you could see if that contractual level met customer need. So CSC might be exceeding the contract requirement, but not the customer need—BAe Contract Manager, Division B.

BAe and CSC recognized the need to supplement the quantitative contractual SLAs with qualitative performance assessment. The process is called the Customer Performance Assessment Reporting System (CPARS). In general, users rate CSC's service using color codes. Blue indicates 'excellent', green indicates 'fully satisfied', yellow indicates 'some problems', and red indicates 'poor/unacceptable'. Key users of IT in the business areas meet monthly with CSC to discuss perceptions of CSC's performance:

> There are two key objectives underpinning these meetings. The first is for both parties to agree how the service will be provided in the coming month or quarter. This discussion will exclude the application of hard measures such as SLAs because it is intended to generate new ideas rather than simply discuss what is already in place. The second objective is to formulate an agreement which is acceptable to both parties. It will then be implemented and will be the subject of the next meting. So far, the company has set up some 250 meetings between key users of the services and the relevant representative from the supplier organization—Quote from a BAe Outsourcing Report.
>
> You may have heard talk about the CPARS process that we use. We use that quite extensively here actually, and it's one of our main sources of contact

with the customer. It looks at how we are performing, where we can improve, and then they will often if there are major issues bring that to the table if we haven't already heard about it through some other means. One of the things about these sessions is that they are quite subjective—CSC Account Executive for one of BAe's Divisions.

The CPARS process is carefully managed because users are motivated to give a red rating in order to get immediate attention. One of the BAe Division Contract Managers serves as a mediator with users and CSC to ensure the problem resolution process is fair:

> If a customer gave a red score, completely unacceptable service performance this month, CSC committed to solve that problem in the following month … It could easily have been just a non-policed process. 'I'll get my job fixed by giving you a red', because we are talking about people, human beings. 'I'll give them a red so I'll get my job done.' Whether it was really on a yellow, green. 'I'm not terribly happy, I'll give them a red, they'll go fix it.' So what we did, we actually had the CSC account manager sit down with the customer representative and the IT team put somebody in-between and said, 'you didn't deliver your commitment CSC', or alternatively, 'You were being unreasonable, service customer.' And so they had an arbitrator—BAe Contract Manager, Division B.

The CPARS process has been considered a success on both sides. Four years into the contract, few disastrous problems existed:

> We find now it's exceptional to get a red. We might find yellow in 10% of the cases—BAe General Contract Manager, 1997.

Implementing Consolidation, Rationalization, and Standardization

On other mega-contracts, suppliers centralize, rationalize, and standardize to reduce costs, and thus increase their margins. CSC made significant strides in the first two areas, but CSC has been contractually prevented from standardizing where they would fail to meet service levels.

Regarding consolidation, CSC successfully consolidated the datacenters in the first year of the contract:

> There were about eight datacenters prior to outsourcing. And within 15 months of outsourcing, we had two. And that was done very professionally and certainly better than we could have done it ourselves—BAe General Contract Manager.

By October 1994, CSC's consolidation would reduce headcount by 250. Such cost reduction tactics were vital in order for CSC to earn any money on this account. Thus, transferred employees felt their instincts about outsourcing leading to redundancies was correct. But CSC Director of Human Resources, Gordon Bottoms, noted:

> We are looking ahead six months and there are 100 jobs vacant in CSC UK, in firms such as Ford and BHS, plus offers of training and redeployment.[5]

On rationalization, CSC implemented new procedures and methodologies. For example, they implemented their system development methodology. From BAe's perspective, this too was successful:

> They've introduced a development methodology. And I understand it to be a particularly good methodology for system development. And that's now well spread around the organization. It's really now that we are starting to see the real business benefit—BAe General Account Manager, 1997.

In the case of BAe, CSC cannot reap the full benefits of standardization because each division has idiosyncratic service-level requirements. For example, when CSC tried to centralize PC procurement, they were not meeting some of the divisional requirements. Instead, CSC had to provide customized solutions:

> The analogy is really that BAe was a famine zone. We opened Sainsbury's— this sophisticated supermarket. People charged through the doors and grabbed all the stuff off the shelves ... What we should have done was throw rice off the back of the truck. Give them standardized products and managed them in a standardized way—CSC Executive.

Validating Services, Costs, Service Levels, and Responsibilities for Baseline Services

In most outsourcing deals, the discovery of undisclosed baseline items triggers customer excess fees. In the BAe–CSC contract, CSC is obligated to pay for undiscovered baseline items. CSC failed to discover two significant items during due diligence. First, CSC found £600 000 worth of software that they would have to support in the fixed-fee structure:

> There is a huge discrepancy in the amount that we pay for software maintenance and the amount of revenue we get from BAe. It is a huge gap, at least on this account. And so it makes it very difficult for me to be charitable or generous when it comes to dealing with software maintenance issues. So I want to take a bit harder line on that. Most other areas, it's not really a big deal—CSC Account Executive for one of BAe's Divisions.

Second, CSC claimed to find £30 million worth of liability for hardware leases, software licenses, pension costs, and British Telecom lines.[6]

These undisclosed items significantly cut into CSC's profits, and creates significant challenges to the relationship:

> Coming from [another CSC client site], there did not appear to be the disputes in that contract that were on this one. I believe because of the way the contract was structured that automatically put us in a bad position in order for us to be profitable. We had to stick to the contract as close as possible and try to take advantage of that to get revenue where we could because I don't believe the contract was set up in a way that enabled us to do that immediately—CSC Account Executive for one of BAe's Divisions.

Most outsourcing contracts require customers to pay for increases in consumption. In the BAe–CSC contract, CSC was obligated to provide baseline services for the fixed fee. In some areas, such as desktops, the increase in demand caused CSC to lose money. As such, they could not, in the first three years, financially provide the level of service they would have liked:

> We have a particularly rough ride on desktops. And this is a very difficult area to deliver in BAe. There are a number of factors for that. One is we are not resourced to meet BAe's requirement and in a sense we've got no ability financially to meet the requirement. Every PC in BAe last year we moved more than once. And because they are all networked, we had to re-cable because they don't have quality infrastructures. That's a huge demand on us because we are doing most of that at our cost—CSC Executive.

Managing Additional Service Requests

New projects are obviously beyond baseline and subject to excess fees. The BAe and CSC IT managers always have hard times explaining to users that CSC is fairly pricing new requests. Users compare CSC quotes with market prices, but they do not consider the total costs of ownership:

> [The purchase cost] is the only cost the individual user sees. Maintaining it costs five times as much as it does to purchase. The purchase price is 20% of the whole thing. And the current head of the central IT unit who manages this whole process for BAe, went into print, he had to go into print to explain [that] to BAe—CSC Quality Manager (transferred from BAe).

In general, however, by the end of the transition period, users were beginning to understand the cost/service trade-offs for additional requests:

> Where previously it was viewed that they didn't pay for a service before, now they are paying for a service. It made it more invisible [before] and perhaps they expected more [after outsourcing]. I think that might initially have

strained the relationship—CSC Account Executive for one of BAe's Divisions.

For example, one business unit manager requested a shop control system that would save him £250 000. But the BAe Contract Manager pointed out that it would cost £500 000 to build! Users also came to realize the cost of tinkering with legacy systems, and they do not spend as much on trivial enhancements. Speaking in mid-1997, the Contract Manager for BAe Division B describes great improvements in user behavior:

> With outsourcing, you go to zero-based costing rather than marginal costing ... In the past, systems were justified on 'well we have all these applications developers who need to develop something anyway'—that type of marginal based costing—BAe Contract Manager, Division B.

Fostering Realistic Expectations of Supplier Performance

A common thread through all transition periods is the need to foster realistic expectations of the supplier's performance. In every mega-contract we have studied, users usually possess an expectation that an IT outsourcer will provide exceptional service for free because, 'they are the IT experts'. It is difficult for users to embrace the notion that suppliers are only contractually obligated for baseline service levels:

> I don't feel like the end user really understands the contract and what we are contractually required to provide. So there is a perception that the service ought to be much greater than what is actually required in the contract financially ... In particular, some of our engineering customers who I believe are already very technically able and so I think they expect a much higher level of service than perhaps the SLA may actually warrant—CSC Account Executive for one of BAe's Divisions.

The gap between expectations and reality was particularly large at the offset, because the parties had to enthusiastically sell the concept of outsourcing to users and IT staff. But on most mega-contracts, the contract is typically delivered by 99% of transitioned people, and thus radical changes are not forthcoming. A CSC representative characterizes the unrealistic expectations:

> At one stage on this site, when we had something like 400 people here, there were actually only two of us on this site who had worked for CSC anywhere other than here. They were all transition staff. That was at BAe's specific request. They wanted the changes in the transition to be—I think the words used were 'evolutionary' rather than 'revolutionary'. But at the same time ... the [expectations were] the services were going to be fantastic. They were

going to have PCs on a desk in 9.5 minutes and God knows whatever else. So the end customer had got this expectation of a step-change, but you were doing it with the same workforce, doing the same things. They've just got a CSC mug and their paychecks have a CSC logo on it—CSC Account Executive, Division A.

By all accounts, most informants thought that CSC has been meeting almost all of the contract service levels for critical services. But by mid-1997 there was a feeling of disappointment on the 'value-added' notion:

Yes, [the supplier] can achieve all the things that were proposed—but where is this famous 'added-value' service? We are not getting anything over-and-above what any old outsourcer could provide—IT Contract Administrator, BAe division, 1997.

Overall, I think statistically, if you look at things in terms of performance against SLAs and things like that, in general we are meeting the terms and conditions of the contract, but I think there is an expectation within the customer that is much higher than what the contract actually states. What we can't do is always go running back to the contract for protection. So we have to move the relationship on. And even if it's not required of us by the contract, we need to be able to work to support the customer. But he also needs to recognize that in providing and receiving a service, there needs to be some compensation. So I guess overall in outsourcing, I think a lot of it revolves around understanding each other's expectations—CSC Account Executive for one of BAe's Divisions, 1997.

A year into the contract, the parties began to realize that the gap in expectations was largely due to the different definitions of 'value-added'. Users defined 'value-added' as getting more IT products and services under the fixed-fee umbrella. BAe managers defined 'value-added' as getting IT to exploit business advantage. CSC manager's defined 'value-added' as delivering the 30% savings, meeting contractual service levels, and providing BAe with scarce technical skills on short-term notice:

One thing that CSC have been able to do because of their international size of operation, they've actually been able to recruit on a scale that we would never have been able to at BAe. To actually draft a team of 40 people within weeks, I've never seen that happen in terms of IT—BAe Contract Manager, Division B.

The parties agreed to define three levels of value-added:

1. *Business value-added*, in which the supplier applies their expertise to help the customer exploit IT for business advantage.
2. *Capacity value-added*, in which the supplier infuses new skills and technologies in an effective manner.

3. *Utility value-added*, in which the supplier provides cheaper IT services.

Clearly, the supplier was delivering utility and capacity value-added. BAe and CSC subsequently attempted to make significant strides on business added value that benefits both parties:

> Value-added, it's one of the goals. It's value adding but has to be done on both sides. CSC has to turn a profit and has to allow BAe to turn a profit. If you were signing up a partner, you wouldn't want your partner to lose money. You want your partner to be successful. So I think the value-added term is used with the implicit understanding that that implies that CSC is also prospering to some level—CSC Account Executive, Division C.

In summary, the transition period focused on operationalizing the contractual agreement. CSC was expected to deliver the cost savings and to meet SLAs. As such, they were treated within the traditional BAe model of exchange-based, customer/supplier relationships. With a track record of solid performance, the relationship is moving into strategic areas:

> Initially, costs were king. This is all about reducing costs ... it is very much like a customer/supplier relationship. Let's be the supplier at the lowest cost. Today, through the work we've done, I think we've put in place the organization and processes that now help us to focus on benefits—CSC Account Executive, Division C.

BAe's Post-Transition: The Middle Years

Mega-contracts typically require a one- to three-year transition period to establish operational structures and processes. This does not mean that problems do not arise after the transition, but it does mean that the parties have developed ways to identify and resolve problems. Certainly, at BAe the CPARS process has been a successful means of problem resolution. And the formal definitions of value-added served to align expectations.

During the middle years of a contract, new challenges arise. The BAe–CSC mid-contract challenges included:

- benchmarking performance to (theoretically) reset prices,
- realigning the contract to reflect changes in technology and business, and
- involving the supplier on more value-added areas.

Benchmarking Performance to (Theoretically) Reset Prices

Many mega-deals include benchmarking provisions to ensure that the customer pays fair market prices. Certainly, benchmarking mainframe datacenters is easily executed and generally effective. However, parties generally agreed that the benchmarking industry for distributed computing and applications was still immature:

> Our experience, being honest, is that I haven't been terribly happy with the benchmarking process. This is not happy for CSC nor BAe. It's just the process seems to be a little bit naive—BAe Contract Manager, Division B, 1997.

For example, application productivity, quality, and cost are benchmarked using function points. CSC is obligated to be 10% of best-of-breed, but best-of-breed is based on managerial practices, such as software standardization, that yield such results. Since CSC cannot standardize software because of idiosyncratic business demands, it is unreasonable to expect CSC to deliver best-of-breed results. Rather than rely on benchmarking, the parties agreed to reset prices in a contract realignment.

Realigning the Contract to Reflect Changes in Technology and Business

A number of technology and business changes had occurred since 1994. The composition of IT services had shifted from mainframe to client server. Deregulation in the telecommunications industry radically reduced market prices. Desktop demand exploded. Both BAe and CSC wanted to realign the contract to be based more on reality.

First, both parties agreed that the fixed price for baseline services no longer reflected IT usage. For example, BAe had falsely assumed mainframe consumption to remain flat over the life of the contract, but demand has significantly decreased. BAe wanted mainframe costs to decrease with volume. Another example: CSC charged a fixed fee for office moves—everytime a BAe employee changes offices, CSC has to move the employee's desktop and reconfigure the network. Since the signing of the contract, the number of desktops increased five times what was expected in the contract, and CSC had to absorb the extra costs of all the moves. Shifting to more variable-based pricing would benefit both parties:

> By mutual agreement, we are trying to make it a little more volume related, but overall it won't change the bottom line, profitability. It's really a readjustment of the pricing mechanisms within the contract, and provides protec-

tion for both sides . . . I see realignment as an ongoing, healthy, fresh aspect of the relationship—CSC Executive.

Prices were realigned for IT man-hours, client/server, telecommunications, and other emerging technologies. For example, the original contract was based on one man-hour rate. That definition caused problems for both CSC and BAe. In instances of rare skill sets, CSC would lose money on the hourly rate. In instances of remedial skills, BAe was paying above market hourly rates. The parties agreed to a three-tiered billing rate for man-hours that considers market prices for technical expertise. In another example, telecommunication prices were realigned to reflect market deregulation:

> But if you think what's happened in the telecommunications market in two years, and yet the contract is based on the 1993/94 view of life. So if you look at the fixed prices in the contract, they pay no account to technology change or market demand for telecom and the competition. So prices are outrageous. They are okay up to 1997, the prices are okay. But in 1998, I think we've halved our telephone prices by choosing different providers. The contract is not recognizing emerging technologies, a real issue for us has been it does not recognize that—BAe Contract Manager, Division B.

Both parties stressed that the 'realignment' was not attributed to 'past mistakes'. Instead, both sides see the contract realignment as a normal progression in customer/supplier relationships:

> We've come to the conclusion that actually what we have, and what we need to do intellectually, is to come to terms with the contract itself. [It] has to be a much more dynamic, moving, changing thing, rather than a set-in-stone thing. And without wishing to change the past, we've jointly been working to realign the mechanisms so that they produce results which are more in keeping with what we went after. But the important factor is that we anticipate to do the same thing again in two to three years time. And then two to three years after that, we will do the same thing again. Not because we got it wrong, but because of the change in technologies and changing user requirements—BAe General Contract Manager.

The learning point here is that the contract still serves as the foundation for the relationship by defining price and service expectations.

Involving the Supplier on More Value-Added Areas

A number of strategic initiatives are underway to focus more on exploiting IT ('rather than exploiting each other', as one informant joked). CSC has been involved in strategic IT planning, re-engineering projects, and major change programs. Both sides recognized that such initiatives financially benefit both parties:

What we are trying to do in the strategic area is really that we've got a program called Operation Efficiency Improvement. And it's really a step change. And CSC work is at the heart of that with BAe staff and what we tried to do is make the thing strategic in not a financial sense, but in a benefit sharing sense … We've actually developed, speaking about the contract, we've just developed another attachment to the contract which is trying to formalize the principles around benefit sharing. But it's still not tangible enough, but it's an attempt—BAe Contract Manager, Division B.

In another example, CSC was instrumental in a planned replacement of 200 mainframe legacy systems in five divisions. They conducted a 15-month evaluation of packages and selected Baan, a Dutch supplier, because of Baan's success at Boeing. A team of 50 CSC and BAe staff were identified to implement the system. CSC's participation on strategic projects, however, does not mean that BAe places less emphasis on IT costs:

Today, as a result of the strategic work we did, we are implementing a whole client/server environment, and buying a lot of PCs. We can demonstrate why we are going to spend all this money, why BAe needs to spend all this money. They bought into it. But we are now negotiating how we can get the price per PC down as low as possible. But they have agreed that client/server architecture that they transferred over to CSC, really will not support their business—CSC Account Executive, Division C.

Although CSC and BAe came to operate more as collaborators on strategic projects, the relationship could still be adversarial when debating operational issues:

We have a schizophrenic relationship. And two compartmentalized debates. So one is entirely a service contract, service level agreement, delivery, value, price/performance debate. And there, compared with other clients, they are very strong and aggressive in that area. On the other end, they have high expectations that we will be strategic, help them change their business. We are involved in some of their most intimate programs—CSC Executive.

This schizophrenic relationship is commonly found during the middle years of a contract. Particularly for the IT managers, the nature of the relationship varies from adversarial to cooperative to collaborative, depending on the task at hand. By this stage, however, even 'adversarial' tasks are based on a foundation of trust earned through years of solid performance.

By 2000 the set of relationships had matured considerably. However, an initial outsourcing budget of some £100 million a year had actually increased by the end of 1999 to over £200 million a year and was set to rise further. Clearly, a lot more was being done with the money; CSC had straightened out a lot of the difficult IT issues they had inherited;

and had installed a lot of desktops, servers, and LANS which, by their own admissions, BAE could not have achieved by themselves. The decentralized running of the contract across several business units was both a strength and a weakness. If business units tended to be getting more of what they specifically wanted, nevertheless there were inefficiencies. For example, there continued to be a lack of common standards across the multiple interfaces of the business units and CSC, and this needed to be pulled together. Six years into the contract it was also widely recognized in BAe that, while there were a number of detailed provisions for exiting from the contract, the switching costs and managerial problems of doing so would be formidable.

Discussion and Analysis of the BAe–CSC Contract

The success of IT outsourcing at BAe can be assessed against the initial objectives. In public presentations, BAe has acknowledged that they realized several expected benefits of outsourcing:

- reduced costs (although informants cite different savings, some claim baseline costs have been reduced by 30%);
- removed assets from balance sheet (CSC paid £75 million to BAe for assets);
- improved service quality (through a more rationalized approach to service requests and a process of expectation management);
- updated technology (such as desktops and client/server systems);
- ability to concentrate on core business.

The other major expected benefit was gaining 'value-added'. Initially, BAe defined value-added as accessing new technologies and skills for 'free':

> We are an IT company, so we can transfuse current IT, state-of-the-art IT, future IT, conceptual IT. But of course that transfusion as far as we are concerned is not free. The big problem is these people think that transfusion is free. All we are contracted to do is drive a service of this level—CSC Quality Manager (transferred from BAe).

Eventually, the parties agreed on a three-tiered definition of 'value-added' that stressed the need for both parties to benefit from transactions.

Partnering in Practice

Many people characterize the success of a contract by the quality of the customer/supplier relationship. By necessity, IT outsourcing relationships are complex because they involve so many stakeholders. IT suppliers must relate to many 'customers': senior managers, business unit managers, IT managers, and a population of end-users that amount to nearly 100 000 people in some organizations. In addition, mega-contracts can involve assimilating thousands of transitioned IT employees. Stakeholders possess different needs, expectations, desires, and measures of 'success'. In most organizations, the customer/supplier relationships vary by these stakeholder groups. Perceived beneficiaries of IT outsourcing contracts applaud supplier performance. Perceived losers attack supplier performance.

Transition Years: Adversarial Contract Disputes During the early days of the contract, BAe stakeholders generally presented a unified front to the supplier. Stakeholders fought to 'win' contract interpretations. This was based on BAe's legacy of managing exchanged-based contracts:

> And it's not that people set out to be adversarial, but in a culture of the organization, the way they've been trained, and the people they see as role models to follow, then always looking for the little more and insisting on the better person or the quicker resolution to the problem. Whatever all those dimensions of the relationship are, there is always them looking for that little bit more. And what can we get off them this time?—CSC Account Manager, Division A.

> Yes, it's undoubtedly true that the contract shaped the relationship in the early days. BAe culturally is used to buying things. It goes along and says, 'I want to buy from you, I want this widget, you are going to make it exactly like this.' And whatever price was quoted, was too much and it's got to be reduced—CSC Quality Manager (transferred from BAe).

In retrospect, some informants thought that the initial adversarial position was due not only to BAe's culture, but to the residual and transitioned IT staff's learning curves. At first, IT people for both sides are more comfortable fighting with each other over IT issues than uniting to sell IT to the business community:

> So all these contractual disputes, and whether it was this mark-up or that mark-up, and whether this was in-scope or out-of-scope, were basically justification for the existence of the significantly large IT retained organization. There were lots of little snippets they could sink their teeth into and send snotty memos and all the rest. And similarly, the CSC account management team...it was a feeding frenzy for them as well...rather than getting out there and spreading the gospel, it was somewhat easier in terms of people's comfort zone to be in the trenches with IT services arguing over the toss—CSC Account Executive, Division A.

Eventually, both parties realized that each must benefit financially from the contract. And in particular, CSC must be allowed to earn a reasonable profit. Rather than try to win every issue, parties began to be more financially neutral overall:

> From time to time we have to negotiate a compromise. Would I like to come out kind of ahead on that financially? Sure, I'd love to, but I don't. There are areas where the contract is not really clear, gray areas. So it's hard to say really who is right and wrong, so we have to negotiate—CSC Account Executive for one of BAe's divisions.

> What you must bear in mind, if you choose to ignore the contract, is that the contract is very complex and it might be that something that appears to be unfair on a spot case is actually compensated for something that's unfair in the opposite direction farther down the track. So you've got to keep your mind open right across the contract to understand—BAe Contract Manager, Division B.

Eventually, contract disputes subsided. The CSC Account Executive, Division A, notes, 'The service level issues are frankly more or less passé now.' BAe managers concur:

> I can't think of an incident in the past year where we were at all confrontational like we were the first year. We have had debates about price or something, whether it's inside the contract or outside the contract, or whether this particular service [is covered]. It really is a different relationship. I think it's better—CSC Account Executive, Division C, 1999.

Middle Years: Divisional Differences   The evolution of the relationship after the first two years is difficult to generalize, because the contract is executed in decentralized and independent divisions. Some divisions still maintained a hard-nosed approach to the relationship. Other divisions chose to by-pass the contract and find work-arounds. The following quotes characterize the different relationships among the three largest divisions:

> BAe is not a uniform organization. The Military Aircraft one is a very demanding customer. It is extremely project driven so their investments surge by project, not by infrastructure investment. Very demanding contractually, they use their muscle very effectively as the largest business unit. I think we broke through there to the degree that we are managing a very large change program with them with a very large enterprise systems integration project. So, on the one hand, they are very demanding on the commodity service provision. On the other hand, we are managing a program which is in the public domain, is several hundred million pounds worth of change program. Airbus is different. We work in a very intimate way with the client because of the particular relationship [the account executive] has with the operating board of Airbus. And typically, [it's] a less contractual and formalized way of working. The dynamics business, which is the third largest

business unit, is much more [contractual] and probably sits between the other two. The day-by-day service is very well controlled and documented and the processes are very good. But the ability to implement large scale strategy has been blunted by affordability—CSC Executive.

In some areas I think we have more of what I would call a partnership type relationship. Some areas are very customer/supplier, throw-it-over-the-wall and we throw it back type of thing . . . it really varies from function to function, from directorate to directorate—CSC Account Executive for one of BAe's Divisions.

In some divisions, BAe and CSC Contract Managers found ways to make the relationship work, even if it meant side-stepping the contract on occasion:

The contract is increasingly left in the cupboard and we find work-arounds and do local initiatives. It's not on that scale a buyer/supplier relationship anymore. But at the same time, it isn't a full strategic partnering—CSC Account Executive, Division A.

In one division, for example, CSC upgraded and expanded BAe's network. Normally, the contract requires CSC to purchase infrastructure investment, then BAe pays for service, training, and maintenance. In the following example, BAe paid the upfront investment, and CSC is responsible for training, and maintenance:

We've laid about 120 kilometers of fiber so far. We've probably spent last year about 3.5 to 4 million on purely networking it at ground level . . . If we study the business case and understand where benefits lie, we will be able to understand—we can put the contract to one side, and understand where the benefits fall. We will be able to understand who should pay for what . . . What we have done is said, 'Okay, we will buy it for you but we won't train you in it, we won't pay for your training which contractually we are obligated to do. We won't pay mark-ups because there's an acquisition mark-up. We won't pay for ongoing maintenance. But we will pay for the upfront investment because we recognize that it's missing from your toolset'—BAe Contract Manager, Division B.

Middle Years: Trust Built on a Track Record of Solid Performance One generalization about the evolution of the relationship is evident: a significant amount of trust had been established. All participants noted that trust was earned through the supplier's track record of good performance.

Trust can only come through people fulfilling their commitments that they've made—CSC Account Executive, Division A.

I suppose trust is being consistent in delivering an output service. You will cultivate trust that way . . . So basically, if we provide the service and they are happy with the service we provide, then relationships will be built and partnerships will emerge—CSC Quality Manager (transferred from BAe).

As trust was built, CSC was invited to expand their responsibilities to more strategic functions. In Division C, for example, CSC had initially suggested to expand the scope of the contract to include engineering systems. At first, the BAe Unit Manager responded:

And he said, 'when you can deliver a PC when you say you are going to deliver a PC, then we'll talk about outsourcing more people to you'—CSC Account Executive, Division C.

Four years into the contract, CSC had a record of performance. When CSC presented a strategic plan to the same BAe Unit Manager, he asked the CSC Account Executive to include engineering systems in the scope of the plan:

He said, 'What about all the engineering software? Who is looking at that? Your strategy isn't covering that.' I said, 'Hey, you were the one who told me not to look at it, that's engineering's.' He said, 'No, you should look at that. We are spending a lot of money on engineering software, that's got to be part of your work.' So without knowing it, the trust needle switched over to the other side—CSC Account Executive, Division C.

Because trust has been built on operational performance, CSC has increasingly been given more responsibilities in IT strategic planning, re-engineering, and change programs. Depending on whether the task was operational or strategic, the nature of the relationship varied from adversarial to collaborative. Recall that one participant characterized the relationship as schizophrenic. The following quotations provide additional evidence:

You have to separate out; whilst there was the battleground going on, at the same time a major strategy exercise was launched in which there was a joint CSC and BAe team sharing the same office. And to some extent it was the same people, who on a frequent basis were involved in contractual skirmishes but who were at the same time in a joint team to define a totally new strategy—CSC Centralized Management Team.

I have two discussions when I go and visit a managing director. Ten minutes might be criticizing me or asking me to take action on the fact that PCs haven't been delivered, then having cleared that conversation, we will move on to probably quite an earnest debate about where his business is going and how IT is or can support him. So you tend to end up with quite compartmentalized debates—CSC Executive.

Maturing Years: Striving for Strategic Relationships   By 2000 parties for both sides were very clear in their aspirations for the remainder of the relationship. Of course, the contract would continue to serve as the foundation of the relationship as evidenced by past and future contract realignments. But IT managers wanted to spend less of their time on operational issues and more time working on strategic issues. While this is a shared goal, both parties have not been able to free themselves yet:

[I] don't want to be sucked into these daily matters. I want to spend more time on IT strategy, educating users on how to better exploit IT, and to teach users to manage CSC themselves—BAe Contract Manager for a Division.

I would like very much to be able to focus on developing and maintaining the relationships within the business unit and to be able to coordinate the provision of services for the customer, to help him really achieve his business goals. That being said, I find that I spend a lot of time, an inordinate amount of my time, dealing with day-to-day service issues, delivery of service, such that I don't have time to go out and do the kind of work and meet the customer in a way that I would like to . . . I feel like we have a lot to contribute if we can be involved with a project or an idea at the conceptual stage. And really be a part of that team. I think we can provide a better service for them at a lower overall cost if we pursue it another way—CSC Account Executive for one of BAe's Divisions.

So I would like to really work on getting out to see more of the customer, not just sitting in front of him as he is assessing my performance, but to develop a business relationship with him. That being said, we have to deliver a basic level of service as per our agreements and satisfy the customer, I think, before we can develop those deeper relationships—CSC Account Executive for one of BAe's Divisions.

BAe Conclusion

The BAe–CSC contract typifies many long-term, 'fixed-price', IT outsourcing contracts. Such exchange-based relationships require a detailed contract because it serves as the major governance structure over the relationship, particularly during the transition years. The transition years are typically adversarial because each side may assume the other will operate opportunistically—opportunistically not because parties are devious, but because each party is obligated to represent the interests of their own organizations.

At BAe and CSC, parties began to institutionalize the relationship by implementing structures and processes to resolve issues in a fair manner. Trust among the parties developed as the record of supplier performance mounted. Disputes are settled in a financially neutral way that benefits both parties overall. Or in some cases, disputes are settled by side-stepping the contract altogether. Such disputes are now argued in a manner similar to spouses—with an underlying comfort zone of safety based on a history of commitment:

> I think we can still have a good relationship and still have contractual disputes—CSC Account Executive for one of BAe's Divisions.

In the maturing years, the threat of opportunism has no longer been an issue. Both parties want the other to succeed. But this said, parties still see the relationship as a commercial one, and the contract still serves as the fundamental governance structure. As such, the contract has been fully realigned once to reflect technology and business changes. Parties anticipate, and have operationalized, contract realignments every two to three years. Both sides are hoping to devote less time to operational issues and more time on exploiting IT for business advantage. Indeed, a number of strategic projects have been completed, and more are underway.

> I think mega-deals can work, but they take a lot of hard work—Quote from BAe Outsourcing Report.

CASE 4: THE INLAND REVENUE

Background

As of 2000, the Inland Revenue (IR) had a staff of over 50 000 people. The IR comprises 23 Executive Offices, a Valuation Office Agency, and 150 local offices throughout the United Kingdom. As a unified department, the IR seeks three objectives:

1. compliance (collect the correct amount of taxes),
2. service quality (through clearly worded forms and leaflets as well as a courteous response to queries),
3. efficiency (keeping costs as low as possible).

The IR strives to meet these competing objectives within a restricted budget annually set by the Treasury Department. In particular, the IR is pressured to keep current systems functioning while simultaneously implementing new tax law and policy changes. During the 1990s, Parliament initiated a number of tax law changes, the most important being Self Assessment, one of the greatest UK tax reforms this century:

> Tax and collection offices are being restructured to bring related activities together and give taxpayers a focal point of responsibility for their affairs. Self

Assessment was introduced in April 1997 which gives the nine million tax-payers, who receive a tax return, the option of calculating their own tax bill.[7]

IT is seen as a key enabler of their strategy. The contract with EDS was motivated not only by the cost savings, but by the promise of quickly adapting systems to policy changes. As an IR bulletin put it in mid-1998:

> An integral part of simplifying and streamlining work processes involves making maximum intelligent uses of available technology. To ensure the best possible advice, skills, and systems, the Department has negotiated a 10-year 'Strategic Partnership' contract with EDS for the provision of IT services.[8]

The Inland Revenue's IT Department Prior to Outsourcing

In 1992, the IR's annual IT budget was £100 million and carried a capital IT investment of nearly £250 million. IT services were supported by a staff of over 2400 IT people. The IR operated 13 datacenters.

In general, the in-house IT function had a good record of performance, though that has not always been the view of users.[9] In some respects in-house capability relative to the market was high. For example, the IR's Worthing datacenter was identified by an external benchmarking firm as more efficient than any private sector datacenter. Civil servant salaries, typically lower than private sector counterparts, contributed to the overall cost efficiency.

Despite the good track record of IT performance, the IR's IT department has always been plagued by meeting Parliamentary-set tax law reforms with Treasury-set annual IT budgets. Thus, both requirements and funding are externally imposed on the organization, sometimes requiring pleas for relief from the Chancellor:

> And where we can't cope, where we've got something that's far too big, we have to make special representation right through to the Treasury and to the Chancellor himself if necessary to get extra funds. None of that is welcomed by the Chancellor, as you can imagine. But if there is no way, we've put every effort in it within IR to meet those demands, and we still can't cope, we've got to actually say, 'Look, the Treasury has to exercise some judgments in terms of our priorities'—IR Account Manager.

The Conservative government mandate to market test public services generally eventually prompted an IT outsourcing investigation. In addition to cost—service efficiency, four other objectives for IT outsourcing were sought:

- gain rapid access to new technologies;
- enhance IT capability to meet ever changing business needs;
- reduce development time, particularly for Parliamentary requirements; and
- improve careers for IT staff.

The Inland Revenue's Outsourcing Decision Process

The outsourcing decision process took almost two years. The IR assembled an evaluation team that comprised 6 to 20 people at different times. The evaluation team included legal, human resource, outsourcing, IT, civil service, property, and contract experts. Their job was to create the Request For Proposal (RFP), evaluate bids, and negotiate a contract. One of these hired experts was an ex-EDS person, who understood the information suppliers needed to make a sound bid. This information included current IT performance, costs, budgets, human resource policies, and pension arrangements. The IR also established a separate team to create an audit trail of the process and outcomes.

In January 1993, four bids were submitted. One bid was a consortium of several suppliers. The three single suppliers were EDS, Hoskyns, and Sema Group. EDS was selected because they were perceived as the only supplier capable of handling such a large account. Contract negotiations began.

A key concern during contract negotiations was the fair treatment of IT staff. The IT staff initially opposed the impending decision, fearing pay cuts and job losses. In April 1993, the IT staff, members of the Inland Revenue Staff Federation union, staged a one-day strike:

> Inland Revenue information technology workers walked out for a day last April, specifically protesting against any outsourcing arrangement, according to an Inland Revenue Staff Federation spokesman. And they have refused to work overtime, also in protest of the outsourcing deal, the spokesman said.[10]

Responsibility for redundancy costs was another human resource concern. The IR wanted all staff who refused to relocate to EDS or refused alternative offers of work to nonetheless receive redundancy payments. EDS wanted to charge the IR £50 million for these unidentified costs. The IR took the position that the EDS offer was a fixed-price bid that should encompass all transition costs, including redundancy payments. By the end of 1994 the employee relation issues were largely settled and the Inland Revenue Staff Federation agreed to transfer arrangements.

Like British Aerospace, the IR identified some 134 risks of IT out-sourcing during contract negotiations. Each risk was tempered by policy or a contractual clause. For example, one risk was the sheer size of transfer—1900 people in all. Initially the risk was reduced by identifying four phases of transfer, but this was later reduced to two. First, the computer operations staff would transfer at the beginning of 1994. Eighteen months later, the 800 IT development staff would transfer. Some 300 staff would stay in-house, while it was estimated that 200 would leave through natural wastage.

The Inland Revenue—Contract Overview

In the public sector, many opponents argue against outsourcing IT to the private sector because of a perceived threat of breach of privacy, confidentiality, and in the case of revenue collection, the threat of theft. When Sir John Bourn, head of the National Audit Office, announced the contract on March 8, 1994, to Parliament, he assured the UK people that the contract included safeguards to protect the interests of the IR, taxpayers, and staff.[11] Detailed aspects of the arrangement include:

- taxpayer confidentiality and security arrangements which are at least as strong as those that existed previously;
- access by the Department and the National Audit Office to EDS's books and records relating to the provision of IR services;
- the IR to share in any profits from the subsequent sale of assets and also in the income generated by the use of assets on non-IR business; retain ownership of their existing intellectual property rights; and obtain future rights created as a result of delivery of the contract services;
- the Department to acquire from the supplier any assets and licences that will be needed to ensure continuity of services following the expiry or termination of the contract;
- staff to transfer to EDS on terms and conditions of employment which are the same or no less favorable than those that applied immediately prior to the transfer, and which were eventually accepted by the trades unions; and whilst the terms and conditions of transferred staff do not provide guarantees of continued employment over the life of the contract, the Department have provided EDS with a financial incentive to minimize redundancies;
- safeguards to ensure continuing price competitiveness, including profit sharing, open-book verification of EDS's costs and profit levels and the re-testing of individual services against the open market.

Pricing

Pertaining to the last point, three provisions are designed to ensure fair pricing during the course of the relationship. First, open-book accounting tracks EDS's costs and caps overall profit margins:

> If EDS makes a greater margin than that average margin, we have a fifty-fifty split of the excess profits. That is actually fundamental to this arrangement because it gives me the confidence to enter into an arrangement with EDS that actually says that if I got it wrong, and you make excess profit EDS, at least I know I'm going to get half that back under the arrangement—IR Account Manager.

[In practice, open-book accounting on other contracts was found to be very difficult to implement because it requires disclosure of anticipated cost structures and an agreed upon accounting methodology.[12]]

Second, pricing schedules ensure that unit costs decline during the contract. The rate of application development serves as one example:

> So that if for instance in a particular area EDS inherited from us a capacity to produce a function point in 20 man-days of application code—and this is an illustrative example only—by the time you are two years into the contract, they've got that down to 12 man-days per function point. If we want to buy more of those function points, we get them at the 12 mark no matter what. So we've got a guarantee that spills out of the way we priced this to drive their efficiency down—IR Account Manager.

Third, the IR retained the right to market test any area of IT, with the possibility of another supplier taking over an activity if it could be done more cost effectively:

> We have the right within the contract to compare any area that they are providing for us with a market test so that we can put that market test to EDS and if they can match it, they will retain the business—IR Account Manager.

Service Levels

The contract has a Master Service-Level Agreement (MSLA) that focuses on 35 different business 'streams'. EDS works with the individual business streams to negotiate any required modifications:

> The MSLA tends to set out the global range of services that the business is acquiring from EDS, and the general framework within those services are acquired. EDS's service delivery philosophy is centered on a one-to-one basis with the business streams. As a partnership, we are very supportive of that. We expect the individual business streams to negotiate from the master service level agreement their own agreement with EDS—IR Account Manager.

EDS agreed to pay the IR £70 million for their IT assets and to eventually transfer 1900 employees. In return, the IR agreed to pay EDS approximately £100 million per year for baseline services. Cost savings of £225 million were promised during the course of the 10-year relationship. The National Audit Office planned to serve as independent monitor of the contract to ensure taxpayers the savings.

The Inland Revenue's Transition Period

Like all mega-contracts, the IR and EDS spent the first two years of the relationship operationalizing their contract by

- distributing and interpreting the contract for the user population;
- establishing the post-contract management infrastructure;
- establishing the post-contract management processes;
- validating services, costs, service levels, and responsibilities for baseline services;
- managing additional service requests; and
- fostering realistic expectations of supplier performance.

Distributing and Interpreting the Contract for the User Population

Our research is finding that most customers decide not to distribute the contract to the user population because it is too difficult for them to understand and interpret. The IR certainly chose not to:

> If you went into our business streams ... They've never seen it. They've only seen an extract from the contract—IR Account Manager.

At the IR, only the 30 individuals in the centralized account team have seen the actual contract. Instead, the MSLA was distributed:

> What they have is the master service level agreement. They have a structure within which they can track their targets with EDS. And that's made painless for them in the sense that the EDS account manager would approach you as the business representative and say, 'let's understand what we mean by that. I need to articulate those needs in the context of this framework' ... he doesn't see the contract—IR Customer Service Manager.

Although most customers find it prudent not to distribute the contract, communicating contractual obligations to the user community is a constant challenge. At the IR, the centralized account team continues to explain the contract to the business units. In particular, the business units must understand what requests are within contract price, and what requests trigger excess fees:

It's really us sitting down with the business counterpart and saying, 'legally this is a reasonable level of service that we can deliver. We are prepared to contract to deliver this and there's no conditions attached.' Then the business can reasonably expect to have that level of service and to complain and seek some form of redress if it doesn't get that. If they want to renegotiate within the terms of commitments already made or funds that are available, then the scope is added—IR Customer Service Manager.

Establishing the Post-Contract Management Infrastructure

From public speeches made by Sir John Bourn, it was evident that the IR was not entirely sure how to manage such a large contract. Thus, the National Audit Office promised to review processes (in addition to assessing outcomes) as the relationship progressed:

> On the future management of the contract, the National Audit Office found that the Department had created a management team with appropriate skills and experience, and established procedures which should help ensure the delivery of the savings and improved services which they seek from EDS. However, it is not yet possible to determine how effective these processes will be during the life of the contract. Once the contract has had time to bed down, therefore, the National Audit Office intend to review the contract management arrangements, including the achievement of benefits and the regulation and control of the contract charges (http://www.open.gov. uk/nao/9495245.htm).

The IR initially assembled a centralized staff of nearly 30 people to manage the contract. The IR planned very tight control of the contract in the beginning (as was the IR's traditional treatment of suppliers), with an intention of loosening control as precedents and supplier performance were established:

> The easy way of managing this contract is the way we've always managed our contracts. That is, in terms of ticking and stamping and not varying from a fairly hard-nosed approach to our suppliers. But even before we led this contract, we knew we didn't want that sort of relationship in the long run. Mainly because we knew that we couldn't possibly predict what our requirements would be and how they would change from day one through the life of a 10-year contract—IR Account Manager.

Another argument against very tight control in the long run was expense:

> We have seen other buyer–supplier types of contract where the tendency is to get more and more aggravated and employ more and more people checking everything that's going on on both sides. You can end up with an enormous team in the middle busy checking everything that the supplier would do and challenging him at every point where he's failing. We saw

that in our references in the States and we were alerted to the fact that we didn't want to jump into that—IR Account Manager.

Thus, the IR sought a balance between costs and risks for supplier monitoring. On the one hand, tight monitoring reduces risks but increases transaction costs because more people are required. On the other hand, loose monitoring reduces transaction costs but increases risk.

Establishing the Post-Contract Management Processes

In the beginning of a relationship, supplier contract compliance is closely monitored until trust is established based on a track record of performance. EDS reports on 1000 measures to the IR every month. Each measure, like other relationships we have studied, is coded red for 'serious problem', amber for 'heading in the wrong direction', and green for 'perfectly acceptable'. This level of detail is quite overwhelming, so an overall picture of service is created every three months. The goal is to ensure a positive trend, i.e. that each quarterly report shows improvement.

Many measures are quite subjective. Initially, users were motivated to rate problems as serious to ensure immediate attention. As the relationship has evolved over the years, however, users have been more likely to indicate a green rating (but see below on problems in 1999):

> If people are feeling relatively comfortable, we'll give the partner the benefit of the doubt—IR Account Manager.

The goal is for service issues to be resolved by joint teams within the business streams, but unresolved issues are passed up the hierarchy to the general account managers. They meet monthly to address problems:

> If we think that there are any stand-offs that are occurring, any differences of opinion we can't get to the bottom of, we attempt to try and sort it as joint teams. Central to this contract, we apply it at the contract level and the two contract management teams, and they are not necessarily called that, but they do have active discussions about particular issues and they consider positions from both sides. And if there's an escalation process where they can't come to some agreement, it comes up to the management hierarchy and will come to myself and an equivalent within EDS to see if we can mediate on these things. So we use the technique of getting people together and trying to find solutions in a fair-minded way—IR Account Manager.

Validating Services, Costs, Service Levels, and Responsibilities for Baseline Services

The first major task of any contract is to validate baseline costs and services. Supplier bids are based on the RFP and discoveries made during due diligence. Any undiscovered items are typically subject to excess fees. After the IR–EDS contract went into effect, the IR had to pay for the following items that surfaced:

- £100 000 for software license fees
- £5 million per year caused by inaccuracies in the original tender offers
- £15 million per year for hardware maintenance

Thus, it appears that the 20% projected cost savings were offset by the illumination of 20% worth of hidden costs. Customers typically re-calculate baseline costs and projected savings when such instances occur. (We will see in the discussion section that the IR still believes it is achieving projected savings on *baseline* costs.)

In addition to the difficulty validating baseline costs, baseline service-level validation was particularly problematic because the IR did not have clearly defined measures prior to the contract:

> This contract is about the same level of service but reducing costs over time. So you start from the basis of what did you actually have before the contract. And that in itself is difficult to know, to write up, because we had some good records in the area of operation systems, we didn't have as good a record in the area of development systems—IR Account Manager.

Software development was a particular source of disagreement. Parties had to agree on the baseline portfolio size, quality, and development productivity:

> We were trying to establish what was it the IR were capable of providing in terms of output to the development area. And our records were not complete. They were open to conjecture and yet we had to try and establish some productivity baselines around the development area. And that was a very hard time. And we had some good meetings. At the end of it we had to make the thing work. In a sense, it's been a real test of the relationship because we've both had to take some pain on that in order to get through it—IR Account Manager.

The first appointed IR and EDS account managers could not settle these disputes. Each felt that they needed to protect the interests of their respective organizations and maintained an adversarial posture (a position they were rewarded for during contract negotiations). Eventually, senior management for EDS and the IR decided they needed to replace the managers:

> At the beginning of this contract, we actually had to change both of the contract managers three months into the contract to get a more reasonable basis for the relationship because the two of them over the opening three

months had continued the negotiations. They were locking horns day in, day out. We had to take both of those individuals out and try to recover that relationship. I think that's been successful—IR Account Manager.

As is typical on other mega-contracts, the parties settled the baseline issues by re-entering negotiations with outside assistance:

We had an issue in post-contract verification where there was a genuine misunderstanding on both sides of what was intended by the contract. We ended up getting advice from lawyers and barristers saying, 'actually there is a view to be had on both sides and we are not absolutely clear'—IR Account Manager.

Managing Additional Service Requests

Services beyond baseline (and thus subject to excess fees), can be triggered by (1) exceeding projected volumes on existing services, (2) changes in the composition of baseline services, or (3) demand for entirely new projects. Every outsourcing customer we have studied experiences all three sources of change.

(1) Concerning projected volumes, the IR underestimated user demand:

What we've seen is of course that we've got an increasing demand for IT and we are ordering more than previously anticipated. Nothing unusual about that—there's an endless appetite for IT. The only difficulty is the endless appetite is matched against diminishing funds. We've actually got more demand for IT within the IR and not the funds to pay for it—IR Account Manager, 1999.

(2) Changing the composition of baseline services is also difficult, not so much because of outsourcing, but because of the integrated nature of technology. For example, the IR had 50 000 16-bit desktop computers. Software upgrades required the eventual upgrade of the hardware fleet to 32-bit computers:

We've got changes in technology that we've become alert to in the last six months or so which is to do with the impact of the move of desktop support services from 16- to 32-bit architecture. And we've got some very heavy dependency in some intricate interim software that we've created ourselves on specific products that are associated with 16-bit architecture. And how we move our desktop terminals, of which there are 50 000, from 16-bit to 32-bit, because the marketplace is not supporting 16-bit any more. And in fact, we are having to make special arrangements if we want to buy something that's still consistent with 16-bit architecture, special arrangements with our supplier for the hardware kit. And we don't want to do that because practically or even strategically that's not an ongoing marketplace we want to be in—IR Account Manager.

(3) In public sector organizations, demand for new projects stems from changes in law and policy. The reality of dictated requirements is particularly troublesome for IT, because elected officials rarely consider the IT costs to implement Parliamentary changes. In 1995, the UK government announced its intention to save some 3000 jobs amongst tax staff by introducing a self-assessment tax scheme to be operational from April 1997. When the IR first drew up its outsourcing plans it was not aware of this project, first announced in general terms by the government in 1993. It represented probably the biggest single reform of UK tax administration for 50 years and was highly dependent on supporting information systems being in place. Not surprisingly, this systems development created considerable anxiety amongst EDS and IR senior IT staff. Neither wished to be seen to fail on such a high profile development project, now called the Computerized Environment for Self Assessment (CESA) project.

EDS believed that the system should be kept as simple as possible. Off-the-shelf packages could provide the capability to record who should receive the forms and the payment history of each taxpayer. The difficulty was that two systems would have to be maintained, because the new system would not interface immediately with the existing systems holding all current records. Moreover, the new 'simple' system would not facilitate spot-checks on the accuracy of taxpayers' returns. IR management therefore wanted a tailored package to meet its specific requirements but this greatly increased the risk of failing to deliver a robust system on time.

Development was also marked by uncertainties. The cost of the project was unknown as at mid-1995. An estimate that the system would have to handle 90 million transactions annually was not that dependable. EDS managers questioned whether the chosen technology was sufficiently expandable. Also the system—ICL VME mainframes linked to servers and thousands of terminals—was dependent upon ICL Goldrush superservers that had never before been used on such a large project. EDS also worried that the ICL equipment seemed to cost more than twice as much to buy and run as equivalent IBM hardware.

For EDS managers the project represented high risk in terms of short timescales, technical complexity, and a major change in the way business would be conducted. Furthermore, the project was only to come under EDS control when the remaining 800 IR development staff were transferred to them in early 1996. This added a further risk, as senior managers in both organizations conceded, with management of the project being transferred in mid-flight to an outside supplier. By mid-1995 EDS managers were asking for control of the project to be handed over earlier. They felt that they could not give a guarantee of delivery before they had control, and had arrived at agreement over the choice of systems.

IR senior managers were willing to concede this control to give EDS an improved opportunity to deliver. Failure would reflect badly on both sets of managers, but also on the outsourcing contract as a whole. In these circumstances, it seemed likely that the cost of the project would be less of an issue than on-time delivery of a robust system. Additional resources would be needed, either from diverting staff from other IR projects, or buying in additional resources from EDS above the original contract price.

Fostering Realistic Expectations of Supplier Performance

Contracts specify a set price for a baseline level of service, but users typically expect a vastly improved service. They argue, 'IT outsourcers are the IT experts—they should do this better.' Every contract management team is challenged by this misalignment of contractual obligations and user expectations. The situation at the IR was no different:

> The contract is about the same level of service provided by the IT Divisions and our customers were never thoroughly satisfied with us in the past—IR Account Manager.

The centralized account teams serve as mediators of realistic expectations among the user population:

> There is always some hot spot somewhere or another that's not working entirely the way either side is expecting. And usually it's a misunderstanding of what people can expect from the contract, expect from the relationship. So once you get in there, it's not always difficult to find some way to improve the relationship. It's just that you don't always know until there is a bit of a stand-off—IR Account Manager, 1997.

One positive outcome of most outsourcing relationships is that users begin to understand cost/service trade-offs. A supplier's formal charge-back mechanism serves to associate a price with above-baseline requests:

> I think one of the things that the contract does is drive out a much better understanding with the individual business streams. What it is they are acquiring; they are forced to consider what it is they need in the first place. And they have to accept, like any commercial undertaking, that there is a price to pay—IR Customer Service Manager, 1996.

In summary, the IR's transition years focused on operationalizing the monolithic contract. During the early days, the relationship was hampered by ambiguous baseline service levels, vast changes in tax law, and by unrealistic user expectations. During the middle years, the relationship has stabilized.

The Inland Revenue's Post-Transition: The Middle Years

We are witnessing across our cases that relationships are much improved during the middle years. Disputes still occur because each party must represent the interests of their own organizations, but issues are resolved with an underlying foundation of trust based on a history of commitment and performance. As the IR and EDS faced the following middle-year issues, parties actively sought to understand the other's position, and the rule of fair-mindedness governed resolutions. In particular, the parties have encountered the following:

- market-testing to negotiate prices
- realigning the contract expectations
- involving the supplier on more value-added areas

Market-Testing to Negotiate Prices

The Inland Revenue, like other mega-outsourcing customers, initially planned to use market-testing to ensure fair prices during the course of the relationship. In practice, however, customers find that this option is a bit naive because EDS's presence is so all-encompassing; it is virtually impossible to carve out areas for another supplier. Instead of formal market-testing, the IR uses 'informal' market-testing on a limited basis to help negotiate better prices:

> Generally we wouldn't go into a formal market test. Because the way we would invoke market test is that we informally test the market against the EDS price and provided that was reasonable, we wouldn't go to a formal market test at all—IR Account Manager.

Thus, the intention of informal market-testing is for EDS to ultimately provide the service. For example, the IR has used informal market-testing in the area of hardware supply to successfully negotiate a lower price with EDS:

> It worked out fine. EDS was able to respond and take advantage of the marketplace and provide those particular items to us at a cheaper rate—IR Account Manager.

In the area of applications development, the IR occasionally uses outside experts to help negotiate a price. For example, the IR hired the Gartner Group to help price the Year 2000 project. Amounting to millions of pounds, such a large project could be competitively bid according to the contract. But the reality is that EDS runs the applications:

> There's no prospect of us asking a third party to dig in on some of our application and change that and then hand it back to EDS for them to operate, or anything of that nature. As soon as we are confronted with something like [the Year 2000] project, we go into direct discussions with EDS as our supplier. Because they are our single systems integrator for our IT services in the IR—IR Account Manager.

The parties agreed on a fixed price for the project. This way, the IR has cost certainty and EDS is responsible for earning a return, regardless of what they uncover:

> [EDS] has got full responsibility for making that conversion work … We took advice from Gartner in assessing whether this was a good deal for us. And we became convinced that it was better to do [a fixed price] rather than try and instigate a pay-as-you-go basis, which would leave us with the total risk of what they might find—IR Account Manager.

Realigning the Contract Expectations

Like the experience at BAe, the IR found that the original contract was becoming obsolete as technology advances, requirements change, and false assumptions become illuminated. Parties were expecting things from each other that were not always realistic, such as the user belief that EDS should upgrade technology as part of the 'strategic partnership'. In 1997, both sides initiated a Perceptions Exercise. EDS and IR teams met separately to document perceptions of each other:

> Then we shared those perceptions. We put them into some shape and presented them to the other side. They were obliged to listen to them and not react. Even if they felt it may not be factual, to recognize that perceptions had a meaningful role to play—IR Account Manager.

The next step in the Perceptions Exercise was to assign joint teams to address the 68 areas of major concern. The teams report monthly to the general account managers on their progress:

> We meet every month. We assigned pairings from that joint partnership meeting to get to the bottom of the way we rated those issues. We analyze those issues, put them into certain categories, and we task them to examine

them and to set out a workplan of how they solve those particular issues, each one of them—IR Account Manager, 1997.

For example, both sides wanted to dismantle the bureaucracy for ordering human resources. The IR was contractually required to provide a 13-month forecast of required manpower on 48 skill sets. They found this task nearly impossible, and subsequently simplified the process:

> If you look at the way our central resource ordering process worked and compared it over the three years to the contract, it's significantly simplified now. We now run it with about 25 resource types rather than over 50. We run it on a quarterly basis rather than monthly. So we've come to an accommodation jointly as to how we handle that—IR Account Manager.

Another example: invoice-clearing was re-engineered because it was perceived as too cumbersome. And finally, the pricing of new capital equipment was changed because the contract initially rewarded EDS for over-spending:

> We have changed the contract over the course where we thought it would be mutually beneficial. And one particular area is where we've introduced an incentive for EDS to reduce the capital costs of IT. Prior to that, they had an active disincentive in the contract because they get an agreed mark-up on any capital item they buy for the provision of our service. And if it costs less, they got less of a mark-up. So we introduced some arrangement within the contract that meant that it was worth their while to drive some harder bargains and deals and we would share the benefit of those decreased costs—IR Account Manager.

The goal of the Perceptions Exercise was to be fair-minded. As such issues are resolved, they are approved and documented:

> We agree at a joint partnership level that that's what we would both be interested in doing. And we would have papers going up both of the organizations internally to counter-sign those changes to the contract. Most of those are written up in the procedures, we don't necessarily change the contract unless it's particularly important—IR Account Manager.

Involving the Supplier on More Value-Added Areas

In the early days of the contract, the IR had expected EDS to offer suggestions for redesigning business processes to achieve greater savings to IT. In the beginning years, this expectation was seen as naive— outside suppliers are not motivated to suggest such cost savings. This is not a criticism of the supplier because the supplier has only a limited amount of resources and needs to focus on the execution of the agreement. In the middle years, the supplier gets a better understanding of which service areas are costing them excessive resources to support. Thus, any proposals to streamline business processes must benefit both parties:

> We had one attempt [at redesigning processes to save IR money] in the early days, which was not terribly successful. But I think our relationship has improved since then. I think we get a lot more cooperation from EDS now on that sort of approach. Because now they are in a position to know what's expensive for them to support, which may actually not have high business value. Now we discuss around the balance of low-cost/high-value and high-cost/low-value—that sort of paradigm—IT Account Manager.

One of the major strategic challenges of the IR's IT department has been to try to maintain existing services while simultaneously incorporating policy changes. The IT department has yearly negotiations with the Treasury for their upcoming budget. In theory, the budget should be increased to cover policy changes, but the reality of restricted funding makes negotiations and prioritizing IT spending very difficult:

> We have an annual budget that is negotiated with Treasury. And within that, we are expected to be able to provide a certain element of policy change and adaptation to our main tax systems. In fact, at the moment, because we've just had a change of government, we've got some far more significant policy changes being considered. Some of which have been announced within previous budgets, some of which have been announced through the House, and some of which will no doubt be announced in the budget coming up. All of which is significantly more than we've had previously. What we have to do is to assess what can we cope with with existing funds and how we prioritize the money spent on IT with IR and whether we can get other funds—IR Account Manager.

As at 2000, EDS serves on the budget committee because their input is vital to understanding the IT cost effects of proposed tax changes:

> It's a Committee chaired by the Deputy Chairman, and actually we have representation from EDS on that committee. So we have joint representation on that committee and of course when we are providing estimates of what certain policy changes would cost, estimates are coming from the EDS camp. We've got [EDS and IR] people collaborating with our feasibility appraisal team in what those estimates would be and what the costs would be—IR Account Manager.

EDS also participates in monthly strategic planning meetings:

> We have full involvement of EDS in our strategic planning forums. So we have a big departmental implementation committee which is chaired by the Deputy Chairman of the investment committee, has other Deputy Chairmen on the board and EDS sit on that. And that's a monthly meting which is actually agreeing what projects are within the departmental priority. So we've

got EDS as fully paid-up members of the departmental committee, and behind all that, our resources ordering process, all our contractual arrangements are all met in with that. So we are providing information about our long-term plans for coming out of two years of man power plans, and 10 years of capital and infrastructure plans—IT Account Manager.

EDS's participation on more strategic projects and committees serves as testimony to the growth and maturing of the relationship.

Maturing of the Contract

By 1999 the IR–EDS deal was running an installed hardware base worth more than £250 million. Datacenters had been consolidated with those of the Department of Social Security (also run by EDS). The economies of scale achieved meant that for about the first time EDS was able to make a reasonable profit from that part of the deal. There were also 30 large Sequent Numa-Q or HP V-class servers, 800 Bull Unix servers (later replaced by 800 NT servers), and more than 200 million pieces of output. By mid-2000 56 000 workstations had been largely upgraded to NT. Moreover, amongst other things, EDS had delivered the £200 million Self Assessment system on time with relatively few problems.

However, in 1999–2000, the roll-out of Infrastructure 2000 (i2K) was not without considerable problems that raised questions amongst many in the user communities. The roll-out of desktops and Windows NT 4.0 systems and the replacement of local office Unix servers inevitably affected performance and morale in the UK's 600 tax offices.[13] However, by November 1999 the head of i2k at EDS felt able to announce that the service was stable, and improving, and that there had been no new issues for three months. IR management admitted to teething problems, but pointed out that the huge infrastructure changes had been delayed due to Y2K, and the need to ensure Self Assessment systems had been introduced successfully. According to John Yard, IR IT Director, problems were largely a result of the scale, complexity, and volume of the changes.

By 2000 the value of the contract had risen from £1 billion to £2 billion. The IR's dependence on computers had increased, the inter-relationships between the systems had become more complex, and EDS had been given more IT business as its work became inextricably intertwined with that of the IR. These factors were explicitly recognized in a further National Audit Office report on the IR–EDS deal in 2000, which concluded, generally, that the outsourcing arrangement was both well managed and offering value for money.

Discussion and Analysis of the Inland Revenue–EDS Contract

The success of any decision is typically assessed by comparing outcomes with initial objectives. In public sector IT outsourcing cases, participants are primarily accountable for realizing projected cost savings for the taxpayer. In the case of all IT outsourcing, however, it is very difficult to rely on initial cost objectives because volumes and the composition of IT services during the contract dramatically differ from baseline volumes and composition. And in the case of the IR, estimated cost savings were predicated on a presumed baseline cost that was later discovered to be 20% under-identified.

IR contract administrators, however, have determined that baseline costs have been achieved using an initial baseline model. The model is invalid as far as the actual volume and composition of service, but the UK government requires an audit of actual versus projected savings. An IR contract administrator explains how baseline cost savings are assessed:

> This contract was signed against a model that we set up that said over 10 years, we will save £225 million. And we are constructing a unit cost model which says how much we have saved from what we can determine this year. We've done it on the concept of constant volumes, so that we have volumes that we associated with the start of the contract. And if all that was ordered in year one we ordered today, what cost reduction have we managed to achieve? And what the model is telling us at the moment, and it isn't a model that's actually been verified by the National Audit Office yet, but it will be one that they look at when they do a value-for-money audit [this year]. What it's telling us is that we are ahead of target to achieve £225 million on our constant volumes—IR Account Manager.

The IR must also track every change to the baseline so that they can justify any deviations from the contract:

> That's very difficult for us because we've always got the prospect of our National Audit Office hanging over us who are bound to make a report to Parliament at some point about the validity of this contract. And in fact, they start a big audit this year. So we've got to have a reasonable account of the changes in the relationship—IR Account Manager.

Thus, the IR contract administrators maintain two models at all times: (1) the baseline volumes and services, and (2) actual volumes and services to assess the cost effects of IT outsourcing.

In practice, by 1998, the overall cost of the IR contract with EDS had already risen 60% to £1.6 billion since it was signed in 1994. Value for money in the deal became the subject of close monitoring by the National Audit Office from 1997. Their positive review in 1998 focused on the additional work given to EDS since the original contract was signed. In the four years since 1994, EDS had received an extra £280 million to cover increasing work volumes arising from new projects, £220 million to cover changes in the value of resources transferred to EDS, and £100 million to cover inflation.

Returning to the other objectives of IT outsourcing, the IR also sought rapid access to new technologies, reduced development time, and enhanced IT capability. EDS has carried out many projects, such as the CESA Project, in the required time frames (though often at the expense of functionality). In addition, EDS eventually delivered the pay-and-file system (despite inherited problems from the IR), a national system that allows employers to submit expenses and benefits information on magnetic media. EDS also helped to pilot an Electronic Data Interchange system to allow employees to electronically submit starting and leaving information. The pilot ran until April 1999 when it was evaluated as eventually offering good cost efficiency and service quality. A Year 2000 project was also a vital contribution to the IR.

Partnering Practice

The success of outsourcing is also assessed by the quality of the customer/supplier relationship. As with all contracts, relationships are quite complex owing to the dimensions of time (the relationship evolves), individuals (some adapt better than others), and stakeholder expectations (different populations expect different things from the relationship). In general, the relationship has improved considerably from the early days.

Transition Years: Adversarial Contract Disputes   During the early days of the contract, IR stakeholders generally presented a unified front to the supplier. Without a history, stakeholders primarily rely on the contract to 'win' disputes:

> For any disputes, we always get a matter of fact account of how that dispute manifests itself in terms of the contract. So we are always looking at what the clauses in the contract are saying about this area. We are looking at whether we believe that the contract was comprehensive in that area, whether it needs to have some changes because we are quite open to changes in the contract if they are beneficial. But we always view that in the context of what the contract is saying about this area of work—IR Account Manager.

Early disputes required re-opening negotiations to interpret the contract. Soon, parties realized that the adversarial posturing would not work in the long run. Instead of relying on the strict wording of the contract, parties began to discuss the 'spirit of intent' of the contract:

From time to time, if we are not absolutely certain what the contract is saying—and the contract is a very complicated vehicle—we are actually saying, 'what were we intending by this process? What did the bid from EDS say and how has it worked out subsequently?' So we may have to go right back and ask: What was the intention to do here, and how has that presented itself in the clauses we are now examining?—IR Account Manager.

Some individuals were replaced to facilitate an agreement. Key individuals must strike a delicate balance between representing organizational interests and facilitating compromise:

So you've got the intent straight and the people who are inclined to make the thing work in the most fair-minded way. We rely on our contract manager to have a very subtle role. One of being able to say absolutely objectively what the contract says about this particular issue, but secondly, to be able to suggest what might be a fair-minded movement from that—IR Account Manager.

Middle Years: General Account Managers Unify to Manage Stakeholders
During the middle years, the general account managers still represent the interests of their perspective organizations. As such, the IR and EDS will never be true partners—i.e. they will never have joint ownership, shared revenues, or be responsible for each other's debts. However, the general account managers present a united front to the business streams, the public, and other constituents.

Consider, for example, the continuing struggle in the business stream trenches:

That's the question: How do we manage the relationship at the operational level? And the answer is: Not very well. There are a number of instances where it's a more antagonistic view of EDS that I don't feel comfortable with after working with them. A natural tendency for the blame culture that probably has been inherited from the old days, but has not improved with EDS. And variously, we are trying to address those—IR Account Manager.

The general account managers strive to identify and quickly resolve disputes in the business streams:

What we've actually got, we've got a relationship where there's interfaces taking place at what we call the operational interface—taking place between our business community and the EDS account managers. Every hour, every day—in theory. And any one of those can be taking a wrong turn. And we may not know about it until it goes sour for one reason or another. Then we'll get in and try and sort it out just in terms of some fair-minded approach. We try to get them away from the nuts and bolts and into more cooperative working arrangements—IR Account Manager.

Overall, though recognizing difficulties, IR management have been pleased with the way the relationship has evolved with EDS. Relationship improvement was facilitated by a combination of contractual changes, filling key account manager roles, mounting trust based on past successes, and EDS's involvement on the IR's strategic projects and committees:

> The relationship has developed substantially from the start. We've got a far more open relationship now. And close to the center of the partnership, I think we've got those relationships of the sort we want—IR Account Manager.

Maturing Years: Continued Adaptation   Both sides have continued to actively review and monitor the relationship in the maturing years:

> We periodically sit down and ask, 'where is this relationship taking us?' And 'is it actually achieving something to our mutual advantage?' We address the difficulties. And it may well be it's just the approach we've adopted previously that's given us the problem. It may well be that it's an aspect of our business that is giving us a problem. But it does enable us to continuously re-appraise what our objectives are. It's not just setting these things in concrete and saying we are going to trend them over 10 years—IR Customer Service Manager.

And even while the parties are still in the middle years of the contract, termination issues loom ahead. For example, the IR relies on EDS to make infrastructure investments on their behalf. EDS bears the investment costs, which are then recovered in service fees over time. As the contract matures, both sides must make sure that EDS has an opportunity to gain a return on investment:

> Unless we can some way manage a revenue stream for them beyond the contract, that's going to be increasingly difficult if we are asking them for investment. We are both jointly aware that that's a real difficulty for us. We've got to re-explore how we are going to cope with that. Otherwise we are going to stultify entirely as we get closer and closer to the end of the contract—IR Account Manager.

The Inland Revenue—Final Points

At the IR, an important driver of IT outsourcing was the desire for cost savings and the assumption that private sector suppliers could deliver IT more efficiently than public sector departments, even while making a profit. The 20% cost savings regularly touted at the beginning of the project would seem to have been partly offset by the unanticipated £20 million extra cost incurred within a year of project commencement. When the Self Assessment development project is then taken into account, it becomes clear that cost savings were, even by 1996, becoming a much lower priority, though the original *operational* cost savings of £220 million were still protected by contract. By 2000, it was clear that the anticipated economics of such a long-term deal were regularly being overtaken by massive changes in business requirement, technology, and IT labor markets. The challenges of contracting for and developing ways of managing through such changes are exhibited in the two cases in this chapter.

The IR case also illustrates the political and technical uncertainties that can plague public sector projects. The government-mandated introduction of the Self Assessment scheme by April 1997 represents merely a large-scale high profile example of the additional risks engendered when having to develop new systems during an outsourcing contract. In previous work we have pointed to examples of senior government ministers developing government policy without a real understanding of the IT implications, and of the difficulties involved in providing information systems support (Willcocks 1994). In the IR case this factor would seem to have a bearing both on the (Conservative) government's commitment to tight deadlines for the delivery of the Self Assessment scheme, but also to its predilection for privatizing IT services wholesale. In the case of the IR, it may well have been looking for a domino effect with the IR deal having managers and a supplier committed to making it a high profile success, thus leading the way for other government departments. And indeed, the predilection for large-scale outsourcing did not cease with the election of a new (Labour) government in 1997.

CONCLUSION

The South Australian Government, DuPont, British Aerospace, and Inland Revenue cases have a number of striking similarities (see Table 3.1).

- *In all four organizations, outsourcing decisions were sponsored and supported by senior executives or government officials in cooperation with IT management.* Mega-deals require the political clout and muscle of senior executives to conquer resistance, enforce standard approaches, and to negotiate favorable deals. As one VP of Operations at EDS noted, the deal at South Australia would have died 1000 deaths along the way without the full support of the Premier.
- *All four organizations expected cost savings.* Although many people argue that cost savings are no longer a major reason for outsourcing, clearly cost savings on baseline measures are sought. No organiza-

Table 3.1   *Comparison of mega-deals*

	South Australia Government	DuPont	British Aerospace	Inland Revenue
Decision sponsor: senior managers (or government officials) and IT managers	Yes	Yes	Yes	Yes
Impetus for the decision	Desire to build an IT industry in South Australia	Economic downturn led to core-competency focus strategy and reduction of overhead costs	Economic losses led to core-competency focus strategy and reduction of overhead costs	Forced market testing by UK government
Non-cost expectations	Economic development	Avoid renewal investment; move from fixed IT costs to variable IT costs	Sought 'value added' from supplier	Rapid development of new IT
Cost expectations	10%–15% cost savings	7% cost savings	10%–30% cost savings	20% cost savings
IT function prior to outsourcing	Highly decentralized; duplicate functions; poor service in many areas	Considerable rationalization, standardization, and consolidation reduced IT costs by 45% prior to outsourcing; IT skills shortage due to drastic cost cuts	Highly decentralized; highly skilled IT employees	Good record of performance, but difficulty renewing scarce IT skills
Length of decision process	1.5 years	1.2 years	1.5 years	2 years
Hired outside experts to help evaluate and negotiate contract?	Yes	Yes	Yes	Yes

	South Australia Government	DuPont	British Aerospace	Inland Revenue
Internal bid	None because internal IT department could not develop economy	None because IT already rationalized by internal IT department	Internal bid used to leverage customer's power during contract negotiations	None mentioned
Number of bids	2	4	3	4
IT employee union?	Yes, early union buy-in sought	No union	Initial union strike, later cooperation	Initial union strike, later cooperation
Contract price structure	Variable price based on volumes	Variable price based on volumes	Fixed price regardless of volumes	Variable price based on volumes
Price adjustment provisions	External benchmarking	External benchmarking	External benchmarking; open-book accounting with margin caps	External benchmarking; open-book accounting with margin caps
Contract service levels	Hundreds of service levels defined at agency level	Hundreds of service levels defined; master service-level agreement, but customized for each decentralized location	Hundreds of service levels defined; master service-level agreement, but customized for each decentralized location	Hundreds of service levels defined; master service-level agreement, but customized for each business stream
Need to simplify SLA during post contract management?	Yes	Yes	Yes	Yes
Contract distributed to users	Summary document only	Summary document only	Summary document only	Summary document only
Problem resolution process using 'red', 'yellow', and 'green' codes?	No	Yes	Yes	Yes
Customer/supplier responsibility matrix?	Yes	Yes	Not mentioned	Not mentioned

(Continued)

Table 3.1   *Continued*

	South Australia Government	DuPont	British Aerospace	Inland Revenue
Centralized contract management team?	Yes	Yes	Yes	Yes
Decentralized customer/supplier liaisons?	Yes	Yes	Yes	Yes
Contract interpretation disputes during transition?	Yes	Yes	Yes	Yes
Under-estimated pent-up user demand for IT?	Yes	Yes	Not mentioned	Yes
Contract realigned during middle years?	No (just starting middle years)	No (still in early years of contract)	Yes	Yes
Has composition of baseline volumes dramatically increased?	Yes	No (still in early years of contract)	Yes	Yes
Did customer underestimate number of employees needed to manage the relationship?	Yes	Yes	Yes	Not mentioned

tion was willing to outsource if it cost the same or more money. In particular, government market-testing in public sector organizations often mandates at least a 10% savings from outsourcing. However, as relationships progressed, original cost saving estimates became increasingly obsolete because the volume and composition of services radically changed. Instead of asking, 'Did we save money?' customers eventually ask, 'Are we getting a fair market price?' (In our two public sector cases, we note that South Australia and the IR must still maintain a burdensome and obsolete baseline model to demonstrate cost savings to taxpayers.)

- *In addition to cost savings, all four organizations sought other strategic objectives.* South Australia government wanted to build an IT industry base in Adelaide. DuPont wanted to avoid the cost of renewing IT assets and sought to refinance IT from a fixed expense to a variable expense. BAe sought 'value-added' from partnering with a supplier. And the IR sought rapid development of new IT and better IS career paths.

- *All four organizations took between one and two years to finalize their sourcing decisions.* Mega-deals cannot be evaluated and signed within a few months. The process from RFP, bid invitations, bid analysis, due diligence, and contract negotiations required between 14 months and two years for these case companies.

- *All four organizations attracted four or less external bids.* Given the size of these mega-deals, only a handful of suppliers are able to compete in this market. EDS, CSC, IBM, and AC were frequent bidders in the mega-deal market.

- *All four organizations defined hundreds of service-level agreements in the contract.* Detailed service agreements are necessary to create contractual service obligations. In prior studies, organizations that failed to detail SLAs regretted the decision, leading to accusations of declining service and even supplier incompetence. Ironically, all four organizations claim they cannot manage these many service levels in practice, and sought to identify a few key indicators of performance. However, no participant regretted the detailed SLAs—they are there if needed.

- *All four organizations only distributed summary documents of the contracts to employees.* Given that contracts can be 30 000 lines long and written in legal jargon, they are difficult to translate into daily work practices and expectations. All four organizations decided not to distribute the contract among employees. Instead, one of the first tasks of the centralized contract administrators was to create a summary document explaining the contractual obligations. The documents explain what services and service levels are provided for in the contract, as well as what additional volumes or services are not included, and thus subject to excess fees. But even these summary documents were open for interpretation and caused disputes among the user community.

- *All four organizations have a centralized contract management team to manage the supplier, as well as decentralized customer/supplier liaisons.* Centralized contract management teams monitor supplier performance, review invoices, manage supply and demand, mediate disputes, coordinate among multiple suppliers, manage finances, negotiate additions, explore new dimensions to the relationship, benchmark costs and performance, and develop IT strategies. Decentralized liaisons monitor local SLAs, help define user requirements, help explain cost/service trade-offs of IT options, work with users and suppliers through change management processes, and interface with the centralized contract management team.

- *All four organizations experienced contract disputes during the transition phase.* No matter how detailed the contract, the four organizations discovered that the contract is always open to interpretation. For example, the BAe contract specified that network enhancements are free, but expansions are extra. But the words *enhancement* and *expansion* were certainly open for interpretation. During the transition phase, customers and suppliers are each motivated to take a hard stand on contract interpretations because they set precedents that span 10 years and millions of dollars. In the end, the four organizations sought a fair or 'financially neutral' resolution to interpretations. Everyone was willing to win some and lose some, as long as the balance of power was equal between the customer and supplier overall.

- *All four organizations under-estimated the number and type of employees that should be retained to manage the relationship.* Participants claimed they should have kept more technical people internally. Technical people are needed to make technical decisions with the best interests of the customer in mind. In addition, technical people are needed to assess the quality and fairness of price of technical changes and additional bids beyond baseline. Other skills under-estimated include financial modelers, and generalists capable of hiring in and harnessing a specialist's expertise. The next chapter, in particular, addresses the core IT capabilities that must be insourced, regardless of the size of mega-deals.

Other common practices found among the cases include a color-coded problem resolution system (BAe, DuPont, IR), joint supplier/customer teams (DuPont, IR), and the refinement of a responsibility matrix (SA and DuPont). Although each organization participating in the research regards these practices as competitive secrets, practices are nearly identical across mega-contracts. We are witnessing an institutional isomorphic effect where outside experts, such as Technology Partners and Gartner Group (consultants on three of the four contracts), seed client organizations with similar standards and methods. In addition, three of the four organizations belong to the ITTUG group, which provides many opportunities for information exchange. In this way, organizational learning is transferred across organizations, and proven practices are more quickly disseminated.

NOTES

1. This seems to be a common issue across all of the mega contracts, but we also find it typical of any outsourcing arrangement of any size. Our survey (Appendix A) found noticeable gaps between expectations and what is actually delivered by suppliers. Four lessons emerging from that separate research are very pertinent on this point for suppliers: Help customers set realistic expectations; fully explain staffing policies to the customer; ensure the customer has a proper infrastructure to manage and coordinate the contract; develop relationship and customer management capability beyond customer service and account management.

2. The story is told in CSC's Howley Rockets to Success With BAe, *Computer Weekly*, November 25, 1993.

3. Harris, D. (1994). How BAe is Spending £1 Billion to Save Money. London, *The Times*, September 5, p. 21.

4. In fact this number never decreased markedly over the first seven years of the contract.

5. Quoted in Ex-BAe Staff to go as CSC Revamps Centres, *Computer Weekly*, October 13, 1994.

6. Collins, T. (1995). Services Giant Lands BAe with £30 Million Claim. *Computer Weekly*, cover story, July 20.

7. Cited on May 3, 1998, on http://www.open.gov.uk/inrev/introd.htm.

8. Cited on May 3, 1998, on http://www.open.gov.uk/inrev/introd.htm.

9. See Dyerson, R. and Roper, M. (1990). Building Competencies: The Computerisation of PAYE. Technology Project Paper No. 6. London Business School, London. See also Willcocks and Currie (1997) and Willcocks and Kern (1998). For a user perspective, see Smith, S. (1996). Taxed to the Limit. *Computer Weekly*, October 31, p. 48.

10. Halper, M., in *Computer World*, November 22, 1993, p. 12.

11. A discussion can be found on http://www.open.gov.uk/nao/9495245.htm.

12. See Shepherd, A. (1997). IT Outsourcing in A Changing World. Research and Discussion Paper. Templeton College, Oxford.

13. An account of user disaffection is provided in Collins, T. (1999). Chaos at UK Tax Offfices. *Computer Weekly*, October 28, pp. 1, 3.

4
Proven Practices in Evaluating and Negotiating IT Outsourcing Deals

Outsourcing contracts are agreed in concept, but delivered in detail, and that's why they can break down; the devil is in the detail—Account Manager, Major Supplier.

Basically we negotiated a tight contract, then put it to one side, which was the intention, so that we could run the thing as a partnership. But you've got to be protected—IT Manager, Entertainment Company.

This is also the honeymoon year. You interview me a year from now and I will probably feel different—CIO, US Bank.

INTRODUCTION

This chapter presents the proven practices for evaluating and negotiating deals extracted from in-depth case studies of over 116 sourcing decisions. This case study research represents a long-term investment in studying 76 organizations over an eight-year period (1992–2000). Such longitudinal research, involving continuous revisiting and tracking of the participant organizations, has been rarely carried out in the outsourcing field. However, it is the only real way of pinpointing practices and their outcomes, and finding out enough detail, including changes, in order to draw conclusions about causes, reasons, impacts, and connections between contexts, events, and factors.

We interviewed 271 business executives, chief information officers, outsourcing consultants, and supplier account managers in the United States, the United Kingdom, Europe, and Australia. Over 800 documents were gathered and reviewed, including annual reports, organizational charts, IT budgets, Request For Proposals, bid analysis documents, internal memos, press releases, and contracts.[1] A number of practices discovered in our parallel 1999–2000 survey research (summarized in Appendix A) are corroborated in this chapter. For example, the case study data found that selective sourcing was not only the most common practice, but the most successful practice. And like the survey data, the case study data stress the need for detailed, short-term contracts. But unlike survey data, the case study data allows us to examine the underlying causes for success and failure in detail.

The proven practices that we can identify from the case study experiences include:

Proven Practice 1: Selective outsourcing decisions and total insourcing decisions achieved success more often than total outsourcing decisions.

Proven Practice 2: Senior executives and IT managers who made decisions together achieved success more often than when either stakeholder group acted alone.

> **Worst Practice 2a:** Senior executives realized their sourcing expectations only 33% of the time when they alone sponsored outsourcing decisions.

> **Worst Practice 2b:** IT Managers realized their sourcing expectations only 56% of the time when they alone sponsored insourcing decisions.

> **Proven Practice 2c:** IT Managers realized their sourcing expectations 82% of the time when they alone sponsored selective outsourcing decisions.

Proven Practice 3: Organizations that invited both internal and external bids achieved success more often than organizations that merely compared a few external bids with current IT performance.

Proven Practice 4: Short-term contracts achieved success more often than long-term contracts.

Proven Practice 5: Detailed fee-for-service contracts achieved success more often than other types of contracts.

In addition to the five proven practices, one other finding provides insight into the sourcing experiences of our case companies:

Finding 6: Older contracts experienced *failure* more often than newer contracts.

Although contract date cannot be manipulated by organizations (unlike managerial practices), Finding 6 does provide additional insight. In particular, the lower success rates of older contracts indicates that customers may be learning to make better decisions and to negotiate more favorable deals.

RESEARCH METHOD

We give details here of the research method, not to bore the reader but to allow the reader to make his/her own judgment about the confidence to be had in the findings. Since the findings have considerable significance for IT outsourcing practice, it is important that such confidence is very soundly based.

In total, we interviewed 271 people about 116 sourcing decisions made in 76 organizations (Figure 4.1). We wanted to get as many perspectives on IT sourcing decisions as possible, and therefor sought interviews with multiple stakeholders in each organization. The 271 participants included 64 IT managers, 56 supplier managers, 52 chief

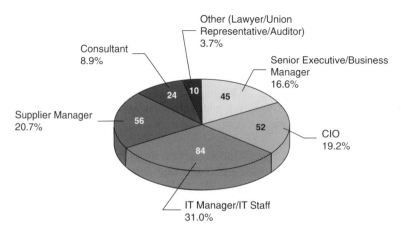

Figure 4.1   *Job titles of 271 people interviewed*

information officers (CIOs), 45 senior business executives, and 24 consultants and IT experts. All interviews were tape-recorded and transcribed in over 2000 pages.

We also sought experiences from a variety of industries in a number of countries (Table 4.1.) Indeed, we have representation from public and private sectors, service and manufacturing sectors, and consumer and industrial products from over five countries.

This large body of case data needed to be interpreted in a succinct and meaningful way to clearly flush out best practices. We investigated six factors that we considered potential differentiators of success and failure in our cases:[2]

1. *Decision scope*: total outsourcing versus total insourcing versus selective outsourcing.
2. *Decision sponsorship*: senior executive sponsorship versus IT manager sponsorship versus joint sponsorship.
3. *Evaluation process*: no formal bid process versus external bids only versus internal and external bids.
4. *Contract duration*: short-term contracts versus long-term contracts.
5. *Contract type*: standard versus detailed versus loose versus mixed fee-for-service contracts.
6. *Contract date*: recently signed contracts versus older contracts.

We also collected data on outcomes and levels of success and failure. In Table 4.2 we summarize the findings on these seven dimensions. See

Table 4.1 *Industries represented by 76 case studies*

Industry	US	UK	Europe	Australia	Total
Banks	3	3	1	0	7
Chemicals	3	1	1	0	5
Consumer products	1	4	0	0	5
Defense/aerospace	2	3	0	0	5
Financial services	0	4	0	1	5
Industrial products	2	3	1	0	6
Mines and minerals	2	1	0	0	3
Other	3	2	0	0	5
Petroleum	4	1	1 .	0	6
Public sector	4	5	0	1	10
Retail	2	6	1	0	9
Transportation	1	0	1	0	2
Utilities	0	6	2	0	8
Total	27	39	8	2	76

Table 4.2   *Summary of data categories*

Categories	Values and percentages	Empirical indicator
Decision Scope (n = 116 sourcing decisions)	(28%) Total outsourcing (16%) Total insourcing (56%) Selective outsourcing	Percentage of annual IT operating budget outsourced
Decision sponsorship (n = 116 sourcing decisions)	(25%) Senior executive only (26%) IT manager only (49%) Joint senior Executive/IT manager	Open-ended questions about the roles of stakeholders, including sponsor
Evaluation process (n = 116 sourcing decisions)	(19%) No formal bid process (10%) Compare vendor bids with newly-prepared internal bid (18%) Compare one to two vendor bids with current IT costs (53%) Compare three or more vendor bids with current IT costs	Open-ended questions about the evaluation process
Contract duration (n = 97 outsourcing contracts)	(36%) 0 to 3 Years (37%) Longer than three years but shorter than eight years (27%) Eight years or longer	Open-ended questions about the contract terms; copies of contracts were analyzed
Contract type (n = 97 outsourcing contracts)	(4%) Standard contracts (73%) Detailed contracts (7%) Loose contracts (12%) Mixed contracts (4%) Strategic alliances	Open-ended questions about the contract terms; copies of contracts were analyzed
Contract date (n = 97 outsourcing contracts)	(19%) Before 1991 (44%) 1991 to 1994 (37%) After 1995	Open-ended questions about the timing of the decision; contracts also specified date
Decision outcome: were expectations met? (n = 116 sourcing decisions)	(58%) **Yes**, most expectations met (22%) **No**, most expectations not met (9%) **Mixed** results: some major expectations met, other major expectations not met (11%) **Too Early to Tell/** unable to determine	Expected cost savings achieved, assessed through interviews and documentation

also the case histories in Appendix B at www.umsl.edu/~lacity/cases.htm for more detail.

Indicator of Success

We wanted to develop an indicator of success based on whether the outcome of IT sourcing decisions met expectations. We first assessed expectations, then assessed whether expectations have been met, then compared the two to determine the extent of success.

When asking participants to describe sourcing expectations, we also asked participants to provide evidence of their expectations, such as archived documents. For example, if a participant cited cost savings as an expectation, they provided evidence such as a press clipping after the contract was signed indicating expected savings during the life of the contract. Not surprisingly, participants cited a variety of expectations (anticipated and hoped-for outcomes) and reasons (justifications or explanations) for their sourcing decisions. We created four categories to capture 12 'expectations/reasons' cited by participants for sourcing: financial, business, focus strategy, and technical (see Table 4.3). The four most commonly cited expectations/reasons were IT cost reduction, better service, ability to focus IT staff on core IT activities, and financial restructuring of the IT cost structure.[3]

We also asked participants to what extent their expectations had been realized. Rather than solely base this on opinion, participants were asked to support their opinions with substantial evidence, including documents, budgets, press announcements, memos, reports, etc. We then created an indicator of success with four possible outcomes:

- **Yes**, participants achieved most of their expectations.
- **No**, participants did not achieve most of their expectations.
- **Mixed** results—participants achieved some major expectations but other major expectations were not achieved.
- **Too Early to Tell** whether expectations were achieved.

Three examples serve to illustrate how the success indicator was determined for sourcing decisions.

Example 1: A US commercial bank (BANK1) achieved its major expectation of 15% cost savings. In the late 1980s, BANK1 suffered meager earnings due to the recession which halted housing starts. The CEO sought corporation-wide cost reductions. The Senior Vice President of Operations asked the VP of IS to cut her $US25 million annual IT budget. She hired an outside consulting firm to assess IT costs.

Table 4.3   *Common participant expectations/reasons*

Category	Expectation/reason
Financial	*Cost reduction*: Many participants were seeking corporate-wide cost cuts, including IT costs, which were prompted by economic recession, increased industry competition, and other business factors.
	Improved cost control/structure: Many participants wanted to restructure IT budgets from fixed costs to 'pay-for-use' variable costs. Also, participants expected suppliers to improve control of IT costs through better chargeback mechanisms and stricter change control procedures.
	Reduce IT headcount: Downsizing trends in the 1990s prompted participants to seek leaner IT organizations with fewer full-time staff.
	Reduce capital cost/improve balance sheet: Total outsourcing deals were often motivated by the desire to sell large investments in IT assets to a supplier in exchange for buying back services. For example, the supplier paid (AERO1) nearly $US300 million for their IT assets.
Business	*Mergers and Acquisitions*: Many participants found that mergers and acquisitions were hindered by IT's inability to integrate systems. By outsourcing, participants expected that a supplier could help facilitate integration. For example, MINE acquired 13 companies in one year, which nearly crippled the IT department. Outsourcing helped to alleviate the problem by quickly bringing in extra supplier IT staff (for a price) to meet short-term increases in demand.
	New start-up business/privatization: In several case companies, senior management outsourced IT rather than invest in IT assets and resources. For example, CHEM1 was a start-up company. As a result of a leveraged buy-out, the new company was too debt-ridden to invest in IT so it totally outsourced for seven years. In UK government, privatization of the gas and water utilities prompted IT outsourcing to meet new market forces and challenges.
	Market test requirements. In the public sector, forced market-testing of government services prompted IT outsourcing evaluations, particularly in the UK and Australian public sector organizations studied.
Focus strategy	*Focus on core business competencies*: Participants (particularly senior executives) wanted to focus organizational resources on core competencies while outsourcing non-core competencies. IT was seen as a non-core competency suitable for outsourcing.
	Refocus IT onto Core IT activities. In a similar vein, some participants viewed IT as a portfolio of activities, some of which require

Category	Expectation/reason
	idiosyncratic skills best provided by internal IT staff, while non-core IT activities could be safely outsourced. In particular, mainframe processing was often outsourced so in-house staff could focus on the development of new client/server applications.
Technical	*Better Service*: Participants were seeking faster and better IT services. In some cases, participants found that a sourcing evaluation served to temper user expectations of what IT services can be provided at what cost.
	Access to technical expertise: Many participants claim that a global IT shortage of skills prompted their sourcing evaluations. Suppliers are perceived as providing superior training and mobilizing critical skills (such as supplier 'red teams') much better than internal IT functions.
	Access to new technologies: Other participants viewed outsourcing as a way to access new technologies, such as industry-specific software, technical software, or superior equipment.

The results of this study indicated that BANK1's small applications department was very cost competitive—they even sold systems to the US Treasury Department. However, the bulk of IT costs (over $US20 million) were spent on datacenter operations, which ran back-office systems. The datacenter was outdated and needed to be upgraded. The VP of IS notes, 'They basically said that you run a great shop if this was fifteen years ago.' Rather than incur investment costs, the VP of IS outsourced datacenter operations to a single supplier for 10 years at an estimated cost savings of 15%–18%. She hired a number of IT consultants and lawyers to negotiate a detailed contract. Within the first year of the contract, the supplier migrated BANK1's datacenter to one of their datacenters in Atlanta. When the VP of IS was first interviewed in 1991, expected cost savings have been achieved because the monthly bill was 15% less than previous costs. But she indicated, 'This is also the honeymoon year. You interview me a year from now and I will probably feel different.' In 1994, she conducted an outsourcing seminar at the University of Virginia. She documented how cost savings continued to be realized for datacenter operations (although subsequent outsourcing of applications was not successful).

Example 2: A US aerospace company (AERO1) had mixed results with IT outsourcing. In the early 1990s, AERO1 suffered huge financial losses due to cuts in the federal military defense budget. The company needed to downsize and lay off a significant number of people to survive. IT outsourcing became a very attractive possibility. A supplier offered to pay the company $US300 million for their immense investment in IT assets and to transition 1500 employees in return for a 10-year, $US3 billion contract. Four years after the deal was signed, it was evident that the results are mixed. First, the outsourcing contract was financially successful in providing much needed cash up-front and in helping to restructure the balance sheet. Second, the infrastructure (mainframes, networks, and telecommunications) part of the contract is running well. Third, other parts of the contract were not running well and subsequently cancelled in the first year. The customer claims that the supplier lacked the idiosyncratic business knowledge required to maintain highly strategic design and engineering systems. Fourth, the customer has discovered they gave monopoly power to the supplier. Although the contract says AERO1 can bid out new work, IT is often too integrated to bring in a second supplier. For example, when AERO1 used a second supplier for a hardware upgrade, they inadvertently negated the contract:

> Our contract says we can go elsewhere. When [the supplier] wanted to charge us $2500 to upgrade each of our HP workstations to 2 gigabyte harddrives, we went elsewhere and bought them for $1000. Now [the supplier] won't support our machines because we put somebody else's hardware in them—User, AERO1, year two into a 10-year contract.

The **Mixed** result assessment is based on an interview with the Director of Processes and Tools as well as three separate teams of AERO1 employees making presentations and papers on the outcome of the outsourcing deal as their MBA student projects.

Example 3: A US-based company in total outsourcing (DIVERSE1), a chemicals company (CHEM1), and a rubber and plastics manufacturer (RUBBER) did not achieve their sourcing expectations. The clearest indication of complete failure is threat of litigation and early termination of the contract. Although these three organizations have different reasons for failure, early termination is a strong indicator of failure. Their unique circumstances are covered in this chapter.

In our work we examined both 'sourcing expectations' and 'expectations achieved' for all 116 IT sourcing decisions. We used 'expectations achieved?' as our decision outcome indicator. Specifically, we categorized the 116 sourcing decisions as follows:

- In 67 decisions, **Yes**, participants achieved most of their expectations (58%).
- In 25 decisions, **No**, participants did not achieve most of their expectations (22%).
- In 10 decisions, participants experienced **Mixed** results; some expectations were achieved, other major expectations were not achieved (9%).
- In 14 decisions, it was **Too Early to Tell** whether expectations were achieved (11%). (We continue to track our case companies and will eventually determine outcomes for many of these decisions.)

In this chapter we dropped the 14 decisions that do not have outcomes from the analyses. Thus, findings are based on 102 decisions with discernible outcomes.

PROVEN PRACTICES FROM THE SOURCING EXPERIENCES

Proven Practice 1—Sourcing Strategy: Selective outsourcing decisions and total insourcing decisions had higher relative frequencies of success than total outsourcing decisions.

The cases represent a wide range of sourcing decisions. Some organizations almost exclusively used internal IT functions to provide IT services. At the opposite end of the spectrum, other organizations engaged in 10-year, multi-billion dollar contracts with external providers for most of their IT needs. Still others assumed a 'middle-of-the-road' approach by contracting for only select subsets of IT activities. We defined these three sourcing options as we did on our mail survey (in Appendix A):

- *Total outsourcing*: The decision to transfer the equivalent of more than 80% of the IT budget for IT assets, leases, staff, and management responsibility to an external IT provider.
- *Total insourcing*: The decision to retain the management and provision of more than 80% of the IT budget internally after evaluating the IT services market.[4]
- *Selective outsourcing*: The decision to source selected IT functions from external provider(s) while still providing between 20% and 80% of the IT budget internally. This strategy may include single or multiple suppliers. In practice, by 2000, a selective sourcer most typically outsourced between 20% and 30% of the IT budget.

With total outsourcing and total insourcing arrangements, over 80% of the IT budget is almost always provided by *one* supplier, either the internal staff or one external supplier. BP Exploration (PETRO1) and the UK Social Security Department (PSB9) were the only cases in which more than 80% of the IT budget was outsourced to multiple suppliers. However, sub-contracting was very prevalent amongst the other, ostensibly single-supplier, total outsourcing deals.

Using these definitions, we categorized the sourcing decisions with discernible cost outcomes as follows:

- 29 decisions resulted in total outsourcing (28%)
- 17 decisions resulted in total insourcing (17%)
- 56 decisions resulted in selective outsourcing (55%)

Selective Outsourcing

Selective outsourcing decisions were generally successful (77%) (see Table 4.4). With selective outsourcing, organizations could select the most capable and efficient source—a practice some participants referred to as 'best-of-breed' sourcing. The most commonly outsourced functions were mainframe datacenters, software development and support services, telecommunications/networks, and support of existing systems. (A similar pattern is observable in our survey findings—Appendix A.) In most cases, suppliers were judged to have an ability to deliver these IT products and services less expensively than internal IT managers. Sometimes, the ability to focus in-house resources to higher-value work also justified selective outsourcing.

Table 4.4   *Sourcing decision scope*

Sourcing decision	Yes, most expectations met	No, most expectations not met	Mixed results	Total
Total outsourcing	11 (38%)	10 (35%)	8 (27%)	29
Total insourcing	13 (76%)	4 (24%)	0 (0%)	17
Selective outsourcing	43 (77%)	11 (20%)	2 (4%)	56
Total number of decisions	67	25	10	102

(*n* = 102 sourcing decisions with discernible outcomes)

Total Outsourcing

In general, total outsourcing decisions achieved their expectations less frequently than selective outsourcing decisions or total insourcing decisions. With total outsourcing, only 11 of 19 companies achieved expectations (Table 4.4). BANK1 was already introduced as a total outsourcing success. Likewise British Aerospace and the UK Inland Revenue (Chapter 3). The success of BP Exploration is explored in Chapter 6. UK British Coal (COAL) was also successful. This was a short-term contract to assist in the IT aspects of privatization of the business. Another example of a total outsourcing success is Philips Electronic's (ELECTRIC1) arrangement. ELECTRIC1 spun off their IT department to a wholly owned subsidiary. Because the new company's only source of revenue at the time of our interviews was from ELECTRIC1, they were highly motivated to meet ELECTRIC1's cost expectations. A third example of a total outsourcing success was the South Australian Government's economic development package with EDS (PSB5). The supplier (EDS) has exceeded yearly targets for delivering $US200 million in economic development during the nine-year contract. Note, however, that other aspects of the deal were less successful (see Chapter 2 for the full case study of South Australia government).

About 27% of total outsourcing decisions led to mixed results in which some major expectations were achieved, while other major expectations were not achieved. AERO1 was already introduced as a total outsourcing decision which had mixed results. The financial restructuring expectations were met, but service and costs in other areas are problematic.

In 10 of the 29 total outsourcing cases (35%) with discernible outcomes, however, expectations were not realized. Participants encountered one or more of the following problems:

- excess fees for services beyond the contract or excess fees for services participants assumed were in the contract;
- 'hidden costs' such as software license transfer fees;
- fixed prices that exceeded market prices two to three years into the contract;
- inability to adapt the contract to even minor changes in business or technology without triggering additional costs;
- lack of innovation from the supplier;
- deteriorating service in the face of patchy supplier staffing of the contract

We will show that such problems are endemic to senior executive sponsorship and to long-term, fee-for-service contracts.

Total Insourcing

Exclusive sourcing by an internal IT department was generally success-ful (76%, see Table 4.4). We found, however, that such success stems from a potential threat of outsourcing. Only through the threat of competition did internal IT managers have the power to overcome organizational resistance to change, to implement the cost reduction tactics used by suppliers, and to temper realistic service-level expecta-tions against available resources. Once empowered through the threat of competition, internal IT managers often had cost advantages over suppliers (such as no marketing expense, no need to generate a profit). In addition, they often had service advantages, such as idiosyncratic knowledge of business applications.

De facto insourcing, however, without the potential outsourcing threat, rarely led to success. In four of our total insourcing cases, internal IT 'monopolies' promoted complacency and erected organizational obstacles against continuous improvement. IT managers who exploited total outsourcing failures and adamantly refused to deal with outsour-cing suppliers were often blamed when their own IT departments failed to demonstrate value for money. For example, the VP of IS at a waste management company (DIVERSE2), tried to deflect his CEO's interest in outsourcing by producing a white paper highlighting outsourcing fail-ures. The CEO eventually dismissed the white paper and signed—six months after our interview—an outsourcing contract for all applications development and support.

Proven Practice 2—Decision Sponsor: Joint senior executive/IT manager decisions or IT managers acting alone had higher rela-tive frequencies of success than senior executives acting alone.

We were interested to know which sponsors—senior executives, IT managers, or users—made the most successful sourcing decisions. We defined decision sponsor as the person who initiated or championed the sourcing decision and who made or authorized the final decision. Using this definition, we asked participants to identify the decision sponsor (which may have been the interviewee), the sponsor's job title, their reporting level in the organization, and the extent of the sponsor's participation in the decision process.

If the sponsor's reporting level was above the IT department, the sponsor was categorized as a 'Senior Executive'. Job titles in this group included CEO, CFO, Controller, and Treasurer. If the sponsor was from the IT department—including the head of the IT depart-ment—we categorized the sponsor as an 'IT Manager'. Job titles in this group included CIO, VP of Information Systems, and Manager of Information Systems. (In no cases were users identified as a sponsor.)

If participants identified multiple sponsors, we categorized them on the basis of their job titles and reporting levels. For example, at TRANS, the CEO and CFO jointly sponsored the decision; thus we categorized the decision as 'Senior Executive Sponsorship'. If a senior executive and an IT manager jointly sponsored the decision, we categorized this as 'Joint Senior Executive/IT Sponsorship'. For example, at ELECTRIC1, the IS Director and the Marketing Manager jointly sponsored the decision.

Using these definitions, we categorized the 102 sourcing decisions with discernible outcomes as follows:

- 28 decisions were sponsored by senior executives (27%)
- 28 decisions were sponsored by IT managers (27%)
- 46 decisions were jointly sponsored by senior executives and IT managers (45%)

In our study, sourcing decisions made jointly with both senior executive and IT input had the highest success rate (76%) (see Table 4.5). It appears that successful sourcing decisions require a mix of political power and technical skills. Political power helped to enforce the larger business perspective—such as the need for organization-wide cost cuts—as well as the 'muscle' to implement such business initiatives. Technical expertise on IT services, service levels, measures of performance, rates of technical obsolescence, rates of service growth, price/performance improvements, and a host of other technical topics were needed to develop Requests For Proposals, evaluate supplier bids, and negotiate and manage sound contracts. In some cases, this mix of

Table 4.5 *Decision sponsor for sourcing decisions*

Decision sponsor	Yes, most expectations met	No, most expectations not met	Mixed results	Total
Senior Executive	12 (43%)	10 (36%)	6 (21%)	28
IT Manager	20 (71%)	6 (22%)	2 (7%)	28
Joint Executive/IT	35 (76%)	9 (20%)	2 (4%)	46
Total number of decisions	67	25	10	102

($n = 102$ sourcing decisions with discernible outcomes)

political power and technical knowledge was encompassed in one stakeholder group, as evidenced by 12 successful decisions sponsored solely by senior executives and 20 successful decisions sponsored solely by senior IT managers.

The UK British Broadcasting Association (PSB4) provides an example of joint sponsorship. In 1988, senior executives of this broadcasting organization were approached by a major supplier. The supplier offered a 40% reduction in IT costs, additional disaster recovery, lower in-house management involvement, career opportunities for transferred staff, and redirected capital from ownership of IT assets to core business activities. Working together, a senior executive (a program manager) and in-house IT managers produced a detailed, less promising analysis of the supplier's assumptions. The supplier's estimated £11 million saving over five years was based on unrealistic assumptions of no growth in workload or change in requirements. It was unclear where staff cost savings of 33% could be made. The supplier's legitimate cost reduction idea proposed savings by consolidating five mainframe datacenters to two. The joint business/IT decision was to implement cost savings in-house, partly through datacenter consolidation and refinancing hardware leases:

> We decided we could do just as well internally as they would. In fact, do better. At that point, we still had a growing mainframe workload ... we were operating a significantly large number of mainframes, so nearly all the ways that the vendor could reduce costs were open to us. They had an edge on us in staffing costs, but of course we were not charging a management fee, which they would. So the decision was to stay in-house—Production Manager, PSB4.

This joint senior executive/IT manager decision exploited the supplier bid to prompt in-house-led improvements. Three years later, the same sponsors made a financially successful decision to selectively outsource the datacenters when technical and business conditions changed.

The value of joint sponsorship is most apparent when outsourcing and insourcing decisions are analyzed separately:

Worst Practice 2a: Senior executives realized their sourcing expectations only 33% of the time when they alone sponsored outsourcing decisions.

When senior executives sponsored decisions that led to outsourcing, a low percentage of decisions were successful (refer to 'Senior Executive' row in Table 4.6).

Senior executives often focused on the short-term financial aspects of outsourcing, primarily because their companies were in poor financial straits, and they saw outsourcing as a way to refinance the company. As

Table 4.6 *Decision sponsor for outsourcing decisions*

Decision sponsor	Yes, most expectations met	No, most expectations not met	Mixed results	Total
Senior Executive	8 (33%)	10 (42%)	6 (25%)	24
IT Manager	15 (78%)	2 (11%)	2 (11%)	19
Joint Executive/IT	31 (74%)	9 (21%)	2 (5%)	42
Total number of decisions	54	21	10	85

($n = 85$ outsourcing decisions with discernible outcomes)

Strassmann noted in 1995, 'Strategy isn't driving outsourcing. Statistics show the real reason companies outsource is simple: They're in financial trouble'.[5] Suppliers offered senior executives attractive financial proposals by transforming IT capital budgets to fixed-fee operating budgets, paying cash for IT assets (worth $US500 million we noted in the case of AERO1), purchasing company shares, and/or postponing payments until the later part of the contract. From a net present value perspective, senior executives viewed outsourcing as a sound decision. Such evaluations were based on false assumptions, including the belief that IT requirements would remain stable over a long-term relationship—or if they changed, that the supplier would willingly adapt under the spirit and trust of a 'strategic partnership'. While these 'CEO-handshake' deals may have saved companies money in the short term, the relationship deteriorated in several cases as the consequences of a poorly negotiated deal became evident.

> What generally happened is senior managers way up here at the 40 000 foot level cut the deal. The people who have to implement it are down here. They are really faced with a different set of problems—Supplier Account Manager, Prior VP of Computer Utility, DIVERSE1.

Worst Practice 2b: IT Managers realized their expectations only 56% of the time when they alone sponsored insourcing decisions.

Granted, IT managers fared better at making insourcing decisions than senior executives fared at making outsourcing decisions. But in four cases, IT managers did not appear to conduct an 'objective' evaluation but rather used the guise of an outsourcing evaluation to prevent senior management from conducting the evaluation themselves (refer to 'IT Manager' row in Table 4.7). In three of the four IT manager-sponsored

Table 4.7   *Decision sponsor for insourcing decisions*

Decision sponsor	Yes, most expectations met	No, most expectations not met	Mixed results	Total
Senior Executive	4 (100%)	0 (0%)	0 (0%)	4
IT Manager	5 (56%)	4 (44%)	0 (0%)	9
Joint Executive/IT	4 (100%)	0 (0%)	0 (0%)	4
Total number of decisions	13	4	0	17

($n = 17$ insourcing decisions with discernible outcomes)

insourcing decisions which did not result in any improvements, IT managers initiated outsourcing evaluations after learning that a supplier was wooing their senior management.

By initiating their own evaluation, IT managers may have hoped that the best defence was a good offense. Their evaluations were either cursory, such as simply calling a few suppliers on the telephone, or else the evaluation was sabotaged through suspicious numbers:

> It really came down to an exercise. We did not try to make outsourcing work. What we were really trying to do was to come up with the justification for why we shouldn't outsource. That's what it boiled down to—Manager of Technical Support, US Petroleum Refining Company (PETRO4).

In the four IT manager-sponsored insourcing decisions that were not successful, senior management either did not believe in the IT manager's outsourcing evaluation and subsequently outsourced (two diversified services firms in the United States (DIVERSE1, DIVERSE2); a UK food manufacturer (FOOD2)) or fired the IT manager (US chemicals manufacturer (CHEM2)).

> I honestly attempted to be as objective as possible, but I admit that even when I presented to [the vice president and controller]—I probably would not ever be perceived as completely unbiased and non-prejudiced—Manager of Data Processing, CHEM2.

Proven Practice 2c: IT managers realized their sourcing expectations 78% of the time when they alone sponsored outsourcing decisions.

We do note, however, that IT managers do make sounder outsourcing decisions. Fifteen of the 19 outsourcing decisions sponsored solely by IT managers were successful (see Table 4.6). And, more noteworthy, 14 of the 15 successes were selective sourcing decisions. IT managers have considerable knowledge about their current IT costs and services and therefore have the technical knowledge (and healthy skepticism) to make good selective outsourcing decisions. Because the scope of selective sourcing decisions is smaller than total outsourcing decisions, IT managers appear to have enough political clout to make successful decisions without the help of senior management.

Proven Practice 3—Decision Process: Organizations that invited both internal and external bids had a higher relative frequency of success than organizations that merely compared a few external bids to current IT performance.

We wanted to know: Which evaluation process was most successful in terms of achieving cost savings and expectations? During the interviews, participants were asked to describe the sourcing evaluation process in detail. After analyzing the transcripts, we defined four general evaluation processes:

- *No formal bid process*: The organization made the sourcing decision without creating a Request For Proposal or inviting external bids.
- *Compare one or two supplier bids with current IT costs*: The organization made the sourcing decision by creating a Request For Proposal and inviting external bids from service providers. One or two supplier bids were compared with current IT performance.
- *Compare three or more supplier bids with current IT costs*: The organization made the sourcing decision by creating a Request For Proposal and inviting external bids from service providers. Three or more supplier bids were compared with current IT performance.
- *Compare supplier bids with newly prepared internal bids*: The organization made the sourcing decision by creating a Request For Proposal and inviting external bids from service providers as well as a bid from the internal IT department.

Using these definitions, we categorized the evaluation processes for the 102 sourcing decisions with discernible outcomes as follows:

- 20 decisions were made based on no formal bid process (20%)
- 19 decisions were made by comparing one or two supplier bids with current IT costs (19%)
- 51 decisions were made by comparing three or four supplier bids with current IT costs (50%)

- 12 decisions were made by comparing external supplier bids with newly submitted internal bids (11%)

The decision process that most often led to realized expectations was the one that allowed internal IT departments to submit a competitive bid along with external suppliers (83% successful) (see Table 4.8). We believe that this was because formal external supplier bids were often based on efficient managerial practices that could be replicated by internal IT managers. The question was: If IT managers could reduce costs, why didn't they?

In some cases, IT managers could not implement cost reduction tactics because the internal politics of user departments often resisted tactics such as consolidating datacenters, standardizing software packages, and implementing full-cost chargeback schemes. For example, users in two divisions at FOOD1—a US-based food manufacturer—did not want to consolidate their datacenters into the corporate datacenter:

> In 1986, [the two divisions] didn't want to come to corporate IS in the first place. They didn't want to close their datacenters, a control thing, 'my car is faster than your car' thing—Datacenter Director, FOOD1.

Senior executives at FOOD1 felt that IT costs had become too expensive and decided to outsource its large corporate datacenter. The Datacenter Director lobbied to submit an internal bid. Once granted permission, he prepared an internal bid that beat an external bid on cost. Within three years, the internal IT department cut costs by 45% by consolidating and standardizing.

Table 4.8 *Evaluation process*

Decision process	Yes, most expectations met	No, most expectations not met	Mixed results	Total
No formal bid process	11 (55%)	9 (45%)	0 (0%)	20
Compare vendor bid(s) with internal bid	10 (83%)	1 (8.5%)	1 (8.5%)	12
Compare one or two vendor bids with current IT performance	8 (42%)	6 (32%)	5 (26%)	19
Compare three or more vendor bids with current IT performance	38 (75%)	9 (17%)	4 (8%)	51
Total number of decisions	67	25	10	102

($n = 102$ sourcing decisions with discernible outcomes)

In other cases, IT managers were not motivated to improve costs, particularly if the legacy of insourcing had created an environment of complacency. For example, the unionized IT employees at a US telecommunications major (TCOM) had maintained inefficient work practices to protect their jobs. It was not until the union was threatened with losing the job site through outsourcing that union representatives acquiesced and improved efficiency. One of the union representatives expressed the following view: 'When you are in the frying pan, you get creative.'

In all our cases, however, the IT managers had to convince management to allow an internal bid submission. The following quote provides an example of IT management's initiative in establishing an internal bid:

> The IS management said that there is no reason we should be excluded from the party. You cannot assume, it's not fair to say that we'll just do what we've been doing. We ought to have some freedom to make decisions that the outsourcers are making—Corporate Manager of Technology, US Petrol Company (PETRO3).

In some cases, senior management granted a request for an internal bid more as a 'morale-preserver' than as a serious contender against external bidders. Once given free rein to compete based on cost efficiency, internal IT managers often surprised senior management by submitting the low cost bid. Furthermore, in eight of the nine cases involving internal bids, IT managers subsequently achieved expected cost savings. The threat of outsourcing in the future may have been a driving force behind implementing the internal bid proposals:

> The repercussions of this exercise are that I suspect we will go through this exercise in another year or two—if we find out that we can do it cheaper outside, we have to seriously consider that option—Assistant Treasurer, US Petrol Refiner (PETRO4).

Proven Practice 4—Contract Duration: Short-term contracts had a higher relative frequency of success than mid-term or long-term contracts.

We were interested in the contract duration to determine whether short-term or long-term contracts were more successful. We classified contract duration into three categories: '1 to 3 years', '4 to 7 years', and '8 or more years'. We selected '1 to 3 years' as the first cut-off point because many participants expressed that they could not define their IT requirements past a three-year time horizon. We selected seven years as our second cut-off point because most participants described seven or more years as 'long-term'.

Using these contract duration categories, the 85 outsourcing decisions with discernible cost outcomes are classified as follows:

- 32 outsourcing decisions were sealed with 1- to 3-year contracts (38%)
- 32 outsourcing decisions were sealed with 4- to 7-year contracts (38%)
- 21 outsourcing decisions were sealed with contracts 8 years or longer (24%)

Among these 85 outsourcing cases, short-term contracts realized expectations more frequently than long-term contracts (88% successful) (see Table 4.9). Short-term contracts involved less uncertainty, motivated supplier performance, allowed participants to recover from mistakes quicker, and helped to ensure that participants were getting a fair market price.

One reason for the success of short-term contracts is that participants only outsourced for the duration in which requirements were stable, thus participants could adequately analyze the cost implications of their decisions. Pilkington plc (GLASS), for example, initially only signed a two-year contract for their datacenter and systems development:

> Here we are dealing with a terrific amount of change within the business and within the head office. We didn't know what it was going to look like in the end . . . so a long contract would have been quite inappropriate here. There is too much change involved—Manager of IS, GLASS.

Second, some participants noted that short-term contracts motivated supplier performance because suppliers realized customers could opt to

Table 4.9 *Contract duration*

Decision process	Yes, most expectations met	No, most expectations not met	Mixed results	Total
0 to 3 year contracts	28 (87.5%)	4 (12.5%)	0 (0%)	32
4 to 7 year contracts	19 (59%)	10 (32%)	3 (9%)	32
8 to 25 year contracts	8 (38%)	6 (29%)	7 (33%)	21
Total number of decisions	55	20	10	85

($n = 85$ outsourcing decisions with discernible outcomes)

switch suppliers when the contract expired. As the IS director of the Civil Aviation Authority (AVIATION) commented, 'It's no surprise to me that the closer we get towards contract renewal, it's amazing what service we can get'.

Third, in some cases short-term contracts allowed companies to recover faster from mistakes. A retail and distribution company (RETAIL3) provides an example of this. In 1990, the IT director of RETAIL3 outsourced corporate telecommunications as a discrete commodity service to achieve an estimated 25% savings in a three-year contract. However, the contract was not detailed enough:

> The supplier largely wrote it and we signed it ... many of the contractual statements were ambiguous in the way they had been written—Contract Manager, RETAIL3.

Contract disputes were driven by poorly defined service levels. The contract resulted in cost savings that were achieved primarily through deteriorating service levels. RETAIL3 motivated an improvement in supplier service only after assigning additional workload to another supplier. When the first contract expired, RETAIL3 selected another supplier and detailed a much better contract, resulting in higher cost savings and higher service levels.

Finally, short-term contracts ensured that the participant's fixed prices were not out of step with market prices. While a supplier's bid to discount current IT costs by 20% may have sounded appealing in year one, by year three contract prices were often above market prices. For example, a US metals manufacturer (METAL) agreed to pay $US100 per processed form in 1990, but by 1993 the supplier was charging $US50 per processed form to other customers. Because of METAL's fixed-price contract, they had been unable to achieve the lower rate. Another related problem with most fixed-fee contracts was that the customers in our study were required to pay for a minimum volume (50%–100% of baseline volumes), even if their volumes significantly declined during the contract. For example, the US waste disposal firm DIVERSE1 signed a 10-year total outsourcing contract in the late 1980s. At that time, the majority of the company's systems were running on mainframe technology. With the advent of client/server technology, the company wanted to migrate to the smaller platform. They found that their outsourcing contract obligated them to pay a fixed fee for the mainframe, regardless of the reduction of use. In the end, business unit managers were forced to use discretionary funds to build client/server systems, while still meeting their contractual obligations for the increasingly obsolescent mainframe.

Proven Practice 5—Contract Type: Detailed fee-for-service contracts had a higher relative frequency of success than other types of contracting models.

Many different types of contracts are used to govern IT outsourcing relationships. In general, IT outsourcing contracts can be categorized as follows:

1. *Fee-for-service contract*: A customer pays a fee to a supplier in exchange for the management and delivery of specified IT products or services. Among the 85 outsourcing decisions with discernible outcomes we studied, 81 are fee-for-service contracts. We further categorized fee-for-service contracts using the following definitions:

- *Standard contracts*: the customer signed the supplier's standard, off-the-shelf contract.
- *Detailed contracts*: the contract included special contractual clauses for service scope, service levels, measures of performance, and penalties for non-performance.
- *Loose contracts*: the contract did not provide comprehensive performance measures or contingencies but specified that the suppliers perform 'whatever the customer was doing in the baseline year' for the next five to ten years at 10%–30% less than the customer's baseline budget.
- *Mixed contracts*: for the first few years of the contract, requirements were fully specified, connoting a 'detailed' contract; however, participants could not define technology and business requirements in the long run, and subsequent requirements were only loosely defined, connoting a 'loose' contract.

2. *Strategic alliance/partnership*: Collaborative inter-organizational relationships involving significant resources of two or more organizations to create, add to, or maximize their joint value. In the contract, the partners agree to furnish a part of the capital and labor for a business enterprise, and each shares in profits and losses. Among our cases, only four outsourcing relationships are strategic alliances—a European electronics firm (ELECTRIC1), the South Australian government's deal (PSB5), a European retailer (RETAIL9), and an Australian finance and property services company (FINANCE1.) (These cases are discussed in the Managerial Implications section below.)

3. *Buy-in contract*: A customer buys in supplier resources to supplement in-house capabilities, but the supplier resources are managed by in-house business and IT management. Because the customer retains responsibility for the delivery of IT services, we have labeled this option

'insourcing'. (This contract type is also discussed in the Managerial Implications section below).

Focusing the analysis on the 85 contracts with discernible outcomes, the contracts are categorized as follows:

- 4 standard fee-for-service contracts (5%)
- 60 detailed fee-for-service contracts (70%)
- 7 loose fee-for-service contracts (8%)
- 11 mixed fee-for-service contracts (12%)
- 4 strategic alliances (5%)

Among them, detailed, fee-for-service contracts achieved expectations with greater relative frequency (75%) than other types of contracts (see Table 4.10). These organizations understood their own IT functions very well, and could therefore define their precise requirements in a contract. They also spent significant time negotiating the details of contracts (up to 18 months in some cases), often with the help of outside experts. For example, the Financial Manager at a US commercial bank (BANK1) spent three months negotiating the datacenter contract, assisted by the VP of IS, internal attorneys, and two hired experts:

> And that's when [the VP of IS] and I and the attorneys sat down everyday for three solid months of drafting up the agreement, negotiating the terms, conditions, and services—Financial Manager, BANK1.

Table 4.10   *Contract types*

Contract type	Yes, most expectations met	No, most expectations not met	Mixed results	Total
Detailed	45 (75%)	9 (15%)	6 (10%)	60
Loose	0 (0%)	7 (100%)	0 (0%)	7
Mixed	6 (55%)	1 (9%)	4 (36%)	11
Strategic alliance	2 (67%)	1 (33%)	0 (0%)	3
Standard	2 (50%)	2 (50%)	0 (0%)	4
Total number of decisions	55	20	10	85

($n = 85$ outsourcing decisions with discernible outcomes)

In contrast to the success of the detailed contract, all seven of the loose contracts were disasters in terms of costs and services. Two of these companies, CHEM1 and RUBBER, actually terminated their outsourcing contracts early and rebuilt their internal IT departments. One of these companies, DIVERSE1, threatened to sue the supplier. Senior executives in these companies had signed flimsy contracts under the rhetoric of a 'strategic alliance'. However, the essential elements of a strategic alliance were absent from these deals. There were no shared risks, no shared rewards, and no synergies from complementary competencies. Instead, these loose contracts created conflicting goals. Specifically, the customers were motivated to demand as many IT services as possible for the fixed-fee price by arguing 'you are our partners'. Supplier account managers countered that their fixed-fee price only included services outlined in the contract. The additional services triggered supplier costs which were passed to the customer in terms of excess fees. Because the customers failed to fully specify baseline services in the contract, the customers were charged excess fees for items they assumed were included in the fixed price.

Six of the 11 'mixed' contracts with discernible outcomes achieved expectations. The contracts contained either shared risks and rewards or significant performance incentives. We have already noted that ELECTRIC's mixed contract involved a spin-off of the IT department to a wholly owned subsidiary in 1991. Because the newly formed company's only source of revenue was from ELECTRIC, it was highly motivated to satisfy ELECTRIC's needs. Since this subsidiary has become successful at attracting external customers besides ELECTRIC, the relationship has evolved into more of a strategic alliance.)

Pilkington plc (GLASS) initially signed only a two-year contract with the supplier for datacenter operations and systems development, provides another example of a successful mixed contract. The promise of contract renewal and additional work in GLASS's multinational divisions motivated supplier performance. In addition, the relationship dimension was strong because the in-house IT manager became the supplier account manager. The initial contract was so successful that it was renewed for three years, and again subsequently.

In contrast, other mixed contracts were less successful. Expectations were not met for a variety of reasons. In European oil major PETRO1, for example, cost inefficiencies were driven out prior to signing three total outsourcing agreements. Although there were additional expected savings of 15%–25% for PETRO1's seven divisions, PETRO1 participants experienced problems trying to coordinate additional savings among the three suppliers. On cost, the overall effect was cost containment rather than cost reduction. At Whitbread (BREWER), the company outsourced primarily to provide jobs to IT employees rather than make them redundant. Although the goal of the contract was to break-even on costs, poor pricing of future work triggered higher than expected costs. A UK food manufacturer (FOOD3) signed a mixed contract for factory software development. Because business requirements were loosely defined, FOOD3 paid twice the original contract price due to excess fees triggered by undocumented requirements. In hindsight, participants believe the wrong activity was outsourced. They perhaps should have bought in supplier expertise to work on an in-house project development team, rather than contract management and delivery of the system to a third party.

In addition to the five best practices, we also studied contract date. Although this 'variable' cannot be manipulated by an organization as in the case with managerial practices, it does shed significant light on the sourcing experiences.

Finding 6—Year of Decision: The oldest contracts had the highest relative frequency of failure compared to newer contracts.

The contract date was analyzed to determine whether customers were getting better at negotiating contracts. We classified decisions into three categories: '1984–1990', '1991–1994', and '1995–1998'. We chose 1990 as the first cut-off point because this was the year after Kodak's outsourcing decision may have triggered a bandwagon effect throughout *Fortune* 500 companies.[6] We selected 1994 as the second cut-off point because it represents the midpoint between 1991 and 1998— 1998 was the contract date we studied. Using these categories, we classified the 85 outsourcing contracts with discernible outcomes as follows:

- 18 contracts were signed prior to 1991 (21%)
- 42 contracts were signed between 1991 and 1994 (49%)
- 25 contracts were signed after 1994 (28%)

It is evident that older contracts had the highest failure rate (56% failures) (see Table 4.11). We offer two explanations. First, customers had little experience with IT outsourcing in the 1980s. Second, the outsourcing market was not mature—there were fewer suppliers than today, and services were less differentiated. Certainly the results of our 1999–2000 survey indicate a much wider spread of maturity amongst both suppliers and customers than was the case a decade before.

In contrast, deals made between 1991 and 1994 had the highest success rate of 79%. By this time, customers were getting better at negotiating deals. In fact, some of our participants adopted incremental outsourcing

Table 4.11   *Contract date*

Year decision was made	Yes, most expectations met	No, most expectations not met	Mixed results	Total
1984–1990	7 (39%)	10 (56%)	1 (5%)	18
1991–1994	33 (79%)	3 (7%)	6 (14%)	42
1995–1998	15 (60%)	7 (28%)	3 (12%)	25
Total number of decisions	55	20	10	85

($n = 85$ outsourcing decisions with discernible outcomes)

precisely to develop an in-house knowledge base learnt from the initial outsourcing experience. With incremental outsourcing, organizations outsourced a small and discrete part of its IT activities, such as third-party maintenance or shared processing services. The experience gained from this first incremental approach was then fed back into further outsourcing. In two cases, PETRO1 and ELECTRIC (see above), organizations found themselves ultimately engaging in total outsourcing.

Also by the early 1990s, the outsourcing market had been changing in the customer's favor. Once dominated by a few big players, the IT outsourcing market had fragmented into many niche services. As competition in the outsourcing market increases, companies have more power to bargain for shorter contracts, more select services, and better financial packages. For example, in the 1980s, CHEM1 and RUBBER received only one supplier bid. In 1992, a UK county council (PSB3) received many responses, 'We put an advert in the press looking for interested parties, and had about 22 responses'—Manager of IS, PSB3. In 1993, PETRO1 reviewed a list of 115 potential suppliers. By 2000 we were noting in our advisory work many more players and ways organizations were contemplating using them—as we predicted in our 1995 *Harvard Business Review* article (Lacity, Willcocks and Feeny 1995). However, suppliers capable of delivering a consistent service globally on even a specific aspect of IT were, even in 2000, still few and far between.

We do note a dip in the success rate (from 79% in the early 1990s to 60% in the late 1990s) of the most recently signed contracts. We attribute these results to two phenomena. First, experimentation with new kinds of deals described in Chapter 2 may require a few years of trial-and-error before the newer models are successfully tweaked. For example, one Australian finance and property services company (FINANCE1) experimented with an equity stakeholder model that failed to align customer and supplier goals as they had hoped. They subsequently negotiated a more detailed fee-for-service contract, and during 1999 also brought back in-house elements of the IT service. A Swiss bank's equity share deal, signed in 1995 for 25 years and $US6 billion plus, was negotiated down to a 10-year deal and $US2.4 billion by 1997, and terminated in 2000 (BANK4).

Second, organizations that have never outsourced before may make mistakes. For example, one insurance multinational (INSURE3) signed a standard off-the-shelf supplier contract in 1996, despite the common wisdom against this practice at the time. Subsequently the contract was radically restructured, with much more detail and cost savings resulting (Appendix B case 66). Perhaps best practices are not as transferable as they should be or we like to think, and each organization may have to learn from their own experiences.

MANAGERIAL IMPLICATIONS: FEE-FOR-SERVICE CONTRACTS OR STRATEGIC ALLIANCES?

IT outsourcing has been a widely publicized and much debated practice. In particular, practitioners and academics have argued about the validity of long-term, total outsourcing. We believe that the debate is clarified by distinguishing among three types of IT outsourcing contracts: fee-for-service contracts, strategic alliances/partnerships, and buy-in contracts. By highlighting the critical elements of various contracting models, we hope to reconcile some of the apparent discrepancies in past findings about best ways to outsource IT.

Fee-for-Service Contracts

The vast majority—81 of our 85 outsourcing relationships—were governed by fee-for-service contracts. We found that fee-for-service relationships require *detailed contracts* that fully specify requirements, service levels, performance metrics, penalties for non-performance, and price; and *short-term contracts* that last only for the duration for which requirements are known. We have found from the mid-1990s that these contracts have, wisely, increasingly taken on more flexible characteristics (see Chapter 1, Practice 8), for example regular reviews of price/performance and quality against the market or other customers of the supplier.

In our research, we found that a fee-for-service contract was best suited to IT activities where companies could clearly define their needs in an air-tight contract. For example, where the technology was mature and stable (particularly mainframe operations), case participants could negotiate detailed contracts that subsequently realized cost and other expectations (examples include BANK1, GOODS, BANK2, and FOOD3).

Fee-for-service contracts were not suited to IT activities in which the technology was ill-defined, immature, or unstable. In these cases, the customer's inability to define baseline requirements, together with subsequent unreasonable expectations that additional/undocumented services would be provided without additional costs, caused relationships to deteriorate.

An important insight is that several of our case companies signed fee-for-service contracts, but mis-labeled them as strategic alliances or strategic partnerships. The rhetoric of a 'partnership' prompted the signing of loosely-defined, fee-for-service contracts (perhaps more aptly labeled 'flimsy' contracts). Suppliers' bids were based on the ill-defined baseline services the customers originally specified. Customers believed suppliers would provide additional services free or at reduced prices under the spirit and trust of the 'partnership'. In reality, additions or changes to the fee-for-service contract triggered additional supplier costs that were recovered through excess fees. Such excess fees contributed to the customer's inability to realize expected cost savings. We have noted how four of our 'loose' contracts were originally labeled as 'strategic partnerships' by participants—DIVERSE1, CHEM1, RUBBER and a European bank (BANK4).

A government department, the UK Inland Revenue (PSB1) provides another example (see also Chapter 3). PSB1 signed a fixed-fee-for-service, 10-year, £1 billion contract for most of PSB1's product and services. In 1994, when the interviews were first conducted, the IT Director referred to the supplier as a 'strategic partner':

> As to why we have gone for a single strategic partner rather than a number of partners each doing different things, much of a modern IT business like ours is an integrated business and carving it up does not become sensible—IS Director, PSB1.

By 1995, excess fees included £100 000 for unexpected software license transfer fees, an additional £5 million a year to cover inaccuracies in the original tender documents, and an additional £15 million a year for hardware maintenance. Furthermore, PSB1 could not meet some of the contractual terms, such as specifying requirements for 48 skill types 13 months in advance. In follow-up interviews in 1996 and 1998, the IT

Director had ceased referring to the supplier as a strategic partner. With unrealistic expectations abandoned (through a Perceptions Exercise), the relationship improved immensely. The IT teams for both parties understood each other better. Together, they worked with business streams to temper realistic expectations of the supplier's contractual obligations and to focus on more strategic issues such as budgeting and setting priorities.

Participants from other cases also decided that it was best to abandon the rhetoric of partnerships when deals were essentially fee-for-service:

> There is a lot of rubbish talked about partnerships. What are called 'strategic partnerships' are easy when everything is going well. It's good if you can work together, but it's not a true partnership unless you have a joint financial venture—IS Director, WH Smith (RETAIL3).

In the reasonably successful highly detailed contract in a UK aerospace company (AERO2), one manager told us in 1999:

> After nine months we banned the 'P' word from all discussions with the supplier. We needed to focus on service and implementing the contracts. As an aside it may well be that we went too far the other way, but I for one felt a lot safer with all this measurement stuff in place on such a big contract ... but we have had to continually revisit it—Contract manager, AERO2.

Strategic Alliances/Partnerships

In the context of IT, the idea that outsourcing suppliers should be treated as 'strategic partners' may be attributed to Eastman Kodak. A Kodak manager overseeing the contracts told an audience of practitioners, 'We think of our alliances as partnerships because of their cooperative and long term qualities' (Lacity and Hirschheim 1993b). Kodak's original contracts were only a dozen or so pages long. The importance of Kodak's IT outsourcing model cannot be over-stated—statistical analysis shows that the IT outsourcing trend can be attributed to the imitative behavior of Kodak's decision.[7] What few people comment on is that, firstly, the alliance was actually with three partners, not one, i.e. was a multiple supplier deal though it subsequently influenced the development of single supplier 'strategic partnerships'. Secondly, at least two of these relationships were not very successful.

In 1994 Kanter conducted over 500 interviews on 37 strategic alliances.[8] She found eight essential factors for successful alliances:

1. *Individual excellence*: both partners are strong and have something of value to contribute.
2. *Importance*: the relationship plays a key role in both partners' long-term strategic plans.
3. *Interdependence*: neither can accomplish alone what both can do together.
4. *Investment*: partners invest in each other.
5. *Information*: communication is reasonably open.
6. *Integration*: partners develop organizational linkages so they work together smoothly.
7. *Institutionalization*: the relationship extends beyond the deal-makers and cannot be broken on a whim.
8. *Integrity*: the partners behave in honorable ways towards each other.

Given these criteria, only four of our cases can be described as strategic alliances—Philips Electronics (ELECTRIC1), a European retailer (RETAIL9), an Australian financial and property services firm (FINANCE1), and South Australian government (PSB5).

ELECTRIC1's joint venture with a Dutch software company is one. ELECTRIC1 provided 1000 IT employees and owns over 30% of the venture. The Dutch software company provided sales and marketing capabilities. The partners develop and support application software for external customers.

RETAIL9 formed a strategic alliance with an IT supplier to help enable a globalization strategy. The deal was signed in 1996 and even in 2000 it is too early to declare a definitive outcome, with the results being quite mixed; there have been problems in 'globalizing' the contract.

FINANCE1 formed a strategic alliance in 1995. FINANCE1 believed that their 35% equity share in the supplier would align the supplier's goals with their goals. In actuality, the equity deal created many problems. In order for the supplier to generate revenues (and thus give a return on FINANCE's investment), it was motivated to run the base contract at a minimal service level and to try to sell excess services to FINANCE1 for excess fees. FINANCE1 wanted many additional services for free (wouldn't you charge your partner less?). The conflict has led to a recent contract realignment based more on a fee-for-service contract.

PSB5 signed an economic development package that exceeded yearly targets for developing the South Australian economy. Before the strategic alliance, EDS only had 30 people working in South Australia. By 1998, EDS employed over 600 people and established in Adelaide an

Information Processing Center (one of only 16 EDS mega-datacenters world-wide), an Information Management Center (one of only three EDS global network management centers world-wide), and a Systems Engineering Center (one of 40 EDS centers world-wide). In addition, EDS established an Asia/Pacific Education Resource Center, which has provided training courses for over 6000 EDS employees throughout the region, on site and remotely. EDS has been able to help a number of small Adelaide software companies access international marketing channels. And EDS has also attracted other global players to Adelaide. For example, EDS and Microsoft announced a deal in which EDS will establish one of Microsoft's four major global Internet datacenters in Adelaide. The multiplier effect of EDS's base in Adelaide includes housing starts, hotel bookings, meals, and rental of government/university property. (See Chapter 2 on mega-contracts for a full case history of the South Australian government deal.) The downside has been in other aspects of the deal to do with operational IT performance. Not least of the problems was the loss of skilled staff when EDS secured other long-term total outsourcing deals in Australia, for example with Commonwealth Bank.

Outside of the cases we studied, see the discussion in Chapter 1 for a number of reported IT strategic alliances that may meet most of Kanter's criteria. In principle, these strategic alliances will combine strengths to add value by selling jointly developed IT products and services to the external marketplace. Because each party will share in the revenue generated from external sales, the deals are not based on fee-for-services, but rather on shared risks and rewards, often accompanied by joint investment. While such deals have high expectations for success, the partners must truly add value by offering IT products and services demanded by customers in the market. We also note that many of these strategic alliances are renegotiated to more fee-for-service contracts. Thus, in a parallel study, Kern and Willcocks (2000) found much renegotiation and restructuring in the much touted Xerox—EDS deal signed in 1994 for 10 years and an initially estimated $US3.2 billion.

Buy-in Contracts

One contract model that emerged from our study was the buying-in of supplier resources to supplement in-house abilities. We labeled this an insourcing option because the customers managed the IT activity and supplier resources internally. This strategy was most successful for the development of applications dependent upon new technologies. In these cases, companies wished to access the supplier's technical expertise but could neither negotiate a detailed contract (because they did not fully understand requirements), nor could they afford to miss a learning opportunity. An example of this buy-in strategy is the development of a first client/server system. Companies we studied—FOOD2 and INSURANCE2, for example—lacked the technical skills to develop the systems, but felt that their own business expertise was required for the client/server applications, which included manufacturing scheduling, claims processing, and customer order processing. Outside experts were hired on an hourly basis to participate on the project team. After the systems were completed, the knowledge had been transferred and the companies opted to support the systems internally. Other examples from ICI Paints (CHEM3), WH Smith (RETAIL3), Barclays Bank (BANK3), Pilkington (GLASS), and an electricity supply company (UTILITY2) included buying-in supplier expertise to help develop applications using new technologies such as relational databases, neural networks, and expert systems.

In summary, we believe that the three general contract models identified above provide a good starting point for understanding customer/supplier relationships. These definitions also reconcile some of the apparent debates in the literature. For example, McFarlan and Nolan (1995) studied over a dozen total outsourcing contracts. Their findings are contrary to our own on a number of points, including their assessment of the viability of long-term IT outsourcing and a call for flexible contracts. The differences in their findings and ours may be attributed to the types of deals we each studied. McFarlan and Nolan primarily studied strategic alliances; we studied primarily fee-for-service contracts, though many of these initially—and incorrectly—called themselves 'strategic alliances'. At the same time we need to observe that all the long-term, large-scale outsourcing contracts we have observed and advised, do by their inherent size run into problems on another order of magnitude from the more selective, focused approaches. This makes risk mitigation for them, as discussed in Chapter 6, a central key activity.

CONCLUSIONS

Sourcing information technology capability remains a problematic area. The increasing number of suppliers and services available in the marketplace provides more opportunities, but also complicates decision-making, contracting, and management issues. As the market evolves and long-term contracts mature, our understanding of IT sourcing and the implications for sound practices will also evolve. There are many opportunities for further research in the area, including identifying IT capabilities that can and cannot be outsourced, adapting sourcing decisions to changes in business and technology and the e-business world, and developing alternative legal arrangements such as strategic alliances or creative variations on fee-for-service contracts.

Our case studies contribute to the mounting experience base, particularly in the area of fee-for-service contracts. Detailed, short-term contracts worked well for the firms we studied if participants clearly defined their requirements. This ensured they were paying market prices, motivated supplier performance (perhaps with a threat to switch suppliers when the contract expired), allowed organizations to gradually learn how to outsource competently, and, in some cases, allowed organizations to recover from their mistakes more quickly. Our ongoing research finds a number of emerging practices that in principle will achieve success through other means. Such practices will need to be monitored and studied before assessing their viability. These practices include flexible pricing, competitive bidding beyond the baseline contract, beginning long-term relationships with a short-term contract, and performance-based contracts—as discussed in Chapter 1.

In conclusion, practitioners want to source their IT portfolios to minimize costs, maximize service, and leverage resources to deliver real value, today and in the future. The five practices that we identified from prior company experiences are viable practices to help achieve sourcing objectives. These practices were selective outsourcing, joint IT/senior executive sponsorship, comparing external bids with newly prepared internal bids, short-term contracts, and detailed fee-for-service contracts. Our research also provides insights into why practices such as strategic alliances and variations of fee-for-service contracts are emerging. Emerging practices stem from organizational learning about the benefits and pitfalls of past IT outsourcing experiences. Future research in this area will serve to uncover additional practices that ensure that sourcing expectations are met. We now move on, in the next four chapters, to look at three critical tasks in preparing for outsourcing: developing sourcing (Chapter 5) and risk mitigation strategies (Chapter 6), developing core in-house IT capabilities (Chapter 7), and how to post- contract manage effectively across the six phases of any IT outsourcing deal (Chapter 8).

NOTES

1. A preliminary version of this research, covering 61 sourcing decisions in the 1990–1996 period, appeared in Lacity and Willcocks (1998). We continued to track these decisions, and a further 55, into 2000, and this work forms the basis of the findings described in this chapter. An earlier summary of these findings is in Willcocks and Lacity (1999b). The case studies that form the basis of our

research for this chapter can be seen at http://www.umsl.edu/~lacity/cases.htm.

2. Although participants identified other critical factors, these other factors were idiosyncratic to a particular case and therefore not useful in explaining the experiences in other cases. Full details of the cases are available on our web site (see note 1). Throughout the text the pseudonyms used also refer to the case details on this web site. Idiosyncratic factors included: a new CIO at a US-based university (UNIVERSITY) who was previously a senior executive at IBM—he knew how to replicate supplier practices without outsourcing; two companies facing bankruptcy—a US petrol refining firm (PETRO3), also a transport firm (TRANS)—and therefore were seeking a cash infusion; a unionized IT department at a telecommunications company (TCOM) that had erected barriers to IT improvement; a mining company that selected their supplier account manager on the basis of his prior experience as a demanding customer for General Motors before joining the supplier (MINE); and a manufacturing company whose new account manager was a previous employee (GLASS) and therefore understood the customer's operations.

3. Note all case names that are pseudonyms in this chapter refer to the case histories documented on our web site.

4. Included in our definition of insourcing is the buying-in of supplier resources to meet a temporary resource need, such as the need for programmers in the latter stages of a new development project or the use of management consultants to facilitate a strategic planning process. In these cases, the customer retains responsibility for the delivery of IT services—supplier resources are brought in to supplement internally managed teams. Sometimes we have distinguished between in-house sourcing (only in-house resources) and insourcing (a mix of in-house and buying-in of resources). The distinction becomes important when deciding on core IT capabilities needed in-house (see Chapter 7). But even there, as we shall see, tight labor markets make it difficult to staff such an in-house core capability initially, and a judicious use of buying-in resources can facilitate the evolution of the IT function to the mature model we describe.

5. Strassmann, P. (1995). Outsourcing—A Game For Losers. *Computer World*, August 21. See also Strassmann, P. (1997). *The Squandered Computer*. Information Economics Press, New Canaan.

6. Loh, L. and Venkatraman, N. (1992). Diffusion of Information Technology Outsourcing: Influence Sources and the Kodak Effect. *Information Systems Research*, **3**, no. 4, 334–358.

7. Loh, L. and Venkatraman, N. (1992) *op. cit.*; Applegate, L. and Montealegre, R. (1991). *Eastman Kodak Co: Managing Information Systems through Strategic Alliances*. Harvard Business School Case 9-192-030, Boston, Mass.

8. Kanter, R. (1994). Collaborative Advantage: The Art of Alliances. *Harvard Business Review*, July–August, 96–108.

5
Making IT Sourcing Decisions: A Framework

Large-scale outsourcing is something for a mature company to undertake ... otherwise severe problems can occur. In our Group companies often used to come to outsourcing from a low understanding of IT and might see the cost advantage but not have the understanding of the relationship between themselves, the IT strategy, the use of information and the use of outsourcing agents—CIO, Manufacturing Multinational.

Most of the large outsourcing deals are built on voodoo economics—CEO Gateway Services, 1993.

The customer from hell is the naïve buyer—CEO, Major IT Service Supplier.

The failing organizations outsource problems, and things they do not understand; they see outsourcing as about spending (and as little as possible) not managing; they expect too much from the vendor, and not enough from themselves. Generally, even now, suppliers are better at selling services, than customers are at buying them—Leslie Willcocks, MIS Outsourcing Roundtable, November 1999.

INTRODUCTION

As the previous chapters noted, IT is outsourced for many reasons, ranging from a bandwagon effect from the subject's high profile to cost pressures due to competition and economic recession. However, industry watchers often attribute the growth of the IT outsourcing market to two main phenomena. First, interest in IT outsourcing is largely a consequence of a shift in business strategy. During the 1990s, many companies abandoned their diversification strategies—once pursued to mediate risk—to focus on core competencies. Senior executives came to believe that the most important sustainable competitive advantage is concentrating on what an organization does better than anyone else and outsourcing the rest. As a result of the focus strategy, IT came under scrutiny: is IT a competitive weapon or merely a utility? Senior executives frequently view the entire IT function as a non-core activity, and reason that IT service suppliers possess economies of scale and technical expertise to provide IT services more efficiently than internal IT departments.

The second reason for the growth in outsourcing is uncertainty about the value delivered by IT. In many companies, senior executives perceive that IT failed to deliver the promise of competitive advantage propagated in the 1980s.[1] Consequently, many senior executives view IT as a necessary cost to be minimized. The CEO of an American conglomerate of petroleum, natural gas, and chemicals expressed to us his frustration with IT:

> All we see is this amount of money that we have to write a cheque for every year. Where is the benefit? IS says, 'Well, we process data faster than we did last year.' So what? Where have you increased revenue? All you do is increase costs, year after year and I am sick of it. All I get are these esoteric benefits and a bunch of baloney on how much technology has advanced. Show me where you put one more dollar on the income statement.

These two phenomena—refocus to core competencies and the perception of IT as a cost burden—prompt many senior executives to sign outsourcing deals. Although many senior executives approach IT outsourcing like any other make or buy decision, this approach can be a mistake. Senior executives must understand the distinctive and idiosyncratic nature of IT when making sourcing decisions. Unlike other functions—such as mailrooms, cafeterias, legal departments, manufacturing, distribution, and advertising—IT cannot be easily handed over to a supplier. IT is distinctive in a number of ways.

In this chapter we first address how IT is distinctive from other 'non-core' activities, then present an IT sourcing decision framework. This framework is empirically derived from our 76 case companies listed on our web site (see http://www.umsl.edu/~lacity/cases.htm), and has been successfully adopted by over 16 large global organizations. The framework is based on the value of selective IT sourcing, which had the highest relative frequency of success in our case-based research (Chapter 4). The framework presumes that the organization is also considering the nine core IT capabilities described in Chapter 7.

Once these core IT capabilities have been identified and established, the remaining IT activities may be considered as potential outsourcing fodder. The selective sourcing frameworks comprise three matrices to help assess the outsourcing potential of IT activities based on business, economic, and technical criteria.

THE DISTINCTIVE NATURE OF IT SOURCING DECISIONS

We are frequently told that IT is just another resource and should not be evaluated, and managed any differently from any other resource. It is important, often critical, but there is nothing that much distinctive about it that makes it any different from outsourcing, for example advertising, catering, the human resource function. Indeed, we saw in Chapter 1 that many organizations are increasingly outsourcing not just IT but large sections of certain business processes, and functions such as human resources and accounting. There is a need to stand back from this perspective on IT, and more carefully consider the specifics of any IT we put forward as an outsourcing candidate.

1. *IT is not a homogeneous function, but comprises a wide variety of IT activities.* Some IT applications uniquely enable business operations and management processes. Other IT activities, such as accounting systems, may appear less critical, but closer scrutiny often reveals that the value of such systems lies in the cross-functional integration of business processes—in many organizations, IT integrates product design, material purchases, manufacturing processes, sales, and customer service. The ubiquitous penetration of many IT applications across business functions hinders outsourcing because IT cannot easily be isolated, unlike other commonly outsourced functions such as legal departments. Outsourcing such activities can hinder business performance because suppliers lack an understanding of the implications IT has on other business processes. For example, one UK food manufacturer outsourced the development of its factory automation system, only to discover that the supplier did not understand the critical interfaces with other business units such as purchasing and inventory control. The system was delivered two years late and was twice as expensive as the food company expected. This and other examples strongly suggest the need for a selective rationale for outsourcing—while some activities can be outsourced, many others require management's attention, protection, and nurturing to ensure current and future business success. As we shall see, this selective sourcing logic must also apply in e-business initiatives.

2. *IT capabilities continue to evolve at a dizzying pace; thus, predicting IT needs past a three-year horizon is wrought with uncertainty.* Although companies initially perceived that suppliers would provide access to new technologies, mega-deals are usually contracted around current technologies with only vague references to future technologies. Most companies find that by the third year into an outsourcing deal, the original contract actually hinders their adoption of new technologies. For example, DIVERSE1, a US petro-chemicals company, signed a 10-year total outsourcing contract in 1988. At that time, the majority of the company's systems were running on mainframe technology. With the advent of client/server technology, the company wanted to migrate to the smaller platform, but found their outsourcing contract erected significant obstacles. In the end, business unit managers were forced to use discretionary funds to build client/server systems, while still meeting their contractual obligations for the increasingly obsolescent mainframe.

3. *There is no simple basis for gauging the economics of IT activity.* Although price/performance improvements occur in every industry, in few industries do the underlying economics shift as fast as IT. A unit of processing power that cost $US1 million in 1965 costs less than $US20 000 today. Today's computing resources may well cost 30%– 40% less next year. The rapid change in the underlying economics makes it extremely difficult for senior executives to evaluate the long-term costs of outsourcing. While a 20% reduction of current IT costs for the next 10 years may be appealing to a senior executive today, a few years into the contract he or she may be paying the supplier above-market prices for computer resources. The economics of desktop computing, in particular, change quickly and many managers have been reluctant to lock themselves into a fixed-price outsourcing arrangement:

> Price competition is such that prices change every three months, that's how fast the life cycle is. When the price drops, you don't want to lock yourself into a long-term contract. You have to pay that negotiated price, unless somehow you have some complicated flexible pricing system. That would also make us have a monopoly supplier which would be a considerable risk— Contract Administrator, South Australian Government.

There is another side to the coin, of course. The price of IT skills will continue to be volatile, and in areas of high demand and shortage, escalate, sometimes quite unpredictably. Staying alive to these switches remains a key skill for client and suppliers alike. Otherwise profit margins for the supplier can erode quickly; and declining service to the client may be a consequence (Willcocks and Lester 1999).

4. *Economic efficiency has more to do with IT practices than inherent economies of scale.* Although there are indeed economies of scale in some aspects of IT, they occur at a size achievable by many medium-sized and most large-sized companies. For example, small development teams are markedly more productive and successful than larger ones. Even in the early 1990s, in the area of datacenter operations, convincing evidence stated that economies of scale were being achieved at 150 'MIPs' (processing power equivalent to one large mainframe) (Lacity and Willcocks 1998). Because many companies operate IT functions large enough to achieve economies of scale, how do suppliers propose to cut costs? Our research suggests that supplier bids are based more on improvements in management practices than inherent economies of scale. For example, suppliers may cut costs through chargeout mechanisms that motivate business users to manage demand, by consolidating datacenters from multiple sites to one site, or by standardizing software. From our experiences, many IT managers can duplicate these cost reduction tactics if empowered by senior executives to overcome user resistance. For example, IT costs at RETAIL2, an American shoe manufacturer/retailer, were high because users refused to let IT managers consolidate their datacenters. Once senior management threatened users by inviting outsourcing bids; users acquiesced and agreed to let IT managers consolidate. IT costs subsequently dropped by 54%.

5. *Most distinctively of all, large switching costs are associated with IT sourcing decisions.* In most areas of business operations, management can protect itself against poor sourcing decisions in a number of ways—by dual sourcing of component supply or annual contract reviews of an advertising agency. These techniques are often inapplicable or ineffective for IT outsourcing, particularly when a total outsourcing approach is taken. The CFO from TRANS, an American airline, who signed a 10-year total outsourcing contract in 1991, perceives that switching costs pose a major risk:

> Once you sign with a vendor, you have no options other than onerous contract terms, so when you get into that situation it's a lose/lose for both parties. What are you going to do? Sue them? Fire them? Stop buying services? There is nobody else, in a short period of time, who you can buy services from—CFO, TRANS.

Those who approach outsourcing in all-or-nothing terms either incur the great risks involved in total outsourcing, or forgo the potentially considerable benefits of selective sourcing by committing to a policy of total insourcing.

BEYOND ALL-OR-NOTHING: SELECTIVE OUTSOURCING

We believe that the media focus on mega-deals has obscured the real issue. The key question is not, 'Should we outsource or insource IT?' but rather 'Where and how can we take advantage of the developing market of IT services?' On the basis of our research, successful companies carefully select which IT activities to outsource, rigorously evaluate suppliers, tailor the terms of the contract, and carefully manage the supplier.

Business Considerations: Selecting Which IT Activities to Outsource

Selecting which IT activities to outsource and which to retain in-house requires treating IT as a portfolio. Successful sourcing begins with an analysis of the business contribution of various IT activities. Conventional wisdom has it that 'commodity' IT functions—such as payroll or datacenter operations—are potential outsourcing fodder, while 'strategic' functions—such as on-line reservation systems— should be retained in-house.[2] Our study indicates that this delineation is too simplistic for two reasons. First, generalizations about which IT activities are 'commodities' or 'strategic' are often fallacious. For some companies, alleged IT commodities such as payroll, accounting systems, and datacenter operations actually serve to critically differentiate them from competitors. For example, in one security guard firm, payroll is a strategic application because on-time payment attracts a better quality of staff, leading to superior customer service. Also, applications often migrate from 'strategic' to 'commodity' within each industry as competition ebbs and flows. For example, while early adoption of automated teller machines (ATMs) once represented a strategic advantage by attracting more customers, universal adoption has delegated ATMs to mere commodities, as we found in our banking cases. Thus, each company must analyze the delineation of IT activities in its own business context, rather than accept generalities.

Second, many companies do not operate highly visible competitive systems, so senior executives may mistakenly classify all IT activities as commodities. In many cases the business contribution of IT may be masked by accounting for IT as an overhead, which serves to highlight only the costs of IT. In PETRO2, an American petroleum company, the CEO continually asked his CIO why IT costs were rising when other departments had managed to cut costs:

He would sit there and pistol-whip me to death about my expenses and I had to answer to everyone of them. I wasn't making him happy because he wasn't getting me to agree to reduce my costs. I said I'd be glad to cut expenses ... anything my user organization doesn't need, just let me know. If the marketing guy doesn't want me to do invoicing, we'll shut her down tomorrow— CIO of PETRO2 describing a conversation with the CEO.

The CIO also explained that other departments primarily reduced costs through IT—transportation costs were cut when IT automated 16 truck terminals and market costs were reduced when IT implemented a new credit card system. Through the CIO's aggressive education of the CEO and senior management about the contribution of IT, they eventually abandoned the view of IT as a cost to be minimized. This CEO realized IT's business contribution and he subsequently rejected an outsourcing supplier's request to bid in 1998:

He says. 'I'm not interested in letting other people'—that's the CEO talking—'have access to our data. I don't have to go outside for use of our data, so prepare a letter back to the chairman of [the outsourcing supplier] and say we appreciate your offer, but at this time we consider our information technology as part of the strategic work that we have'—CIO, PETRO2.

We have found that companies that consistently succeed in their selection of what can be outsourced to advantage use a richer vocabulary. They distinguish between two ideas—the contribution that an IT activity makes to business operations, and its impact on competitive positioning. These dimensions, which are depicted in the Business Factors Matrix (see Figure 5.1), are explored further below.

Some IT activities can differentiate a company from its competitors while other IT activities merely provide necessary functions. Some well publicized examples of IT products that have successfully differentiated companies from their competitors include American Airline's SABRE, American Hospital Supply's Order Entry System (subsequently acquired by Baxter), and Merrill Lynch's Cash Management System. These systems created barriers to entry, increased switching costs, and changed the nature of competition. Most IT activities, however, are viewed as commodities. Although IT commodities do not distinguish a company from its competitors in business offering and performance terms, these types of activities need to be performed competently. Examples of 'IT commodities', depending on the specific company, may include IT products, such as accounting systems in a UK water company (UTILITY1) and aviation authority (AVIATION), or IT services, such as datacenter processing in a US commercial bank (BANK1), a UK clothing and food

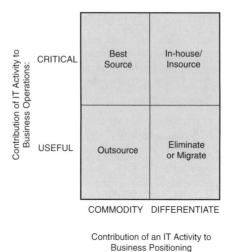

COMMODITY   DIFFERENTIATE

Contribution of an IT Activity to
Business Positioning

Figure 5.1   *The Business Factors Matrix*

retailer (RETAIL4), and Citibank (BANK2). Are enterprise resource planning systems 'commodities' in this sense? They could be, and indeed, as we shall see in Chapter 9, there is an increasing market for applications service provision, in which a variety of software is made available and supported externally.

Some IT activities are viewed as critical contributors to business operations, whereas other IT activities are viewed as merely useful because they only make incremental contributions to the bottom line. For example, US petroleum refining company PETRO2 views an information system that monitors the refining process as a critical contributor because it prevents fires and ensures product quality. Conversely, the company views an employee scheduling system as a useful contributor to business operations, but not a critical contributor.

After mapping an IT activity's contribution to business positioning and business operations, four categories of potential outsourcing candidates emerge.

1. *'Critical Differentiators'—IT activities that are not only critical to business operations, but also help to distinguish the business from its competitors.* A European ferry company—P&O—considers its reservation and check-in systems to be 'critical differentiators'. The company has ships similar to those of rivals, and operates them from the same major ports across the Channel between Britain and France. It also has to compete on these

dimensions against Channel Tunnel and hovercraft crossings. Its competitive strategy is to differentiate through service, including the speed and ease with which passengers and their cars complete the boarding process. It is constantly making innovations in this respect, and the systems are instrumental in achieving this. While the company outsources a number of its IT activities, the reservation and check-in systems are retained in-house. This protects their ideas, expertise, and continuing ability to rapidly innovate. As three examples, we found similar 'critical differentiators' in a comprehensive customer management system at a UK-based insurer (INSURE1), a product development support system at ICI Paints (CHEM3), and a foreign exchange system in Citibank (BANK2). Although such systems should be managed internally, we have seen organizations boost their in-house IT capability by bringing in specialists from an external supplier. However, these 'outsiders' work alongside in-house people, under the company's own management.

2. *'Critical Commodities'—IT activities that are critical to business operations but fail to distinguish the business from its competitors.* A major British airline views its IT systems that support aircraft maintenance as 'critical commodities'. Like its rivals, the airline must obviously maintain its fleet to specification or face very serious consequences. However, the maintenance activity and supporting systems respond to the mandated requirements of the manufacturers and regulatory authorities. There is no benefit from over-performance. Although the airline has not yet outsourced these systems, it is in principle prepared to do so. Because of the risks involved for the business, such a decision would be based on clear evidence that an external supplier could meet stringent requirements for quality and responsiveness, as well as offer a low price. The policy is 'best source', not 'cheapest source'. A more standard 'critical-commodity'—the provision of an emergency/standby computer center—is commonly outsourced by businesses because many high-quality suppliers are available.

3. *'Useful Commodities'—the myriad IT activities that provide incremental benefits to the business, but fail to distinguish it from its competitors.* In our experience, payroll, benefits, and accounting systems are the first examples of 'useful commodities' volunteered by most businesses. But sweeping generalizations cannot be made, even within industries, as we have noted with the security guard firm. 'Useful commodities' are the prime candidates for outsourcing. We found many such examples in the cases, such as personal computer support at US chemicals major

CHEM1, accounting services at BP Exploration (PETRO1), and main-frame operations at a US bank (BANK1). External suppliers are likely to have achieved low costs and prices through standardization. The business makes further gains if it can free up internal management time to focus on more critical activities. But the expectation of outsourcing must be validated through analysis of economic considerations.

4. *'Useful-Differentiators'—IT activities that differentiate the business from its competitors, but in a way that is not critical to business success.* 'Useful differentiators' should not exist, but we have found that they frequently do. One reason is that the IT function is sometimes relatively isolated from the business and subsequently pursues its own agenda. For example, the IT department at CHEM3, a European paint manufacturer, created a system that precisely matched a paint formulation to a customer's color sample. IT managers envisioned that the system would create competitive advantage by meeting customers' wishes that paint should match their home furnishings. However, senior management had established the company's strategy as color innovation. They failed to market the system because it ran counter to their strategy, and the system became an expensive and ineffective distraction. The system was eventually eliminated.

A more common reason for the creation of 'useful differentiators' is that a potential commodity has been extensively reworked to reflect 'how we are different' or to incorporate the 'nice-to-haves'. This was an extensive phenomenon at Philips, the Dutch electronics multinational resulting in very problematic and high cost software maintenance. The CIO of the company subsequently implemented a policy requiring that all needs for 'useful' systems be met through standard software packages, with strict limits to customization. 'Useful differentiators' need to be eliminated from or migrated within an IT portfolio, but never outsourced merely to reduce their costs. One can remark that the initial phase of Internet usage by existing corporations has been replete with 'useful differentiator' web sites, often reflecting flawed strategic thinking, underfunding, and a belief in outsourcing to speed the move to the Net and fortune.[4]

In summary, treating IT as a portfolio helps to identify outsourcing candidates by analyzing not only an IT activity's contribution to competitive strategy, but also its contribution to business operations. Through these two dimensions, senior executives more easily identify the value of IT. In addition to business contribution, economic considerations—which are often prematurely assumed to favor the supplier—are an important consideration in confirming the viability of IT outsourcing candidates.

Economic Considerations: Comparing Supplier Offerings with In-house Capabilities

Many senior executives may assume that a supplier can reduce their company's IT costs because suppliers possess inherent economies of scale that elude internal IT departments. But we have noted that a distinctive feature of IT is that economies of scale occur at a size achievable by many medium to large organizations (see Lacity and Willcocks 1998 for a full analysis of IT size and economies of scale). If this is true, how can a supplier under-bid current IT costs? Often, the answer is that suppliers implement efficient managerial practices that may be replicated by internal IT departments if empowered to do so. Successful companies we studied compare supplier bids not against current IT offerings, but against a newly submitted bid prepared by internal IT managers.

As previously noted, many IT managers possess a plethora of ideas to reduce costs, but internal user resistance—or even outright user sabotage—may have hindered their efforts in the past. The problem stems from stakeholders within organizations who have different performance expectations for IT (see also Chapter 8). Senior executives—who typically write the check for IT every year—often set cost minimization as the performance expectation for IT. Business units and users—who actually consume computer resources—often demand service excellence as their primary performance expectation. These expectations are in conflict because service excellence drives up IT costs. For example, users perceive software customization, local datacenters, fast response time, and 24-hour help-lines as elements of service excellence—practices that drive up IT costs. IT managers are left to resolve the dilemma: how to provide a Rolls Royce service at a Chevrolet price.

Senior management's threat of outsourcing often serves to align IT performance expectations, typically with the cost minimization agenda. IT managers are then free to prepare bids which include cost reduction tactics practiced by suppliers. These practices include chargeback systems to curtail user demand, employee empowerment to reduce supervision costs, consolidation of datacenters to one physical site, standardization of software, automation of datacenter operations, and the archiving of inactive data. Users understand that if their internal IT managers—who are at least familiar to them—do not implement these practices, a horde of supplier employees will.

We studied a number of turnaround cases where previous attempts by IT managers to reduce costs failed until senior management invited external and internal bids. These were in an insurance multinational (INSURE2), a petrol refiner (PETRO3), a US university (UNIVERSITY), a food manufacturer (FOOD1), a telecommunications company (TCOM), a public health authority (PSB2), the BBC (PSB4), an aerospace firm (AERO2), and a European airline (AIR1). To ensure fair play, internal bid teams are removed from the organization—in the case of US company PETRO3, from Tulsa offices to a Dallas bunker—and treated with the same formality as suppliers. For example, all bidders submit questions in writing and responses are distributed to all parties. In these companies, the internal bids not only beat current IT costs, but significantly beat supplier bids. After insourcing, IT managers from FOOD1, reduced costs by 45% through software standardization. UNIVERSITY, reduced costs by 20% by reorganizing the IT department and eliminating redundant staff. PETRO3, an American petroleum company, reduced costs by 43% by consolidating three datacenters into one. Prior to the outsourcing threat, users in all these companies except TCOM resisted cost reduction practices. At TCOM, an outsourcing threat served to mobilize a more formidable opponent than users—an IT trade union:

TCOM: Using an Outsourcing Threat to Empower Internal IT Managers

Senior executives at TCOM, a US telecommunications company, decided to outsource after reading about Kodak's success. They rightfully perceived that the internal IT department was not cost competitive due to a strong IT labor union which promoted inefficient work practices. In particular, the labor union specified narrow job descriptions which caused excessive manpower. For example, datacenter managers were forbidden to touch the hardware and software; a union manager was required on every shift; and both a manager and a worker were called in for emergencies. Although the IT manager had tried on numerous occasions to negotiate better terms, the strong labor union resisted. Only after the Request For Proposal had attracted two external bids, did the labor union agree to allow the internal IT department to include revised union rules in their internal bid—the labor union either had to succumb or risk losing the entire work site. The internal IT subsequently reduced headcount by 46%.

We have incorporated these two economic considerations—in-house economies of scale and adoption of leading practices—into a matrix to guide senior executives through these issues (see Figure 5.2).

If the internal IT department has reached critical mass and has adopted leading management practices, it is unlikely a supplier will be able to reduce costs further because suppliers have to earn a 15%–20% profit, whereas internal IT departments merely need to cover costs. If the in-house IT department possesses theoretical economies of scale but has

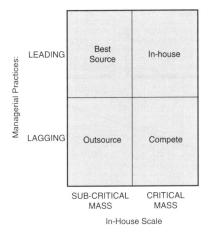

Figure 5.2 *The Economic Factors Matrix*

failed to implement efficient managerial practices, we recommend that senior executives allow internal IT managers to compete against supplier bids. As we have seen in the previous cases, the competition serves to empower IT managers to overcome user resistance to the idea of reducing costs. If the internal IT department is of sub-critical mass but has adopted efficient practices, it is quite possible that a supplier's size advantage may be negated by their need to generate a profit. We recommend best source in these cases; that is, test the market to determine the economic validity of outsourcing. Finally, if the internal IT department is of sub-critical mass and has failed to adopt efficient practices, there is a strong economic justification for outsourcing. But even companies that fall in this quadrant may wish to empower IT to implement the practices they can before outsourcing to avoid giving the supplier the lion's share of the easy savings.

But what happens when external supplier bids beat internal bids? Prudent managers question where and how the supplier proposes to earn a profit while still meeting the bid. In the most desirable scenario, suppliers clearly out-bid internal IT departments on the basis of a number of valid reasons—superior management practices which could not be replicated by the internal staff, inherent economies of scale, or superior technical expertise (see Figure 5.3). But in many cases, supplier bids may be based on 'voodoo' economics—customers are offered long-term, fixed prices which are attractive in year one but will be out of step with price/performance improvements a few years into the contract. Or the supplier may be trying to buy market share in a fiercely competitive market. Once the contract is signed, the supplier may

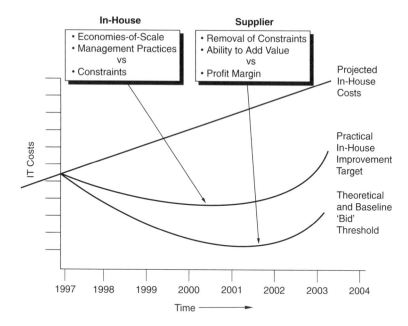

Figure 5.3   *Managing the economics of the supplier bid*

recoup losses by charging exorbitant excess fees for any change, realizing that customers are captive. Supplier bids may contain hidden costs. For example, a US bank (BANK1) failed to question a software transfer fee licence clause which ended up costing half a million dollars.

How is it possible to manage and avoid 'voodoo' economics? In Figure 5.3 we show that the objective should be *not* to compare a supplier bid against projected in-house costs, but rather against a carefully arrived at, practical, in-house improvement target. This improvement target would be the result of re-analyzing the in-house performance during a three to five month baseline period. Once a clear view is gained of in-house cost/performance, detailed investigations can proceed on whether further economies of scale can be achieved, and whether superior IT management practices can be applied. In advisory work in the 1998–2000 period we continued to see examples of up to 40% cost reductions achieved through this process, the majority typically through management practice improvements. However, changes were not always supported; much depended on political factors, and how the IT function was perceived. There was often a range of size and budgetary constraints holding back further in-house improvements.

A supplier can often remove many of those constraints, and may well bring economies of scale and superior management practices to bear. However, these must be offset against the fact that profit margins mean that on one, not insignificant, dimension at least, the vendor bid will be more expensive than any in-house proposal. The problem then arising is how to ensure you are comparing like with like across the in-house and supplier proposals. One technique is funneling. We saw this in the UK Inland Revenue supplier assessment process. (see Chapter 3). Using a pro forma document, detail all the types and size of costs for the practical in-house improvement target. Then get both the in-house function and supplier(s) separately to detail the estimates for their performances. Identify and get these to explain differences. Include estimates of reasonable profit for each supplier.

If a supplier's bid is close to the baseline 'bid' threshold and the in-house IT function is only making at best the practical in-house improvement target, then outsourcing looks the cost-effective option. But if there are other good non-cost reasons for outsourcing and the supplier is close to the practical in-house improvement target, then outsourcing may still be a viable alternative. The trick in either case is not to allow the supplier to pick all the low-lying fruit in cost reduction, but argue from strength that, since in-house could improve its performance considerably, then the client and supplier should agree a basis of sharing the gains from the proposed cost reductions achievable through outsourcing. In our cases this happened at both UK Inland Revenue and in the BP Exploration cases (see Chapter 6).

On looking at our work on the economics of supplier bids, 10 lessons emerge:

- Customers may be able to achieve similar savings as those offered by a supplier.
- Some savings may be more real than others.
- In-house IT costs may already be falling.
- Be careful not to compare total in-house costs against a supplier's selective bid (the 'apples against pears' problem).
- Suppliers may not get better deals on hardware and software, or may shunt some costs on to the client.
- Outsourcing can carry hidden costs (see Appendix A)—e.g. management, excess fees, contract ambiguities.
- The economics of different sourcing options can change over the length of a contract.
- Make sure the supplier makes a reasonable profit.
- The supplier bid can reveal ways of improving in-house performance.

A final note: some companies may actually seek a purely economic package based on financial manipulations rather than inherent best practices or efficiency. Two of our case studies—TRANS, a US transportation company, and AERO1, a US aerospace company—used outsourcing to escape financial peril. The CFO from the transportation company signed a 10-year outsourcing contract when his company went bankrupt. Senior executives from the aerospace company signed a 10-year contract after several years of negative profits. These arrangements bought in multi-million dollar cash infusions when the supplier purchased IT assets, transferred 2000 employees in one case and 1600 employees in the other to a more stable supplier, and postponed fixed fees until the later portion of the contract.

Technical Considerations: Selecting an Appropriate Contract

Regardless of the impetus for outsourcing, once senior executives are convinced of the validity of supplier bids, the process continues by selecting appropriate contracting options. In Chapter 4 we introduced three general contracting models:

- *Fee-for-service contract*: A customer pays a fee to a supplier in exchange for the management and delivery of specified IT products or services.
- *Buy-in contract*: A customer buys in supplier resources to supplement in-house capabilities, but the supplier resources are managed by in-house business and IT management.
- *Strategic alliance*: Collaborative inter-organizational relationships involving significant resources of two or more organizations to create, add to, or maximize their joint value.

Another contracting model includes a preferred supplier:

- *Preferred supplier*: A customer's past experience with a chosen supplier has established trust based on prior performance, allowing a degree of flexibility and creativity in establishing a contract for a new set of IT activities.

In practice, selecting an appropriate contracting model depends on several important technical considerations. The danger in ignoring technical considerations is that senior executives may sign flimsy contracts that strongly favor suppliers. Suppliers negotiate many deals each month and understand the technical implications of contracting, while the customer company may have little or no experience with outsourcing. To counter-balance their negotiating power, senior executives must have a sound understanding of their specific service requirements associated with the outsourced technology. We have determined from our research that the degree of technology maturity and the degree of technology integration are two key technical considerations.

The degree of technical maturity determines a company's ability to precisely define their requirements to suppliers (Willcocks, Feeny and Islei 1997). We describe an IT activity as having low technology maturity when the technology itself is new and unstable, when the business has little experience with a technology that may be better established elsewhere, and/or when the business has embarked on a radically new use of a familiar technology. Examples include an organization's first venture into imaging, client/server, intranet, or extranet technologies, or the development of a major network to support a new business direction of globalization. In these instances, all that senior executives know for sure is that requirements will change over time, based on experience and the availability of new options.

Outsourcing technically immature activities engenders significant risk. Ironically, these are precisely the IT activities many senior executives wish to outsource. For example, many companies choose to outsource their first client/server application, reasoning that suppliers possess the technical expertise lacking in-house. This practice often proves disastrous because companies are in no position to negotiate sound contracts. In addition, such companies lose a valuable learning opportunity, leaving them dependent on the supplier after implementation. Consider the experiences of RUBBER, a US rubber and plastics equipment manufacturer, in which outsourcing the delivery of new technology led to failure. The important lesson at RUBBER is that the company was in no position to write a detailed contract because of technical immaturity:

RUBBER: The Potential Consequences of Outsourcing the Delivery of New Technology

Senior executives at RUBBER outsourced the conversion from one mainframe environment to another. They reasoned that the supplier was in a better position to perform the conversion and to provide continued management after installation because of their vast expertise with the new environment. They soon discovered that it was unwise to outsource what they did not understand because they could not evaluate supplier performance. For four years, senior management questioned the supplier about the escalating costs of IT. When the supplier provided justifications for the expense, internal IT managers lacked the technical knowledge to validate the response. When IT costs rose to 4% of sales, participants terminated the contract early and brought the environment back in-house. After a painful adjustment and conquering of the learning curve, IT costs subsequently dropped to 1.5% sales.

On the other hand, companies in this position may well benefit from an injection of external expertise to support their voyage of discovery. The recommendation is to 'buy-in' this expertise, but to integrate external resources into an internally managed team. The business retains full management control and visibility of the project, capturing as much learning as possible about the technology and its application. A US petroleum company used this pattern to develop its first 'expert system' application—a system designed to calculate sales tax for material transfers to and from pipe and wallhead warehouses. A specialist expert systems supplier seconded resources to the in-house team, which retained management of the project. The project was completed successfully, and the in-house IT staff now had the capability to take full charge of the ongoing support and development of the system.

In contrast to the risks of outsourcing in conditions of low technology maturity, there is significantly less risk in outsourcing activities characterized as 'technically mature'. We can describe an IT activity as having high technology maturity when it represents the well-established use of familiar technology. Mainframe-based datacenter operations and accounting systems were highly mature activities for many of our case companies. In these cases, the business has conquered the learning curve and reached a point where its requirements are well specified and reasonably stable.

Outsourcing technically mature activities provides less risk to organizations because they can define their requirements precisely. Customers can negotiate a fee-for-service contract which assigns service delivery management and responsibility to the supplier. For example, BANK1 outsourced its mainframe operations to a supplier. The CIO was able to negotiate an air-tight contract because of her experience and understanding of the requirements and costs of her mainframe operations. In the contract, she fully specified the service levels required, such as response time and availability, service-level measures, cash penalties for non-performance, and adjustments to changes in business volumes. Four years into the contract, she has achieved the anticipated savings of 15%.

A second important technical consideration is the degree of integration with other business processes. In the simplest case, an IT activity is easily separated out and handed over to suppliers. For example, CHEM2, a US chemicals company, successfully contracted out support for personal computers using a fee-for-service contract. At that time—late 1980s—users operated stand-alone personal computers which ran word processors and electronic spreadsheets. The CIO wanted to outsource because the growing adoption of PCs forced him into regular and poorly received requests for additional headcount. Through his two-year outsourcing contract he reduced costs and avoided further requests for staffing.

In cases where technical integration with other business processes is high, the risks of outsourcing increase. For example, we discussed FOOD2's experiences with outsourcing the development of factory automation. Soon into the contract, managers realized that the new system had profound implications for almost every business unit in the company. Although the supplier was an expert in factory automation software, it lacked an understanding of business interfaces. The system took four years to develop instead of two.

In contrast, one financial services company successfully outsourced the development of a highly integrated system using a 'preferred supplier' model. This company invested in imaging technology to replace paper records (such as customer letters) with an electronic file. The company first explored the technology through a discrete R&D project. Senior executives reached a point at which they were convinced of the benefits of large-scale adoption but realized that many of their existing systems would now be affected. At this stage the company turned to its preferred IT supplier, a supplier with a very broad product line, with whom it had worked for many years. Resisting the supplier's instinct to develop a detailed fixed-price agreement, the company set up an enabling, resource-based contract. The project was completed successfully, providing competitive advantage for both the business and its supplier, which had established a reference site for its own imaging products.

Technical considerations—the degree of technical maturity and degree of integration—strongly suggest the need to limit the length of contracts. A typical view from our research is that three years is the maximum period for which one could assume requirements would be stable. Returning to the case of the outsourced personal computers, the CIO was wise to limit the contract to two years because the company subsequently integrated the PCs onto a client/server network. Thus, the degree of integration and degree of maturity were only stable for two years. After that time, new management and possibly new outsourcing arrangements are required.

We have mapped the two technical considerations—technology maturity and integration—in the Technical Factors Matrix (Figure 5.4).

We caution when using the term 'strategic alliance'. The 'strategic alliance' contracting model has been widely recommended as the preferred governor of outsourcing contracts.[5] But we have seen the rhetoric of 'strategic alliance' or 'strategic partnership' used as an excuse to sign a poor contract, and this led to the failures of five of our total outsourcing cases (waste disposal company DIVERSE1, US chemicals major CHEM1,

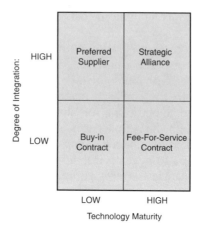

Figure 5.4   *The Technical Factors Matrix*

US rubber and plastics firm RUBBER, European insurance company INSURE1, and consumer products manufacturer GOODS). We argue that strategic partnerships require shared—or at least complementary—risks and rewards. Indeed, we have two successful strategic alliances that met the shared risk/reward requirement among the four studied: European electronics company ELECTRIC1 and (part of) the South Australian government contract PSB5. (See Chapters 2 and 4 for more details.)

ELECTRIC1 (Philips, the Dutch electronics company), for example, used a strategic alliance for technically mature and highly integrated IT activities. When ELECTRIC1 decided to reduce costs by outsourcing datacenter operations and support of existing systems, they mediated risk by entering into a joint venture with a software house. By establishing a jointly owned company, they created shared goals which prevented supplier opportunism. Because of technical maturity, ELECTRIC1 could negotiate a detailed contract in which the supplier is responsible for the management and delivery of an IT activity. Because of the high integration with other business processes, ELECTRIC1 developed a close relationship to maintain the integrity of interfaces. To ensure supplier performance, the company constructed an incentive-based contract that ensures shared goals.

CONCLUSION

The outsourcing market has been changing in the customer's favor. Once dominated by a few big players—EDS, Andersen, CSC, and

IBM—the IT outsourcing market has also fragmented a lot more into many niche services. Developments in e-commerce from 1996–2001 have also stimulated the development of niche IT product and service providers. As competition in the outsourcing market increases, companies have more power to bargain for shorter contracts, more select services, and better financial packages. Also in the customer's favor is a growing experience base with IT outsourcing, which allows customers to intelligently evaluate and negotiate outsourcing deals. In fact, many of our respondent companies adopted incremental outsourcing precisely to mitigate risk and develop in-house learning from outsourcing over time. Our evidence points to long-term total outsourcing as a possible option only for those highly experienced in IT outsourcing contracts and in managing major, long-term relationships with suppliers. In practice, especially on the latter point, we uncovered considerable immaturity not only among customers, but also among suppliers. It may well be that long-term total outsourcing deals are more likely to occur with a maturing of the capability to handle them; however, even supporters of such deals regularly point to the considerable difficulties experienced in getting them right.

More importantly, juxtaposed with the growing evidence, including our own, of the problems with an 'all or nothing' approach to IT outsourcing are the benefits of selective sourcing. When companies properly select and contract for specific IT activities by treating IT as a dynamic portfolio, companies maintain management and control of core IT activities—such as strategic planning, scanning the environment for new technologies applicable to business needs, developing of business-specific applications, and supporting critical systems—while still accessing supplier expertise and economies of scale for well-defined, isolated, or mature IT activities. These lessons continue to be as valid for the next round of technologies and business circumstances as they have been for the 1990–2000 period we have studied. Further consideration of this proposition is made in Chapter 9.

NOTES

1. Feeny, D. and Ives, B. (1997). Information Technology as a Basis for Sustainable Competitive Advantage. In Willcocks, L., Feeny, D. and Islei, G. (eds), *Managing IT as a Strategic Resource*. McGraw-Hill, Maidenhead.
2. McFarlan, W. and Nolan, R. (1995). How to Manage an IT Outsourcing Alliance. *Sloan Management Review*, Winter, 9–23.
3. See Clemons, E. and Row, M. (1998). McKesson Drug Company—A Case Study of a Strategic Information System. *Journal of Management Information*

Systems, **5**, no. 1, 36–50; McKenney, J. (1996). *Waves of Change*. Harvard Business Press, Boston;
Ciborra, C. (1993). *Teams, Markets and Systems*. Cambridge University Press, Cambridge.

4. Plant, R. and Willcocks, L. (2000). Moving to the Net—Leadership Strategies. In Marchand, D., Davenport, T. and Dickson, T. (eds), *Mastering Information Management*. FT Prentice-Hall, London.
   Also Sauer, C. and Willcocks, L. (2000). *Building the E-business Infrastructure*. Business Intelligence, London; Willcocks, L. and Sauer C. (eds) (2000). *Moving to E-business*. Random House, London.

5. See Henderson, J. (1990) Plugging into Strategic Partnerships: The Critical IS Connection. *Sloan Management Review*, Spring, 7–18. Also McFarlan and Nolan (1995) *op. cit.*

6
Preparing for Outsourcing—
Risk Mitigation for Business
Advantage

There was a real risk when we took this over of the wheels falling off, that all the contractors would walk out, and that Polaris's credibility would just plummet, because they'd say—they've outsourced it, it can't be any good...—Steve Burnett, Logica.

Failure to outsource our commodity IT will permanently impair the future competitiveness of our business—John Browne, CEO British Petroleum.

INTRODUCTION

The growth in the number and size of outsourcing deals has been paralleled by rising concern with how these deals can be managed, and in particular how the risks they represent can be controlled. Risk here is taken to be a negative outcome that has a known or estimated probability of occurrence based on experience or some theory. Risk is the likelihood of loss as a consequence of uncertainty. Risk has emerged as a key issue in IT outsourcing, not least because of the very mixed picture on success emerging from the trade press and the academic evidence.[1]

Our research into the 1991–2000 period, described in Chapter 4, finds that long-term, large-scale, single-supplier deals have been particularly risky. Indeed, even proponents of this approach, such as McFarlan and Nolan (1995), point out that it can be a high risk strategy.[2] Even so, such deals have continued to be entered into, with for example the Inland

Revenue–EDS, Sears–Andersen Consulting, and British Aerospace–CSC arrangements signed since 1994 in the United Kingdom (UK), and similar deals signed elsewhere in the mid-1990s—for example, Xerox–EDS in the United States, Lend Lease–ISSC in Australia, and United Bank of Switzerland–Perot Systems in Switzerland.

If such deals exhibit the highest risk, then, as we saw in Chapter 4, nowhere does the outsourcing of IT emerge as anywhere near a low risk enterprise, unless those risks are offset by the adoption of specific proven practices (see also Appendix A). The emerging practices described in Chapter 1 can also be seen partially as—less tested—attempts to mitigate risk. However, practitioners have not been aided by the surprisingly scant systematic attention given to risk issues. Of course there is already a long history and knowledge base about *information technology* adoption as a high risk, hidden cost process. In particular, risk, and its mitigation, in the areas of software development and project management has been heavily researched.[3] However, although many of the case examples in this literature have involved external IT suppliers, this has rarely flowed into detailed analyses of risks in IT outsourcing. In practice, in fact, our detailed review of the last decade finds the surprising fact there are all too few systematic studies of types of IT outsourcing risks, their salience, and how they can be controlled.[4]

TOWARDS ANALYZING RISK

Given this state of affairs, and the fact that on conservative estimates IT outsourcing may well represent, on average, 30%–35% of IT budgets by 2002 (Lacity and Willcocks 2000a), a primary motivation for this chapter is to build on previous studies and provide much needed empirical and analytical work in a critical area for IT outsourcing decision-making and management.

Although there is a limited literature upon which to draw for the identification of salient risk, an exploratory analytical framework can be distilled from case study and survey work by Lacity and Willcocks (1998, 2000a) and others.[5] The framework has also been productively utilized, and further developed for present use, in parallel case work (see Willcocks, Lacity and Kern 2000). There we found the framework providing sufficient generic coverage of salient risks to allow complementary detail to be explored in an insightful, qualitative manner. Drawing on this combined work, the main reasons for failure/negative outcomes in IT outsourcing deals have been various combinations of the factors shown in Table 6.1.

Table 6.1 *Risk Factors in IT Outsourcing*

1. Treating IT as an undifferentiated commodity to be outsourced
2. Incomplete contracting
3. Lack of active management of the supplier on contract and relationship dimensions
4. Failure to build and retain requisite in-house capabilities and skills
5. Power asymmetries developing in favor of the vendor
6. Difficulties in constructing and adapting deals in the face of rapid business/technical change
7. Lack of maturity and experience of contracting for and managing 'total' outsourcing arrangements
8. Outsourcing for short-term financial restructuring or cash injection rather than to levering IT assets for business advantage
9. Unrealistic expectations with multiple objectives for outsourcing
10. Poor sourcing and contracting for development and new technologies

Much of the attention in IT outsourcing has focused on the two areas that we investigate further in this chapter, namely decision-making frameworks and contracting. But, for risk mitigation, what has lacked serious attention are two critical areas that demand managing. As will be detailed in Chapter 7, one of these is retained in-house capabilities. The second area, dealt with in detail in Chapter 8, comprises the formation, development, and sustaining of client/vendor relations. It is widely acknowledged that IT outsourcing agreements are founded on inter-organizational relationships due to the resulting dependencies that arise.[6] Paradoxically, though, with a few notable exceptions,[7] the area in IT outsourcing that has received the least attention so far is this relationship issue, and particularly the characteristics that determine effective and ineffective outsourcing relationships.

The two case studies in this chapter offer an opportunity to examine these issues, and how the client organizations sought to mitigate risk across three differently constructed outsourcing deals. The two cases were selected from our database of 116 case histories see Appendix B at `http:www.umsl.edu/~lacity/cases.htm`) as different examples of creative contracting and management for business advantage.

Polaris is an innovative, selective IT outsourcing deal where the supplier operates as an applications management service for a company whose main line of business is selling software products and services in the UK insurance sector.

Our second case—BP Exploration—is an example of total outsourcing to multiple suppliers on five-year contracts explicitly in order to mitigate the risks from long-term single supplier deals discussed in

Table 6.2   *Overview of the case studies*

Customer	Supplier	Contract signed	Contract duration	Value of contract	Scope of contract
Polaris	Logica	1996	3.5 years renewable to 7	$US22 million	• Appns. mmt • Helpdesk • Training • Software development • Maintenance • Consultancy
BP	Sema Group	1993	5 years	$US175 million	• Datacenter
Exploration	SAIC BT/Syncordia		5 years 2 years renewable		• Client server • Telecoms and WANS

earlier chapters, while achieving significant business leverage through IT usage (see Table 6.2).

By the end of 2000 Polaris was nearly five years into its contract, while the BP Exploration (BPX) contracts finished in mid-1998. Subsequently at BPX some of these deals were revised and renewed, others terminated, while in some cases new suppliers were brought in for the next round of outsourcing—all issues we will comment upon. Both cases provide immense learning on how risks can be mitigated across different sorts of deals. The lessons are detailed in sections after each case study, and in the general analysis section at the end of the chapter. From these lessons we also generate a risk analysis framework for use when preparing for outsourcing.

CASE 1: POLARIS IN INSURANCE—CREATIVE CONTRACTING FOR BUSINESS ADVANTAGE

Polaris was set up in 1993 by seven major UK-based insurance companies. The objective with Polaris was to 'cooperate in order to compete'. By creating and utilizing a common set of standard software tools, the insurance companies using the indirect broker–customer channels hoped to compete more effectively against the direct insurers coming into the market. By 2000 over 40 insurance companies and syndicates, together with their brokers and software houses, were using Polaris software in the UK market. There were also possibilities of utilizing the software in Internet and satellite distribution channels, and for more complex insurance products.

Background

In the early 1990s direct writers, particularly the highly successful Direct Line company, made major competitive inroads into the very large UK markets for commodity products such as motor and household insurance. As new start-ups with no legacy systems, and dealing directly with customers through the telephone, direct insurers typically could achieve a cost advantage of between 5% and 10% off the price of insurance premiums compared with the more traditional insurance company–broker–customer channel. Tim Ablett, a Director of Polaris indicates the further business problem:

> Before Polaris it could take up to 6 months to code up a new insurance product, and two months just to change an existing product. This meant that if the premium structure altered it was taking up to two months to get the information disseminated into the different broker software packages, during which time you could be writing business with poor premiums for the customer, or unprofitable for the insurance company.

There was the added problem of thousands of brokers holding different information about the same products:

> It's not so much that there's somebody in the middle, it's the fact that there are so many—hundreds or thousands—who could be in the middle, and that they should all be having the same information—Steve Burnett, Logica.

The net result was that the broker-based channels used by the major insurance companies were losing significant amounts of business.

Polaris was set up to reduce significantly the costs of the broker distribution channel to insurers, software houses, and brokers, and allow insurers to provide better, competitively priced products and amend their rates, terms and conditions quickly. The issue was to give the broker channel the same sort of competitive costing and response time possessed by the direct channel. These business goals were to be realized by creating a common platform for new software for licensing to insurers and software houses, instead of allowing each software house to use its own development methods. Software houses would need to undertake the one-time task of incorporating interface programs—provided by Polaris—into their own systems.

In the past insurers had used a number of software houses to develop their products, each using their own methods. This approach pushed up the costs of bringing products to market. It also meant brokers were using different software products. A further point of concern for the insurers was that the software houses had assumed a large measure of control over the production and distribution of insurance policies.

The Polaris Solution

Polaris's plan was to develop a single platform of industry-standard software templates and formats to help insurers and software houses to bring products to market more cost effectively. As a consortium the members sponsoring Polaris did not want to invest in building a large infrastructure for the project. A small team of people was seconded from the member companies to manage the development. Initially the team relied heavily on consultants and contract programmers to do the programming and systems analysis and design. In practice the volume of software grew more rapidly than expected as the initiative expanded from motor policies to household, small business insurance and other other lines:

> I guess it was a measure of its success that this thing actually started to run away with itself and before they knew it this small team of contractors had grown into quite a large one, and to some extent self-fulfilling, and was starting to behave like a software house, which in many ways it was— Steve Burnett, Logica.

Over the next three years two major pieces of software were developed. Sitting in the insurer's office, Productwriter was designed to enable insurers to define insurance products—the data to be captured, type of policy and form to be produced, the insurance rates and algorithms to be used on those rates, and the format of electronic trading messages. The insurer can produce a diskette, or send the product electronically to the software house. Here a second software product called Run Time Environment (RTE) was designed to integrate Productwriter with software house and broker systems, allowing for onward distribution of products to brokers. The objective was to achieve the dissemination and availability of product and rate changes within 48 hours. Brokers gain by also obtaining a wider choice of up-to-date products from many more insurers, plus the benefits and speed of electronic trading. This is across the whole product processing cycle including fast and accurate quotations, mid-term adjustments, and policy renewals.

The overall operation is shown in Figure 6.1. This also illustrates how the insurance industry standards body—the Association of British Insurers (ABI)—provides data standards to Polaris, which is then also responsible for maintaining a data dictionary of standard insurance information drawn upon by underwriters in the insurance companies. The ABI is responsible for market data in the dictionary, but Polaris is wholly reponsible for the data dictionary and its distribution and integration. Members of the Polaris community requiring enhancements to

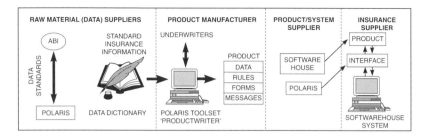

Figure 6.1   *Polaris: Enhancing The Intermediary Business*

the live dictionary make their requests directly to Polaris who then manage the ratification process through the ABI.

Moving to Outsourcing

After two years of development, Polaris managers found they were more engaged in running a software house than an insurance business. Too much time was spent on looking after the system and not enough on how to extend its coverage in the market amongst insurers, brokers, and software houses. They also had some expensive contractors on board, allied to a lack of management clarity and control in the IT area:

> It's fair to say that quite a lot of the money going into Polaris was actually being wasted because it wasn't being spent on things that would really improve its coverage in the market; it was perhaps playing around with interesting technology—Steve Burnett, Logica.

Moreover, there was a lack of commercial discipline in the relationship between Polaris and its shareholders. Was Polaris to make money as a software house, or was it a strategic investment with the benefit coming back indirectly to investors through more insurance business? By 1996 the weight of director and shareholder opinion was that Polaris needed to be profit-generating through software development and that it needed a partner who understood the software business to develop and maintain its existing and future commercial systems:

> The hardware was irrelevant, the value was all in the software. What we wanted was a very professional company with a good understanding of the insurance business to take responsibility for the future of our software—Tim Ablett, Director, Polaris.

Six vendors bid for the outsourcing contract, and these were reduced to a shortlist of three. Martin McLachlan, Managing Director of Polaris, outlines the selection criteria used:

> The basis of decision factors were, firstly, quality in terms of the delivered product and the way the software was developed and maintained. There's a lot of maintenance in this software. Cost saving was fundamental—the Polaris directorate were concerned about the growth in development costs and wanted that more tightly managed. We also wanted to reach the stage where we could look for more stability in the software—by knowing what base we were working from.
>
> We also realised that other technologies were coming along—like the Internet and digital television—that the Polaris solution was suitable for, but we did not want to build up expertise in these ourselves. Thus the range of expertise and the ability to pull in specialist skills easily and quickly were important. We also needed an uncontroversial outsourcing partner because there were already software houses in this market, so we needed one acceptable to all because of its reputation.

In early 1997 Logica was confirmed as the preferred supplier, and after a due diligence period of three months, the companies signed a seven-year £14 million ($US22 million) plus contract. The highlights are:

- The price was fixed for 3.5 years with Polaris having the right to terminate at that point if they wished.
- Subsequently six months notice of termination would be required from either side, with Logica obligated to smooth any transition to any other arrangement or supplier.
- Logica were contracted to provide a helpdesk service on the existing software and dictionaries, training, development and implementation capability, and support for new releases including to software houses and insurers (100 person-days per quarter), software maintenance, technical consultancy, and technical support to the selling process.
- This was to be paid for on a fixed-fee basis which subsequently covered 90% of Logica's revenue from the contract, with extra work charged by time and materials:

> It's provision of an applications management service ... it's primarily people. It really is the outsourcing of essentially a software business that forms a discrete entity within a group of insurers. What's nice about it is it's very clear what its business is—to build and support a first-class software product for the business benefit of the sponsors so that they can enable the intermediaries to do better business—Steve Burnett, Logica.

In fact, Logica had not been in the business of application management for very long, but then nor had any of their competitors. Polaris chose to mitigate risk by retaining responsibility for general management, sales, marketing, financial control overall, and, in terms of the systems, for the logical business descriptions of the functionality required. This was to cover logical process and data descriptions, and building the logical data models against which the Polaris dictionaries are written.

Before the contract was signed the two sides spent much time designing a service-level agreement that covered every aspect of the work, with over 20 sets of measures of performance, and also points at which terms could be varied. Thus, service levels were set in terms of critical software faults fixed in a defined time period, and response within a defined time, and tasks were defined in terms of, for example, number of days development time, or number of training courses.

Progress at Polaris 1997–2000

In the four years from 1997 to 2000 the Logica systems team stayed a relatively stable 30 in number, with 16 staff on the Polaris side. External contractors were initially reduced from 25 to 15 in number, these now becoming paid and under the control of Logica. The total number was expected to reduce as major developments came to an end. Cost efficiencies were achieved by:

- replacing external contractors with permanent Logica staff,
- introducing better procedures in the support effort,
- utilizing Internet and e-mail communication for administration, and
- fully documenting processes and the software, once developed.

Additionally, as part of the new disciplines, Logica now made sure that a business case was presented to the Polaris advisory board for every major development in the systems area.

Logica's first priority was to stabilize, then improve, the level of service:

> There was a real risk when we took this over of the wheels falling off, that all the contractors would walk out, and that Polaris's credibility would just plummet, because they'd say—they've outsourced it, it can't be any good … —Steve Burnett, Logica.

These two objectives were achieved through 1997–1998, with service-level benchmarks being revisited annually.

While Logica brought control and clarity into management and service, Polaris also sought to mitigate risk by their own policy on retained skills. In the 16-strong Polaris group were people building the logical data dictionaries, doing accreditation testing of electronic data interchange (EDI) messages, managing the contract, providing consultancy support to insurers writing products using Productwriter, and doing systems support and project management. The group included a considerable amount of technical know-how, but of a specified type:

> You cannot give up technical know-how, it just doesn't work ... we have technical knowledge in EDI message design, the use of Productwriter to build business products, in-depth know-how on the dictionary. Where Logica is involved is more in the development of the underlying tools, and changes to those or to the physical dictionaries. We are on the logical side, they (Logica) are on the physical side, but we do maintain a degree of technical expertise in the application of the business skills. I haven't given that away and have no intention of doing so either—Martin McLachlan, Polaris.

Additionally, a business planning group was formed to develop a view of Polaris several years out. While the insurers and brokers represented provide very much a business view, at the same time they produce a view of what the technology must do at the logical level, and Logica, also represented on the group, then determine how it can be physically implemented, and make the business case to the Polaris board.

Polaris also mitigates risk through three people responsible for detailed monitoring of the contract. These deal daily with the Logica service delivery manager, while there is also a monthly review meeting of the four main Logica and Polaris managers. The service-level agreement and measures act as the mainstay for both client and supplier, while development falling into or outside of the 100 person-days per quarter fixed price is controlled and signed off through the business planning group.

Price changes for Logica staff have been tested against the market, although the way the contract is written, Logica offer their rates at a discount from their standard rates. There are change control procedures also written into the contract where either party can ask for the pricing and measurement mechanisms to be varied in the event of major changes, such as that occasioned by the 1998 expansion of Polaris into business and commercial lines.

Future Developments

By early 1999 Logica had stabilized and improved the service and Polaris was functioning very successfully in the market with over 36 companies and syndicates using the software and plans for 50 or more within three years. Cost savings were coming through individually for the main insurer, software house, and broker stakeholders. The technology was also allowing brokers to focus on factors in the insurance products other than just price. The indirect market was holding up well against the direct insurers, and Polaris was assisting in that process. In mid 1998 a merger between Polaris and CLMI—operating in commercial lines—expanded the insurance products that Productwriter would cover:

> I think the way Polaris will go forward is we will broaden the number of business classes and within each business class we'll become capable of handling more complex business—Martin McLachlan, Managing Director, Polaris.

Moreover, Polaris technology allowed new channels, in particular Internet and digital TV, an easy way of developing and selling insurance products. Ironically this meant that Polaris could also be sold to direct insurers, enabling them to cut their costs as increased competition in the direct markets—not least from traditional indirect channel insurers also using direct channels—pushed up the marketing costs. By 2000 these possibilities were becoming a reality as Polaris pushed into new technologies and markets. Meanwhile, the contract with Logica was extended.

In all these scenarios Logica, or any other supplier operating as the development shop for Polaris, remained a fundamental building block for the development of future business, providing support to brokers and insurers, development and refinement of software, technical understanding, and control and clarity in technical management.

RISK ANALYSIS OF THE POLARIS–LOGICA DEAL

The power of IT outsourcing for achieving business advantage for Polaris cannot be fully appreciated without understanding the business context in which the IT supplier—Logica—is being relied upon to perform. Polaris and its software products have been at the heart of a significant competitive strategy designed by major players in the general insurance market aimed at bolstering failing profitability and growth in the indirect broker channel against the direct insurers. The original aim was to reduce costs and so be price competitive in the major motor and household insurance markets.

But by the late 1990s Polaris products were expanding to other insurance classes, in particular commercial lines, could handle more complex forms of insurance, and could also support product differentiation in different insurance markets. It could also be plugged relatively easily into more direct channels, for example Internet and digital TV. In these circumstances outsourcing represented a refocusing strategy allowing Polaris staff to develop the business, a cost containment strategy, and a way of guaranteeing up-to-date technical skills and know-how in a difficult, supply-led IT labor market.

At the same time high dependence on the supplier represents a significant, if conscious, business risk for Polaris. The creative, risk aspect is allowing a supplier to be so responsible for aspects of a commercial IT product and service as opposed to back-office tasks and the more obvious 'useful commodities'. This means that the initial selective sourcing and vendor selection were in fact business-critical decisions.

Moreover, active management, creative contracting on an ongoing basis, and close working with the supplier are undoubtedly business-critical tasks. The risk-mitigating practices adopted at Polaris are shown in Table 6.3 versus the risk factors discussed earlier.

Given that the business risk from outsourcing was so high, and that Polaris has been effective in both business terms and in its outsourcing arrangement, it is valuable to analyze in more detail how risk was

Table 6.3   *Polaris—Approaches to risk mitigation*

Risk factors	Practices at Polaris
1. IT treated as undifferentiated commodity	• Core/non-core split • Retained business logic and analysis, outsourced technology implementation • Clear about what IT gives business advantage
2. Incomplete contracting	• Complete contract • Jumping-off point at 3.5 years • Six months notice thereafter • Smooth termination guaranteed in contract
3. Lack of active management of the supplier on (a) contract and (b) relationship dimensions	• Active daily contract management • Regular business–supplier management reviews
4. Failure to retain requisite capabilities and skills	• Business-facing technical know-how retained • Contract management capability • Business systems thinking and relationship building retained *But* • Lacking in in-house IT strategy and technical fixing capability

Risk factors	Practices at Polaris
5. Power asymmetries developing in favor of vendor	• Highly dependant on vendor, but stabilized software made switching costs low • Retained ownership of software assets • Carefully delineated performance measures through SLA
6. Difficulties in reconstructing/ adapting deals for business and technical change	• Fixed price plus mechanism • Regular reviews of price/ service/requirement against market
7. Lack of maturity/experience of contracting and managing long-term 'total' outsourcing deals	• Staged 3.5-year to 7-year contract • Keen, competitive price/service terms • Kept most key capabilities in-house while outsourcing technology tasks.
8. Short-term financial restructuring or cash injection rather than leveraging IT for business advantage	• Objective is long-term business advantage on cost-competitive contract • Outsourcing allows refocus from technology to growing the business
9. Unrealistic expectations about what can be achieved by outsourcing	• Careful delineation in contract of limited expectations from both client and supplier perspectives
10. Poor sourcing and contracting for development and new technologies	• Stabilized software before outsourcing • Polaris understood systems and products • Contracted on a market-competitive resource and service basis • All work has a business case to be signed off by Polaris senior management • Retained ownership of all software.

mitigated and what risks remain. We do this by blocking the analysis into five primary areas that emerge from the case and subsume the points made in Figure 6.1 into this discussion.

Outsourcing: Type and Scope

Earlier chapters have shown that organizations run large risks when they are not clear about the overall business rationale, cannot clarify to themselves the detailed financial and technical reasons for going down the IT outsourcing route, and fail to carry out the necessary analysis needed to arrive at realistic expectations about what IT outsourcing can achieve (see especially Chapter 5).

The strength of the Polaris approach to outsourcing has been the very clear business rationale to outsourcing—it allows Polaris staff to focus on growing the software business, while the supplier provides development capability and implements and supports the technology/software. Moreover, the interrelated financial and technical reasons were strong and clear. On detailed analysis, given the small scale of Polaris and the reluctance of its shareholders to move further into technical capability, a supplier could provide more effective cost and operational management of the development and maintenance shop. Moreover, suppliers were available who could provide the requisite up-to-date technical expertise at more competitive prices than Polaris itself could achieve.

Polaris also made clear distinctions between 'core' and 'non-core' business and IT assets and activities, only outsourcing what they perceived as the 'non-core'. Thus Polaris retained intellectual property rights and ownership of all its software products and services, essentially only outsourcing technical 'doing' skills and their management. The outsourcing of software development has often been experienced as high risk. However, the software products were largely stabilized before outsourcing and some in-house technical understanding was maintained. Moreover, for future systems development business and logical requirements were the preserve of Polaris staff while the supplier was mainly responsible for their technical implementation.

It was also clear that the small size of Polaris allowed a degree of partnering and mutual learning to develop over time. This offset the risk all too commonly affecting development effort, especially as a consequence of outsourcing, namely that of disconnection between business requirement and technical development because of failure to work as a multi-disciplinary team.

At the same time much of the technical effort at Polaris has been support and maintenance. The outsourcing arrangement might prove less effective if the business required major new software developments, in which case the lower risk approach would be to contract-in resources to work under Polaris management, and also build up in-house technical understanding (see Chapter 7).

Vendor Selection Criteria and Process

In reviewing the case histories in Chapters 2 and 3 (see also Appendix A) it is clear that poor vendor selection criteria and process have been one source of relative lack of success in IT outsourcing deals. Polaris offset the latent risks by being very clear about the requirement. It was also clear that—because quality of resource was business-critical—cost was not, and could not be, the dominant discriminating criterion.

Previous research has shown that selecting the lowest bid can incur risks of deteriorating service and opportunistic behavior (Lacity and Hirschheim 1995a). At Polaris, the detailed specification pointed to a niche player with a good understanding of the insurance business, and with a successful track record of providing skilled technical resource on a project management basis. Because the provision of high-quality skills was paramount, the supplier also had to have a good track record of working successfully on small as well as large contracts. This specification ruled out virtually all the big outsourcing players as strong candidates.

Risk was also mitigated by inviting competitive bids and comparing these with the internal service—something identifed as a best practice in the review of 116 case histories in Chapter 4. A further risk-mitigating practice suggested by previous research (Lacity and Hirschheim 1993a; Willcocks, Lacity and Fitzgerald 1995) was Polaris establishing detailed metrics against which supplier performance could be monitored. Moreover, this was achieved in a three-month due diligence period and included in the contract before the contract was signed, thus reducing the risk of subsequent extra-contractual disputes diverting management effort.

The Contract

In the Polaris–Logica case there is no doubt about the consciously central role of the contract in mitigating risk. Long-term contracts, historically, have turned out inflexible in the face of business volatility and rapid technological changes (Chapter 4). Consider how Polaris has mitigated risk:

- One recent trend has been more staged contracting. This can be seen in the Polaris deal with the possibility of termination after 3.5 years, and a right to terminate with six months notice thereafter, though the declared intention is a seven-year contract period.
- Risk is also mitigated by a continuity clause requiring the vendor to smooth transition to any preferred arrangement in the event of termination.
- The contract also has highly detailed price–service-level resource requirement stipulations, with mechanisms in place for regular review to ensure all prices are competitive.

- Regular reviews build in the contractual flexibility needed to deal with changes in volume and/or type of business and technical requirements.
- There are also a battery of 20 sets of performance measures against which the supplier is monitored regularly, and can be penalized on.

Active Management of the Supplier

Robust contracts mean little if the client then sees outsourcing as 'spending, not managing' and turns away from active management of the supplier. The significant risk here lies in consequent failure to leverage (and redirect as necessary) vendor performance.

In fact Polaris maintains very active management of the supplier, reflecting the high business dependence on the supplier's ability to perform. Three people monitor Logica's delivery against contract and ongoing requirements, and there are regular reviews between operational and senior management staff from both companies. The business planning board meets regularly to set future direction and also acts as a sounding board and sign-off for business cases for IT changes suggested by the supplier.

Polaris staff become much more involved in hands-on management of IT rather than just monitoring the supplier, the closer the tasks move to eliciting detailed business requirement. At the same time Polaris does not retain all four capabilities required for active management detailed in Chapter 7, namely informed buying, contract facilitation, contract monitoring, and vendor development. The strongest areas would seem to be contract monitoring and vendor development. The risks of not having high performing capabilities in all these areas, but diluting these roles across a few individuals, is partly explicable by the relatively small size of Polaris, and so of the management task.

Additionally, the small size means much more personal interaction and informal facilitation between supplier and Polaris staff generally, thus developing the relationship dimension more strongly than is often possible in larger deals. This can offset the risk by providing more informal channels for active management of the supplier.

Retained Capabilities and Skills

We argue in Chapter 7 that nine core IS capabilities need to be retained in the modern corporation in order to run any IT sourcing regime effectively. As we shall see, organizations with weaknesses in any of these nine areas incur difficulties. Some struggle on while others have been observed to offset such risks by gradually developing the type of capabilities that are initially missing. In the case of Polaris the first point to make is that the relatively small size of the business and of the IT operation will inevitably mean a dilution of the fully fledged model detailed in Chapter 7, though one would still expect the nine components to be represented within the in-house team.

The second point is that, in fact, Polaris have not outsourced their in-house IT—a small in-house IT office function has been retained, and its role and relationship with the business managers of Polaris remains unproblematical. It is also the case that the business side of Polaris—dealing with and selling to the insurers, software houses, and brokers—is very much the preserve of Polaris staff. However, as Logica staff's understanding has grown they have been increasingly utilized in support roles here, as technology experts—an indication of the growth of the relationship dimension in the outsourcing arrangement, and another risk-mitigation factor. Polaris have also retained business systems thinking capability in their management group, expressed in the Business Planning Board. Relationship-building is a less distinctive capability and is spread through several roles, but is less necessary because of the small size of the business and strong interactions that have developed between Polaris and supplier staff.

A much more significant area, however, where risks are paramount and need to be offset, is in the creation of, and maintenance and support for, the Polaris software products and services. The issue of retained skills for leveraging supplier performance have already been discussed above. Polaris would seem to have offset much of the risk of handing over its technology future to a supplier in two main ways:

- The first was to be clear that Polaris itself would be responsible, and retain skills for arriving at the detailed business requirements, for all future technical developments. In this scenario Logica have been responsible for technical implementation only—a lower risk route, recognized as such by our research (see Chapter 7).
- Secondly, Polaris retain a great deal of 'doing' technical know-how in specific areas—building logical data dictionaries, EDI message design, use of software to build business products, systems support, and project management. According to Martin MacLachlan, Director of Polaris, these essentially involve 'technical expertise in the application of business skills'.

Interestingly, however, what Polaris have ceded to the supplier, quite consciously, is the 'technical fixing' capability relative to the software products—something that our own research shows should be retained in-house. This, perhaps, is the creative part of the Polaris–Logica contract but also is the biggest reason for dependence on the supplier, and so represents the biggest business risk in the contract.

Undoubtedly this continues to be the most significant business risk, but it has been offset by careful choice of a suitable supplier, strong contracting and monitoring practices, relationship development over time, and retention of some technical capability in-house. There is also the high profile nature of the work and reputational aspects in the market incenting supplier performance. Countenance also the business risk of not using the supplier. After all, Polaris could not provide for itself high-quality, cost-effective, well-managed development people during a critical period in its business development. Outsourcing has successfully allowed Polaris to redirect its fundamental attention into the business and away from technical areas.

CASE 2: BP EXPLORATION—MULTI-SOURCING AS RISK MITIGATION

In 1993 BP Exploration, a $US13 billion division of the BP Group that explores for and produces oil and gas, signed IT outsourcing deals with three vendors for five years, worth in total about $US35 million a year. Why did they develop this strategy of multiple alliances, how was it managed, and with what results? And what impact did a subsequent 1999 merger with Amoco have on IT outsourcing arrangements?

Background: The Outsourcing Rationale

By the late 1980s, through business pressures, senior management in BP and BP Exploration (BPX) identified the need to reduce costs greatly, and radically change the organization and its performance. Organizationally the legacy had been high costs, complexity, inflexibility, and duplication. In a changing competitive business environment, senior managers saw the way forward as through cost management, process simplification, and the use of integrated teams. An important element of the business strategy was organizing around the the notion of core competence.

Forms of outsourcing had been a common way of operating at BPX, and indeed this was true for the industry as a whole. By 1990, in a worsening financial situation, BPX senior management became much more focused on the core competence argument, suggesting that BPX's key competence was exploration and its key intelligence was in its explorers, not its IT or in its Accounting, for example. Non-core activities should be outsourced or be managed through alliances with partners who added complementary capabilities. In fact, in 1991 BPX outsourced its accounting services, including computer systems and 250 staff, to Andersen Consulting in a five-year £55 million ($US82 million) deal, one of the few of its kind in the world at the time. The deal was expected to save £3 million annually. Following this logic, it also became important to outsource those IT activities identified as non-core. In the words of John Browne, subsequently BP CEO:

> Failure to outsource our commodity IT will permanently impair the future competitiveness of our business.

However, the core competence philosophy was to lead not to traditional outsourcing, but to the development of a series of 'partnerships' or 'strategic alliances', viewed as increasingly important for the company's future:

> ... for us to remain, and in fact become an even stronger player in the exploration production market in the next 10 years, we are going to need the skills of not just an in-house traditional organization, but we need to move towards, what we would probably call, a constellation of partners—George Fish, BPX, 1993.

Closely related to this general strategy the company was also facing a change in its core business from a relatively narrow focus in the 1970s and 1980s to becoming a much more diversified production company in the 1990s. Consequently, they required a presence in a number of areas they were not previously identified with, and in which they did not really have the necessary in-house experience and skills. The chosen strategy was to identify partners, and work with organizations that had the relevant experience and skills. An example from the IT area was in the field of wide area networking (WAN), where the company felt they were lacking, but nevertheless they identified WAN as a key strategic requirement. As one company manager commented in 1993:

> ... the identification of a partner who could assist us in the application of telecommunications from quite immature telecoms infrastructures, is pretty key to us. That partner could add a lot of value to us in terms of cost efficiency, improvements in service, in the traditional telecoms world, but also could be a significant partner to us in the new areas we are seeking to exploit.

The Changing Role Of IT

The problems experienced with in-house IT further drove the emerging BPX approach to IT outsourcing. Historically, the majority of people and resources in IT were focused on infrastructure and applications with only a very few people devoted to thinking about the role of IT, where it should be going, and how it could help the business. According to George Fish of BPX this situation:

> ... would be one that many companies would recognize and ... it is a very stable and resistant-to-change type structure, and it doesn't really have a lot to do with improving the performance of your IT department.

In 1989, IT in BPX was a supply-driven, fixed-cost, functionally based, service-only function. The aim became to shift the function to a demand-driven, activity-based service that also added value, but at variable cost. The shift that occurred in the 1989–1993 period is shown in Figure 6.2. Substantial resource would now be devoted to the role of 'IT thinking' and internal consultancy, supplemented by external information services. The applications and infrastructure would now be outsourced mainly to a number of partners with only a few key staff retained in the IT area. As one BPX respondent commented on outsourcing:

> ... it's a method of rebuilding the focus of your organization so that you start to focus on what is important to the company and not what's important to the traditional IT world.

Figure 6.2 represents a new view of the role of the IT function. In-house expertise should be focused on value-*creating* activities dealing with business processes and information. Value-*realization* activities related to IT applications and infrastructure could largely be outsourced. The outsourcing rationale was related to changing the performance levels of the IT function. In the traditional structure it was felt that performance would decline slowly over time. It may be improved from time to time by an injection of strategy or consultancy that set it on a performance upturn for a short period, but inevitably it would then resume its previous decline. The new structure would have the opposite performance slope, everything helping to push the business performance and focus in an upward direction. In 1993 a senior manager commented:

> The purpose of the internal consultancy structure supplemented by external partners with a core internal consultancy, i.e. putting your effort into 'IT thinking', is that you are constantly improving performance, you've got nothing established or set in concrete in your organization, and so you find a steady but continuous improvement over time. That's what we've seen so far anyway on our performance indicators. Over about five years the difference in performance would probably be actually a radical transformation.

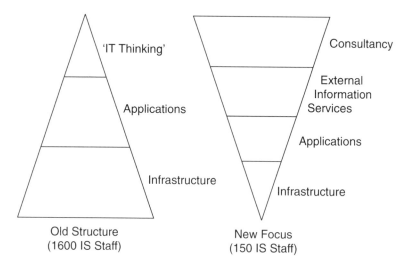

Figure 6.2   *Reconstructing in-house capability*

The IT Cost Management Phase 1989–1992

In the period 1989–1992 BPX sought significant cuts in IT costs while preserving the IT service to the business. In IT there were five routes to achieving these objectives:

- eliminating human resource duplication;
- making large reductions in staff numbers;
- forming single 'centers of excellence' to provide support for all sites;
- rationalizing applications; and
- outsourcing IT.

This period saw the consolidation of seven IT departments into one global department, the standardization of systems across the company, and the closing of all but two datacenters. The objective was to make the running of IT as efficient as possible. This approach was largely successful. Costs were reduced from $US360 million to $US150 million ($US110 million in 1994). Staff numbers went from 1400 to 500 (150 in 1994). Computing power increased while new technologies were implemented. A considerable reduction was achieved in the complexity and duplication of infrastructure and applications. Quality and information management were improved, while the IT service to the business was maintained.

At the same time BPX was having mixed experiences with its selective outsourcing of IT. Some of these deals had been inherited during the

1980s acquisition of Standard Oil, Lear Petroleum, and Britoil. From the late 1980s other one-year renewable deals were signed with a variety of suppliers for items including desktop equipment maintenance, maintenance of selected applications, and helpdesk services. BPX gained a lot of learning out of these deals, and most provided the benefits anticipated.

However, although these contractors often performed their individual tasks on an adequate basis, the overall effectiveness of these arrangements in terms of business performance and contribution was poor. The contracts were drawn up in ways that did not encourage cooperation between vendors. This left BPX a range of inter-contract problems arising from what was described as 'the cracks' between vendors. BPX ended up with the considerable task of having to manage not only each individual sub-contractor but also the relationships and interfaces between them. According to one contract manager:

> It's not just like having a crack between your applications and infrastructure within the departments, but like having ten cracks right across the department! . . . We got very little benefit out of that.

Moving to Multiple Alliances

BPX examined various options. From looking at other deals, long-term 10-year contracts seemed to be inflexible. Changing business requirements would need new technology solutions that would be beyond contract and costly. Nor did BPX management believe that one single supplier could provide all their IT needs to a 'best-in-class' level. At the same time selective outsourcing without re-focusing on core processes and driving down IT costs first would mean paying vendors to do what BPX should and could do themselves.

BPX sought a consortium of outsourcing partners to handle their IT. In early 1992, 65 companies had responded to the Request For Information (RFI), and this was reduced to a short list of 16. Some of these failed to meet key criteria. Thus, according to John Cross, Head of IT at BPX at this time, some vendors, even at senior levels, were not clear on the market they were targeting, or how they saw the market evolving. Others seemed less innovative and flexible, and less aggressive about cost control, than BPX required.

The BPX board encouraged an incremental approach to outsourcing, getting each of the decentralized businesses to buy into the advantages of IT outsourcing. The short list was reduced to six. BPX needed to assess the ability of the prospective suppliers to work with one another and so provide a seamless service. It was felt that contracts alone could not guarantee this objective. They concluded that they needed different partners for different activities requiring differing skills, but all with the ability to work together, so eliminating the 'cracks' that had caused such problems earlier. They wanted them to work together as a consortium—to present a united interface to the company, and deal with any issues amongst themselves, thereby minimizing BPX involvement:

> We started to look for more for partners that we could pull into our value chain, challenge on their own long-term business strategy, their cultural fit with us, their approach to quality ... We were looking for those partners not just to save us some money, that's not really been the dominant feature. It's important that they add value with their skills, and it is the sharing of risks and rewards that will help to achieve this. I think if you pursue outsourcing purely and simply as a short-term, cost-saving measure, you are going to be disappointed—Contract Manager, BPX.

The key to this was partnership, not only between the client and the vendor but also between the vendors themselves. This was quite a challenge for the vendors involved, who in other situations were competitors. The six suppliers agreed to participate in a one-week workshop to collaborate in developing proposals. Cost performance targets were expected to be ambitious; an alliance of between two and four suppliers was required; and proposals had to meet BPX's detailed specifications.

At the end of 1992 BPX identified three major partners and signed five-year contracts with two, and a two-year renewable with Syncordia, worth a total of roughly $US35 million per year. All the partners were identified as capable of covering the company's requirements globally, which was identified as an important criterion. Sema Group was selected to handle the datacenter operations. The strengths of Science Applications International Corporation (SAIC) in developing distributed and leading edge systems and scientific applications were to be used to develop and innovate in client/server type systems. Syncordia, a subsidiary of British Telecom, had the maturity, flexibility, and range to manage BPX's telecommunications and WANs.

The final details of the contracts and the arrangements between the vendors took a great deal of arranging and negotiating: 'we want the three to work together as if they were one company, but it's not proving as straightforward as we'd expected' said one BP executive. However, agreement was eventually arrived at and the three suppliers began initially to operate at sites in Glasgow, Harlow, Aberdeen and Stockley Park in the United Kingdom, and telecommunications and networks mostly world-wide.

According to John Cross, commenting in December 1992, the objective was not simply to reduce costs but to put the whole of the IT in the company on a different and more effective footing. He suggested that the IT restructuring and outsourcing partnership arrangements would save the company the cost of finding a new oil field, providing the equivalent of a £10 billion ($US15 billion) cash influx:

> We've already halved our IT costs and next year's IT budget ... will save another 30% ... and we will have only 10% of our previous staff, 20% of our mainframes, and 10 times as many MIPs on the desktop ... By the end of next year all the IT infrastructure will be in the hands of its outsourcing alliance partners. They deal with the suppliers, I don't buy technology any more, and I have no capital budget—John Cross, Head of IT, BPX.

Managing Multiple Vendors 1993–1998

In February 1993 BPX drew up separate contracts with each vendor. BPX deliberately avoided long-term contracts. There were five-year framework agreements with Sema Group and SAIC, and a two-year agreement with Syncordia, in fact renewed in 1995. The latter reflected BPX's determination to revisit regularly the arrangement in the face of high price volatility in the telecommunications market.

Despite these separate contracts, the need was for the vendors to provide combined services to all BPX business sites. Seamless service was a critical requirement. By 1995 each of the eight major business sites had one supplier operating as primary contractor, coordinating the services provided by all three. This arrangement continued until June 1998 when the contracts came up for renewal. The rationale here was vendor motivation: each vendor was a primary contractor somewhere, and ultimately responsible for seamless service to a major business site. This engendered co-dependence. A further feature was the use of framework agreements. These defined for each vendor the generic services provided, legal provisions, financial targets, margins, and performance review, quality and incentive practices. Each of the eight business sites then negotiated further with its IT suppliers for customized services. Suppliers then invoiced the sites who recovered costs from their business units. Costs were closely controlled:

> The three suppliers' books are open to us; they itemize all costs clearly in quarterly or annual invoices, distinguishing among direct, allocated, and corporate overhead costs charged to BPX ... Our agreement stipulates that we can audit our suppliers' accounts of services to us, if it is necessary—John Cross, Head of IT, BPX.

Contracts, measurement, and their regular updating were critical to managing the multiple suppliers. New performance contracts were negotiated each year. The performance metrics shifted from traditional

IT measures to a balanced scorecard approach to assessing service value. Thus suppliers came to be assessed not just on response and downtime, but on a weighted points system for areas of value to the business—for example financial management, innovation, customer focus, organizational learning. The results influenced the profit margins suppliers earned. A further feature was benchmarking:

> We retain with our outsourcing partners an agreement about benchmarking their performance, and also a requirement for them to employ best-in-class sub-contractors ... if you can demonstrate through benchmarking that someone else can do the job better, they will incorporate them as a sub-contractor—Contract Manager, BPX.

BPX also built risk/reward sharing into the agreements with suppliers. They were paid a remuneration agreed every year, but this could be increased. According to George Fish: 'they have a figure which we expect them to manage the cost for a year, just as an internal department does'.

However, if they achieved cost savings the results were split equally between BPX and the supplier responsible. Performance targets were set with each supplier every year. While negotiations over these took nearly two months in 1993, by 1998 this was down to a single day.

Notions of partnering ran through the management of the three vendors. This extended to IT policy, which was managed through a particular board with representatives from each vendor. Generally, policy was set in collaboration:

> BP has the right itself to set policy but generally we formulate it in collaboration. This is valuable, you get some good external views on what's sensible and what isn't ... They now understand our business well and can make very useful contributions—Senior Manager, BPX.

Retaining and Developing Skills

The deals also involved the transfer of about 150 staff in total, but the changes were larger than this. The company put in place, as part of the restructuring, a two-year program of human resource development in IT. This was to enhance the skills for the new IT world. As one contract manager commented in 1993:

> It's not feasible or even sensible to say we are going to throw away all the experience we've got and recruit a whole load of new people to perform the internal consultancy role.

At the start of the restructuring the company had about 750 people world-wide in IT and by 1998 they had slightly more than 150. Of these the largest number, about 90, were performing a business consultancy role, about 25 in a technology consultancy role, 25 in the role of contract and vendor management, and the remaining 10 in general IT management—each site, for example, having a regional manager. The in-house capabilities at this time are indicated in Figure 6.3. Working with vendors and the consultancy roles were seen as particularly important:

> We put people in the vendors' organizations for months, even years to help them understand our needs ... the in-house staff changed from a system delivery group to a consulting group which would question the need to have the system to begin with. They're expected to work from a global perspective. It took massive re-skilling—Larry Gahagan, Principal Consultant, BP.

Learning how to operate as a service and consultancy group in fact took a great deal of time. Another important emerging issue was the development of a more relationship-orientated type of management

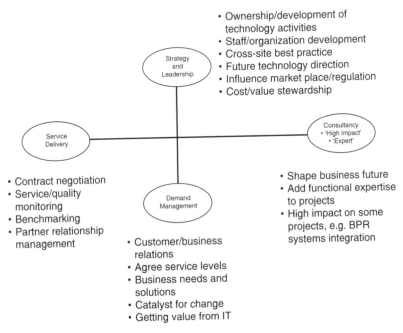

Figure 6.3   *BPX retained capabilities and skills*

style both amongst BPX and vendor staff, whilst ensuring that strict contractual elements and monitoring remained in place.

Emerging Issues 1995–1998

Clearly, over the years BPX put in place a number of key mechanisms and processes for managing multiple vendors. Difficulties did occur. In 1995 John Cross pointed to three challenges, some of which still existed in 1998. At the beginning, one supplier staffed the work mainly with ex-BP staff, resulting in no change to the service. Improvements came about when the supplier's middle managers at the relevant sites were changed. Another supplier failed to take new initiatives and worked as if in a traditional outsourcing relationship, continually looking to BPX and the contract for direction. A shift in the measurement regime away from cost reduction and on to business value and customer responsiveness helped both these situations.

As in any multi-vendor outsourcing, a perennial issue was to manage potential and actual conflicts between the partners. As well as needing to collaborate, the suppliers were also competitors for future business at BPX and elsewhere. One consequence was a reluctance to share best practice, learning, and information. Managing technical change amongst competing suppliers also proved difficult. As one example, in 1995 upgrading the telecommunications network meant the need for a set of common protocols. But:

> For competing suppliers, protocols are a battlefield. BP's adoption of one standard over another may affect the balance of either company's future business with us. If we did effectively choose one company over another, we would contradict our efforts to outsource our operations to multiple suppliers—John Cross, BP.

There were also further challenges where new vendors were added to the alliance, as for example happened in 1994 when CTG took over applications support for Alaska, while I-Net took over datacenters and IT services at Houston. Not only did these two new suppliers have to learn to work together, but they also needed to learn to work closely with the existing suppliers, since all their work inter-penetrated. While BPX's experience in dealing with multiple vendors helped in this, nevertheless a much more complicated set of relationships subsequently needed to be managed.

Effective working relationships between the BPX operating businesses and the IT providers developed over time as each got to understand the others' expectations and requirements. Up to 1998 the quality of the work and service had been rated highly on the performance measures that were in place and there were no serious disputes. John Cross pointed to greater flexibility in systems, higher quality service, declining costs, and the availability of technical skills and ideas that could no longer be developed inside BPX. However, there always remained the potential for conflicts as well as added value cooperation between suppliers and with BPX, and the mechanisms and retained skills would seem to be critical for their management. This became even more vital when the switching of costs out of total outsourcing and into recreating a fully operational in-house IT function had become so prohibitive that BPX would probably never even contemplate that option.

1998–2000: Revisions

In mid-1998 the contracts with SAIC, Syncordia (already renewed after the initial two years), and Sema Group came up for renewal. In fact the termination of these contracts coincided with a longer term plan to integrate IT, infrastructure, and processes across the Group. According to John Cross, by 1997 Group CIO:

> It's a very complex set of contractual processes that we are gradually beginning to rework and redefine. We are right in the process now (February 1997) of entirely reviewing all the outsourcing experiences we have. Time has moved on, our experiences and learning have moved on.

As one sign of future direction, and BP's search for integrated global services, by 1997 BT Syncordia had already become the world-wide telecommunications supplier for the BP Group as a whole, on a £110 million per annum contract.

A number of things emerged from the five-year experience. One was that while suppliers had been expected to optimize on costs, the main impulse behind outsourcing had not been cost reduction—most efficiencies had been achieved before 1993—but to re-engineer and refocus the IT function. In this BPX were very successful. Several suppliers had been too operational, and not strategic enough, in their thinking and behavior. All sometimes found it difficult to keep up with BPX's radically changing technology base and service demands. During the five years, for example, BPX moved to a Unix, Microsoft, NT, server-based IT platform. The suppliers also found it difficult to move to an increasingly globalized set of services.

At BPX the three suppliers were retained, but in some cases on much reduced contracts. At the same time the vendor alliance concept was dropped:

It's very difficult to get multi-vendors to work in alliance. We did look at it but didn't feel we would get the benefit of economies of scale, and of getting the innovation out of the suppliers . . . . We decided to go for the one-supplier option. We don't really have formal alliances any more, rather a loose relationship between the suppliers where we say to them you've got to work together, to sort specific issues out as they arise—Simon Lees, Commercial Development Manager, BP Chemicals.

There were two further developments in late 1998. In August BP took over Amoco for £30.3 billion, forming one of the top three groups in terms of oil and gas production, reserves, and refining capacity. This had some complicating implications for IT outsourcing strategy, though Amoco had previously not outsourced IT extensively. In the same month BP (not just BPX) confirmed that it was reversing its previous policy, and for the desktop was replacing its three outsourcing partners with EDS in a £180 million ($US300 million) five-year deal. Existing contracts would not be renewed as they ran out over the following 18 months. Among problems cited were 'fragmented service with differing quality in different geographic regions'. The aim was greater consistency and reliability. EDS was judged to be one of the few suppliers who, world-wide, could run 35 000 desktops, helpdesks, printers, and LANs without sub-contracting. The IT outsourcing deal was designed to support BP's drive to compete with Royal Dutch Shell and Exxon on a global basis. It also signaled the delivery of what was long known within BP—the need to get commonality across the Group, and now also across the newly merged entity.

Late 1998 and early 1999 were spent managing the handover of desktop infrastructure to EDS, and the development, for example, of several common helpdesks around the world offering 24-hour service. Subsequently the plan was to develop more global suppliers for specific sets of IT activities. BT Syncordia was already in charge of telecommunications world-wide (with a few exceptions), Sema Group was in the frame for managing datacenters, while several applications service suppliers were mooted, rather than one global one. The transition period, together with managing the IT implications of the BP Amoco merger, was sheduled to run from late 1998 to mid-2000.

Some feel for BP Amoco's position on outsourcing comes from two business process deals in 1999 and 2000. In June 1999 the company renewed a £63 million five-year deal with Andersen Consulting to run its finance and administrative services. This meant that the Group now had Andersen Consulting and PriceWaterhouseCoopers running separate parts of its financial operations, and its IT support, on a world-wide basis. Meanwhile in early 2000 BP Amoco signed a £400 million five-year deal for US-based start-up Exult to manage the whole of the merged company's Human Resource operations (including IT support).

ANALYZING RISK AND MULTI-SOURCING AT BP EXPLORATION

The 1993–1998 BPX case is an example of total outsourcing of IT with multiple suppliers, on two- to five-year contracts. The type and content of IT outsourcing were influenced by a number of factors. First, the overall philosophy and strategy of the company mandated a refocusing of internal attention on those activities perceived as 'core'—and this implied large-scale IT outsourcing. Second, the company desired to restructure and refocus IT on the business, and away from more traditional IT preoccupations. Third, BPX's previous experience of outsourcing suggested that a transaction-based relationship did not work, leading them to demand partnering relationships based on the sharing of risk and reward and including participation in policy-making. The sheer size of the company and the requirement to have more than one partner led to a consortium of partners that could work together. Looking at some of the more recent contracts discussed in this book, this may be a direction that many large organizations will explore and take more seriously in the future.

The risks experienced, and how they were mitigated at BPX, are outlined in Table 6.4. We will analyze the case further below, subsuming the points made in Table 6.4 into the argument, and also commenting on subsequent developments at BP Amoco and the implications of the Group's 1998–2000 approach.

Building on Experience

One key risk-mitigating factor throughout this case was BPX's ability to learn from experience. From the late 1980s to 1993 they built up their knowledge base on outsourcing through a selective and incremental approach with several suppliers. The learning built a knowledge platform and experience base from which they could move to the next stage of structuring and managing 'total' multiple-supplier outsourcing.

The learning from the 1993–1998 experiences, together with changing business requirements, also fed in some radical changes to subsequent outsourcing deals. The alliance model was abandoned as largely unworkable; the lower risk approach was direct relationships with each supplier, and beginning to segment IT activity into global slices, each to be managed by a single supplier with key capability in the

Table 6.4 *Risks and practices at BP Exploration*

Risk factors	Practices at BPX
1. IT treated as undifferentiated commodity	• Explicit core/non-core split • Retained value-creating activities—consultancy, information management, strategy, leadership, demand management, and monitoring • Outsourced technology infrastructure/applications/'doing' activities • Clear about what IT gives business advantage
2. Incomplete contracting	• Complete contract for five years (Syncordia two years, renewable) • Regular updating of performance/payment criteria • Service continuity in the event of termination guaranteed in contract *But* Lack of innovation and sharing of best practices
3. Lack of active management on (a) contract and (b) relationship dimensions.	• Active daily contact management • Regular business–supplier management reviews • Operational demand–supply relationships *But* • Demand managers became overwhelmed or were not of necessary quality in some regions. • Alliance basis created conflicts and need for a lot of refereeing
4. Failure to retain requisite capabilities and skills	• Business-facing technical know-how retained • Contract/service management capability • Demand management retained • Strategy and leadership retained *But* • Lacking in in-house IT strategy and technical fixing capability • Too few in-house 'high impact' consultants were of the necessary world-class quality

Continued

Table 6.4 *Continued*

Risk factors	Practices at BPX
5. Power asymmetries developing in favor of the vendor	• Dependence offset by multiple vendors on short-term contracts, and competitive situation. • Retained ownership of many technical assets • Well constructed and managed performance measures through SLAs
6. Difficulties in reconstructing/ adapting deals for business and technical change	• Resource price plus market mechanisms • Regular reviews of price/service/ requirement against market • Supplier performance/reward mechanisms • Five-year contracts • Contracts written around today's and future business *But* • Saw two generations of technology and major merger in six year period
7. Lack of maturity/experience of contracting and managing long-term 'total' outsourcing deals	• Built up experience of managing outsourcing in 1988–1992 period by selective outsourcing • Five-year contract and multiple suppliers • Keen, competitive price/service terms that incented suppliers on performance • Kept most key capabilities in-house while outsourcing technology tasks.
8. Short-term financial restructuring or cash injection rather than leveraging IT for business advantage	• Financial restructuring a major objective, but in the context of long-term business advantage on cost-competitive contract • Outsourcing allowed refocus from technology to growing the business— successful in this. *But* • Little technical innovation from suppliers
9. Unrealistic expectations about what can be achieved by outsourcing	• Careful delineation in contract of limited expectations from both client and supplier perspectives • Stabilized and updated the technology platform; move to desktop globally

	But
	• Many of the business leveraging activities expected from suppliers did not materialize
10. Poor sourcing and contracting for development and new technologies	• Contracting done quite well • Developed the desktop platform first before handing it over to EDS to manage
	But
	• Sometimes over-dependent on suppliers and sub-contractors in development and new technology area. • Before 1998 retained too few technical skills.

specified area. The other type of global slice ripe for outsourcing now was a 'commodity' business process with IT support—as in the case of accounting and finance and human resource functions.

Outsourcing: Type and Scope

BPX management turned away from a single-supplier long-term deal. They decided that no one supplier had a monopoly on the 'best-in-class' IT and services that BPX needed. At the same time the suppliers needed to have complementary capabilities and an ability to work with one another. BPX also consciously rejected long-term deals as too risky, seeing real risks in contracting too inflexibly for periods of considerable but unspecifiable business and technological changes. At the same time, BPX were careful to delineate 'core' IT activities relating to value creation, and retain these in-house, though there were subsequently question marks about some of the quality of those capabilities retained (see Figure 6.3).

By 1998 it was fairly clear that the switching costs of returning to a substantial in-house operation were far too prohibitive, thus closing off one path to subsequent risk mitigation, and adding further weight on BP's ability to scope, contract, and manage future IT sourcing strategy. However, the multi-sourcing strategy, though requiring more management—which BP showed every sign of being willing to build and maintain—also diffused risk by isolating supplier effects to specific activities, though, of course, supplier work necessarily overlapped at certain points.

Vendor Selection Criteria and Process

Suppliers were selected on their core capability to deliver specific types of service, but also on their ability and willingness to cooperate in an alliance, to drive down on costs, and to innovate and be proactive. BPX adopted an innovative, and effective, approach to selection by getting prospective suppliers to form bidding alliances, and, in some senses, to get the suppliers to select themselves. In all this BPX were especially thorough. Nevertheless, and as a demonstration of the risks in IT outsourcing, BPX managers subsequently commented on the reluctance of several suppliers in some regions to go beyond traditional fee-for-service type behavior, and a lack of innovation and strategic proactivity coming through. This, of course, puts even more pressure on in-house management to turn the expectations they have of suppliers into reality.

The Contracts

There were framework agreements standardized across all BPX regions, but further detailed contracts were also negotiated in each region. BPX's considerable experience in contracting led not only to detailed contracts, but also to regular updates in terms of service levels, price, expectations judged against market benchmarks, internal customer satisfaction, and changing business requirements. The contracts also incented the suppliers by rewarding exceptional performance by higher profit, and by sharing in any cost reductions achieved. Another vital element was flexibility:

> The deal was struck on the basis of BPX as a very dynamically changing organization, and every year we were going to need to redefine the nature of the services, the quantity, as well as the cost and quality. Building contracts on some fixed view of financial outgoings always strikes me as an extraordinary model because you have locked yourself into a cost base and structures that your organization may not want subsequently. We did not want the straitjacket of a predicted view of the future to set around ourselves—John Cross, CIO, BP.

The risk-mitigating practice here was to have regular reviews of every aspect of performance, price and requirement, and overall this proved an effective approach to incenting the supplier while keeping the contracts flexible in the face of market pricing, technical, and business changes. In a further risk-mitigating move, BPX also included detailed agreements for smooth transition in the event of termination or substantial change to contracts.

One of the problems in the contracts was lack of incentive for innovation on the part of suppliers. In the event, by 1997 an innovation fund had to be set up. This provided a pot of money which the client organization and suppliers could variously bid for. As a mechanism this achieved some, but not a significant, level of innovation.

Active Measurement and Management of Suppliers

Short-term contracts and detailed measurement and benchmarking with regular reviews and renegotiations were seen as vital elements in the regulation of performance and relationships. The measurement regimes put in at BPX proved robust and helped greatly in the process of managing supplier performance. The risk/reward deals, and mechanisms enhancing mutual activity and learning, contributed to developing relationships and fed through into enhanced IT service and business performance.

Post-contract management was less successful in its attempts to increase supplier motivation and reduce conflicts by getting vendors to manage themselves. There was no one primary contractor. All suppliers had a primary contractor role, and in theory this made them interdependent and induced cooperation rather than conflict amongst them.

In the event, this experiment was patchily successful. Respondents reported a lot of competitiveness and finger-pointing, frequent failures to share best practices and help one another, with BPX having to do quite a lot of refereeing between the parties. One account manager commented in retrospect that a better way of managing multiple suppliers would have been to have an independent supplier do this. Importantly, such a primary contractor should not be not part of service delivery to BPX, and it would need strategic consulting skills not normally possessed by traditional suppliers. In the event, from 1998 the BP Group went down another risk-mitigation route of managing each supplier directly.

Retained Capabilities and Skills

As we saw in the Polaris case, retained skills and management capabilities are critical, especially where, as at BP, switching costs continue to be so prohibitive that large-scale outsourcing is virtually irreversible.

Many new capabilities needed to be developed in this large-scale, multiple-vendor deal. This proved time-consuming. Because so much depended on these capabilities and skills, it was important to ensure that the few retained people were high performing (see Chapter 7). In Figure 6.3 we see a fairly sound theoretical perpective on what needed to be kept at BPX. Whereas on the whole this model worked to mitigate risk effectively, in practice it also ran into a number of problems worth highlighting:

- It is probable that BPX did not retain enough technical understanding and 'doing' capability to keep full control of its IT destiny, not just at the strategic but also at the operational day-to-day level.
- BPX tended to staff the new in-house positions with retained staff who did not always possess the requisite skills, orientations, attitudes, motivations, and behaviors. Staff development was high on the agenda, but nevertheless, as Chapter 7 will show, the person profiles needed to staff a high performing IT function of the sort BPX envisaged are distinctive and often quite different from those of more traditional IT staff. In retrospect, an influx of differently skilled staff might have been a more risk-mitigating policy.
- Demand or 'partner relationship' managers eventually had to be appointed at the different BPX sites in order to handle the rising problems of coordinating demand. Much depended on the quality of these individuals. As one BP manager put it subsequently: 'If X was in post, nothing much got done; but when he was replaced by Y, things really moved—much depended on the individuals in post. It applied to the supplier managers too.'
- The 'high impact' consultants were not always of the 'world-class' caliber required. There were few—up to 16—of them, and this made each one a core IT asset. Again high performers are required in such a retained IT function; without them, the risk of poor IT development and supplier control increases. In practice, charged with a brief to innovate, it was also the case that sometimes this group had the effect of stifling innovation that originated elsewhere in BPX or amongst suppliers.

CONCLUSIONS: LESSONS ON RISK MITIGATION IN IT OUTSOURCING

The two case studies in this chapter illuminate many of the key issues and concerns of managing outsourcing arrangements. There is no doubt, in our assessment, that both Polaris and BPX formed and operated successful IT outsourcing deals. The purpose of the chapter has been to learn from their experiences, build on their effective practices and find ways of improving their less successful ones.

We uncovered a range of risks relating to: outsourcing type and scope, vendor selection criteria and processes, the contract terms, measurement systems, retained capabilities and management processes, and vendor–client relationship processes. It was also clear that an ever present set of high risks that had to be managed related to often unanticipatable changes in business contexts and strategies, dynamic technical developments, and changes in IT services markets in terms of supplier capabilities, labor supply, and pricing. We delineated the ways in which these risks were mitigated either by conscious management planning and action or by a combination of circumstances and features.

The analytical framework proved to be sufficiently comprehensive to enable us to make sense of much of the rich data. Basically, Tables 6.3 and 6.4 show what generic and specific risk-mitigation practices Polaris and BPX adopted in order to be successful users of IT outsourcing for business advantage. However, discussing the cases in such detail has also enabled the identification of two further distinctive risk areas. The business contexts and the suppliers' capabilities and long-term market strategies also emerged as significant distinctive risks. In terms of developing the analytical framework, the evidence from our case analysis and related work by Willcocks and Lacity (1999a) is that supplier capability and long-term market strategy could be usefully added as a further distinctive risk area, as could business external and organizational contexts for the period contracted for. Both would receive endorsement from earlier work on IT project risks by Willcocks and Griffiths.[8]

In Figure 6.4 we put together a distillation of previous and current findings on the risks in IT outsourcing that have been emerging as distinctive and significant, as a guide for practitioners and for further research.

Some common themes emerge from reviewing the two case histories in this chapter. Effective risk mitigation for business advantage seems to result from applying the following lessons:

1. Polaris and BPX developed IT outsourcing strategies that had as twin goals the maximization of flexibility and control within changing business and technical and IT service market contexts. Neither focused merely on cost reduction, but sought multiple, business leveraging objectives that were not compromised by an undue focus on slimming supplier margins and achieving cost reductions (see also Chapters 4 and 5).

2. Both organizations possessed and retained the ability to make sourcing decisions and arrive at a long-term IT sourcing strategy, building in learning, and taking into account business, technical, and economic factors. Interestingly, on this front, while both took the total IT outsourcing route, each found sufficient effective practices and processes to mitigate the associated high risks.

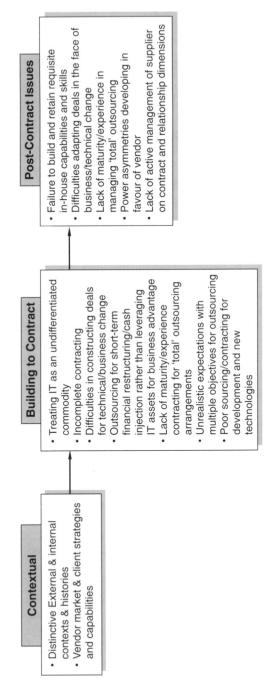

Figure 6.4 *IT outsourcing risk analysis framework*

3. Both organizations understood the IT services marketplace, the capabilities and weaknesses of relevant vendors, and what their business strategies were, and implied, in any likely IT outsourcing deal embarked upon. Even so, BPX still ran into some difficulties over unrealized expectations with some suppliers. Our research shows two proven practices here. First, informed buying is a core IT capability for all contemporary organizations (see Chapter 7). Second, organizations that invite both internal and external bids achieve success more often than organizations that merely compare a few external bids with current IT performance (see Chapter 4). If understanding supplier long-term market strategy is as widely neglected as some authors suggest,[9] it nevertheless emerges once more as a vital, risk-mitigating task.

4. Both Polaris and BPX had a strong capability to contract over time in ways that incent the supplier(s) and ensure that they got what they thought they agreed to. Chapter 4 showed that two proven practices here are that short-term (four years or less) contracts achieve success much more often than long-term contracts (seven years or more); and that detailed fee-for-service contracts achieve success more often than other types of contracts.

5. Both organizations also demonstrated the ability to post-contract manage across the lifetime of the deal in ways that secure and build the organization's IT destiny, and effectively achieve the required service performance and added value from the supplier. The evidence is that this is one of the weakest areas in IT outsourcing practice and is rarely adequately thought through at the front of outsourcing deals. Not surprisingly, some weaknesses became apparent even in the retained capabilities at Polaris and BPX. Typically, a minimum of nine core IS capabilities emerge as necessary in response to problems confronted during contract performance. As the next chapter will show, these cover leadership, informed buying, vendor development, contract facilitation, contract monitoring, technical fixing, architecture planning, relationship-building, and business systems thinking.

6. Both organizations had a strong perspective on and orientation towards getting the relationship dimensions right in their outsourcing deals. Kern and Willcocks (2000a,b) found that securing the mature client/supplier relationships we observe in the Polaris case is much more difficult in multiple-vendor situations such as at BPX, but their achievement becomes both an expression of, and a significant contribution to, effective risk mitigation in IT outsourcing (see also Chapter 8).

Organizations fail when they hand over IT without understanding its role in the organization, and what the vendor's capabilities are. One rule of thumb is: never outsource a problem, only an IT activity or set of tasks that a detailed contract and performance measures can be written for. Too many client companies see IT outsourcing as spending—and as little as possible—and ditching their problems, not managing. In fact IT outsourcing requires a great deal of in-house management, but of a different kind, covering elicitation and delivery of business requirements, ensuring technical capability, managing external supply, and IT governance. A cardinal insight from our research is that organizations still expect too much from vendors and not enough from themselves; or, put another way, vendors are still much better at selling IT services than their clients are at buying them. The two cases here show how to remedy these all too common fatal flaws. The next chapter describes a vital component of the remedy, namely the core IT capabilities necessary to mitigate the risks and manage any IT sourcing strategy.

NOTES

1. See, for example, Ang, S. and Straub, D. (1998). Production and Transaction Economies and IS Outsourcing: A Study of the US Banking Industry. *MIS Quarterly*, December, 535–542; Collins, T. (1999). End of the EDS Dream. *Computer Weekly*, October 28, pp 1, 22; Collins, T. and Phillips, S. (1999). Utility to Pull Plug on Perot Systems Deal. *Computer Weekly*, March 25, 1; Dempsey, M. (1999). Outsourcing Refusenik Enjoys His Vindication. *Financial Times—IT Review*, August 4, p. 3; Lacity and Willcocks (1996, 1998); Loh, L. and Venkatraman, N. (1992). Diffusion of Information Technology Outsourcing: Influence Sources and the Kodak Effect. *Information Systems Research*, **4**, no. 3, 334–358; Poston, T. (1997). Lloyds Ditches 50 Million Pound Outsourcing Contract. *Computer Weekly*, January 30, p. 1; Strassmann, P. (1998). *The Squandered Computer*. Information Economics Press, New Canaan: Thomas, K. and Schneider, K. (1997). Ernst and Young Scraps 45 Million Pound Model FM Deal. *Computer Weekly*, March 13, p. 1; Vowler, J. (1996). Management: Lessons in Outsourcing. *Computer Weekly*, 26.
2. See McFarlan, F.W. and Nolan, R. (1995). How to Manage an IT Outsourcing Alliance. *Sloan Management Review*, Winter, 9–23.
3. For software development see, as examples: Boehm, B. (1991). Software Risk Management: Principles and Practices, *IEEE Software*, January, 32–41: Charette, R. (1991). *Application Strategies for Risk Analysis*. McGraw-Hill, New York; Griffiths, C. and Newman, M. (eds) (1996). Risk Management and Information Systems. *Journal of Information Technology*, Special Issue, **11**, no. 4; Lyytinen, K., Mathiassen, L. and Ropponen, J. (1998). Attention Shaping and Software Risk: A Categorical Analysis of Four Classical Risk Management Approaches. *Information Systems Research*, **9**, no. 3, 233–255; Ropponen, J.

(1999). Risk Assessment and Management Practices in Software Development. In Willcocks, L. and Lester, S. (eds), *Beyond the IT Productivity Paradox*. Wiley, Chichester.

Examples for project management are: Keil, M. (1995). Pulling the Plug: Software Project Management and the Problem of Project Escalation: Morris, P. (1996). Project Management: Lessons from IT and Non-IT Projects. In Earl, M. (ed.) Information Management. Oxford University Press, Oxford; Willcocks, L. and Griffiths, C. (1996). Predicting Risk of Failure in Large-Scale Information Technology Projects. *Technological Forecasting and Social Change*, **47**, 205–228.

4. The main studies have been Earl, M.J. (1996). The Risks of Outsourcing IT. *Sloan Management Review*, **37**, no 3, 26–32; also Klepper, R. and Jones, W. (1998). *Outsourcing Information Technology, Systems and Services*. Prentice-Hall, New Jersey. Both are somewhat anecdotal in character. Ang, S. and Toh, S-K. (1998). Failure in Software Outsourcing: A Case Analysis. In Willcocks, L. and Lacity, M. (eds), *Strategic Sourcing of Information Systems*. Wiley, Chichester, provides a detailed case history of a failed software development project, and derived guidelines. Jurison, J. (1995). The Role of Risk and Return in Information Technology Outsourcing Decisions. *Journal of Information Technology*, **10**, no. 4, 239–247, provided a theoretical risk–return analytical model for making IT outsourcing decisions. Willcocks and Lacity (1999a) investigated risk-mitigation tactics in a single case history. Lacity and Willcocks (1998) derived risk-reduction guidelines from studying 40 organizations and their IT sourcing practices. Outside these, there are many other studies that deal with IT outsourcing but do not choose to focus on providing a comprehensive analysis of salient risks and/or risk-mitigation approaches.

5. See Ang and Straub (1998) *op cit.*; Ang, S. and Toh, S-K (1998). Failure in Software Outsourcing: A Case Analysis. In Willcocks, L. and Lacity, M. (eds), *Strategic Sourcing of Information Systems*. Wiley, Chichester; Auwers, T. and Deschoolmeester, D. (1993). The Dynamics of an Outsourcing Relationship: A Case Study in the Belgian Food Industry. Paper at the Outsourcing of Information Systems Services Conference, University of Twente, The Netherlands, May 20–22; Currie and Willcocks (1998); DiRomualdo, A. and Gurbaxani, V. (1998). Strategic Intent for IT Outsourcing. *Sloan Management Review*, **39**, no. 4, 1–26. Klepper and Jones (1998) *op. cit.*; Kumar and Willcocks (1999); Lacity, Willcocks and Feeny (1996); Thomas and Schneider (1997), *op. cit.*

6. Grover, V., M. J. Cheon, et al. (1995). Theoretical Perspectives on the Outsourcing of Information Technology. Working Paper, University of South Carolina, Columbia, 1–27; Kern and Willcocks, (2000a); Kirkpatrick, D. (1991). Why Not Farm Out Your Computer? *Fortune*, 73–78; McFarlan and Nolan (1995) *op. cit.*

7. The notable exceptions include Henderson, J.C. (1990). Plugging into Strategic Partnerships: The Critical IS Connection. *Sloan Management Review*, Spring, 7–18; Klepper, R. (1994). Outsourcing Relationships. In Khosrowpur, M. (ed.), *Managing Information Technology with Outsourcing*. Idea Group Publishing, Harrisburg, PA.; Klepper, R. (1995). The Management of Partnering Development in IS Outsourcing. *Journal of Information Technology*, **10**, no. 4, 249–258; McFarlan and Nolan (1995) *op. cit.*; Willcocks and Choi (1995).

8. See Willcocks, L. and Griffiths, C. (1996). Predicting Risk of Failure in Large-Scale Information Technology Projects. *Technological Forecasting and Social Change*, **47**, 205–228.
9. This is a very under-researched area. Two useful sources are: Michell, V. and Fitzgerald, G. (1997). IT Outsourcing, Vendor Selection and the Vendor Marketplace. *Journal of Information Technology*, September. Also Kern and Willcocks (2000b).

7
Preparing for Outsourcing: The Core IT Capabilities Framework

The concept of your IT person being part of the management of the company, not just a technician sitting on the sidelines, is something that, in fact, keeps you from outsourcing certain roles—Vice President of IS, US Petroleum Company.

... A building doesn't change its basic purpose over 20 years, whereas with IT it is only for at most three years. And there is a much closer relationship between the business and the technology. Other services you might procure are not as dynamic. But there still is this perception that you can manage IT contracts like any other contracts—Contract Administrator, Australian Government Agency.

We originally identified these as non-core and targets for outsourcing. But, in fact, our applications support people have an understanding of the business, and of the specific applications context, that amounts to a core IT competency...—Technical Director, B&Q.

INTRODUCTION

Over the last decade, shaping and staffing the IT function has presented a perennial, often intractable set of issues. By 2001 the continuing problems related to dynamic changes in the wider global and national economies, increased competitive pressures in most sectors, together with cost-containment drives, mergers and acquisitions, rapid developments in information-based technologies, and regular reorganizations and organizational changes to anticipate or react to fluctuating markets and financial results. In all this much of the pressure comes from the constant fire-fighting. Thus, a 1999 study of more than 220 companies found that the millennium bug, supporting existing systems, upgrading legacy systems and infrastructure investments were all ongoing priority issues. As a result:

> if strategies are to be delivered, companies must rethink the way IT is structured and managed. Otherwise, with the best will in the world, highly skilled IT personnel will still be unable to move away from their day-to-day support role and focus on innovations for the future.[1]

In the face of these pressures, one concern has been to restructure the IT function.[2] The degree of centralization has been a prime subject of debate, and, in search of balance, many IT functions have regularly been moved up and down the centralization–decentralization continuum to reflect specific contingencies. Throughout the last decade IT has also become variously a corporate service, an internal bureau, a business venture, and, in the 1990s, the subject of various degrees of outsourcing. In large complex organizations we found the federal structure the major trend in configuration in the early 1990s. An important finding by Hodgkinson (1996) was the need for the structure of the IT function to reflect, and not be in tension with, that of the wider organization.[3]

Another ongoing concern has been with the difficult task of aligning business and IT/IS strategies.[4] However, even where achieved, such alignment has seemed to have had little effect on the catalog of implementation problems revealed in a range of studies. One research-based explanation suggested by Walton (1989) and Willcocks and Currie (1997) has been the frequent lack of follow-through on alignment from strategy through the development and implementation stages into routine operations. Other reasons cited for implementation difficulties include poor project management, slow systems development methods, and lack of line management involvement in the implementation process.[5]

A further piece in the jigsaw of explanation has been referred to as the 'culture gap' between IT and the business. Closing the gap means working on both bringing the business closer to IS, and IS closer to the business. Particular areas of study here have been the central role played by CEO/CIO relationships; the advantages gained from bridge-building mechanisms; user–IS co-location and joint working processes; and the need to reshape skill mixes, including the development and role of hybrid managers.[6]

In rethinking these strands, it becomes clear that restructuring, strategic alignment, improving project management expertise, providing better development tools and methodologies, and making line managers/users more responsible for IT, and more IT literate, are necessary but not sufficient conditions for successful IT. In particular, we note two further points. First, the focus of attention has shifted from structuring the IT function towards issues of IT–user relationships, processes, and skills. Second, a particularly neglected area is that of capabilities and skills within IT functions themselves. Our research over the last five years has focused on these missing, critical, and essentially human resource elements in the equation—the capabilities and skills required to run a business-value-adding IT function.

A focus on key capabilities and skills reflects a resource-based approach to how organizations can survive, pursue stakeholder objectives, and compete. Early exponents of the theme of competitive advantage and strategic necessity through IT tended to adopt positioning frameworks for locating the role of IT; by implication the supportive role of the IT function was to deliver the systems required.[7] Latterly, we have seen more resource-based theories applied to how effective IT can be developed and sustained.[8] This fits with moves in the broader strategy and organization literature toward resource-based theories and notions of core competence.[9]

In practice top management are seen to be debating whether IT is core or non-core/peripheral to the future of their business; and what arrangements for IT best reflect their analysis. However, an uneasy juxtaposition of concepts bedevils this debate. For example, as we have seen, large IT outsourcing deals are signed but regularly labeled 'strategic partnerships', recognizing that IT exploitation remains a 'critical', but somehow 'non-core', element in the future of the business. Here we argue that resource-based theory needs to be unequivocally applied not just to the organization but also to the IT function itself. In doing this a key, but neglected, question is produced; namely, which IT capabilities are core to the business's future capacity to exploit IT successfully?

Here we address this issue in the context of delivering an IT sourcing strategy. First, we detail the major contextual pressures shaping IT functions in the last five years. In the light of these pressures, we develop a perspective on the emerging shape of the IT function. The key capabilities and skills are then detailed. Here IT capability will refer to an assembly of skills, techniques, and know-how developed over time that enable an organization to acquire, deploy, and leverage IT investments in pursuit of business strategies. The challenges and implications of developing and applying these capabilities and skills will be discussed, and related to the issue of sourcing IT capability.

PRESSURES ON THE IT FUNCTION

Before examining these core capabilities and skills, it is important to understand in more detail the key forces that are shaping their development. There are four main pressures, and we see no let up in these over the 2000–2004 period. The first is the increasing business reliance on information technologies that are subject to rapid change. In some industries the IT infrastructure is becoming almost synonymous with the organization structure. As one CIO at a major bank commented: 'If the bank was without its major IT systems for 24 hours we would go out of business.'

As IT penetrates to the core of operations, so its reliability, the speed with which IT solutions can be delivered, and understanding of new technologies and their potential application, become business critical. The growth of business process re-engineering—remembering that moves to e-business imply a new bout of re-engineering and what has been described as 're-engineering on steroids'—has also concentrated minds. Research, by ourselves and others, shows that IT is regarded as a key enabler of the process-based organization. Within these trends, IT delivery and support become key performance indicators for the IT function.

Second, successive recessions, allied from the mid-1990s with intensive competition across sectors, have led to pressures for cost containment and headcount reductions together with ever more concern for IT to demonstrate the business value it represents.

Third, there is evidence of a long-term shift in the way organizations are configured and managed. In pursuit of 'core competence' strategies, an increasing number of firms, and indeed governments, have sought to apply the principles embedded in a core–periphery model of functioning (for a strong example, see BP Exploration in Chapter 6). An organization, it is argued, can only be effective at a few core activities, and should concentrate on developing these to world class. Anything else should be eliminated, minimized, or outsourced. This raises important questions about whether the whole, or parts, of the IT function itself are perceived as core or support. On applying the core competence concept to the IT function at BP Exploration (part of BP Amoco), an IT manager commented:

> It's a method of rebuilding the focus of your organization so that you focus on what is important to the company, and not what's important to the traditional IT world.

As earlier chapters have shown, a related fourth trend has been the growing number, size, and maturity of external IT services providers.

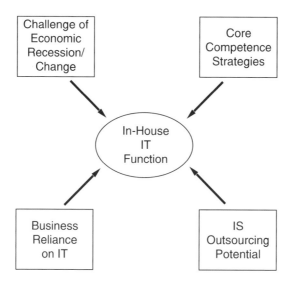

Figure 7.1 *Forces shaping the future IT function*

Senior executives have been attracted by the outsourcing potential for IT, driven by supplier promises of up to 40% IT cost reductions, the 'bandwagon' effect, disappointment with in-house performance, skills shortages, the need to do things quickly, and the desire to focus on core activities in difficult economic and competitive climates. Earlier chapters have shown that selective IT outsourcing in particular can realize a range of financial, business, and technical advantages for organizations, provided it is carefully entered into and managed.

These trends raise key related issues of performance, business value, relevance, and alternative sourcing that provide considerable challenges for more traditional IT functions (Figure 7.1).

This chapter provides an extensive review of our thinking on the multiple capabilities and skills mix that organizations require to manage successfully over time the supply and demand for IT services. Our research leads us to conclude that, in the face of the trends and challenges outlined above, a critical emerging need is for the development of what later we call the 'high performance' IT function.

THE EMERGING CORE IT CAPABILITIES MODEL

The view presented here of core IS capabilities and the 'high performance' IT function has been developed from several strands of research carried out in the 1992–2000 period.[10] In reviewing this research, organizations seemed to be converging on core capabilities concepts from two different directions. Some organizations can be characterized as starting with the principle that IT is to be outsourced, and the main question was: 'What if any capability should be retained in house?' These organizations tended to have particular insights into the various capabilities required to contract for and manage externally provided IT services. By contrast, other organizations had worked from the premise that IT represents an important strategic resource, and focused their analysis on what must exist to ensure their continuing ability to exploit it. These latter organizations tended to have sharper insights into the capabilities required to understand and articulate business-driven IT needs, and those that relate to developing the appropriate technical platform. They were often less sophisticated in their definition of supply management capabilities even though they often accepted that much IT service would become externally sourced in the fullness of time. By synthesizing the learning that was being achieved from these two different start points, we can provide a rich picture of the core capabilities required in IT functions in the new decade.

The first step in the synthesis is represented by Figure 7.2. Here we present the four faces of the target, or emergent, IT function. We will present this model followed by the nine key research-derived capabilities that populate it, and then discuss the implications and challenges this form of IT function represents. Some points on terminology are in order. Throughout we employ a working definition of the IT function as the set of activities, personnel, and IT assets set up to define and ensure delivery of the IS requirements of the business. Of course, such a function will be variously structured, physically located, and staffed within different organizations. Figure 7.2 represents a development from existing terminology in the IT literature. Following Earl (1996), and in a continuation from previous work where the conceptual clarification proved consistently useful, we now distinguish between information management (IM), information systems (IS), and information technology (IT) strategies.[11] Additionally, the growth in IT outsourcing in the 1990s, together with a maturing and expanding IT service market, leads us to make explicit the need for an IT/IS sourcing strategy and supportive capabilities within the contemporary organization. Some brief description of these four faces, or tasks, is now provided.

- The business 'face' is concerned with the elicitation and delivery of business requirements. The domain of *Information Systems Strategy*, capabilities here are business-focused, demand-led, and concerned with defining the systems to be provided, their relationship to

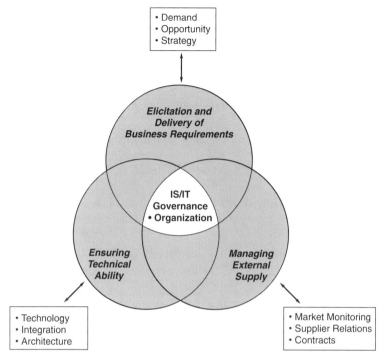

Figure 7.2 *Four 'faces', or tasks, of the emerging IT function*

business needs and, where relevant, the inter-relationships and inter-dependencies with other systems. A further focus here is a strategy for delivery, together with actual IS implementation

- The technical 'face' is concerned with ensuring that the business has access to the technical capability it needs—taking into account such issues as current price/performance, future directions and integration potential. This is the domain of *Information Technology Strategy* that is defining the blueprint or architecture of the technical platform that will be used over time to support the target systems. IT presents the set of allowable options from which the technical implementation of each system must be selected. A further concern is to provide technical support for delivery of the IT strategy.

- The 'governance' face is concerned with *Information Management Strategy*, which defines the governance and coordination of the organization's IT/IS activity. It elaborates such issues as:
  — the role/mission of IS/IT within the business;
  — the respective responsibilities of IS/IT and business staff in achieving that role;

— the people and processes involved in the creation of the IS strategy to support the business;

— the people and processes involved in achieving the chosen approach to systems implementation;

— the principles which should guide the development of IT strategy;

— the processes that will be used to evaluate any proposals for IS/IT investment or services;

— the purpose and scope of any standards which should apply to IS/IT activity.

- The supply 'face' encompasses the understanding and use of the external IS/IT services market; its activity is driven by decisions about the sourcing of activity. As such it is the domain of *IT/IS Market Sourcing Strategy*. Particularly critical here are decisions on what to outsource and insource, on which external suppliers to use and how. A further concern is ensuring appropriate delivery of external services contracted for.

REQUISITE CAPABILITY IN THE EMERGING IT FUNCTION

In this section we further develop the model of the future IT function by detailing nine capabilities required to render it dynamic and fully operational. These capabilities, expressed as roles, are shown in Figure 7.3. It should be noted that the nine capabilities populate seven spaces. As will emerge, these spaces are not accidentally arrived at. Three are essentially business, technology or service facing. One is a lynchpin governance position covered by two capabilities (see Figure 7.3— Leadership and Informed Buying). Finally, there are three spaces that represent various interfaces between the three faces. The capabilities that populate these spaces are crucial for facilitating the integration of effort across the three faces. We now move to detailing each of the nine capabilities.

Capability 1—IS/IT Governance

Integrating IS/IT effort with business purpose and activity.

At the heart of Figure 7.3, in the overlapped space of the three faces, is the need for effective IS/IT governance. Effective IS/IT leaders devise the organizational arrangements—structures, processes, and staffing—to address each challenge area and manage their interdependencies.

BUSINESS and IT VISION

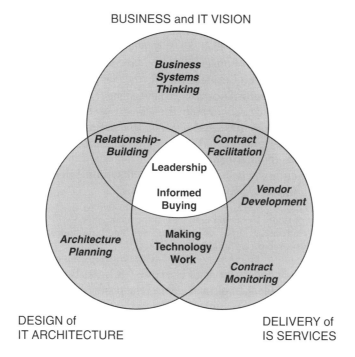

DESIGN of
IT ARCHITECTURE

DELIVERY of
IS SERVICES

Figure 7.3 *Nine capabilities in the emerging IT function*

They set goals and direction in each area. Leaders also influence the overall business perception of IT's role and contribution, and establish strong business/IT relationships at the executive level and leverage those relationships to achieve a shared vision of IT. At the same time leaders determine the values and culture of the IT function and instill the belief that an IT staff's first duty is to contribute to the business.

Leadership is of course the traditional role of the CIO or Director of IT, although the future of that role is sometimes questioned. But our experience consistently reinforces our colleague David Feeny's view that the CIO is personally instrumental in organizational exploitation of IT, whether the IT is outsourced or not. Consider the example of East Midlands Electricity in the United Kingdom (UTILITY6) (Full details of all case studies can be found at our web site: http://www.umsl.edu/ ~lacity/cases.htm). In 1992 the company outsourced its IT department and transferred almost the entire computer staff of 230 people in a 12-year, £230 million deal with Perot Systems. In 1995 senior managers accepted that systems were critical to the evolution of the company's business strategy as East Midlands sought to implement major new client/server systems.

The company recognized the need for a high-performance CIO to provide the necessary IT/IS leadership and manage the new IT organization. According to Andy Halford, the new Group IS Director, his job was to 'strengthen the in-house resource . . . recognizing just how critical IT is going to be to the business during the next two to three years'. Then Managing Director, Norman Askew, believed that rebuilding the in-house team would also enable the company to improve control, revise the IS/IT strategies, and review the sourcing approach with Perot Systems. He remarked: 'You cannot outsource these things and then not manage them adequately.'

A complementary view was put by a senior IT manager of a petroleum refining company (PETRO2):

> The concept of your IT person being part of the management of the company, not just a technician sitting on the sidelines, is something that, in fact, keeps you from outsourcing certain roles.

The precise role and qualities of effective CIOs has been the source of much debate. In Table 7.1 below we detail the profile of the CIO required to lead a fully operational 'high performance' IT function. Later we will discuss how organizations can evolve into this model over time, and the different types of CIO required at different stages to facilitate this process.

Table 7.1   *Capabilities and skills in the emerging IT function*

| Capability | Exhibited behaviours in role | Skills | | | Drivers |
		Technical	Business	Inter-personal	
1. IS/IT Governance	• Establishes and maintains executive relationships • Strives to achieve shared and challenging vision of role of IT in the business • Develops the culture and orientation of the IT/IS function • Searches for and promotes best practice in information management	Medium	High	High	• Adding value to the business • High concern for acceptance and exploitation of IT • Continuous business and personal development
2. Business Systems Thinking	• Contributes to development of business strategy and operation • Identifies/communicates current patterns of organization and activity • Envisions potential new patterns • Identifies connections and inter-dependencies	Low/Medium	High	Medium/High	• Adding value to business • Holistic understanding • Innovation/creativity

Table 7.1   *Continued*

Capability	Exhibited behaviours in role	Skills			Drivers
		Technical	Business	Inter-personal	
3. Business-IT Relationship Building	• Develops user understanding of potential of IT • Helps users and IT specialists to communicate and work together • Ensures user ownership and satisfaction	Medium/High	Medium	High	• Adding value to the business • Curiosity about individual personalities and motivations • Concern to achieve progress
4. Designing Technical Architecture	• Analyses trends in development of a range of technologies • Develops vision of integrated technical platform • Formulates policies to ensure necessary integration and flexibility of IT services	High	Low/Medium	Medium	• Fascinated by new technologies • Holistic thinking and design • acceptance as technology thought leader
5. Making Technology Work	• Focused on action and problem-solving • Understands internal design of IT systems • Delivers very high programming productivity • Comfortable with wide range of technical regimes	High	Low	Medium	• Hobby as work • Getting the right result • Recognition for professional prowess • Freedom to perform
6. Informed Buying of IT Service	• Monitors available services of external suppliers • Analyses nature of service requirements for immediate and longer term • Structures tendering process • Oversees contract negotiations	Medium	High	High	• Understanding bargaining structures • Involvement in negotiating • Achieving hard but fair results
7. Contract Facilitation	• Facilitate/manage people relationships • Devise/pursue processes for conflict resolution • Interpret business and technical issues within established contract framework	Medium	Medium	High	• Achieving day-to-day progress • Building and sustaining partnerships • Protecting business interests
8. Contract Monitoring	• Monitoring results against goals • Benchmarking existing contracts against developing market capability • Negotiating detailed amendments • Identifying/protecting against potential precedents	Medium	Medium	Low/Medium	• Delight in detail • Focus on hard measures • Professional standards and networking

Table 7.1   *Continued*

Capability	Exhibited behaviours in role	Technical	Business	Inter-personal	Drivers
9. Vendor Develop-ment	• Analyses emerging structure of services market • Assess specific vendors – goals and capabilities • Explores potential for new vendor services • Identifies opportunities for added value to business and vendor	Medium	High	Medium	• Innovation • Potential from partnership • Industry analysis orientation

The "Skills" heading spans Technical, Business, Inter-personal columns.

Capability 2—Business Systems Thinking

Envisioning the business process which technology makes possible.

We are frequently told that business thinking should precede consideration of technology; that processes must be redesigned before being automated. The truth is more complicated. Business processes should be redesigned in the light of technology potential. Within the exclusive space of Figure 7.3's business face, the key capability needed is the business systems thinking which brings together ideas of business strategy and technology application. In best practice organizations, business systems thinkers from the IT function are important contributors to teams charged with business problem-solving, process re-engineering, and strategic development. The information systems strategy emerges from these teams' recommendations, with the technology components of solutions to business issues already having been identified.

Consider as one example the role of the vice president of IT in US oil major Texaco:

> Our Operating Committee are the top executives in the business. They are making decisions outside the IT world. And they look to my expertise, my management expertise and my knowledge of technology to help them make the right decisions.

Companies that have this capability, such as a major retailer in our research, automatically include IT as an equal partner in every significant business development initiative. By contrast, in a large aerospace business, the CIO was frustrated at her inability to get IT representation in any of the business process re-engineering task-forces underway. The managers planned to involve the IT group later, after the primary thinking and design were complete, and the CIO could not convince them that any of her staff could contribute at a more formative stage.

Such neglect can be disastrous for projects involving external suppliers. Thus, in the late 1990s one major insurance company we studied contracted a major supplier to deliver a strategic IT system aimed at transforming administrative and customer service systems. Despite warnings from a person with, in fact, business systems thinking skills and know-how, that the project needed to be conceived as a re-engineering rather than a largely IT project, that the supplier did not have enough insurance understanding, and that the business needed to take more responsibility itself, the supplier was given most responsibility and set aggressive deadlines. In the event the supplier failed to deliver detailed business requirements on time, and the project was cancelled at the first milestone after nine months.

Capability 3—Relationship-Building

Getting the business constructively engaged in IS/IT issues.

While the business systems thinker is the individual embodiment of integrated business/IS/IT thinking, the relationship-builder facilitates the wider dialogue between business and IT communities. Specifically, relationship-building involves developing users' understanding of IT's potential, helping users and IT specialists to work together, and ensuring users' ownership and satisfaction. Extensive research has pointed to the difficulty in achieving this dialogue and has referred to the culture gap between 'techies' and 'users'. While this gap can develop in delivering IT services, we have found the most important contribution of relationship-building to be in the creation of mutual confidence, harmony of purpose, and successful communication amongst those focused on the business and technical agendas. Through education (of both sides) and facilitation, the relationship-builders bring together in constructive dialogue people who previously found it difficult to talk to each other. In many instances, a single individual has transformed the relationship between an area of the business and the IT function. As a departmental head in one retailer commented: 'Things are quite different now: we feel our new contact point with IT is really one of us'.

Capability 4—Architecture Planning

Creating the coherent blueprint for a technical platform which responds to present and future business needs.

Designing technical architecture, or IT strategy, is the main task within the technical face. The principal challenge to the architect is, through insight into technology, suppliers and business directions, to anticipate technology trends so that the organization is consistently able to operate from an effective and efficient platform—without major investment in energy-sapping migration efforts. Planners shape what has been called the IT infrastructure and what increasingly may well be known as the e-business infrastructure.[12] They do this through developing the vision of an appropriate technical platform, and through formulating associated policies that ensure necessary integration and flexibility in IS/IT services across the firm.

Quite a number of study organizations assumed that, having made recent commitments to a largely outsourced environment, the task of architecture planning was now one for the suppliers. Examples have also been found—in the face of lack of skills and the need to do something quickly—for outsourcing this task in e-business projects as well. However, without in-house expertise, a company cannot understand the viability of addressing new demands or the potential for meeting existing demands on a new technology platform with better economics. Nor will an external supplier place priority on moving to a lower-cost platform, unless it results in higher profits, rather than lower revenues, for the supplier. Consider the following comment by the Contract Administrator for a major government outsourcing contract (PSB5):

> You shouldn't outsource technical architecture. Let's take our supplier. They have a standard operating environment and a global roll-out. As it turns out in our situation, they happen to overlap, like *MS Office* on their desktop. But if you go to a different organization you may not have that synergy. They are going to take your architecture where their business is going, not where you want to go ... It is dangerous to let all your architects go ... and we have an exposure there, and now (1998) I am skilling up my group to build an expertise that can keep up. It's probably most contentious in the mainframe area—suppliers want vanilla and customers want chocolate, and we even have discussions on the supplier's standards, including their standard security environment which is not our preferred one.

By comparison, in a successful total outsourcing deal renewed for three years (and again subsequently) a multinational glass manufacturer (GLASS) retained the skills to identify and manage the common standards required to achieve inter-relationships and efficiencies across its businesses.

Capability 5—Making Technology Work

Rapidly achieving technical progress—by one means or another.

Operating in the overlap between the challenges of IT architecture design and delivery of IT services is the core capability of making technology work. The technical fixer requires much of the insight of an architecture planner, together with a pragmatic and short-term orientation. In today's environment of highly complex, networked, multi-supplier systems, the technical fixer makes two critical contributions: to rapidly troubleshoot problems that are being disowned by others across the technical supply chain; and to identify how to address business needs which cannot be properly satisfied by standard technical approaches. Fixers who excel are highly productive in programming and can work within a wide range of technical regimes because of their understanding of IT's fundamentals (rather than specifics).

The need to retain high quality technical 'doing' capability was widely recognized amongst the organizations we studied. Thus UK retailer The Kingfisher Group consists of leading retailers Woolworths, B&Q, and Comet. B&Q (RETAIL7) was the last to outsource its aging mainframe operations in a three-year deal signed in 1996. Its objective was to free internal IT staff to refocus on building and deploying midrange and distributed client/server systems. Following his own experiences the IT Director of Woolworths advised B&Q to retain in-house technical skills to deliver applications development and support related to the mainframe environment. According to B&Q technical director Pete Hanson:

> We originally identified these as non-core and targets for outsourcing. But, in fact, our applications support people have an understanding of the business, and of the specific applications context, that amounts to a core IT competency. After outsourcing, the company also found that it had to put even more effort into technical interface tasks.

Organizations that successfully totally outsourced IT also recognized the need to retain key technical skills. Thus, Alan Pollard, in charge of a five-year deal at the British Army's Logistics IS Agency (LOGIST), commented:

> We can't retain too much skill because we will be paying twice for it. But we are retaining a modicum in the systems analysis and requirements definition area, and for rapid application development and prototyping and hybrid skills, for example. There can be a flaw in any outsourcing, if you are actually outsourcing your basic, core skill. There will come a time when you can no longer call yourself an intelligent customer, unless, in some way, you are growing the seed corn of tomorrow's intelligence.

Capability 6—Informed Buying

> Managing the IS/IT sourcing strategy which meets the interests of the business.

A second core IT capability that overlaps all three challenges is informed buying. It involves analysis of the external market for IT services; selection of a sourcing strategy to meet business needs and technology issues; and leadership of the tendering, contracting, and service management processes. In an organization that has decided to outsource most of its IT service, the informed buyer is the most prominent role behind that of the CIO. One respondent described their role in this way:

> If you are a senior manager in the company and you want something done, you come to me and I will ... go outside, select the vendor and draw up the contract with the outsourcer, and if anything goes wrong it's my butt that gets kicked by you.

By 1994, Philips Electronics (ELECTRIC1) had 'totally' outsourced its IT. The arrangements have proved successful. One development was to push informed buyers, with IT, management and contract skills, into the businesses:

> Philips have got control of their IT through business-based IT managers who are absolutely critical ... they are now responsible for buying IT products and services from our two preferred suppliers.

Even companies that retain 80% or more IS/IT activity in-house recognize the importance of informed buying. Typically, as spending on outside services gets closer to 20% of the IT budget, the informed buying capability develops and becomes separate from the CIO role. There are two trends here. First, business managers require reassurance that the in-house option is truly appropriate and competitive compared with external options. Second, where datacenters and other operational activities are consolidated to achieve efficiencies, informed buyers will underpin in-house services with more explicit, quasi-contractual agreements.

Capability 7—Contract Facilitation

Ensuring the success of existing contracts for IS/IT services.

Arrangements for the delivery of IT services are complex. Typically a large population of users within the business are receiving a variety of services from multiple supply points in detailed, lengthy service agreements. Contract facilitation operates in the overlap between Figure 7.3's business and supply faces, trying to ensure that problems and conflicts are seen to be resolved fairly and promptly within what are usually long-term relationships. It is an action-oriented capability. If service agreements and suppliers were perfect, contract facilitation would not be a core IT capability. But as one interviewee noted:

They [users] have been bitten a few times when they have dealt directly with suppliers, and it's a service we can provide, so now we do.

In our experience, both users and suppliers place high value on effective contract facilitators. The role arises for a variety of reasons:

- to provide one-stop shopping for the business user;
- the supplier or user demands it;
- multiple suppliers need coordinating;
- it enables easier monitoring of usage and service; and
- users may demand too much and incur excessive charges.

Although contract facilitation is sometimes set up to manage excessive user demand and cost overruns with suppliers, in general it is a coordinating role. But a fundamental task would seem to be that of managing expectations on all sides. As a supplier Account Executive in the BAE–CSC deal (see Chapter 2) explained:

Overall, I think statistically, if you look at things in terms of performance against SLAs, we are meeting the terms and conditions of the contract, but I think there is an expectation within the customer that is much higher than what the contract actually states.

The role of contract facilitation in such situations is demonstrated by this manager commenting on the UK Inland Revenue Service deal with EDS (see Chapter 2):

There is always some hot spot somewhere that's not working entirely the way either side is expecting. And usually it's a misunderstanding of what people can expect from the contract and relationship. So once you get in there, it's not always difficult to find some way to improve the relationship. It's just that you don't always know until there is a bit of a stand-off.

Capability 8—Contract Monitoring

Protecting the business's contractual position, current and future.

As organizations exploit the burgeoning external market for IT services, contract monitoring becomes a core IT capability. While the contract facilitator is working to 'make things happen' on a day-to-day basis, the contract monitor is ensuring that the business position is protected at all times. Effective contract monitoring involves holding suppliers to account against both existing service contracts and the developing performance standards of the services market. It enables the production of a 'report card' for each supplier that highlights their achievement against external benchmarks and the standards in the contract.

While all our outsourcing case study companies recognized contract monitoring as a core IT capability, we found that they frequently underestimated the extent and nature of the task. Following a major outsourcing deal in the defence industry, an IT manager in the company commented:

> We need a significant number of people in-house to monitor vendor service performance. In one business unit alone we have 16 people working on contracts, six exclusively on the monitoring side. Admittedly we are still in the settling-in period, but I can't see the work declining that much.

In a 1995 'total' outsourcing deal in Australia, the Contract Administrator commented in 1999:

> Some people think that managing an IT contract is like managing a cleaning or building contract. But a building doesn't change its basic purpose over 20 years, whereas with IT it is only for at most three years. And there is a much closer relationship between the business and the technology. Other services you might procure are not as dynamic. But there still is this perception that you can manage IT contracts like any other contracts.

Nor would it seem that the role is about merely monitoring a static contract. According to one contract manager (AERO2):

> We've come to the conclusion that actually it has to be a much more dynamic, moving, changing thing rather than a set-in-stone thing. We've been jointly working (client and vendor) to realign the mechanisms so that they produce the results more in keeping with what we went after. But the important factor is that we anticipate to do the same thing in two to three years time, and then two to three years after that. Not because we got it wrong, but because of the changes in technologies and user requirements.

Capability 9—Supplier Development

Identifying the potential added value of IT service suppliers.

The single most threatening aspect of IT outsourcing is the substantial switching costs. To outsource successfully requires considerable organizational effort over an extended period of time. In one case, it took more than 50 person-years to arrive at a contract for a 10-year deal worth around $US700 million. Sizable implementation requirements followed. To subsequently change suppliers may require equivalent effort. Hence it is in the company's interest to maximize the contribution of existing suppliers, and also, when outsourcing, to guard against what we call 'mid-contract sag'. A supplier may be meeting the contract after two or more years, but none of the much talked-about added value of outsourcing materializes. As one IT Services Director commented in an aerospace company:

> Yes [the supplier] can achieve all the things that were proposed—but where is this famous 'added-value service'? We are not getting anything over and above what any old outsourcer could provide.

As the contract manager in a major US bank commented after his firm consolidated and outsourced its datacenters:

> Sure, the suppliers deliver the contract, but to the letter. They've incurred only one penalty in more than two years. But trying to get them to identify the added value we both talked about at the beginning, let alone deliver it, is very difficult. They've had changes in management staff, so they are driven by what is written down rather than by some of our initial understandings.

In supplier development, organizations look beyond existing contractual arrangements to explore the long-term potential for suppliers to create the 'win–win' situations in which the supplier increases its revenues by providing services that increase business benefits. A major retail multinational (RETAIL4) has many ways to achieve this, including an annual formal meeting:

> It's in both our interests to keep these things going and we formally, with our biggest suppliers, have a meeting once a year and these are done at very senior levels in both organizations. There are certain things we force on our suppliers, like understanding our business and growing the business together ... and that works very well.

CAPABILITIES, HIGH PERFORMANCE AND CONTINGENCIES

We have established that there are nine capabilities that can be identified for any effective future in-house IT function. We have briefly described the nine with reference to their roles in delivering the four overlapping tasks of Figure 7.2. But are there contingencies that make different capabilities more, or less important? Earlier we flagged that the emerging IT function would also seem to need to be a high performance function. High performance is mainly a function of who is recruited and their ability to work together as a team. But one initial finding is that the high performance IT concept properly embraces all nine capabilities. What has been interesting in the research is the degree to which when a particular capability is missing or is stretched across too few people, pressure arises pushing towards the full complement of capabilities and skills. For example, a common tendency when outsourcing is to initially appoint a contract manager, conceived as some mix of the informed buying and contract monitoring roles. However in one major US bank (BANK2):

> I am not physically managing anyone in the datacenter environment . . . but a lot of my time is being taken up as being not contract management but service relationship management . . . dealing with senior managers in the bank who are coming to me to explain service issues on a day-to-day basis. We are having to do lots of work we thought we had outsourced.

In fact, the contract manager was being stretched across four of the 'service face' capabilities, and the supplier development capability did not exist.

The under-estimation of capability and skills required came through several times in companies that had outsourced, as in this retail operation (RETAIL3):

> I was managing central systems, EDI and telecommunications. Only the latter had been outsourced but it took up 70% of my time . . . luckily we kept on someone who happened to know about telecommunications . . . it's what saved us in the end . . . —(IT manager).

Clearly the manager was being spread across technical, business, and service faces, and little thought had been given to requisite capability and skills in a selectively outsourced IT/IS environment. In an electronics company where major outsourcing had taken place in the early 1990s, a senior IT manager commented subsequently:

> The IT people we put into the business end became isolated, their IT skills were not wide ranging enough for their new roles that also needed a lot more contract management skills than they possessed . . . .

Here again the company was not only conflating several capabilities—in this case informed buyer, technical fixer, and relationship builder—into a one-person role, but also only learning by experience the type of skills needed to support each capability.

However, while we argue that all nine capabilities are needed, it is clear that their relative importance can vary. To date we have identified five factors which differentiate: three are aspects of the business context—concerned with the structure, mission, and nature of the activity; and two are functions of the IS/IT context—the maturity of IS/IT exploitation, and the experience of IT outsourcing. Each factor and its general consequences are briefly discussed in turn.

Structure

Here consideration needs to be given to the degree to which the business is physically and/or logically dispersed. Multiple locations increase the need for relationship-building capability. Relationship-builders need to physically and emotionally locate within the relevant part of the business; they cannot operate well across multiple locations or logical units. Secondly, if the business is physically dispersed but logically centralized, the technical architect role increases in importance— whether or not the IT service is outsourced.

Mission

The distinction is between a business or unit with a stable/well-defined/ bounded role, and one that is more externally oriented. The more the focus is on changing the external world—linking to other departments, or third-party organizations, for example—the more important will be the chief information officer and business systems thinkers, followed by technical fixers to ensure delivery of IS/IT commitments.

Business Activity

We are thinking of the relative emphasis between policy development and operational service. Policy-orientated units will benefit primarily from relationship-building capability and technical fixers. Operations-orientated units should be more concerned with the chief information officer, business systems thinker, and technical architect roles.

IT Exploitation

Businesses with limited experience of IT exploitation have a particular need for relationship-building capability. As experience increases, so does the need for business systems thinkers, informed buyers, and technical fixers.[13]

Experience of IT Outsourcing

The need, or more precisely the recognition of need, for various supply-oriented roles develops with experience of IT outsourcing. Every organization needs the information-buying capability; as its use of external IT services grows, so does its reliance on contract monitoring. Although there are real and immediate benefits from contract facilitation, many organizations do not seem to recognize the role until they have had

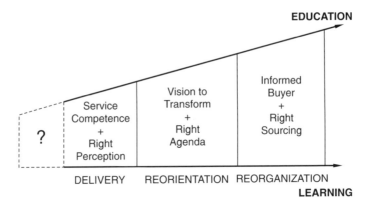

Figure 7.4   *Evolution in the management of IT*

painful experience in its absence. And it is our research experience that too few have so far understood the importance of supplier development.

These points also lead us to stress that the model in Figure 7.3 cannot be taken as static. A specific organization will need different emphases on different capabilities at different points in its history. We strongly recommend that all nine capabilities be represented at some level. In parallel research Feeny (1997) and Ross and Feeny (2000) observed three typical phases through which an IT function would be expected to evolve into the web-based era (see Figure 7.4).[14]

The objective in the first phase—delivery—is to establish the credibility of the IT function. The CIO's energies here are harnessed to achieve a reputation for excellent operational service, and successful completion of development projects; in other words, to achieve the reputation for, and reality of, technical and service competence. In the second phase—orientation—the agenda shifts to gaining the perception in the business of IT as a strategic resource. This requires educating and engaging business managers and users in how IT can be exploited for business advantage. In the third, most mature phase—reorganization—it becomes possible to decentralize IT responsibilities more fully to business units, with the IT function integrated with the business and able to participate in strategic thinking, achieve timely development of new systems that support business initiatives, and provide the operational services now critical to the functioning of the business.

Our work with companies shows that the fully developed core IT capabilities framework will be developed across the three phases, but can only be fully implemented in the third phase. Throughout, the right kind of IT leadership and agenda are vital. In phase one, however, with service and technical competence as priority, contract monitoring, contract facilitating, technical fixing, and architecture planning are the vital capabilities to focus on. In phase two, relationship-building, with the CIO also focusing beyond the boundary of the IT function in relations with senior business managers, becomes key. Our evidence is that only once relationships are in place can business systems thinking then be built and applied effectively. In the mature model the informed buying capability becomes central, with supplier development also required to ensure added value from external suppliers. While the use of external IT services is possible, and indeed may be necessary, at each stage, our evidence is that extensive outsourcing (as opposed to buying-in resources to work under internal management) is managed most effectively under the informed buying and 'rightsourcing' regime inherent in the core IT capabilities framework.

THE CAPABILITY–SKILLS MATRIX

Each of the nine capabilities/roles required to deliver the 'high performance IT' concept implies a set of people behaviors, characteristics and skills. Table 7.1 profiles what our research shows to be the critical attributes for high performance in each role.

In contrast to the more traditional skills found in IT functions, our work suggests four key human resource developments:

1. There needs to be a much greater emphasis on business skills and business orientation in nearly all roles, the exceptions being the 'technical fixer', and to some extent the 'technical architect' roles.
2. There is a significantly increased requirement for 'soft' skills across all roles, the exception being the 'contract monitor' role.
3. The nine roles all demand high performers. The major shift we are observing in organizations such as Esso, ICI, Dupont, and Railtrack, with some experience at developing the IT function along the lines suggested in this chapter, is toward fewer personnel, but of very high quality.
4. Each role requires a specific set of skills, attributes, and drivers. Through possessing one set, a person will be potentially disabled from high performance in the other roles. Our experience to date is that one person could deliver high performance in no more than two or three roles at any single point in their career path. This has considerable implications for staffing, personal, and career development.

We now consider these propositions in more detail.

Business Skills and Orientation

The generic requirement for these in the 'high performance IS' model should not disguise the fact that a distinctive set of business skills is needed in each role. A review of Figure 7.3 and the location of roles within business or supply faces will help to illustrate this. The business skills required by a CIO will relate to developing business vision and strategy, identifying business opportunities for IT, and the business potential of new technologies. The business systems thinker will be even more concerned with these issues, and from a more holistic business rather than technical perspective. The informed buyer has high business skills but these are focused on extracting value from suppliers, through monitoring the market and specific suppliers, negotiation, and supply management. The relationship-builder is highly concerned to add value to the business but the business skills are more operational in their focus, as is the case with the contract facilitator and contract monitor. With the other roles in place, business skills are less important for performance of the more technically focused 'architect' and 'fixer' roles.

The 'Soft' Skills

The importance of interpersonal skills in seven of the roles reflects the greater external 'face' that the modern IS function requires as IT becomes pervasive in organizations, and also the increasing dependence on external IT provision. In the 'high performance' model there are also fewer retained staff resulting in greater contact with business users/managers; team-working within the group also becomes critical. The type of interpersonal skills will vary across the roles. Again, reference back to Figure 7.3 is helpful here. Many of the roles are defined within the overlap between two or more faces. Bridge-building is critical in these roles. Leadership skills are prominent in the CIO, informed buyer, and to a lesser extent in the systems thinker role. Communication, team-building, and facilitation skills are highest in the CIO, relationship-builder, contract facilitator, and informed buyer roles. Negotiation skills are a prime requirement for informed buying, relationship-building, and contract facilitation.

The 'High Performance' Team

The nine roles form a team in two senses: the roles are complementary and interdependent; and the role-holders need to be able to work together interpersonally. The roles require high performers, i.e. people who outperform others by a considerable margin. Subject to the qualifications made above, our research shows some evidence that these high performers share three characteristics. First, they are achievers with a projects/results orientation. They tend to set high standards for themselves, are decisive and tough-minded, with good communication/influencing skills. Second, they have a learning orientation. They are motivated by change, have a high learning capability, are imaginative and enjoy experimenting. Finally, they are adaptable with flexibility in their management style profile, and a networking/partnership orientation.[15]

Given that these high performers have distinctive styles and motivations, there is a potential threat to the teamwork in the high performance IT function. However, looking at Esso, ICI, and similar companies that have extensive outsourcing arrangements and have adopted aspects of the core IT capabilities model, mutual respect for ability, together with the network orientation of most role-holders, does allow creative rather than destructive tension.

Distinctive Sets of Skills and Drivers

A further point illustrated by Table 7.1 is that while high performers may share many characteristics, in specific roles they will also require different assemblies of skills and motivations. We have already argued that it is a mistake to assume that the same business and interpersonal skills are required to carry out each role. For these reasons we envisage the high performer being adaptable and capable enough to fulfill two or three adjacent roles only—business systems thinker and relationship-builder is an example combination from our experience so far. When the high performance requirement is removed, it becomes more possible for people to move around the different roles. However, the attractions of this approach are outweighed by considerable disadvantages. Within the context of a small residual IS group, individual capability is very visible. One observation we can make is that neither users nor IT personnel seem to have much patience with an unconvincing colleague.

A final point needs to be made on technical skills. In some cases we have seen the high performance IT concept founded primarily on a mix of business and interpersonal skills. The downplay of technical skills is particularly inherent in the notion of outsourcing IT supply. Technical know-how is spread thinly through all the roles and retained to the degree that a watching rather than a doing technical brief can be delivered. In this scenario the technical fixer role is discarded, and the architect role retained but with less technical skill. Alternatively, it too is combined with another role, typically that of CIO. In our view this approach is seriously mistaken. Significant technical expertise and build capability must always be retained to enable the organization to maintain a degree of control over its IT destiny. This should apply even, or perhaps especially, in total outsourcing deals, as several pieces of research demonstrate—to guard against risks and irreversibility of contract (see, for example, Lacity and Hirschheim 1993a,b,c).

As one example, in 1990 First Fidelity bank outsourced all datacenter operations and systems conversions to EDS in a \$US450 million 10-year contract. Although EDS had hire/fire power over the systems developers throughout systems conversions, 250 systems developers remained on the bank's payroll during and after the conversion projects. This was to protect the bank's ability to maintain new systems in the future.

HUMAN RESOURCE AND ORGANIZATIONAL IMPLICATIONS

We have argued for a larger function—in terms of capabilities and roles—than seems generally expected amongst organizations as they increasingly look for supply from the external IT services market. Nevertheless, we are talking about a small group of people, particularly when a contrast is made with the typical size of in-house IT functions in the early and mid-1990s. This section points to some major challenges in getting and retaining such staff. Furthermore, we highlight some contextual features that influence the degree to which a high performance IT function can be effective in larger organizational terms.

Human Resource Challenges

The argument for high performers wins strong support from the experiences of respondents in over 30 organizations where IT was seen as a strategic resource; and in the selective and total outsourcing histories we studied in Chapter 4. As two total outsourcing examples, one respondent manager from a multinational oil company commented: 'You've got to be able to upskill your organization and to have a human resource policy which provides such training to people in your organization.'

On a similar theme, the logistics manager of a major retail company said: 'To be honest, we had to recruit a few people'.

In practice, recruitment and retention of a small high quality group is a major challenge in human resource management terms. The people being targeted here would look more familiar as senior professionals within a major management consulting firm. Even though they are largely self-driven, and job satisfaction oriented, how, in the tight labor market of 2001 and beyond, can an organization:

- pay them at a level that is 'within striking distance' of that provided by alternative employers?
- provide them consistently with the level of challenge they look for in the job?
- provide them with a career path despite the very small numbers?

These are major challenges in the IT functions of private and public sector organizations alike. In several respondent organizations, and across sectors, we have witnessed a reactive rather than anticipatory approach to human resource issues in IT. Many firms have some sense of operating a core–periphery model, the notion being that core workers have superior working terms and conditions, employment security, training and development opportunities, and long-term career paths within the firm. Core workers give stability in key areas together with functional flexibility. Meanwhile non-core workers on more limited contracts offer financial and numerical flexibility. In reality, in a volatile labor market with many IT-based skills in short supply, we find full-time IT staff frequently on disadvantageous contract terms, inflexible reward and promotion systems, a high use of contract staff on high pay rates, and the more marketable in-house staff induced away by offers of significant pay increases.[16] Clearly, in such organizations the erosion or absence of the 'core worker' concept in the IT function would need radical re-examination and action if our proposals are to be taken seriously.

We have observed an additional disadvantage accruing in organizations where there is a lack of understanding of the IT contribution demonstrated by senior executives. This threatens the availability of any of the 'transformational' excitement which high performers hold most dear.[17] One conclusion is the need to consider carefully the career management/ownership—and therefore deployment over time—of individuals who fulfill the roles comprising the high performance IT function. The highest value of such individuals is usually the availability of a stream of learning and change opportunities. This is much more easily delivered through centrally coordinated career management. A second possibility, discussed below, is that a richer model of IT sourcing may point to other ways of staffing, at least some of the roles.

A further human resource challenge rests with what one respondent termed 'the legacy people' problem. In other words, what about existing IT staff that the high performance model specifically excludes? Some approaches we have observed in various combinations are: early retirement, redundancy packages, making people redundant as the in-house legacy systems become redundant, and relocation and retraining. In outsourcing situations one common response has been to transfer such staff to suppliers. In 1999–2000 we found staff reductions occurring in 63% of cases, with the average reduction in these cases being over 40%, with 32% of staff being transferred to the supplier (see Appendix A). One difficulty is that suppliers, understandably, prefer to take only the better motivated and skilled staff; sometimes the result has been that the staff that remain are not sufficiently motivated, or capable, of delivering on the in-house high performance requirement.

A final point made to us by some respondents is the role of suppliers in supporting the high performance concept. In specific projects or services, they need to have complementary rather than competing or duplicating capabilities and skills. Furthermore, it is important to develop mutual cooperation and understanding between the in-house and supplier groups. In some cases, however, different terms and conditions have been a source of friction and resentment; suppliers may turn lack of in-house skills to their own opportunistic advantage; and in-house employees may stand back and let supplier staff take all responsibility (Lacity and Hirschheim 1993a,b,c; Willcocks and Lacity 1998). Some of the ways in which firms sought a more constructive relationship are indicated by the following:

> We put people in the vendors' organizations for months, even years, to help them understand our needs. They [the in-house staff] changed from a systems delivery group to a consulting group which would question the need to have a system to begin with ... it took massive reskilling—Principal Consultant, Oil Company.
> They [the supplier staff] are part of my team, they sit with my team, so for all intents and purposes they could be working for me. We have brought them into the organization almost because they are running a very important production system for us ... they also deal directly with the business users of the system ... it's worked well because they actually get a sense of responsibility for the service like the internal people—IT Manager, UK Retailing Company.

Organizational Issues

The 'high performance team' concept in IT provides additional challenges for the wider organization, and assumes, for its operationalization, a supportive environment that was not always prevalent in respondent organizations.

Human Resource Policy

Outdatedness, mismatching, and inflexibility in the human resource policy of the wider organization often disadvantage the in-house IT function *vis-à-vis* the external labor market. Wider studies of labor markets indicate all too often a short-termism, reliance on buying in staff, a lack of training, development and career paths, and considerable neglect of a human resource strategy generally. A particular concern is the degree to which internal human resource policies fail to align with the quickly changing realities of the IT labor market.

Project Management

There is no explicit mention in Figure 7.3 of project management capability. In dynamic business environments, the emphasis has shifted from hierarchical, functionally based organizations toward task and project-based ways of operating. The assumption here is that project management skills will be spread throughout such organizations—that it must be an organizational core capability, and not the preserve of one function or department. Whatever the IT component in a project, in practice its project manager can come from anywhere in the business, the main primary criterion being his/her credibility, which in turn relates to proven successful project experience.[18] Without this, in a pharmaceuticals company we saw a project manager, appointed from the business to implement a MRP2 system, fail through lack of technical credibility. In a bank and insurance company several projects managed by IT personnel failed to deliver effective business systems through a narrow, technical view of the requirement.

In terms of Figure 7.3, depending on how user-driven the project needs to be, candidates for project management would most likely be found in the relationship-builder and technical fixer roles. In connection with projects, two other roles are usually mentioned in addition to project manager, namely project sponsor and project champion.[19] Depending on the technical content of the project, and its importance, these roles are most likely to be held by senior business managers, though from Figure 7.3 the CIO may be a candidate.

Location

The issue of the physical location of the nine key capabilities in the organization structure can be largely answered by referring to the findings and prescriptions from work already cited.[20] A vital requirement is that a person fulfilling a key IT capability can be in easy and regular contact with his/her salient senior management, user, and IT function constituency. Thus, a relationship-builder is more likely to be located and spend time within business units; a technical architect may be located centrally in a planning unit; a contract facilitator needs to be located close to both users generating requirements and supplier staff; but for all these much depends upon the specific contingencies, problems and projects of the day.

SOURCING IT/IS: THE CORE–PERIPHERY MODEL REVISITED

So far we have outlined the emerging nine key capabilities required for any future high performance IT function. We have also discussed the issues around how such a function can be operationalized. This final section returns to the notion of core capabilities and relates it more explicitly to the growing use of the external market for IT services. This yields further insight into the sourcing strategy, and the capability needed to support it.

Over many years organizations have consistently used the external market to some degree to source their IT whether in the form of technology, services, or human resources. However, in the 1990s, as a response to the four pressures described earlier, we increasingly saw advanced a view of the in-house IT function as having primarily what has been variously described as a 'strategic', 'residual', 'governance', or 'intelligent customer' role. Essentially this definition emphasizes full in-house involvement in 'upstream' activities—particularly IM and the continuing development of IS strategy to meet business needs—followed by a 'procure and manage' role related to 'downstream' activities such as systems development, operational service, and support. This perspective incorporates much of the thinking that underpins how major, or even total, outsourcing of IT services may be supported by a demand-led, strategy-focused, residual IT function. One unfortunate consequence of such thinking is where 'residual' becomes all too accurate a phrase for the human resource capabilities and skills remaining to plan for future needs, administer outsourcing contracts, and look after the organization's IT/IS destiny.

The dilemma is illustrated in Figure 7.5. As discussed earlier, every organization must somehow ensure that it has in place the IM, IS and IT components of an overall information strategy. For each element there is a spectrum of activities required, represented by the horizontal axis of Figure 7.5. Some of the activities are necessary enablers of the strategy process, such as relationship-building and information-gathering. Then there is the strategy-creation process itself, involving analysis, brainstorming, evaluation, and so on. At all three levels there is the requirement to enable/create/build/operate/improve, with at least some level of activity in each phase of the process all of the time. Sourcing decisions

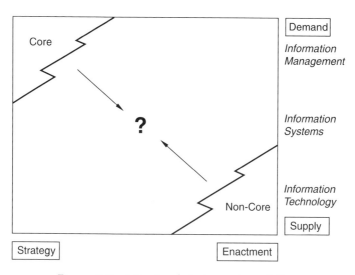

Figure 7.5 *Mapping choice in sourcing activity*

need to be made along the demand–supply and the strategy–enactment axes.

A key question arises: How do resource-based concepts of core capabilities/distinctive competencies relate to this model of IS/IT activity in the light of the developing external market for IT services? The minimalist view—which some organizations have taken—is that core capability occupies a small space in the top left corner of the map. The information management strategy—to outsource—is owned by the business, and the rest of the space is occupied by a supplier who is a 'strategic partner' responsible for creating and implementing the IS and IT strategies, as well as implementing IM. Our experience strongly and consistently challenges this view. No organization can remain informed of its demand-side needs and in control of its IS/IT investment without a richer definition of core capability in the IT function. But where should the line be drawn? Figure 7.6 suggests how the concept—together with its IM, IS, and IT dimensions—needs to be populated by the nine capabilities that describe the high performance IT function. Figure 7.6 seeks to illustrate what our research evidence shows strongly, namely that IT core capabilities cannot be different from, but must be virtually synonymous with, what we have defined as the high performance IT function.

It is worth considering this proposition in a little more detail. The terms core competence/distinctive competence were coined to distinguish those things an organization does particularly well relative to

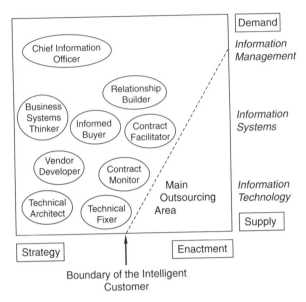

Figure 7.6   *Core capabilities and sourcing strategy in IT*

its competitors, and that are fundamental to a firm's performance and strategy.[21] Our research reveals nine key capabilities that need to be developed that enable an organization to acquire, deploy, and leverage IT investments over time as a basis for sustainable survival and competitive success. Clearly, much depends upon the quality of these capabilities, and the degree to which they are supported by the wider organization, relative to competitors. Feeny and Ives (1997) describe three bases for sustainable competitive advantage through IT: generic lead time, competitive asymmetry, and preemption potential.[22] They note that projects that rely solely on generic lead time for advantage are at risk. Sustainability is much more likely where the prime mover in the sector earns a decided advantage by going first, or where competitive asymmetry makes it difficult or impossible for a competitor to respond. Core IT capabilities contribute by providing the organizational and knowledge sources from which competitive asymmetry can be developed. But they also provide the capability to both identify the prime moves that can be made, and ensure that preemption is not imitable.

In researching 16 companies Runge and Earl (1988) found competitive advantage from IT developing from 'marginal' managers operating on the edge of the organization and close to external customers, with strong business sponsorship, outside formal procedures and the IT department, together with strong internal marketing. Plant and Willcocks (2000) made a similar finding in the context of organizations leading in the adoption of e-commerce.[23] Three points arise. First, Runge and Earl found that competitive edge systems mostly developed incrementally over time, and outside, planning systems. Second, processes, power, and relationships were an important source of getting the IT investment off the ground. Third, the organizations and their IT departments were configured mainly on functional and hierarchical lines. On the first two points the high performance model offers the capability to match the requirement closely. In particular, research into respondent organizations suggests that the relationship, roles, and how they are fulfilled bridge real gaps in previous organizational arrangements, facilitating a flow of information and ideas and creating support mechanisms for leveraging IT investments. Moreover, business systems thinking that spans organizational and IT-based systems represents a significant development for the capability of developing business-based systems (see Figure 7.6). On the third point, the model of the emergent IT function also offers, on our evidence, much-needed ways of reconfiguring some major barriers to leveraging IT effectively.

However, we have said little so far about IT market sourcing strategy and its relationship to organizational performance. Figure 7.6 delineates four critical capabilities for dealing with external suppliers. A richer picture of the sourcing options needs to be supplied to show how optimal decisions can be arrived at and delivered on. This will also help to indicate how at least some of the human resource challenges presented by the high performance IT function may be met.

All too often the trade press, and some academic studies, tend to present IT sourcing decisions as binary choices: in-house or outsourced. We have consistently promoted a more complex model. A key distinction can be made between contracts that specify a service and result which the market is to provide (outsourcing); and contracts which call for the market to provide resources to be deployed under the buyer's management and control (insourcing) (see Chapter 5). The purchasing style can either be consistently open tender (i.e. competition for each market transaction), or relationship oriented (i.e. single tender to a preferred supplier provided certain conditions are met). This analysis suggests five different sourcing options. Three of them—buy-in, preferred supplier, and in-house—we refer to as 'insourcing'. Two others—contract out and preferred supplier are 'outsourcing'. In practice these multiple options offer more opportunities for gaining leverage from external and internal IT services, but also provide more potential pitfalls. We are also finding many large organizations moving to a complex set of sourcing arrangements where all five options are taken up to some degree simultaneously. The high performance model specifically provides the capability in-house to make choices in this complex arena, and also enforce those choices.

Finally, insourcing options may also be used to address some of the human resource challenges presented by the high performance model. The CIO, informed buyer, business systems thinker, relationship-builder, and contract facilitator all fall within the 'business' face of Figure 7.3. These are the priorities for in-house resourcing, which provides the best opportunity for ongoing business orientation. But four other roles— technical architect, technical fixer, contract monitor, and supplier developer—lie outside the business face. If these roles are 'insourced' to a preferred supplier, they may successfully provide a check and balance on the contractors to whom service provision has been 'outsourced'. Moreover, an important remit to the insourcer would be to build up that capability as a form of succession planning. Better, surely, to insource on this basis than to deprive the high performance IT function of some of its facilities.

CONCLUSIONS

This chapter has sought to provide fresh thinking on the key capabilities required in the IT function in contemporary organizations. Three research strands showed the importance of capabilities and skills— essentially human-resource-based—in identifying, delivering and operating IT for organizational advantage. In particular, in some instances organizations seemed to be making incremental moves, and in others planned moves, toward an emergent model of the IT function. Our analysis has distilled these moves into nine key capabilities and posited the need, if the promise of IT is to be fully exploited, for a high performance IT function.

At the same time as developing, from research, the notion of the high performance IT function, we have been deeply aware of the challenges it poses for organizations. Historically, in both IT and the wider organization, human resource issues have been neglected, and are still rarely the subject of anticipatory, let alone strategic, action. Resource-based approaches and notions of building long-term core capabilities also appear more regularly in the academic literature and in a few high profile cases of success, than in actual organizational practices. However, there have been many encouraging signs in the organizations we have studied. Moreover, there are many indications that, if most organizations fail to move in the direction of the high performance model, then those that do would gain even more sustainable advantage than might otherwise be the case.

NOTES

1. Orb Consultancy (1999). *The IT and Corporate Performance Report.* Orb Consultancy, London.
2. Earl, M. (2000). Local Lessons for Global Businesses. In Marchand, D., Davenport, T. and Dickson, T. (eds), *Mastering Information Management.* FT Prentice-Hall, London. Also Marchand, D. (2000). Hard IM Choices for Senior Managers. See also Willcocks, L., Feeny, D. and Islei, G. (eds) (1997). *Managing Information Technology as a Strategic Resource.* McGraw-Hill, Maidenhead.
3. Hodgkinson, S. (1996). The Role of the Corporate IT Function in the Federal Organization. In Earl, M. (ed.) (1996). *Information Management: The Organizational Dimension,* Oxford University Press, Oxford.
4. Weill, P. and Broadbent M. (1997). *Investing in the New IT Infrastructure.* Harvard Business Press, Boston. Henderson, J. and Venkatraman, N. (2000). Five Principles for Making the Most of IT. In Marchand, D., Davenport, T. and Dickson, T. (eds), In Marchand, D., Davenport, T. and Dickson, T. (eds), *Mastering Information Management.* FT Prentice-Hall, London.
5. Walton, R. (1989). *Up and Running.* Harvard Business Press, Boston. Also Willcocks, L. and Currie, W. (1997). Does Radical Reengineering Really Work? A Cross-Sectoral Study of Strategic Projects. In Willcocks, L., Feeny, D. and Islei, G. (eds) (1997). *Managing Information Technology on a Strategic Resource.* McGraw-Hill, Maidenhead. Willcocks, L. and Griffiths, C. (1997). Management And Risk in Major IT Projects.
6. See, for example, Feeny, D., Earl, M. and Edwards, B. (1994). Organizational Arrangements for IS: The Role of Users and IS Specialists. *OXIIM Research and Discussion Paper RDP94/6,* Templeton College, Oxford. Also Markus, L. (2000). Organizing a Better IT Function. In Marchand, D., Davenport, T. and Dickson, T. (eds) *op. cit.* Also Taylor-Cummings, A. and Feeny, D. (1997). The Development and Implementation of Systems: Bridging The User-IS Gap. In Willcocks, L., Feeny, D. and Islei, G. (eds) (1997) *op. cit.*
7. McFarlan, W. (1984). Information Technology Changes the Way You Compete. *Harvard Business Review,* May–June, 98–103.
8. Resource-based theories applied to how effective IT can be developed and sustained appear in Ciborra, C. (1993). *Teams, Markets and Systems.* Cambridge University Press, Cambridge. Also Feeny, D. and Ives, B., Information Technology as a Basis for Sustainable Competitive Advantage. In Willcocks, L., Feeny, D. and Islei, G. (eds) (1997) *op. cit.*
9. For the broader strategy and organization literature on resource-based theories and notions of core competence, see Grant, R. (1995). *Contemporary Strategy Analysis.* Blackwell, Oxford. Also Hamel, G. and Pralahad, C. (1994). *Competing For The Future.* Harvard Business Press, Boston.
10. The first strand of research concentrated on the role, person, and experiences of the CIO. Three parallel studies used a variety of techniques, including face-to-face interviews and psychometric tests, to provide rich data on IS leadership in 61 organizations. The research program led by David Feeny of the Oxford Institute of Information Management also provided insights into the capabilities which leading CIOs believed to be crucial to the IT function.

    In the second strand, David Feeny and colleagues investigated four of the capabilities that were consistently highlighted by CIOs. Twelve participating organizations identified 53 individuals who were considered to demonstrate outstanding ability in one of the target areas. Data on these individuals were captured using personal background and perceived ability questionnaires, critical event interviews, and a variety of psychometric testing instruments. The research provided insights into both the way target capabilities were delivered, and the profile of individuals who delivered them.

An extensive third strand has involved research into IT/IS outsourcing experiences. This has consisted of four surveys in Europe and the United States in 1993, 1997, 1998, and 1999 (see also Appendix A). Further data from organizations have been collected by face-to-face interviews with multiple stakeholders in 76 case study organizations across the 1992–2000 period (see Chapter 4). Significantly for our purposes here, many of the case study organizations were found to be addressing the question of what they often referred to as the scope of the 'residual' IT in-house function; that is, what minimum capabilities should remain after outsourcing.

11. Earl, M. (ed.) (1996) *op. cit.* Also Willcocks, Feeny and Islei (1997) *op. cit.*

12. See Sauer, C. and Willcocks, L. (2000). *Building The E-business Infrastructure.* Business Intelligence, London.

13. Feeny, D. (1997). The Five Year Learning of Ten IT Directors. In Willcocks, L., Feeny, D. and Islei, G. (eds) *op. cit.*

14. Feeny, D. (1997). The Five Year Learning of Ten IT Directors. In Willcocks, L., Feeny, D. and Islei, G. (eds) *op. cit.* See also Ross, J. and Feeny, D. (2000). In Zmud, R. (ed.) *Framing the Domains of IT Management Research: Glimpsing the Future Through the Past* (forthcoming).

15. Feeny, D., Abl, V., Millie, E., Minter, A. Selby, C. and Williams, J. (1997). Defining New IS Skills and Competencies. *OXIIM/KPMG Research And Discussion Paper.* Templeton College, Oxford.

16. Even more worrying is the fact that, on 1999 estimates for an economy like the United Kingdom, 30% and more of the IT skills available were with IT service companies, and that in 2000 this figure was rising rather than declining.

17. Feeny, D., Edwards, B. and Simpson, K. (1992). Understanding the CEO/CIO Relationship. *MIS Quarterly,* **16**, 435–448. Also, Feeny, D., Abl, V., Millie, E., Minter, A. Selby, C. and Williams, J. (1997) *op. cit.*

18. Earl (1996) *op. cit.*; Willcocks, Feeny and Islei (1997) *op. cit.*

19. Beath, C., (1996). The Project Champion In Earl, M. (ed.) (1996) *op. cit.* Edwards, B. (1996). The Project Sponsor. In Earl, M. (ed.) (1996) *op. cit.*

20. Earl, M., Feeny, D. and Edwards, B. (1997). Configuring the IS Function in Complex Organizations. In Willcocks, L, Feeny, D. and Islei, G. (eds) *op. cit.* Also Hodgkinson, S. (1996). In Earl, M. (ed.) (1996) *op. cit.*

21. Hamel, G. and Heene, A. (eds) (1994). *Competence-Based Competition.* Wiley, Chichester; Pralahad, C. and Hamel, G. (1990). The Core Competence of the Corporation. *Harvard Business Review,* **68**, no. 3, 79–91. Also Quinn, J. (1992). The Intelligent Enterprise: A New Paradigm. *Academy of Management Executive,* **6**, no. 4, 44–63.

22. Feeny, D. and Ives, B. (1997). Information Technology as a Basis for Sustainable Competitive Advantage. In Willcocks, L., Feeny, D. and Islei, G. (eds) *op. cit.*

23. Runge, D. and Earl, M. (1988). Gaining Competitive Advantage from Telecommunications. In Earl, M. (ed.), *Information Management: The Strategic Dimension.* Clarendon Press, Oxford. Plant, R. and Willcocks, L. (2000). Moving to the Net—Leadership Strategies. In Marchand, D., Davenport, T. and Dickson, T. (eds) (2000) *op. cit.*

8
Managing Stakeholder Relationships Across Six Phases

Suppliers have to make a reasonable margin to stay in business. You don't want them to lose money because the worse their business gets, the worse your business gets—Contract Administrator, South Australian Government.

I think mega-deals can work, but they take a lot of hard work—Quote from BAe Outsourcing Report.

Another concern that we had was that if we did a five-year deal say, what happens at the end of the five years? If we don't get along well, or we want it back and we had transferred the people, then we are in a real bad situation—Corporate Manager of Planning and Administration, Petroleum Company.

INTRODUCTION

All our case and survey findings indicate clearly that gaining a business advantage requires a comprehensive sourcing strategy for the IT function. In previous chapters we presented frameworks, processes, and practices for successful sourcing. But successful implementation of such ideas requires an understanding and management of the political realities. Simply put, sourcing decisions alter people's lives. As such, all decisions affect the balance of power among stakeholders, often resulting in resistance to change, conflict, and even sabotage.

Most of the IT sourcing literature focuses on only two stakeholders—the customer and the supplier. But this dichotomous customer/supplier analysis fails to appreciate the complexity of stakeholder relationships in IT sourcing. 'Customers' include senior business managers who pay for IT, senior IT managers who manage IT, IT staff who deliver IT, and finally the users who actually receive the service. 'Suppliers' include senior management who negotiate deals, account managers responsible for earning a profit on the deal, and supplier IT staff charged with delivery. If IT unions, external consultants, lawyers, sub-contractors, or multi-sourcing are involved, additional sets of stakeholders are added to the party.

Stakeholders can behave antagonistically, cooperatively, and even collaboratively depending on the alignment of goals for the issue at hand. Indeed, relationships are quite dynamic, and we found that those organizations that, rather than seeking a naive harmony, faced the complex realities of shared goals, complementary goals, and conflicting goals learned to function in a healthy and productive manner. With this broader view, activities such as realigning (i.e. renegotiating!) a contract midway through a relationship is not seen as a failure, but as a normal phase in the evolution of the relationship. By understanding that stakeholder goals often naturally conflict, each side appreciates the other's position while still protecting their own interests.

By attending to the expectations and goals of many stakeholders, apparent anomalies in relationships are understood. Why do customer contract managers and supplier account managers *collaborate* to mediate IT user expectations, then feel perfectly comfortable *fighting* over a monthly bill? Quite simply, *the dynamics of stakeholder relationships vary with the task.* In the former example, both customer contract managers and supplier account managers have the shared goal of communicating contractual obligations to users. (No one wants users complaining about services for which they are not entitled.) In the latter example, customer contract managers and supplier account managers have conflicting goals; customers naturally want lower bills, suppliers naturally want higher bills. In principle, each side seeks a fair bill, but circumstances are often ambiguous and lead to each side naturally assuming the more favorable interpretation.

This chapter presents an overall framework for understanding the relationships among stakeholders before, during, and after IT outsourcing contracts are signed. The relationship framework focuses on three key elements:

- IT stakeholders involved in the relationship,
- types of relationships, and
- phases in the relationship.

We begin with the IT stakeholders.

INFORMATION TECHNOLOGY STAKEHOLDERS

An IT stakeholder group consists of people tending to have the same expectations, perceptions, and goals for IT and outsourcing. Rather than merely categorizing people as either 'customers' or 'suppliers', our research identified eight types of IT stakeholders (see Table 8.1). However, while our stakeholder analysis is richer than previous dichotomous analyses, we still note that stereotypes ignore individual personalities. In the conclusion, we address how personal charisma (or abrasiveness) can sometimes supercede stakeholder stereotypes.

In general, we found four distinct customer IT stakeholders and three distinct supplier stakeholders. In cases of multi-sourcing (such as the

Table 8.1 *Stakeholder expectations and goals*

Stakeholder	IT expectations/goals
Customer senior business managers	Customer senior business managers expected demonstrated business value for IT expenditures. Inability to assess the benefits of IT often caused senior business managers to focus on IT costs.
Customer senior IT managers	Customer senior IT managers balanced service excellence expectations from users against cost containment expectations from senior business managers.
Customer IT staff	As technical enthusiasts, customer IT staff focused primarily on service excellence, but within budget and time constraints.
Customer IT users	IT users expected service excellence. Cost implications were often not apparent due to centralized accounting and contracting for IT.
Supplier senior managers	Supplier account managers negotiated deals that would satisfy the customer while maximizing profits.
Supplier account managers	Supplier senior managers balanced customer service and profitability.
Supplier IT staff	As technical enthusiasts, supplier IT staff primarily focused on service excellence, but within budget and time constraints.
Sub-contractors	Sub-contractors were expected to deliver on their contracts. Sometimes sub-contractors also seek more direct relationships with end customers.

sourcing options pursued from 1993 to 1998 by British Petroleum Exploration with three suppliers, and DuPont from 1996 to 1997 with two suppliers) the number of supplier stakeholders, and interactions among stakeholders, increases. The additional complexity of multi-sourcing is often deemed worthwhile because of the benefits of best sourcing, and elimination of the monopoly power of a sole supplier. In addition, it is quite common for suppliers on large IT outsourcing contracts to hire sub-contractors.

Customer Senior Business Managers

Though responsible for achieving business results from IT expenditures, in many of our cases, senior business managers did not have the tools to assess whether the IT function was adding value. They often asked senior IT managers for evidence of business value. In cases where senior managers could not assess the value of IT, they focused primarily on the financing and costs of IT. The questions naturally arose: Can IT be delivered more efficiently? Can IT assets (which may represent up to 20% of all capital assets) be removed from the balance sheet? Can large fixed annual IT budgets be transformed into a 'pay for use' model? And ultimately, 'Can an IT outsourcer save us money?'

Customer Senior IT Managers

Typically these are centralized and responsible for balancing the costs of IT with the services provided to ensure value for money. In general, senior IT managers were often frustrated by their charge. Users often demanded service excellence while their bosses often demanded cost containment. One senior IT manager explains:

> I cannot get any support on how to allocate these resources. And we cannot be the traffic cop in this whole process because it is not right. I'm trying to satisfy everybody and it's not working—Former Director of IS, US Petroleum Company.

In most of our cases, senior IT managers maintained their focus on balancing IT costs and services throughout an outsourcing process. Senior IT managers are rarely threatened by IT outsourcing, which meant their roles being redefined rather than lost. Indeed, most senior IT managers became valuable contributors to outsourcing evaluations, contract negotiations, and post-contract management. Although we discussed the political behavior of a few IT managers biased against outsourcing in Lacity and Willcocks (1998), by far the preponderance of IT managers expressed a goal to balance costs and service delivery.

Customer IT Staff

These staff are responsible for IT service delivery. Although they are expected to meet budgets and deadlines, we found that IT professionals are generally technology enthusiasts who also seek to please users. The internal IT staff were often the stakeholder groups most profoundly affected by outsourcing evaluations. They felt their senior managers were making life choices for them about transition and retention, and often without their input on careers, salaries, and benefits. In cases where IT staff are unionized, the unions were often very vocal against outsourcing. For example, unions initially opposed the decisions at British Aerospace and Inland Revenue (see Chapter 3, and also at another case we researched—Westchester County; Lacity and Willcocks 1997). Ultimately, we found customer IT employees almost always agreeing to transfer to the supplier. Acceptance rates were above 95% in all our cases except at a US public sector organization and at a US metal company.

IT Users

These typically focused throughout all phases on IT *service excellence*, expecting systems to be up and running, to provide business functionality, and to facilitate the execution of their business responsibilities. IT users rarely resisted outsourcing, although they frequently had questions about confidentiality and integrity of data.

In most instances, IT users were supportive of outsourcing because they perceived that the supplier would radically improve IT service. But IT users' expectations for service excellence were often unrealistic, believing that an infusion of new IT and better service would be provided by the supplier virtually free of charge. The gap in expectations and reality often dampened their initial enthusiasm.

Supplier Senior Managers

These stakeholders are responsible for sales and negotiations. They must balance the need to satisfy their customers with the need to generate a profit for their organization. A tremendous amount of judgment, typically based on years of experience, is often needed to assess what can be delivered at what price while still generating a profit.

According to one supplier senior manager, suppliers 'never knowingly sell a deal by reducing IT cost' because the margins are too small. For his company, IT cost reduction deals typically require 50% overhead (25% for supplier corporate headquarters; 25% for profit on the account) while still being able to reduce the customer's costs by 10%–20%. Few IT cost reduction deals qualify. Instead, supplier senior managers typically focus on the value they can add to a customer in terms of improving service, redesigning business processes, providing scarce IT skills, helping customers refinance IT, and developing new added-value systems.

Supplier Account Managers

Supplier account managers are responsible for profitability and customer satisfaction on a given IT contract. Again, supplier account managers must strike a delicate balance between the often conflicting goals of service excellence and cost containment. Because the supplier account manager is so critical to the success of an outsourcing relationship, many customers include approval clauses in the contract for this role.

Supplier IT Staff

A primary concern of supplier IT staff is with providing good customer service. Like customer IT staff, supplier IT staff are generally technology enthusiasts who are anxious to please users. Sometimes their enthusiasm for customer service had to be harnessed by their management to protect profit margins. Most IT staff, however, are well aware of budget and time requirements. Although they aim to please their customers, their organizations must earn a profit:

> We are an IT company, so we can transfuse current IT, state of the art IT, future IT, conceptual IT. But of course that transfusion as far as we are concerned is not free. The big problem is these people think that transfusion is free—Quality Manager, IT Supplier.

Sub-contractors

Sub-contractors are hired by prime suppliers to deliver part of the service to customers. According to International Data Corporation (IDC), 36% of IT outsourcing contracts involve sub-contractors. An *Information Week* survey found an even higher frequency of sub-contractors: 50% of IT suppliers hire contractors. Customers often have limited or no interaction with sub-contractors. Over 15% of 55 IT managers surveyed by IDC stated that their IT suppliers do not notify them when they hire sub-contractors. Half of the suppliers in the *Information Week* survey admitted that sub-contractors sometimes cause problems, including service quality (67%), costs (30%), viruses (17%), and security (10%).

According to surveys, prime contractors hire sub-contractors to access scarce technical skills. Ironically, customers often outsourced for the same reason: to gain access to scarce IT skills of the prime contractor. But prime contractors face the same global shortage of IT skills as everyone else.[1] In our case work we found between 30% and 50% of some contracts actually being multi-supplier outsourced in disguise. Areas where sub-contracting was most prevalent were in technical consulting, desktop (hardware and installation, network and software work), and special projects. Clearly, the widespread usage of sub-contracting brings additional dimensions and issues to outsourcing; our research experience is that these are all too often overlooked by client organizations. In many of the deals we looked at key questions seemed not to be addressed. For example: Does your supplier manage sub-contractors any better than you could? Is the management fee higher than you can do it for? Is there clarity about who is responsible for what? Are there intellectual property right issues? What is in the sub-contracts, and how are risks to the customer mitigated?

In summary, the eight types of stakeholders generally held different IT expectations and goals. Some stakeholders primarily focus on IT costs because they are the ones paying for IT. Other stakeholders focus on service excellence because they are the ones using the IT service. Other stakeholders must strike a delicate balance between service excellence and cost containment. Clearly, such diverse goals and orientations amongst typical stakeholders can have a profound impact on the types of relationships that can develop.

TYPES OF STAKEHOLDER RELATIONSHIPS

As previously noted, stakeholder relationships are quite dynamic. The same two people can fight one minute and collaborate the next, and we found stakeholders regularly operating at different points along the relationship continuum. In general, at least four types of relationships were evident (see Figure 8.1):

- tentative
- collaborative
- cooperative
- adversarial

Tentative Relationships:

Unknown Goals

Collaborative Relationships:

Shared Goals

Cooperative Relationships:

Complementary Goals

Adversarial Relationships:

Conflicting Goals

Figure 8.1 *Relationship types*

Tentative Relationships

These were quite common when stakeholders had no shared history. Thus, stakeholders were unsure whether goals were shared, complementary, or conflicting. Most of the time behavior manifested itself in polite caution, but sometimes a predisposition towards enthusiasm was evident. For example, *customer* and *supplier senior managers* were often quite enthusiastic—albeit tentative—when exploring the possibility for a 'partnership'. At this stage there was no commitment, and thus no motivation to behave aggressively or antagonistically. One informant described senior management talks as a 'peacock dance' because each party was anxious to impress the other with their organization's assets and capabilities.

Another common example of tentative relationships was the first few meetings between *supplier stakeholders* and *customer IT staff* identified for transfer. The tentativeness mostly occurred on the part of the IT staff, who were quite naturally concerned about their new careers, salaries, and benefits. Most supplier stakeholders immediately began to build confidence by guaranteeing equivalent salaries and benefits and by allowing potential transferees to speak with previously transferred employees.

Collaborative Relationships

These occurred when stakeholders' goals were shared. In many cases, shared goals were fostered by being part of the same organization. Customer stakeholder goals were often aligned for a number of negotiation activities:

- *Customer senior business managers* and *customer senior IT managers* typically both wanted to negotiate the best service at the lowest cost.
- *Customer senior managers* and *customer IT staff* typically both wanted to negotiate the best salaries and benefits for employees targeted for transfer to the supplier.
- *Customer senior managers* and *customer IT users* typically both wanted to negotiate the best possible service level agreements with the supplier.

Similarly, *supplier senior managers* and future *supplier account managers* had the shared goal of negotiating a deal with enough leeway to ensure profit margins, even assuming unforeseen events.

Cooperative Relationships

These manifested themselves when goals were complementary. Each party needs something from the other party to succeed. Many IT outsourcing activities are based on the notion of an exchange—the customer pays a fee in exchange for a service. Customer and supplier goals are therefore complementary: the customer needs the supplier to provide the service; the supplier needs the customer to pay the fee. While it is clear these goals are not shared, each party has a vested interest in the other's success. Indeed, sensible customer stakeholders never wanted suppliers to lose money on the account because if the supplier suffers, the customer suffers:

> Suppliers have to make a reasonable margin to stay in business. You don't want them to lose money because the worse their business gets, the worse your business gets. At the same time you don't want them to make outrageous profits at your expense—Contract Administrator, South Australian Government.

Adversarial Relationships

These occurred when stakeholder goals were in *conflict*. Stakeholders were adversarial when the conflict entailed millions of dollars, such as a conflict over an interpretation of financial responsibility in a contract clause. In particular, three activities are inherently adversarial:

- negotiating the original contract;
- establishing precedents for contract interpretation during the transition phase; and
- renegotiating or realigning the contract midway through the contract.

The key here was for the customer and supplier to have equal power to achieve an equitable outcome. When one party had more power than the other, the stronger party clearly dominated the weaker. In the early mega-deals, suppliers clearly had more power due to information impactedness. Oliver Williamson[2] defines information impactedness as follows:

> It exists in circumstances in which one of the parties to an exchange is much better informed than is the other regarding underlying conditions germane to the trade, and the second party cannot achieve information parity except at great cost—because he cannot rely on the first party to disclose the information in a fully candid manner.

Customers were often inexperienced in negotiating IT outsourcing contracts. To balance the power during contract negotiations, customers are hiring more outside experts to represent their interests. In fact, few new IT outsourcing deals were signed without the customer's extensive reliance on outside technical and legal consultants. Customers employed a number of other strategies to balance the power, i.e. they:

- established non-exclusivity clauses that enable the customer to open work up to competitive bids beyond-baseline services;
- multi-sourced rather than give monopoly power to a sole supplier;
- selectively sourced to limit the power of a supplier to a targeted subset of IT activities.

The objective of these strategies, again, is not necessarily to dominate the other party, but to have enough power to favorably and fairly resolve adversarial tasks. Indeed, customer empowerment contributes to our understanding of why more recent contracts have higher success rates than older contracts (Lacity and Willcocks 1998).

In summary, the dynamic nature of stakeholder relationships was clearly evident in case study organizations. The same stakeholders can have tentative, collaborative, cooperative, and adversarial relationships depending on the task at hand. By understanding relationship complexities, customers and suppliers can abandon the naive quest for continual harmony. Instead, stakeholders should accept the ebbs and flows of the evolution of relationships. Stakeholders can occasionally fight, yet still have an effective relationship overall:

> I think mega-deals can work, but they take a lot of hard work—Quote from BAe Outsourcing Report.

RELATIONSHIP PHASES

We identified six outsourcing phases, each comprising multiple activities (see Table 8.2). Stakeholder relationships vary during activities within phases, depending on goal alignment. For each of the phases, we describe the major stakeholder goals, interactions, and outcomes witnessed in our cases.

Phase 1: Scoping

Customer goal: 'Create a strategic vision of IT sourcing.'

The two main activities in this phase were identifying core IT capabilities and identifying IT activities for potential outsourcing. Typically, the *customer senior business managers* and *customer senior IT managers* were the primary stakeholders involved during this initial phase. Senior business managers had agendas prompted by financial pressures. Such pressures often led to a 'core competency' strategy where the organization focused on the 'core', and downsized or outsourced the rest. Because senior business managers viewed much of IT as a non-core competency, they regularly questioned if potentially some or all of the IT function could be outsourced.

Senior IT managers, typically, had coped with a legacy of trying to balance service excellence demands from the user population with IT cost-containment pressures from their senior managers. In the past, there was often tension between CEOs and senior IT managers because the latter often struggled to demonstrate value for IT expenditures to their bosses.

A full-blown investigation of IT sourcing options, however, often served to align goals between senior business and IT managers. As previously noted, because senior IT managers rarely lose their jobs as a consequence of outsourcing, they usually welcomed a reasoned approach to sourcing the IT function. With the support of their bosses, senior IT managers could overcome user resistance and implement cost reduction and outsourcing strategies.[3]

Supplier stakeholders, typically, were not involved until the evaluation phase. However, in a few cases, *supplier senior managers* actually prompted the decision to consider outsourcing by wooing customer senior executives in this phase. For example, the VP of IS at one petroleum company told us that EDS prompted a sourcing decision by offering cash during a major court battle at his company:

> The Chairman of the Board of EDS wrote a letter to our Chief Executive Officer saying that they would be most interested in paying substantial cash for our whole IS organization. That includes all the people, and they would be very happy to meet him, and discuss that with him—VP of IS, US Petroleum Company.

Customer and supplier senior executive interactions were typically characterized by tentative enthusiasm and optimism during the scoping phase. But one lesson that clearly emerged from our body of research is that customer and supplier senior executives should not make outsourcing decisions without IT management's input. The 'CEO handshake deals' typically failed because of inattention to detail. Two CEOs can get very excited about an alliance, but the success of any IT outsourcing deal relies on the details of the cost and service to be delivered.

Phase 2: Evaluation

Customer goal: 'Identify the best source for IT activities.'

The major activities during this phase were:

- measuring baseline services and costs;
- creating a Request For Proposal (RFP);
- developing evaluation criteria; and
- inviting internal and external bids.

Previous chapters have discussed the need for joint senior management and IT management participation in sourcing evaluations. We also discussed the evaluation process that most frequently led to success, namely create an RFP, and invite both external and internal bids. We showed how this practice ensures that a supplier's bid is not merely compared with current IT performance, but with IT performance that could be achieved if internal managers were empowered to behave like suppliers.

Supplier stakeholders became much more active during this phase. In addition to the *supplier senior management* team, a host of supplier experts attended bid presentations. In some cases, like British Aerospace (BAe), suppliers helped to win the bid by talking to many customer stake-

Table 8.2 *IT outsourcing phases*

	Scoping phase	Evaluation phase	Negotiation phase	Transition phase	Middle phase	Mature phase
Activities	• Identify core IT capabilities • Identify IT activities for potential outsourcing using business, economic, and technical criteria	• Measure baseline services • Measure baseline costs • Create RFP • Develop evaluation criteria • Invite external and internal bids	• Conduct due diligence to verify RFP baseline claims • Negotiate service-level agreements • Create responsibility matrices • Price work units • Negotiate terms for employee transfer • Negotiate mechanisms for contractual change, including benchmarking, open-book accounting, non-exclusivity clauses, and pricing schedules	• Distribute contract to IT users • Interpret the contract • Establish post-contract management infrastructure and processes • Implement consolidation, rationalization, standardization • Validate service scope, costs, levels, and responsibilities for baseline services • Manage additional service requests • Foster realistic expectations of supplier performance	• Benchmark performance to (theoretically) reset prices • Realign the contract to reflect changes in technology and business • Involve the supplier on more value-added areas	• Recalibrate investment criteria to reflect shorter time horizon for recouping investments • Determine if the relationship will be terminated or extended

| *Objective* | Identify flexible IT organization, including IT activities for potential outsourcing | Select best and final offer | Sign contract(s) | • Publicly promote the contract | Establish operational performance | Achieve value-added above operational performance | No lapses in operational performance during final transition |

holders. While Computer Sciences Corporation (CSC) obviously talked to senior business managers about finances, they also talked to BAe users about service, to the IT staff about career paths/benefits, and to IT managers about baseline service-level agreements. Several BAe and CSC informants indicated that CSC was successful in winning the bid in large part because of their expertise in aerospace and their ability to talk business language:

> The senior managers within BAe and even more the managers within the business wanted to hear people talking their language, the language of making airplanes. And we were able to do that, we were able to produce these people who talked their language—CSC Quality Manager (transferred from BAe).

Like the previous phase, the customer/supplier interactions—although tentative—were typically characterized by enthusiasm and optimism at the senior management level during the evaluation phase.

The *customer IT users* were primarily concerned with service excellence during the entire outsourcing evaluation. As previously noted, IT users sometimes questioned confidentiality and privacy of data with IT outsourcing. But, in general, IT users typically supported outsourcing because they perceived that suppliers—with their IT expertise—would increase service and provide new IT to the user community.

At the *customer IT staff level*, however, IT professionals were frequently threatened by the impending decision. Some organizations, particularly those with an IT labor union, experienced significant resistance from this stakeholder group. Indeed, BAe and the Inland Revenue's unionized IT staff both held strikes in opposition to outsourcing.

In cases in which IT staff were invited to submit an alternative bid, the internal bid process often served as a galvanizing force. In some cases, senior management granted a request for an internal bid more as a 'morale-preserver' than as a serious contender against external bidders. Once given free rein to compete based on cost efficiency, internal IT managers from eight of our cases surprised senior management by submitting the winning bid. Sourcing evaluations which led to continued insourcing of the IT function, proceeded to a transition phase. The primary activity of the insourcing transition phase is the implementation of consolidation, rationalization, and standardization of the internal bid proposal.

Sourcing evaluations that result in outsourcing were found to proceed through four further phases (see below). Unlike insourcing, IT outsourcing requires significant changes in duties and responsibilities of IT management, staff, and users (Currie and Willcocks 1998; Feeny and

Willcocks 1998). Also, more stakeholders must adapt and learn to inter-act with each other to deliver a cost-effective IT service.

Phase 3: Negotiation

Customer Goal: 'Negotiate a contract to ensure sourcing expectations are realized.'

The previous chapter on contract negotiations discussed some of the principles of negotiating deals, including the proven practices of nego-tiating short-term contracts and detailed contracts. The South Australia Government, DuPont, British Aerospace, and Inland Revenue spent considerably more than a year negotiating contract details. These con-tract details included:

- conducting due diligence to verify RFP baseline claims;
- negotiating service-level agreements for 500 or more IT services;
- creating customer/supplier responsibility matrices for more than 700 responsibilities;
- pricing 20 to 30 units of work, such as CPU minutes, number of UNIX boxes, man-hours of analyst time, etc.;
- negotiating terms for the transfer of employees at equivalent or better benefits; and
- agreeing on mechanisms for contractual change, including bench-marking, open-book accounting, non-exclusivity clauses, and pricing schedules.

It is quite clear that contract negotiations are antagonistic, because the customer stakeholders and supplier stakeholders are each accountable for protecting the interests of their respective organizations. Participants have used the nouns 'war', 'blood bath', and 'battle' to describe negotia-tions. No parties, however, seemed to expect a different type of relation-ship during contract negotiations. Each side expected the other to be a tough negotiator. Indeed, one CSC account executive even complimen-ted BAe on their negotiating skills:

> BAe, say that for Military Aircraft, 70% of the cost of the Eurofighter is brought in from somewhere else. So they are used to, and their whole culture is around one of, deal-making and negotiating and hard-bargaining. And they are brought up in that and they play hard ball extremely well—CSC Account Executive.

During outsourcing negotiations, *customer IT managers* were typically tough negotiators. They fought very hard to represent the interests of their organizations. At a US bank, for example, the VP of IS was adamant that she was not going to pay a $US500 000 software license transfer fee. The supplier threatened to shut down the datacenter (and thus the bank) unless the bill was paid. Here is how the VP of IS and the financial manager responded:

> We called our attorneys. Our attorneys called their attorneys. Ours said, 'How dare you threaten to shut down a national bank. You think you can shut down a national bank?' But that was a very difficult period, after they sent us that shut down letter. Finally, they said, 'I think we better go see these people.' Thursday morning they came in and it was a shouting match back and forth. And they said, 'We don't have to put up with this.' And they got up and left. Their attorneys called me the next day and apologized for their marketers. The next week we negotiated from $US500 000 down to $US110 000.

Despite tough negotiations, the bank's deal ended up being a success. We found similar situations in many organizations: tough battles during contract negotiations between customer and supplier constituents often led to successful arrangements. After a contract is signed, however, the customers and suppliers sought a more harmonious relationship. The South Australian (SA) government even hosted a session between SA IT managers and EDS managers to quickly move from the adversarial posturing of contract negotiations to the more cooperative delivery of the contract.

IT users are another stakeholder group that is involved in contract negotiations. Because IT outsourcing contracts typically rely on a base-line measure of services, users became involved in documenting current service levels and volumes. IT users were generally motivated to actually inflate current service levels. In essence, this would enable them to get the supplier to increase service levels under a fixed-fee baseline price. But suppliers were keenly aware of the motivation, and thus suppliers required a documented and detailed due diligence process to verify baseline claims.

During the negotiation phase, potential *supplier account managers* are often interviewed by the customer stakeholders. Initial meetings were often characterized by tentativeness as each party explored the other's motivations and values. Customer stakeholders were motivated to select a person who would primarily focus on customer service. Supplier stakeholders—who are accountable to their shareholders—needed a person who would protect their profit margins. In many of our cases, customers did not select a person who was part of the supplier negotiating team. When customers experienced a supplier's tough negotiating skills first hand, they naturally retreated from the individual. Instead, a fresh face often helped the transition from antagonism during the nego-tiation phase to cooperation during the transition phase.

In general, all parties agree that even though contract negotiations are antagonistic, the process is worthwhile for both sides. Detailed contracts document expectations and are therefore a pre-requisite for a successful relationship:

> It is important to have a sound base contract. It is important because that's how operating trust is built—VP CSC.

> There should be no ambiguity in the contract as to what is baseline or fixed price or essentially free, in scope. What is actually there to be done and who is paying for it. It should be totally crystal-clear—CSC Account Manager on BAe Contract.

Phase 4: Transition

Customer Goal: 'Establish precedents for operational performance.'

On large contracts, transition activities may last from 18 months to over two years. Our research shows eight main areas of activity here, as we now detail.

1. *Distributing the contract.* Many actual IT outsourcing contracts are impossible to execute from because they are typically massive documents written in obscure legal terminology. Mega-contracts may contain 30 000 lines and require several legal-sized boxes for a single copy. In the early days of a mega-contract, one of the major tasks of the centralized contract management team is to develop user guides to the contract. The guides are designed to describe what the supplier is obligated to provide under the fixed-fee structure in user terms.

The major stakeholders involved in this activity are the *customer IT managers* and the *IT users*. Often the stakeholders goals were in conflict. IT users, particularly division managers, wanted to see the entire contract. IT managers wanted only to distribute summaries of the contract because they felt that every IT user would interpret the contract differently:

> We find anything you write down and distribute to a group of people, those people interpret it differently and they try to execute against their interpretation—Global Alliance Manager, DuPont.

Indeed, on many contracts, *IT users* fought with *supplier IT staff* over the contract. At DuPont, for example, work on 150 major projects was halted due to lack of project pricing. Lower level employees were not sure how to behave—How can we do this work when it has not been properly priced and approved? Once the DuPont IT managers and CSC account managers were aware of the problem, they sent clear messages to lower level employees: do the work and we'll worry about the price:

> But just last week, they had a client that was doing design work for them on the network connection. CSC quoted a price they felt too high. And I looked at it and said, 'We'll just do it, we'll worry about the quote later'—Dual BAe–CSC Account Executive.

2. *Interpreting the contract*. No matter how well the negotiating teams believe they had nailed down the details, the contract was always open to interpretation. Typically, the *customer IT managers* and *supplier account managers* were in charge of resolving contract interpretation issues. Clearly stakeholder goals are conflicting because each side is charged with protecting their own organization's interests. Each side sought a fair resolution, but financial pressures fuelled the tension. A precedent resolved during the transition phase could have millions of dollars worth of consequences during the remainder of the contract: 'What may be only £6000 today might set a precedent worth £10 million—IT Services Manager, British Aerospace.

Some examples serve to illustrate the ambiguity typically found in contracts:

- If the customer needs system maintenance that requires the supplier to bring the datacenter down over the weekend, who pays supplier overtime?
- What is included in the fixed price of a standard hardware upgrade? Is analyst time spent identifying requirements billable or included in the fixed price? Are installation, wiring, and shipping and handling costs included or billable?

DuPont, like other customers, realized that more staff should have been retained to address these issues:

> Had we known that was coming, we would have saved more resources, or kept more resource to help with both the continuing negotiation, definition of the deal, as well as I would say it has taken more resources than anticipated to put in place all these managing processes that are required as part of the transition or start-up of the deal—Global Alliance Manager, DuPont.

3. *Establishing post-contract management infrastructure and processes*. Here, customers typically established centralized teams to facilitate the contract monitoring and vendor development roles. Centralized teams focused on financial and strategic management of the contract. Contract facilitation roles were typically decentralized (see Chapter 7 for details on these roles). Decentralized teams focused on daily operations.

For problem resolution, many customers and suppliers sought cooperative processes rather than unproductive adversarial processes. At DuPont and Inland Revenue in 1999, joint customer/supplier teams were delegated responsibility for solving operational problems. The teams are typically comprised of *customer IT users, customer IT staff,* and *supplier IT staff.* The goal is for the joint teams to resolve the problem before escalating the issue to their superiors:

> If we think that there are any stand-offs that are occurring, any differences of opinion we can't get to the bottom of, we attempt to try and sort it as joint teams ... we apply it at the contract level and the two contract management teams ... have active discussions about particular issues and they consider positions from both sides. And ... where they can't come to some agreement, it comes up the management hierarchy and will come to myself and an equivalent within EDS to see if we can mediate on these things—Account Manager, IR.

Although customers are expected to represent customer interests, and suppliers are expected to represent supplier interests, the joint teams create an environment of compromise. The operating principle of joint teams is to be fair and not to exploit any contract inefficiencies. At Dupont, by late 1998, 120 operational problems had been successfully resolved in this manner.

4. *Implementing consolidation, rationalization, and standardization.* Customer stakeholders were well aware that suppliers' bids were based, in part, on projected savings from implementing cost-reduction practices after the contract was signed. Cost-reduction tactics included consolidating datacenters, standardizing software and hardware platforms, creating stringent service request approval processes, centralizing IT staff, implementing chargeback systems, etc. These practices were often unpopular with IT users because they perceived that such practices would reduce service levels. In fact, insourcing proposals were often rejected because senior executives perceived that internal IT managers lacked the political clout to overcome user resistance to cost-reduction tactics. Once a supplier takes over a customer's assets, however, they clearly had the power to manage resources in a more efficient manner.

Customer IT managers supported *supplier account managers* in their cost-reduction practices. They realized that the supplier needed the savings to earn a profit on the account. Indeed, many customers complimented suppliers on their ability to consolidate, rationalize, and standardize:

> EDS did in 12 months what we couldn't do in four years—Contract Administrator, South Australia Government.

I was so impressed with the preparation activities and the actual execution of the migration to their datacenter. There were few interruptions in service to the users. [The vendor] made this very detailed, complex move look like it wasn't difficult at all—Manager of IS, US Metal Company.

5. *Validating baseline service scope, costs, levels, and responsibilities.* A major transition challenge for all relationships was validating the baseline. Supplier bids were based on the RFP and discoveries made during due diligence. Any undiscovered items were typically subject to excess fees. After the IR–EDS contract went into effect, for example, IR had to pay for the following items that surfaced:

- £100 000 for software license fees
- £5 million per year caused by inaccuracies in the original tender offers
- £15 million per year for hardware maintenance

As far as validating baseline service levels, typically, *customer IT staff* and *supplier IT staff* are charged with the task. At DuPont, for example, baseline service levels are verified by joint teams distributed around the globe. Because failure to meet service levels can result in financial penalties, the stakeholder goals were typically in conflict. Each is motivated to blame the other for service lapses. To avoid disputes during the transition phase, DuPont agreed to suspend cash penalties for non-performance for the first year of the contract. As one DuPont employee noted, '90% of the service lapses were inherited from us'. Because the financial consequence was removed, parties at DuPont are working together to improve service lapses, rather than merely trying to blame one another.

6. *Managing additional service requests beyond baseline.* Services beyond baseline—and thus subject to excess fees—can be triggered by

- exceeding projected volumes on existing services,
- changing the composition of baseline services, and/or
- demanding entirely new services.

Nearly every outsourcing customer we studied experienced all three sources of change. Indeed, a common lament among *customer IT managers* and *supplier account managers* was, '*we completely underestimated user demand*'. During an often two-year outsourcing decision process, many organizations instituted a buying freeze. Once the contract went into effect, user demands were no longer constrained:

The whole process until we had a contract in place was about two and a half years. During that period of time, the government pretty much put a freeze on buying equipment, things like that. So there was a pent-up demand that we all under-estimated. The number of change requests overwhelmed us. The number of change requests so far has been something like 2000. And this is new servers, new LANs, those kind of things. We went, for example, and these are approximate numbers, at the time of taking over the baseline, they had about 1000 LAN servers out there. And there are now about 1800. So that's an example—Vendor VP of Operations in a major central government deal.

Supplier account managers typically have the resources and financial motivation to meet any volume of demand. *Customer IT managers* were typically charged with keeping excess fees to a minimum. Thus, stakeholder goals were often in conflict during this task. At the very least, customer IT managers tried to ensure that users only requested beyond baseline items if the benefits generated covered the excess costs. For example, one business unit manager at British Aerospace requested a shop control system that would save him £250 000. But the BAe Contract Manager pointed out that it would cost £500 000 to build!

7. *Fostering realistic expectations of supplier performance.* We have noted several times that *IT users* often have misperceptions about what the supplier is obligated to provide the customer. Although contract summaries are distributed to IT users, the user community can comprise thousands of individuals.

IT users often expected a step-change in service, but contracts typically required maintenance of current service levels at a reduced cost. Both *customer IT managers* and *supplier account managers* shared the goal of communicating contractual obligations to the IT user community. Customer IT managers wanted users to have realistic expectations for several reasons:

- not wanting IT users to demand a higher level of service that could trigger excess fees;
- not wanting IT users to be disappointed in their management of the contract;
- not wanting IT users to complain unfairly to the supplier because it causes tension and requires management intervention.

Suppliers also wanted users to understand the contractual obligations because customer satisfaction is obviously a goal of all suppliers—and customer satisfaction requires realistic expectations of supplier performance.

Because goals are shared, customer IT managers were generally very supportive of the supplier for this activity. Internal IT managers have historically been in the same position of trying to balance user expectations for service excellence with cost constraints. The contract administrator at the South Australian government, for example, expressed his support of the supplier in achieving realistic IT user expectations:

> I've actually been an outsourcer before.... There is generally an expectation of management on the user side that here is this knight in shining armor, I'll get three times better service at half the price. And also what happens, that expectation grows as you get closer to contract, so you have this large gap in expectations from the start—Contract Administrator, South Australian Government.

8. *Publicly promoting the IT contract.* Another common activity in which customer and supplier stakeholders had shared goals was promoting the IT contract to the general public. Particularly in public sector outsourcing, taxpayers and opposing elected officials were often critical of outsourcing, and thus the *customer senior managers* and *supplier senior managers* would often jointly hold press conferences to explain the benefits of the relationship to the public. Although both sides admit relationships are not always easy, customers and suppliers stress the overall value to taxpayers.

At UK Inland Revenue, the status of the contract is actually reported to Parliament. Both Inland Revenue contract managers and EDS supplier account managers collaborate on parliamentary and strategic planning committees:

> It's a committee chaired by the Deputy Chairman, and actually we have representation from EDS on that committee. So we have joint representation on that committee and of course when we are providing estimates of what certain policy changes would cost, estimates are coming from the EDS camp. We've got [EDS and IR] people collaborating with our feasibility appraisal team in what those estimates would be and what the costs would be—Account Manager, IR.

Phase 5: Middle Phase

Goal: 'Achieve value-added above and beyond operational performance.'

Here, customers seek to adapt and to improve the contract beyond the baseline. Cost reduction, service improvement, and more strategic views of IT service delivery are sought. The major activities in this phase included benchmarking performance, realigning the contract, and involving the supplier in value-added areas. Because of the history of working with the supplier, parties during the middle phase were typically comfortable changing hats from adversaries to cooperators to collaborators, depending on the task at hand. By the middle phase, the complexity of relationships had become second nature, though the relational climate much depended on how the overall outsourcing arrangement was turning out.

1. *Benchmarking performance.* Benchmarking is the practice of comparing a customer's IT performance against a reference group of similar organizations. In this phase, benchmarking is used as a tool to ensure that the supplier's costs and services are among the best-of-breed. Customers view benchmarking as a powerful tool to leverage their bargaining position with the supplier.

The major stakeholders involved in this activity were the *customer IT managers* and the *supplier account managers.* Customers wanted to use benchmarking to reduce prices or increase service levels under the fixed-fee umbrella. Suppliers wanted to use benchmarking to demonstrate that their performance is already superior, and therefore prices need not be reduced. Thus, it is quite clear that stakeholder goals are in conflict. In addition, because benchmarks could reset prices, the financial consequences of this activity could again result in millions of dollars, serving to add to the tension.

In general, benchmarking firms competently measure the cost and service of technical platforms, such as IBM mainframe datacenters, UNIX midrange computing, or LAN performance. But customer and supplier participants both agree that the benchmarking industry is immature in a number of areas, particularly desktop computing and applications development and support. A few customers, for example, used function points to measure application productivity and quality. But benchmarking results were contested by the supplier. Application productivity depends not only on the supplier's performance, but on the quality of the systems inherited from the customer. Over-customized and jury-rigged legacy systems required a significant amount of supplier support. Is it fair to compare their performance against the productivity of application packages?

> Our experience, being honest, is that I haven't been terribly happy with the benchmarking process. This is not happy for CSC nor BAe. It's just the process seems to be a little bit naive—BAe Contract Manager.

Despite the limitations of benchmarking, customers believe it is still a valuable tool because it provides at least some rational data on performance.[4]

2. *Realigning the contract.* Customers frequently found that the original contract became obsolete as technology advanced, business

requirements changed, and false assumptions became illuminated. Technology changes included a shift from mainframe computing to client/server, deregulation of the telecommunications industry, and the emergence of new technologies such as the Internet and enterprise-wide systems (such as SAP). Business requirement changes were prompted by government regulations—such as the Self Assessment project at Inland Revenue—acquisitions, mergers, and divestitures. Illuminated false assumptions included poor estimates of baseline services, volumes, and costs. In addition, original contract mechanisms designed for one purpose may be operationalized in unintended ways. Some customers capped supplier margins which actually motivated supplier under-performance in practice, such as awarding the supplier a set mark-up on new capital IT investments; the more the technology cost, the more the supplier earned.

A number of participants claimed that contracts could not be valid for a period of more than three years. After that, contracts had to be renegotiated:

> The nature of this technology is volatile, that it was extremely difficult to predict for even two or three years, much less ten, with any degree of confidence ... And whether it's two years, three years, five years, you're increasingly going to see involvement in renegotiating to cover the kinds of technology situations that were unforeseeable when you struck the deal— Director of IS Planning, Energy Company.

During a contract realignment, *customer IT managers* and *supplier account managers* were the most active stakeholders. Stakeholder goals were in conflict because each side is motivated to protect the interests of their own organizations. By this stage in the relationship, however, relationships have progressed beyond the tentativeness of original contract negotiations. The customer and supplier constituents had a history of working together, and both were committed to perpetuating the relationship. At British Aerospace and Inland Revenue, both sides wanted to realign the contract to help set realistic expectations. Indeed parties expect to go through a realignment exercise every few years:

> We've come to the conclusion that actually what we have, and what we need to do intellectually, is come to terms with the contract itself. [It] has to be a much more dynamic, moving, changing thing, rather than a set-in-stone thing. And without wishing to change the past, we've jointly been working to realign the mechanisms so that they produce results which are more in keeping with what we went after. But the important factor is that we anticipate to do the same thing again in two to three years time. And then two to three years after that, we will do the same thing again. Not because we got it wrong, but because the change in technologies and changing user requirements—Contract Manager, Aerospace Company.

3. *Involving the supplier in value-added areas.* The primary focus of the transition phase was to establish operational performance. From the number of transition activities discussed in the previous phase, it was quite apparent that customers and suppliers devote all their time and resources to making the IT service work. Once transition tasks have been accomplished, customer and supplier stakeholders alike sought ways to extend the relationship into more value-added areas. Indeed, one of the nine core IT capabilities discussed in Chapter 7 is this 'vendor development' role. Here, the 'value-added' may include cooperative relationships or collaborative relationships, depending on whether goals are complementary or shared. Value-added areas included:

- Supplier participation on steering committees. The idea was to include an IT perspective on business initiatives and strategies.
- Selling customer IT assets and jointly sharing profits. We only have a few limited examples of this activity, such as a supplier selling a customer's data models to a UK retailer.
- Supplier participation on business processing re-engineering projects. Again, we only have a few examples of this value-added, such as re-engineering the invoicing process at UK Inland Revenue.

The search for value-added continues to be a goal—albeit an elusive one—among participants. While everyone was talking about 'value-added', few had actually achieved it. See, for example, the difficulties BP Exploration experienced on this in Chapter 6. The following quotations also express these sentiments:

> Value-added, it's one of the goals. It's value-adding but has to be done on both sides. CSC has to turn a profit and has to allow BAe to turn a profit. If you were signing up a partner, you wouldn't want your partner to lose money. You want your partner to be successful. So I think the value-added term is used with the implicit understanding that that implies that CSC is also prospering to some level—CSC Account Executive.

> One of the things that the customers seem most disappointed in is that they looked at these kind of suppliers as 'you understand the future of IT and what its capabilities are and harnessing IT for the business value'. And from that perspective, they seem to be disappointed that now everything is very technical—how many LANs, WANs, desktops, etc... . They complain that the contract is getting in the way. And I think the contract is getting in the way of that kind of vision. We took IT strategy right out of the contract—Consultant, South Australia Government.

Phase 6: The Mature Phase

Customer Goal: 'Determine and plan for the fate of current sourcing options.'

During the mature phase, the customer's goal is to first ensure continued operational performance if the relationship is not to be renewed. In cases where relationships are extended, the mature phase provides an opportunity to learn from past experiences as well as to explore creative options when constructing a new deal. Assessment of these options will depend as much on business strategic concerns and the nature of the current and future competitive climate as on the strength of relationships and past value of the outsourcing arrangement. Although only a few of our long-term deals have researched this stage, two activities were apparent.

1. *Recalibrate investment criteria.* When suppliers make IT investments on behalf of a customer, the supplier needs time to recoup the investment. As the contract reaches the expiration date, reinvestment becomes a major issue. The suppliers will not want to invest in new capital assets if the customer decides not to extend the relationship. At the IR, for example, both sides must make sure that EDS has an opportunity to gain a return on investment as the contract matures:

> Unless we can some way manage a revenue stream for them beyond the contract, that's going to be increasingly difficult if we are asking them for investment. We are both jointly aware that that's a real difficulty for us. We've got to re-explore how we are going to cope with that. Otherwise we are going to stultify entirely as we get closer and closer to the end of the contract—Account Manager, IR.

2. *Determine if relationship will be extended or terminated.* Some participants were so concerned about what happens at the end of contracts, that they avoided outsourcing altogether:

> Another concern that we had was that if we did a five year deal say, what happens at the end of the five years? If we don't get along well, or we want it back and we had transferred the people, then we are in a real bad situation—Corporate Manager of Planning and Administration, Petroleum Company.

But are customers in a bad position? In general, three options are possible:

- extend the contract with current supplier(s),
- switch supplier(s), or
- bring the IT activity back in-house.

Table 8.3 *Case study contract expiration dates: total outsourcing contracts*

Contract expiration date (year)	Case study organization
2000	BANK1; METAL; LOGIST; FINANCE1; PSB9
2001	TRANS; MINE; CONSULT; RETAIL9
2002	AERO3
2003	AERO1; RETAIL1; PETRO1;
2004	PSB1; PSB5; AERO2; EQUIP2
2005	BANK4; RETAIL5; PSB9
2006	RETAIL5
2007	CHEM4; EQUIP1

Our CIO survey data also shows that all three options are commonly practiced in the US and UK markets: 51% switched supplier, 34% brought the activity back in-house, and 11% renewed the original contract (according to other 1999 surveys, mainland European organizations show much less propensity to change supplier or bring IT back in-house at the end of contract). On termination of agreements in 1998 BP Exploration successfully renewed some contracts, reduced others, and also brought in a new supplier. We have examples of all three options from our case studies. In no situation were the consequences devastating—indeed all three options can be executed without serious disruption in service as long as customers plan for events well in advance. GOODS switched suppliers. ELECTRIC1 opted to renew their contract with the original supplier. CHEM1, RUBBER, and PSB6 brought the IT function back in-house (see at `http://www.umsl.edu/~lacity/cases.htm`):

- CHEM1 migrated off the supplier's mainframe platform to a mid-range system and also rehired 40 transferred personnel.
- RUBBER was a large enough company to migrate the IT activities to a subsidiary's datacenter.
- PSB6's contract was deemed illegal and assets and people were reverted back to the government.

Of the 32 total outsourcing decisions studied, however, 23 are still in their original contract period (see Table 8.3). Thus, we will continue to track our case study companies as they approach the mature years.

CONCLUSION

Many 'partnership' frameworks consider only the 'customer' and 'supplier' as relevant stakeholders. Our research found this duality to be over-simplified and naive. To fill the gap in the popular literature, this chapter focused on the dynamic relationships among at least eight distinct types of stakeholders: customer senior business managers, customer senior IT managers, customer IT staff, customer IT users, supplier senior managers, supplier account managers, and supplier IT staff. And while much prior research has focused on making sourcing decisions, little research has addressed post-contract management transition, the middle phase, and the mature phase. By understanding the common post-contract management activities and the inherent stakeholder goals and relationships during these activities, customers and suppliers can better plan and manage their contracts.

We do, however, note one caveat about stereotyping stakeholders. Our stakeholder analysis described the general goals and perceptions of stakeholder members. While generalizations are an effective tool for summarizing common experiences, they do ignore the role of individual personalities in the success of customer/supplier relationships. In several instances, stakeholder relationships improved when the person was replaced. Customer and supplier account managers, in particular, had a high turnover rate in several of the mega-deals studied. The following participant quotes testify to the effectiveness of new faces:

> I think the major thing that's driven change in the relationship is the fact that there has been a change in the head of IT and there's been a change of CSC account executive. It just so happened that [the CSC account executive] and myself worked in another British Aerospace industry together which was much smaller with less problems so that we were able to develop a good working relationship and we've brought that relationship to MAD—BAe Contract Manager, MAD Division.

> At the beginning of this contract, we actually had to change both of the contract managers three months into the contract to get a more reasonable basis for the relationship because the two of them over the opening three months had continued the negotiations. They were locking horns day in, day out. We had to take both of those individuals out and try to recover that relationship. I think that's been successful—Account Manager, IR.

> I think it's unhealthy in any case to perpetuate the same relationships for too long, because you then know each other so well that you very rarely bring a new perspective onto things, a fresh pair of eyes with a new set of ideas— BAe General Contract Manager.

Thus, relationship management not only requires an understanding of stakeholder goals and expectations, but, as Chapter 9 underlines, a human resource sensitivity as to the individuals who fill these roles.

Indeed, a major concern of many participants in mega-deal situations is the continual renewal of skills and experiences to fill these roles, particularly during a 10-year relationship. At DuPont in 2000, for example, the current team of contract facilitators and contract monitors had 10 or more years experience at DuPont. Thus, they had accumulated an understanding of DuPont's business-specific needs as well as an understanding of how IT supports those needs. As team attrition occurs, DuPont questions how these stakeholders will be replaced.

NOTES

1. Caldwell, B., Violino, B. and McGee, M. (1997). Hidden Partners, Hidden Dangers: Security and Service Quality May be at Risk When Your Outsourcing Vendors Use Subcontractors. *Information Week*, Issue 614, January 20.
2. Williamson, O. (1975). *Markets and Hierarchies: Analysis and Antitrust Implications. A Study in the Economics of Internal Organization*, The Free Press, New York, p. 14.
3. See Lacity and Hirschheim (1995a) for case studies on IT empowerment as a consequence of outsourcing evaluations.
4. For a detailed analysis, see Lacity, M. and Hirschheim, R. (1996). The Role of Benchmarking in Demonstrating IS Performance. In Willcocks, L. (ed.), *Investing in Information Systems*. TB Press, London.

9
Future Sourcing

... if I outsourced tomorrow I might save a dollar or two on each account, but I would lose flexibility and value and service levels—Nigel Morris, President of Capital One, US Credit Card Company.

E-commerce, e-money, e-bay, e-trade ... its e-topia—Jack Kemp, at The 2000 Outsourcing World Summit, February 21–23, Orlando, Florida.

As the labor market gets tougher, and as outsourcing firms beef up their capabilities, we might take a look [at Application Service Provision] again, but only at the generic business applications like payroll, HR and some aspects of financials. But on logistics? That is the core of our business. We'd have to train ASPs on that forever—IT Manager, Medium Sized Retailer, 1999.

We can go from quote to cash without ever touching a physical asset or piece of paper. You've heard of JIT manufacturing, well this is not-at-all manufacturing—VP, Cisco Systems.

INTRODUCTION

IT outsourcing has outlived the five-year period typical of a management fad. From an initial main focus on cost reduction, IT outsourcing is becoming a complementary, routine mode of managing IT. We estimate that global market revenues will be $US150 billion by 2004, with 30%–35% of most large organizations' IT budgets managed by outsourcing arrangements. 'Why not outsource IT?' is no longer, if it ever was, an adequate question from which to make and manage outsourcing decisions. The real question is: 'How do we exploit the ever-maturing external IT services market to achieve strategic business leverage?' In this final chapter we look back at the evidence assembled in this book, and forward at developing trends and practices to discern how organizations are seeking answers to this question.

OUTSOURCING REPORT CARD REVISITED: PRACTICES AND RISKS

It is clear that some organizations have sought strategic business leverage through total outsourcing. Mega-deals, like those at Xerox, Dupont (Chapter 2), McDonnell Douglas (now Boeing), and Continental Bank in the United States, Commonwealth Bank, Lend Lease Corporation, and South Australia Government in Australia (Chapter 2), and BAe and Inland Revenue in the United Kingdom (Chapter 3), have often been referred to as 'strategic alliances'. From media coverage one could be forgiven for believing this type of outsourcing still to be the dominant approach. In fact, a much richer picture emerges from this book of the IT sourcing paths organizations have been taking (see Figure 9.1). In 2000, many still sought tactical IT gains rather than strategic business advantage.

By far the dominant mode has been selective sourcing, especially in the United States and the United Kingdom (respectively 82% and 75% of organizations in 1999—see the Appendix). A mixed portfolio, 'best-source' approach typically has seen 15%–30% of the IT budget under

	In-house Commitment	Selective Sourcing	Total Outsourcing	Total Outsourcing
ATTITUDE	Core Strategic Asset	Mixed Portfolio	Non-Core Necessary Cost	World Class Provision
PROVIDERS	IT Employees Loyal To The Business	'Horses For Courses'	Vendor	'Strategic Partner'
EMPHASIS	'Value Focus'	'Value For Money'	'Money' ⟶ 'Added Value?'	
RISKS	High Cost Insular Unresponsive	Management Overhead	Exploitation By Suppliers	Unbalanced Risk/Reward/ Innovation

Figure 9.1   *IT sourcing: main approaches* (Source: Feeny, Willcocks and Lacity/ OXIIM)

third-party management, with other IT needs met through buying-in resources under in-house management (insourcing), and through internal IT staffing. Many organizations (US 10%, UK 23% in 1999) have no significant IT outsourcing contracts. Here IT is perceived as a core strategic asset, with IT employees loyal to the business and striving to achieve business advantage in ways that external providers are deemed unable to do. Consider Capital One, a US credit card group with 12 000 employees, 1000 of them in IT. In 1999, Capital One lent $US17.4 billion to 18 million customers. According to the president Nigel Morris:[1]

> If you have a business that churns out products, then outsourcing makes sense. But if you are in a business where rapid but tailored products are essential and where listening to the customer is the way you survive, then you need to have business development people who sit next to the IT people ... IT is our central nervous system ... if I outsourced tomorrow I might save a dollar or two on each account, but I would lose flexibility and value and service levels.

Total outsourcing (80% or more of the IT budget under third-party management of a single or multiple suppliers) is a distinctly minority pursuit. In the United States some 8% of organizations took this route in 1999; in the United Kingdom, about 2%. World-wide there were just over 140 such deals as at 2000.

All IT sourcing arrangements have inherent risks (see Figure 9.1). A mainly in-house function needs to be continually assessed against the market to prevent high costs and unresponsiveness. With selective sourcing, one risk is management overhead cost, falling typically between four to eight percent of outsourcing costs, even before the effectiveness of the consequent management arrangements is assessed.[2] Large-scale outsourcing deals can achieve expected cost savings, but often at the risk of IT operational and business strategic inflexibility (see below). Alternatively, incomplete contracts, or negligible profit margins through over-tight contracts, can, and have, promoted hidden costs. Finally, as has been made clear throughout the book, underdeveloped approaches to 'strategic partnerships' can be high risk. Indeed many have seen significant restructuring 18−24 months into the deal.

Despite all the rhetoric on shareholder value and strategic sourcing, surveys continue to show that accessing technical expertise and cutting costs are still major outsourcing drivers. For example, in 1999, Forrester Research Group identified the following motivators for IT outsourcing:

- 55% gaining better technical expertise
- 53% cutting costs

- 38% focusing on core capabilities
- 30% solving IT staff problems

Forrester Research also found that the inability to realize business value was the number one 'pain point' experienced by outsourcing customers. Arcane pricing structures was the second most frequent complaint.

Against this background of risks, during the 1990s most organizations that outsourced IT pursued one of two approaches. In incremental/tactical outsourcing the primary focus has been on cost reduction, efficiencies, and improved IT service. Our 1999/2000 survey suggests that such expected benefits have tended to be achieved (see Appendix A). Moreover, learning about outsourcing matures organizational capability, positioning these organizations for larger scale and more strategic outsourcing in the future. However, one consequence of incremental IT outsourcing has been that a minority of organizations encountered difficult problems impinging on business strategy. Some survey respondents claimed that 'the supplier does not understand our business' (37%); 'corporate strategy and IT no longer aligned' (35%); and 'poor strategic IT planning' (24%). Other organizations have taken a 'hard learning' route, signing significant outsourcing contracts without developing strategic outsourcing objectives—let alone the capabilities to deliver on these objectives.

STRATEGIC DISADVANTAGE?

Given these findings, it is important to pursue further the relationship between business strategy and IT outsourcing. Some studies suggest that strategic *disadvantage* may well be one outcome from outsourcing. In a study of 54 businesses over five years, and reporting in 1998, Weill and Broadbent[3] found those outsourcing at a faster rate had achieved lower costs, but also experienced greater strategic losses compared with organizations that did less outsourcing. These losses included:

- significantly increasing information systems staff turnover;
- longer time to market for new products;
- lower perceived product and service quality than their competitors;
- slower rate of increase in revenue per employee; and
- lower return on assets.

Firms that outsourced were more likely to be in industries where IT was less likely to be a core competence and a source of competitive advantage. *'In industries like retailing, where IT is becoming more of a core competence, we saw a significant reduction in the amount of outsourcing'* (Weill and Broadbent 1998, p. 65). Of course, these judgments of whether or not IT is a core competence will vary over time depending on how firms choose to compete.

Weill and Broadbent point out that cost-reduction benefits from outsourcing will suit firms with low-cost strategies, but they found that the benefits from outsourcing seemed to be restricted mainly to cost-reduction effects—a point endorsed by Nigel Morris at Capital One (above). This suggests that either those firms in their sample pursued primarily a cost-reduction outsourcing strategy, or that other benefits were also expected but not realized. Instead, adverse effects on strategic flexibility were a significant, unanticipated outcome.

But much depends on how firms wish to compete. Weill and Broadbent argue that firms requiring faster time to market and growth are better served by less outsourcing. Such organizations should restrict themselves to outsourcing well-understood commodities like datacenters, telecommunications and network services, and desktop maintenance. Their main point is that one needs to decide what IT capabilities are needed in the context of business strategy before sourcing for those capabilities. This was the central argument of Chapter 5. We discussed how business factors are superordinate to technical and economic factors. In all this, can organizations gain more than mainly cost-reduction effects from IT outsourcing? Is cost reduction that critical any more? Can organizations turn away from the potential for strategic disadvantage and leverage outsourcing for significant business advantage?

FROM TACTICAL TO STRATEGIC USES OF OUTSOURCING

Throughout this book we have described a number of organizations that are achieving strategic business leverage with their IT sourcing approaches. Using these and other examples, we can discern six strategic foci, used in combination or in isolation, by which organizations are increasingly attempting, and sometimes achieving, significant business advantage.

1. *Financial Restructuring: 'Improving the business's financial position while reducing or at least containing costs'.* Cost efficiency has remained a key organizational goal across most selective and total outsourcing customers. However, organizations like British Aerospace, McDonnell Douglas (now Boeing), Continental Bank, and UK retailer Sears have

sought wider long-term, significant changes in their financial position through outsourcing. Such companies were often in financial trouble. Outsourcing provides a significant cash influx from the transfer of IT assets and staff, together with tax advantages, thus helping to improve cash flow, and restructure the balance sheet and profit and loss account. As such, outsourcing represents a long-term financial strategy, supporting a turnaround in the firm's financial and competitive position over time in exchange for annual outsourcing fees.

During the early 1990s, single-supplier, total outsourcing deals were of this character (see Figure 9.1). But after the turnaround, many organizations changed the nature of the original deal. For example, McDonnell Douglas (MD) brought major applications back in-house, and when Boeing merged with MD, more IT functions returned, including servers. Overall the deal achieved its financial restructuring objectives, but a more selective approach has been sought as the company recovered. In British Aerospace's case, outsourcing bought it time to recover its financial position. But by 1999 much more was being done with the technology, and the IT budget as a whole had nearly doubled from 1993 (see Chapter 3).

2. *Core Competence:* 'Redirecting the business and IT into core competencies'. The major business imperative for the 1990s has been 'do what you do best and outsource the rest'. A self-espoused exemplar of this strategy is British Airways' (BA) transition to a 'virtual airline' in order to achieve £1 billion savings and a doubling of profits in the 1996–2000 period. The aim has been to focus on the transportation of passengers and cargo. To this extent, BA only needs to focus on owning its route structure, brand, and IT-based yield management system. Almost all other things can be outsourced, leased, or bought in.

Consider also BP Exploration (BPX) (Chapter 6). By 1990, in a worsening financial situation, BPX became much more focused on the core competence argument. BPX's key competence was exploration, and its key intelligence was in its explorers—not in IT or accounting, for example. The accounting function, including its IT, was outsourced in 1991 in a five-year, £55 million deal. According to John Browne, BP CEO: 'failure to outsource our commodity IT will permanently impair our business competitiveness'. However, this was to be achieved not by traditional outsourcing but by establishing a constellation of partners. In 1993, BPX signed five-year contracts with three suppliers worth $US35 million annually. These suppliers were chosen to support a strategy of becoming a more diversified production company. The suppliers helped move BPX into areas for which it did not have the necessary in-house IT skills. Subsequently, the BPX in-house team focused on business processes, information, and business value creation, while the suppliers focused on more routine applications and technology. One achievement was the dissemination of desktops throughout BPX, widely recognized as not possible without outsourcing. By 2000, the profitable BP–Amoco merger also outsourced its entire human resource function, including IT, to a single supplier.

3. *Technology Catalyst: 'Strengthening resources and flexibility in technology and service to underpin business's strategic direction'*. Outsourcing suppliers are regularly used to 'fill in' for IT skills shortages and to provide competitively priced computing power and service. However, some organizations have used outsourcing more strategically by using suppliers to help transform a traditional IT infrastructure and to achieve a new technology agenda to underpin business strategy. In the case of Polaris (Chapter 6), we saw how an in-house group developed software products for insurance brokering. Subsequently, Polaris used a technology supplier to underpin their strategic business direction.

In 1994, Xerox signed a 10-year global contract with EDS for an estimated $US3.2 billion. It became clear to Xerox that its business restructuring in the early 1990s rendered its existing systems and skills inadequate. The internal service was seen as ineffective, costing a lot of money without significant returns. A new infrastructure, which required an estimated investment of $US55 million just for hardware, was needed. Here outsourcing was designed to allow Xerox to refocus IT on business-critical applications, while the supplier facilitated routine operations, applications, telecommunications, and the move to a client/server infrastructure. The jury is still out on aspects of this deal, however. Moreover where cost reductions did take place they probably incapacitated the ability of Xerox to cope with a major change in marketing structure. In late 1999, Xerox lost control of its billing and sales commissions systems with big consequences for profitability. In early 2000 Xerox's market share value had dropped from above $US90 to below $US20[4] (see also Kern and Willcocks 2001).

DuPont looked for a similar 'technology catalyst' payoff in its $US4 billion, 10-year contracts signed with two suppliers in 1997 (see Chapter 2). Earlier cost-cutting at DuPont caused a lack of renewal of IT assets and skills. The IT infrastructure required several hundred million dollars of investments. Outsourcing became a serious option. DuPont looked to move its fixed IT costs to variable, improved service speed and flexibility, skill renewal, IT career development and further cost reductions. The suppliers bore the upfront investment costs in infrastructure as well as SAP training for 300 people, enabling DuPont to pay a variable fee for the benefits.

4. *Business Transition: 'Facilitating and supporting major organizational change'.* Forms of *transitional outsourcing* have frequently been used and are generally successful. This involves temporarily outsourcing technically mature IT during a period of major transition to a new technology (see Chapter 1). However, some organizations operate even more strategically, incorporating transitional IT outsourcing into a suite of outsourcing contracts to enable major organizational change. Typical times when outsourcing has been used are during mergers and acquisitions, new business start-ups, and major devolution/restructuring of the business, including privatization.

British Gas provides an example. Faced with privatization, deregulation, and devolution in the mid-1990s its IT director commented:

> some of the challenges have probably not been met in many other organizations in the world. We are seeing implementations in timescales thought impossible before. There is also incredible downsizing. One of the implications is you cannot do it all in-house, outsourcing is needed just to meet the challenging projects, their size, our lack of resources and the short timescales.

One effective transitional move in 1995 was to outsource all data-centers in an 18-month, £55 million deal. On a larger front, British Gas used a range of suppliers to assist in re-engineering, and to develop new billing, service, retail, and distribution IT systems for its five autonomous business units.

5. *Business Innovation: 'Using outsourcing to innovate processes, skills and technology, while mediating financial risk to achieve competitive advantage'.* Organizations looking to suppliers for business innovation have often been disappointed. BPX, for example, had to create an innovation fund for suppliers and BPX staff to bid for, such was the lack of innovation forthcoming (Chapter 6).

Yet external suppliers can assist in business innovation. Examples include various Private Financial Initiatives (PFIs) in the UK public sector, 'co-sourcing' deals at Rolls Royce and Citibank, and benefits funding mechanisms used by the US California Franchise Tax Board (CFTB) (Willcocks and Lester 1999). The essential ingredient in these deals is that the supplier uses IT to focus on the client's business objectives. At Rolls Royce, the co-sourcing deal is delivering re-engineered processes. At Citibank, the supplier is developing a Travel Agency commission system. At CFTB, the supplier is improving the accuracy, number, and revenues from tax returns. The supplier takes the investment risk upfront and gets paid on pre-agreed performance measures as business benefits are realized. However, performance-based contracts are perceived by suppliers as high risk and require a culture change in suppliers more accustomed to fee-paying type deals. This accounts for the very small percentage of performance-based contracts world-wide (see Chapter 1).

6. New Market: 'Direct profit generation through joint venturing with vendor partner'. Some organizations have experimented with new ways to generate external profits from their IT assets. Companies have used spin-offs, value-added outsourcing, and equity-holding deals to incent supplier performance, to secure the business relationship, and to make a profit.

As Chapter 1 revealed, some difficulties have been experienced with spin-offs. The new supplier needs to build commercial and marketing skills for a very competitive marketplace. We pointed out how electronics multinational Philips obtained success by taking shares in Dutch software house BSO. Philips transferred its development staff and subsequently its processing operations into a jointly owned company, Origin. BSO had an existing reputation and customer base to build on, and Philips was a ready-made large client. Even so, it took Origin several years to build a wider outsourcing market position.

Many deals have a 'value-added' element in them. Thus Xerox–EDS sought future shared revenues for the development and sale of a global electronic document distribution service. Mutual Life Insurance of New York and CSC sought to market software and services to the insurance industry. But, as Chapter 1 pointed out, partners must truly add value by offering products/services demanded by customers in the market. In several deals, this value-added element was too marginal to the overall fee-based contract to make a difference. Also, under pressure in other parts of the outsourcing contract, client and supplier may become less interested in the investment required to commercialize home-grown systems.

Finally, equity-holding deals such as Lend Lease–ISSC, Swiss Bank–Perot Systems, and Delta Airlines–AT&T have had some attractions. In principle, the mechanism of shared risks and rewards overcomes the previous conflicts inherent in fee-based contracts. However, the incentive of shareholder profit may operate at too high a level to influence performance on the ground. Also supporting the supplier's market and profit growth can conflict with service needs of the original client (see Chapter 1).

In summary, we saw how organizations use IT outsourcing to leverage business advantage. We would expect these practices to continue as well as new practices to emerge. But we would also expect the effective practices we have described in this book to help managers face new challenges described below.

TOWARDS THE NEW E-ECONOMY: TRENDS ... AND ISSUES

The dot.coms are often used as exemplars of the new economy. Many of the new dot.coms are essentially 95% outsourced services with front-end websites. Products are bought elsewhere. Distribution, accounting, financing, and most other business processes are outsourced. A team of often fewer than 50 individuals serves as the 'core'. While such a business model enables rapid innovation, the question remains whether these companies can survive.

By early 2000, many experts were arguing that the early innovators in the dot.com companies would lose significant market share when the Global 1000 companies respond by entering the Internet economy. Many dot.coms will likely be acquired by larger competitors. The smaller companies simply do not have the assets, resources, and name brand recognition to compete with very large firms. For example, industry watchers are looking at the attack of `Barnes&noble.com` on `Amazon.com`'s market share. As another example, `Netbank.com` was one of the first online banks, which incurred start-up costs of under half a million dollars. How will such a bank compete when large players choose to go online? Although Netbank did not incur 'bricks and mortar' costs, large banks have the competitive advantages of name brand recognition and a full range of financial services and products. Clearly, the business model of a small core capability and a large outsourced infrastructure faces considerable developments and testing during the next decade. (This issue is discussed further in the section 'Towards the Digital Assembly Line' below.)

In practice we see 10 additional IT sourcing trends to watch out for over the next few years. We start with the less web-based practices and move on to those much more typical of web-based business.

Backsourcing

Backsourcing involves taking back in-house what was previously outsourced. In our 1999–2000 survey, we found that almost one-third of canceled contracts were brought back in-house. A qualification: very few of any of these deals were total outsourcing contracts. However, there are some examples of canceled total outsourcing contracts. In 1997, Sears canceled a £344 million contract with Andersen Consulting after 17 months. Sears subsequently took back 500 staff and went down a selective outsourcing route (see Chapter 1). US-based chip-maker LSI Logic Corp terminated its outsourcing contract with IBM Global Services in 1997 because it felt locked into an agreement that was not keeping pace with the company's rapid growth. The company hired 50 specialists in 90 days, and focused the team on implementing big projects in discrete six-month stages. In the end, LSI achieved a 33% cost saving. By 2000, the company was only contracting out the operation of a computer server in the United Kingdom.

East Midlands Electricity signed a £150 million, 12-year deal with Perot Systems in 1992. By 1995, East Midlands redefined the importance of IT to the business and began rebuilding its in-house skills. In March 1999, it terminated the contract five years early, taking advantage of a clause permitting this in the event of a merger (East Midlands merged with Powergen in 1998). The business systems were brought back in-house. Similarly, the Australian-based financial service giant MLC chose to rebuild its own application management expertise in 1990. This occurred four years after outsourcing all its IT to IBM Global Services (Australia). According to the CIO, Michelle Tredenick: 'We felt that to be able to compete effectively, we had to have the group that delivered business solutions under our own management and control.'

What is happening here? Backsourcing seems to be used to flex sourcing arrangements as a result of changing circumstances, experience, and learning. Dataquest found 53% of European contracts being renegotiated once under way. Eight percent of those negotiations ended with the company breaking the contract and going it alone. Another 16% switched suppliers. Very few organizations are in fact taking *all* of IT back in-house. One more obvious trend is to move from total to selective sourcing models (remembering that the amount being selectively sourced is predicted to increase to, on average, some 30%–35% of the IT budget). We expect backsourcing to continue to be employed at similar levels over the next five years. One caveat: on e-commerce projects, we are already seeing a pattern of early outsourcing of technical development/provision. Once implemented, customers have tended to take control of further development in-house as e-commerce becomes core. Refocusing resources to e-commerce is often followed by late outsourcing of legacy applications to allow the in-house team to focus on new web-based developments. In such scenarios, backsourcing has a clear role to play in the middle phases.

Shared Services among Industry Competitors

In 1991, oil multinational BP Exploration outsourced accounting services and computer systems and transferred 250 staff to Andersen (see above). The deal has since been renewed twice. On the last round, in mid-1999, BP Amoco signed a new £63 million five-year deal with

Andersen Consulting to run its finance and administrative services. The interesting development has been on the supplier side. Here Andersen Consulting have developed a center at Aberdeen, Scotland, where it also runs such services for seven oil and exploration companies, including Elf, Talisman, and Saga Petroleum. The center has produced a standardized oil industry accounting system, using SAP R/3, Unix-based systems. According to BP, it cut its accounting costs per barrel of oil by 65% in real terms over the 1994–1999 period as a result of using this service. Andersen can deliver a much more cost-efficient service for all concerned.

Of course, the model of shared services is not new. But technical developments and the grounds on which firms compete bring new pressures and possibilities. Clearly these oil commodities operate a core/non-core logic with this business service and its IT components. They choose not to compete based on these services, but rather to minimize costs. Economies of scale and supplier core capability are applied to what we called in Chapter 5 a 'useful commodity'. We will see that similar logic is increasingly being applied in the web-based world—to application service providers (ASPs) and business service providers (BSPs), for example. But often, the fundamental principles that flow through this book are obscured by new vocabulary and market hype. The model is a good one, but its application is not a substitute for thinking through its appropriateness to specific activities and circumstances. The business, technical, and economic matrices provided in Chapter 5 also apply to the evaluation of shared services.

Technology Partnering/Joint Ventures

Throughout the 1990s we saw many companies seek world-class technology supply from their outsourcing contracts and improved business value. Too often they signed contracts that actually were about achieving IT efficiency and a cost/service trade-off. This meant that the supplier would provide a resource pool rather than any distinctive technical leadership. Subsequently, some organizations have had greater clarity and have sought new ways to achieve these further objectives. We would expect this to be a continuing search and testing process.

One example is the joint venture between FI Group and Bank of Scotland (BoS). In June 1998 they formed First Banking Systems. By 1999, the venture comprised 310 people from the Bank of Scotland and 120 people, including many project managers, from FI. Both groups remained employees of their respective companies and both groups kept their own terms, conditions, and pay rates. FBS is joint owned (51% BoS and 49% FI). The deal committed the bank to underwrite

£30 million a year for five years. The contract is fixed price. FI Group agrees to take a loss on any costs over this figure. The joint venture has worked on development projects for the bank, including a new core banking system. In the first year, FBS reduced overheads, introduced new services, and brought in new customers from the Bank of Scotland Group. It also made an unexpected profit.

Prudential Assurance and AMP in Australia also showed innovation in partnering in the late 1990s. While AMP had outsourced most of IT to CSC, it also partnered with Andersen Consulting to help run the IT function. In 1997, Andersen also took control over 800 of Prudential's in-house IT staff. The logic in both cases was to keep expertise in-house, but use Andersen's managerial skills to bring a tighter focus on IT services. The centralized computer subsidiary in each case has been run by an Andersen partner.

These hybrids present very interesting examples of new forms of organization. Each walks a blurred line between the core and non-core IT capabilities described in Chapter 7. Each is an attempt at closer user–IT–supplier relationships especially needed in certain types of IT activity. One can predict two things: that new forms will also come along; and that these present forms will need to be flexed in the light of experience.

e-Business Projects

Does the phrase 'e-business' mean that you can throw away the principles of right-sourcing laid down in this book? Certainly one is given the impression that everything is new; that in the new 'e-Economy' all prior management principles no longer apply. Business's 'need-for-speed' and the lack of key skills exacerbate the situation. Customers want to rely on suppliers that claim core capabilities in e-business areas that they seemingly did not have just a short time ago.

It is necessary to step back and consider carefully the risks of outsourcing e-business projects. e-business projects increasingly will not be about just designing and delivering web sites, but will involve re-engineering infrastructure and business processes. In March 1999, IBM helped toy-maker Lego to deliver its World Shop web site. However, Lego used a special creative designer for the web site itself, Lego provided content, and IBM provided the web, hardware, and software expertise. Reducing the risks of notoriously hidden-cost IT projects will continue to be an enduring game. But in the case of e-business projects, risks are greater because they are fundamentally business projects, not IT projects. Such projects will need to work in a 'user-focused' rather than a 'specialist-focused' manner (Chapter 5, Figure 5.4).

e-Business projects require the same management practices espoused by this book. In particular, e-business projects require multi-functional teams with business sponsors and champions, capable users attached full time to the project, buying-in resources from the market where necessary, and having a full complement of technical staff and project management (see Figure 9.2).

The deeper customers get into web-based technologies and the IT/ business sourcing issue, seemingly the more optimistic, and the less tested, the claims for how much can be outsourced. Cases in point are the next four, fast-growing, trends. The first is Application Service Provision (ASP).

Application Service Providers

ASPs are service firms that provide 'pay-as-you-use' access to centrally managed applications distributed over the Internet and other networks. ASPs often act as intermediaries between client organizations and independent software suppliers. In another variant, the latter may choose to deal directly with the client.

The market size has been predicted to rise from $US150 million in 1999 to between $US11.3 billion and $US21 billion by 2003. The convergence of software and IT infrastructure toward an Internet/net-centric environment has enabled the ASP concept to emerge. By mid-2000, some 200 firms fitted the ASP definition. The market consisted of a diverse range of established and new start-up firms, including internet service provision (ISP), telecommunication and network infrastructure

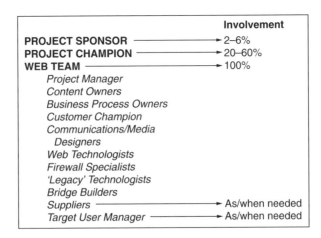

Figure 9.2   *The e-business project team*

provision (Telcos), independent software vendors (ISVs), online software companies, systems integrators, and outsourcing service suppliers. Under the ASP heading we see software providers like Baan, Oracle, Peoplesoft, and SAP offering remote-hosted enterprise software. These are just a few examples amongst many. It is likely that the market will move from single application offerings towards the provision of fully integrated, multiple applications. A full application service might include e-commerce capability, customer relationship management, financial packages, messaging and collaboration, distance learning, and personal utilities.

Early adopters of ASPs were primarily small to medium-sized firms. Large firms had largely invested in the applications they needed or they did not believe application service provision was cost-effective. For larger firms, the main advantages seem to be accelerated application deployment, access to the latest technology and technical support, and transfer of application ownership risk. ASPs could also be used to reduce total cost of ownership, improve efficiency of internal IT staff, level the competitive playing field, and allow focus on more core issues.[5] On the negative side, some worries and risks concerning ASPs have risen.[6] Some ASP customers have experienced problems with

- security of proprietary information
- performance concerns on availability and scalability
- bandwidth capacity
- data and network redundancy
- adaptability of the software to a web-enabled arena
- trade-offs between scope and flexibility for ASPs

It is interesting when looking at ASPs that we come back time and again to the perennial issues addressed in this book. These include: core versus non-core activities; cost reduction versus inflexibility; standardization versus customization; in-house versus supplier capabilities; and problems of maturity and reliability of technology. Customers always need to trade off a variety of good practices and principles against the pragmatics of speed to market, securing labor in short supply, and, for smaller companies, lack of affordability from alternative sources.

Business Service Providers

In 2000, many commentators were predicting a trend evolving from ISPs (information service providers) and ASPs (application service providers) to BSPs (business service providers). ISPs merely provided the infrastructure, ASPs provided applications and infrastructure, but BSPs would provide full-service business processes along with the applications and the infrastructure. While ASP contracts focus on costs and service levels, BSP contracts focus on business results, such as revenue or market growth. In early 2000, a large US chemical company and a small home decor company were using BSPs as a strategy for developing a flexible, variable support infrastructure so that the companies could focus on their core business models.[7] These ideas fit with notions of business process outsourcing, discussed in Chapter 1. Once again, with business service provision, we can gain considerable insight from revisiting the chapters in this book on risk mitigation, core IT capabilities, and the business, technical and economic factors that influence sourcing decisions.

Managed Network Services

Throughout the industry, suppliers are offering more integrated services. According to Denny McGuire, founder of Technology Partners International, Managed Network Services would be the next innovation in infrastructure outsourcing.[8] As at 2000, traditional infrastructure outsourcing provided four towers of service: mainframe computers, midrange computers, application servers, and desktops. Managed Network Services (MNS) included a fifth tower of service—voice communications, including telephone sets, wiring, and PBXs with an increasing focus on bandwidth management across the towers. In addition, MNSs provide engineering, procurement, billing, helpdesk, and monitoring services. While MNSs focus on integration of technology service, customer relationship management (CRM) focuses on integration of customer processes.

Customer Relationship Management

Older models of competitive advantage focus on products, quality, and price. However, some experts argue that there is much parity among competitors along these aspects. Competitive advantage in the new millennium will focus instead on customer relationship management (CRM). For example, Jack Welch, CEO of General Electric, argues that there are only two sources of competitive advantage: '(1) the ability to learn more about our customers faster than the competition, and (2) the ability to turn that learning into action faster than the competition.'

Managing customer *information* is key to managing customer relationships. Customer information includes service inquiries, purchases, account set-ups, billing, self-help, and technical support. Such information is increasingly reliant on information technologies, and thus has the increasing potential to be outsourced.[9] In the United States, International Data Corporation estimates that customer care outsourcing reached $US11.4 billion in 1999, while $US111 billion was insourced. Outsourcing in this area will likely increase because—it is argued—suppliers are better able to deploy new modes of customer communication. Suppliers such as Convergys provide integrated customer contact centers, including e-mail, phone, fax, mail, and web management. Intelligent middleware serves as an interface between the customer, business rules, credit bureau data, and the customer databases.

The March 2000 issue of the *Server/Workstation Expert* argued that the true value of CRM will only be realized when it is fully integrated with enterprise resource planning (ERP) packages. The integration of ERP and CRM will allow customers to track quality of service issues throughout the value chain—from product creation to deployment and use. We again see the merging of multiple trends claiming to deliver on the elusive 'value-added' promise of technology outsourcing.

Supply Chain Management: From 'Preferred Suppliers' to Open Bidding?

During the 1990s, supply chain management principles espoused that customers should develop preferred supplier relationships to ensure quality and to quicken product development. To reduce costs, connect those preferred suppliers over *fixed* networks to enable just-in-time (JIT) inventory, EDI purchase orders and invoices, and electronic payment. With the explosion of the Internet, connections become *virtual*. Will long-term commitment to a few suppliers be replaced by transaction-to-transaction bidding over the web?

Consider the web-based trade exchange for procurement set up by Ford, General Motors, and Daimler-Benz in early 2000. Commerce One and Oracle collaborated on the technology. Component suppliers would bid for work put on to the exchange market by the car manufacturers. The aim was to save billions of dollars through more efficient supply chain management. In March 2000, Toyota agreed to join the exchange but restricted its participation to trading only in basic commodity items and office supplies. The company had several concerns about the exchange, centering on quality assurance and security on an open network. For Taadaki Jagawa, VP of procurement: 'the other companies are our rivals and we are competing on parts. We do not share information about our components,' including information about the price of core parts. Moreover: 'our parts are not purchased through a bidding process. We buy them by building a relationship with suppliers over time.' Essentially, Toyota saw its suppliers as consultants, and believed the close relationships with them gave a competitive edge in quality assurance but also in lead time on new car development.

Towards the Digital Assembly Line

Much of this casting into the future seems to imply much more outsourcing. But more sophisticated, deeper relationships are needed to offset the increased exposure/dependence implied by the activities being touted for outsourcing. Here again we are revisiting some old dilemmas, concerns, and prescriptions in IT outsourcing. The questions here are: What level of exposure does a company undergo when it outsources to a very high degree? How can those risks be mitigated to a sensible level so that outsourcing can leverage significant business advantage? These questions have not gone away. Consider the 'digital assembly line' shown in Figure 9.3. Here we can see that a business can now contemplate web-enabled outsourcing at virtually every stage in its customer resource life-cycle. For both Internet start-ups and 'bricks and mortar' companies moving to e-business, the web enables a high degree of outsourcing as suppliers develop core capabilities in a range of areas.

In practice, e-commerce requires dozens of companies and technologies providing the infrastructure for retail and business-to-business e-commerce. Looking across the entire customer resource life-cycle, there are already service companies like LinkExchange and DoubleClick that deliver targeted audiences to web sites. In stage 2 (Figure 9.3) W.W. Grainger is a major company in the maintenance repair and operations market offering hard good supplies to offices and manufacturers across the United States. Its three web sites achieved $US140 million in 1999, aided by `ondisplay.com` to organize its cataloging and content. In stage 3, customization of products/services is enabled by companies like `Calico.com` that provide configuration software and enable real-time, web-based, build-to-order buying in manufacturing and in PC and consumer electronics sales. To assist transactions (stage 4) companies like `Ariba.com` and Commerce One already offer business-to-business marketplaces for companies such as Cisco Systems and Charles Schwab, and market-making platforms are available from other suppliers, e.g. for insurance and reinsurance exchange. Companies like `eCredit.com` and Paylinx assist payments (stage 5). There is a variety of services that allow online order tracking by customers, and that provide call center capability (stage 6). Still more service providers have been moving into order fulfilment (stage 7), while others analyze customer data to provide adaptive customer profiling services (Figure 9.3, stage 8).[10]

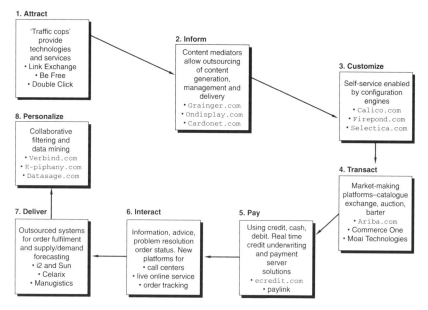

Figure 9.3 *The digital assembly line*

The external sourcing possibilities on the web, and enabled by web-based technologies, are in fact massive both in retail and in business-to-business, and the back office, and within organizations. Cisco Systems is an impressive exemplar of a profitable, fast growing, web-based virtual organization that has taken these outsourcing possibilities to radical and successful lengths. As at 2000, it had outsourced most production to 37 factories, all linked to the Internet. Suppliers made all the components, 90% of the sub-assembly, and 55% of the final assembly. Eighty percent of the company's sales were from its web site. However, despite total outsourcing, and wide use of third-party suppliers, Cisco designed the production methods and used the Internet to monitor operations. According to D. Listwin, VP: 'The source code is developed here and maintained here. So the innovation is all at Cisco.' But the practices adopted here are not so new, though they are web-enabled. Thus, Benetton, the Italian-based multinational, has for decades been operating on very similar principles of using the market as much as possible but retaining control over core aspects. In practice, those contemplating wide-scale use of third-party services—whether for web-based or 'bricks and mortar operations'—can learn as much about effective IT sourcing practices from Benetton as from Cisco Systems.

CONCLUSION

Since 1999 we have been bombarded with calls for more IT outsourcing. The development of the network-centric era has enabled suppliers to offer greater varieties of services, and can help organizations approach competing on a much more focused basis. These are particularly important developments for start-up companies who need to move quickly with few resources. But existing firms also need to be slim, flexible, and responsive against 'bricks and mortar', web-based, and 'bricks-and-clicks' competitors.

While the development of the so-called new e-Economy does represent a real transition, this does not mean that what we have learned about IT sourcing strategy and delivery for business advantage no longer applies. In a time of uncertainty, lack of clarity, and huge hype, we are certain that it means the opposite. It becomes salutary to return to some abiding principles about IT sourcing that are based on extensive experience and research. These practices include:

- the use of a selective sourcing strategy rather than all-or-none outsourcing strategies;
- identifying core IT capabilities to keep in-house;
- identifying non-core IT capabilities for potential outsourcing;
- conducting a rigorous evaluation of market options and supplier offerings;
- clearly defining IT outsourcing expectations and mitigating risk in a contract; and
- implementing post-contract management processes and structures to enable supplier success.

Such practices serve as a foundation for sound sourcing decisions, despite pleas to abandon them. These practices allow customers to maximize both control and flexibility in the face of significant business and technical change.

NOTES

1. Quoted in *Financial Times FT—IT Review*, August 4, 1999.
2. The figure is for post-contract management costs. The costs for getting to contract usually fall between 0.5% and 2.5% of the total value of the contract. Consider the DuPont case, where over 100 people were involved at various stages during a 14-month period. Needless to say such deals can also cost the supplier a lot to bid for. In the UK Inland Revenue case, EDS would have spent well in excess of £2 million winning the contract. These figures are drawn from

analysis of our 250 plus case database held at Oxford Institute of Information Management.

3. See Weill, P. and Broadbent, M. (1998). *Leveraging the New Infrastructure.* Harvard Business School Press, Boston.

4. We thank Paul Strassmann for pointing out this example and that of General Motors.

5. McCullough, S. (1999). *Sizing App. Hosting.* Forrester Research, Cambridge, Mass., December.

6. Kern, T. and Willcocks, L. (2000). Risky Application Sourcing. Erasmus University, Working Paper, March. School of Decision and Information Sciences, Erasmus, Rotterdam.

7. Kevin Campbell of Ernst & Young. Presentation at the 2000 Outsourcing World Summit, February 21–23, Orlando, Florida.

8. Presentation at the 2000 Outsourcing World Summit, February 21–23, Orlando, Florida.

9. Meringer, J. (1999). *Outsourcing's Future.* Forrester Research, Cambridge, Mass., April.

10. An interesting article on this subject is Davis, J. (2000). How it Works. *Business 2.0* February.

APPENDIX A
Findings from the 1999–2000 Survey of IT Outsourcing in the US and UK

INTRODUCTION

Inside IT Outsourcing: A State-of-the-Art Report was published in March 2000 by Templeton College, University of Oxford (see Lacity and Willcocks 2000b). The Report estimated that global revenues would exceed $US120 billion by the year 2002, and possibly $US140 billion by 2004, reflecting a 16% growth rate in the 1997–2004 period. IT outsourcing has outlived the five-year period typical of a management fad. The Report reveals that outsourcing has been becoming part of the routine part of IT management, and estimates that on average 35% of most corporations' IT budgets would be outsourced by 2003.

But is the rapid growth of the IT outsourcing market primarily attributable to the well-publicized and studied mega-deals? Are high-profile, large-scale contracts indicative of the sourcing practices of most organizations? Are customers satisfied with their IT outsourcing practices and outcomes? What more needs to be done to achieve effective contracts and practices?

These questions prompted a detailed review of the authors' previous research, and a new in-depth 1999 survey into IT outsourcing experiences in the lead markets of the United States and the United Kingdom. The survey was distributed to 600 US and UK Chief Information Officers (CIOs) and senior IT managers. This Report presents the in-depth findings of this survey and compares findings with previous surveys and research. It also details major lessons for customers and suppliers, emerging from the study.

SUMMARY OF FINDINGS

1. Selective, multi-supplier outsourcing is preferred.

The vast majority of organizations pursued selective outsourcing (15%–30% of IT budget outsourced) rather than total outsourcing (80% plus of the IT budget contracted out). In 1999 we found 73% of organizations pursuing selective outsourcing, 21% total in-house sourcing, and only 6% total outsourcing. Some differences between the United States and the United Kingdom can be highlighted. On average, UK organizations (30%) totally insourced IT more frequently than US organizations (8%). US organizations (29%) more frequently used a single supplier than UK organizations (9%). UK organizations (50%) used only one stakeholder to negotiate/define contracts compared with US organizations (9%). Differences may be explained by a more mature approach to outsourcing in the United States together with the higher preponderance of larger deals and organizations studied. Some 82% of organizations used multiple suppliers.

2. Against other surveys, supplier performance is quite well rated. This is explained by the dominant practices of outsourcing selectively, on three- to five-year contracts, targeting mainly IT infrastructure and stable IT activities for which detailed contracts can be written.

Respondents were generally providing a healthy report card for information technology (IT) outsourcing. In particular, respondents rated overall supplier performance as 'good', respondents realized some or most of the benefits they expected from IT outsourcing, and respondents characterized the majority of problems/issues as only 'minor' in nature. However, as we shall see, these generalizations concealed some significant problem areas for a sizable minority of organizations.

The healthy IT outsourcing report card is explained by the scope and type of IT outsourcing practiced by responding organizations. The vast majority of respondents pursued selective outsourcing, which is markedly less risky than total outsourcing. Most respondents also used multiple suppliers (82%) rather than a single supplier, which allows for best-of-breed supplier selection. The healthy report card may also be explained by the types of IT activities selected for outsourcing.

Respondents generally targeted IT infrastructure activities—such as disaster recovery, mainframe operations, network management, mid-range operations, PC support, and helpdesk operations—rather than IT development or IT strategy. UK and US practices and outcomes were very similar, although a few exceptions were noteworthy.

3. However, actual benefits from outsourcing are invariably less than those expected. Cost reduction remains a major requirement, though increasingly linked with other objectives.

Overall, there was a noticeable gap, with expected benefits from outsourcing always exceeding actual benefits. Cost reduction remained a major requirement for most organizations, though linked increasingly with other objectives. However, 53% of respondents achieved mainly some, rather than significant, cost reductions. The others achieved no cost reductions, and in some cases cost rises. The second most frequent benefit experienced was refocusing of in-house IT staff (44%), followed by improved IT flexibility (41%), better quality service, improved use of IT resource, and access to scarce IT skills (39% each)—see Table A.1.

4. Several serious problem areas persist for more than a quarter of organizations. These relate to strategic difficulties, cost escalation, supplier not properly staffing the contract, poor service level definitions, IT skills shortages.

The seemingly healthy report card described above does disguise some overall issues, and some serious problem areas for a significant

Table A.1   *Actual benefits from IT outsourcing*

Actual Benefit	US %	UK %	Total %
Cost reduction:	40	64	53
• Some cost reduction	34	39	37
• Significant cost reduction	6	25	16
Refocus in-house IT staff	37	50	44
Improved IT flexibility	46	36	41
Better quality service	40	39	39
Improved use of IT resource	43	36	39
Access to scarce IT skills	43	36	39
Improved business flexibility	26	36	32
Focus on core business	29	34	32
Better management control	17	25	22
Access to new IT	26	16	20
Balanced processing loads	11	9	10
Assist cash flow problems	6	14	10

minority of organizations. As an overall average figure on the 24 issues mentioned, one-quarter of all respondents were encountering serious/ difficult problems during outsourcing. On individual issues this percentage was sometimes higher—see Table A.2.

Table A.2 *Extent of problems/issues encountered with outsourcing*

	Serious problem	Difficult problem	Minor problem	Not a problem	Total
Strategic issues					
1. Supplier's lack of understanding of your business	11	14	30	21	76
2. Failure to align corporate strategy with IT strategy	7	12	18	39	76
3. Poor strategic planning for IT	4	15	16	41	76
4. Defining intellectual property rights	0	8	23	45	76
5. Defining data protection procedures	2	5	27	42	76
Total number of strategic issues	*24*	*54*	*114*	*188*	*380*
	6%	*14%*	*30%*	*50%*	
Cost issues					
6. Cost escalation as a result of contract loopholes	10	10	31	25	76
7. Difficulties in controling/ monitoring costs	8	8	34	26	76
8. Costs for additional services beyond contract	8	15	23	30	76
Total number of cost issues	*26*	*33*	*88*	*81*	*228*
	11%	*14%*	*39%*	*36%*	
Managerial issues					
9. Loss of control over IT operations	3	8	24	41	76
10. In-house staff resistance to outsourcing	8	13	22	33	76
11. Poor supplier staffing of contract	9	23	21	23	76
12. Managerial skills shortage	5	16	29	26	76
13. Lack of supplier training for staff	5	10	19	42	76
Total number of managerial issues	*30*	*70*	*115*	*165*	*380*
	8%	*18%*	*31%*	*43%*	

	Serious problem	Difficult problem	Minor problem	Not a problem	Total
Operational issues					
14. Getting different contract suppliers to work together	9	14	27	26	76
15. Defining service levels	6	23	33	14	76
16. Coordinating IT work with supplier	2	14	39	21	76
17. Communication with supplier	2	10	33	31	76
18. Lack of supplier responsiveness to client needs	8	18	23	27	76
19. Deteriorating service	7	6	28	35	76
Total number of operational issues	*34* *7%*	*85* *19%*	*183* *40%*	*154* *34%*	*456*
Contractual issue					
20. Defining the outsourcing contract	7 *9%*	12 *16%*	25 *33%*	32 *42%*	76
Technical issues					**0**
21. Supplier failure to upgrade IT	3	9	20	44	76
22. Duplication of systems	5	13	16	42	76
23. Policy to recruit inexperienced IT staff	3	10	16	47	76
24. IT skills shortage affecting supplier's service	6	18	20	32	76
Total number of technical issues	*17* *6%*	*50* *16%*	*72* *24%*	*165* *54%*	*304*
Overall total	138	304	597	785	1824
Overall percentage	*8%*	*17%*	*33%*	*42%*	

1. Some 21% experienced serious strategic problems with outsourcing.
2. On cost issues, 31% indicated serious problems with services beyond the contract, 26% with cost escalation due to contract loopholes, and 22% with monitoring/controling costs.
3. The major managerial problem experienced was the supplier not properly staffing the contract (42% of respondents).
4. On operational issues, 38% experienced serious problems due to poor service-level definitions.
5. On technical issues, a significant minority complained of a serious shortage of IT skills (31%), duplicate systems (23%), and inexperienced supplier staff (17%).

6. Some 63% of companies reduced IT headcount as a consequence of IT outsourcing. Most report no problems with transferring staff to the supplier, but 30% of those transferring staff did experience problems.

4. Nearly one-third of organizations have cancelled contracts in the last five years.

Other studies have invariably reported expectations rather than actual cancelation figures. We found that 32% of organizations had canceled one or more outsourcing contract in the last five years. Of these, half changed suppliers, a third brought the IT back in-house, 11% renegotiated the contract, and only 3% went to litigation. Respondents regularly pointed to being inhibited by the large switching costs likely, and actually, to be incurred by canceling contracts.

5. The most common reason for rejecting outsourcing is expense

More than half of the organizations surveyed had at some stage considered but rejected outsourcing some aspect of IT activity. Table A.3 indicates the top reasons for rejection. Interestingly, only 6% rejected outsourcing on the grounds that no suitable supplier could be found. The outsourcing market has clearly matured over the last decade, as discussed in Chapter 1, with many niche suppliers, as well as mega-suppliers and sub-contractors available.

6. Only one-third of organizations have complete contracts by including all important contractual clauses.

The Report identified 10 major clauses that previous research demonstrated needed to be in all outsourcing contracts. The most common clauses found were for confidentiality, service-level agreements, and

Table A.3   *Reasons for rejecting outsourcing*

	US %	UK %	Total %
Outsourcing deemed too expensive	24	22	23
In-house IT able to achieve same benefits	22	16	19
Lack of identifiable benefits	19	18	18
Concern about loss of operational control	17	18	18
IT activity deemed as too strategic	13	19	15
No suitable supplier was found	5	6	6
Company policy not to outsource	0	1	1
Total	100	100	100

early termination. Clauses covering non-performance penalties, named contract managers, warranties, and intellectual property rights were less frequent. The fact that so many US and UK organizations were not focusing on some important contractual clauses must be a matter for some concern.

7. Proven practices in IT outsourcing are confirmed—selective sourcing as the lower risk option; three- to five-year detailed contracts; mitigating the risks in all deals by comprehensive, detailed contracting, a mature active in-house capability (especially for large-scale deals), careful selection of suppliers for tasks they are most suitable, and various forms of creative contracting to motivate suppliers while keeping the arrangements flexible over realistic time-scales.

Nine core IT capabilities need to be retained in-house in order to elicit and deliver on business requirements, manage external supply, plan and keep control of the IT platform, and preserve and enhance the organization's ability to leverage IT for business advantage. IT sourcing decisions need to be based on consideration of a set of six major business, economic, and technical factors. An informed buying capability provides the detailed understanding of an organization's needs, the IT services markets, and of specific supplier's capabilities and strategies that enable the identification of suitable suppliers. A contracting capability is required—often enhanced by external legal and consultancy outsourcing expertise—to ensure that the organization contracts cost effectively for and secures the services and quality it expects. Retained in-house capabilities are required to post-contract manage suppliers and retain control over the organization's IT destiny.

Early total outsourcing deals showed a poor success rate, though this has improved to 38% on our 1999 figures, with a further 27% achieving very mixed results. These improvements can be explained partly by more total outsourcing decisions involving multiple suppliers, on five- to seven-year contracts. Total outsourcing risks are mitigated by proper, comprehensive contracting, a mature active in-house capability for dealing with large-scale IT outsourcing deals, careful selection of suppliers for tasks they are most suitable, and various forms of creative contracting to incent the supplier(s) while keeping the arrangements flexible over realistic time-scales.

8. Emerging lessons for customers and suppliers

The Report concludes by detailing five lessons for customers and six lessons for suppliers emerging from the study.

For customers:

- Involve more skills and stakeholders in outsourcing evaluations.
- Improve communications with in-house IT staff during evaluation.
- Insist on more clearly defined, more detailed and comprehensive contracts.
- Beware of outsourcing too many key people.
- Plan for and regularly improve post-contract management infrastructure.

For suppliers:

- Help customers set realistic expectations.
- Fully explain staffing policies to the customer.
- Ensure the customer has a proper infrastructure to manage and coordinate the contract.
- Develop relationship and customer management capability beyond customer service and account management.
- Note the check-list of serious and difficult problems encountered by a sizable minority of customers during outsourcing. Take preemptive action to ensure the risk of these happening is minimized.
- Reconsider strategy and market offerings in the light of many customers preferring shorter contracts, selective IT outsourcing, and multiple suppliers.

The full Report *Inside IT Outsourcing: A State-of-the-Art Report* is available from Dave.Hall@templeton.oxford.ac.uk
tel: 00 44 (0)1865 422515/500.

Authors' Publications on IT Outsourcing (1993–2001)

BOOKS AND REPORTS

Currie, W. and Willcocks, L. (1998). *New Strategies in IT Outsourcing: Major Trends and Global Best Practices.* Business Intelligence, London.

Graeser, V., Willcocks, L. and Pisanias, N. (1998). *Developing the IT Scorecard: Evaluation and Management Practices.* Business Intelligence, London.

Kern, T. and Willcocks, L. (2001). *The Relationship Advantage: Information Technologies, Sourcing and Management.* Oxford University Press, Oxford.

Lacity, M. and Hirschheim, R. (1993a). *Information Systems Outsourcing: Myths, Metaphors and Realities.* Wiley, Chichester.

Lacity, M. and Hirschheim, R. (1995a). *Beyond the Information Systems Outsourcing Bandwagon: The Insourcing Response.* Wiley, Chichester.

Lacity, M. and Willcocks, L. (1996). *Best Practices in Information Technology Sourcing.* The Oxford Executive Research Briefings, No. 2. Templeton College, Oxford, June.

Lacity, M. and Willcocks, L. (2000a). *Global IT Outsourcing: Search for Business Advantage.* Wiley, Chichester.

Lacity, M. and Willcocks, L. (2000b). *Inside IT Outsourcing: A State-of-the-Art Report.* Templeton Research, Templeton College, Oxford.

Willcocks, L. and Fitzgerald, G. (1994a). *A Business Guide to Outsourcing Information Technology: A Study of European Best Practice in the Selection, Management and Use of External IT Services.* Business Intelligence, London.

Willcocks, L. and Lacity, M. (eds) (1998). *Strategic Sourcing of Information Systems.* Wiley, Chichester.

Willcocks, L. and Lester, S. (eds) (1999). *Beyond the IT Productivity Paradox: Assessment Issues.* Wiley, Chichester. Especially Chapters 9 and 10.

Willcocks, L., Feeny, D. and Islei, G. (1997). *Managing Information Technology as a Strategic Resource.* McGraw-Hill, Maidenhead. Especially Chapters 11, 12 and 17.

REFEREED PAPERS: JOURNALS

Currie, W. and Willcocks, L. (1998). Analysing IT Outsourcing Decisions in the Context of Size, Interdependency and Risk. *Information Systems Journal*, **8**, no. 2, 86–102.

Feeny, D. and Willcocks, L. (1998). Core IS Capabilities for Exploiting Information Technology. *Sloan Management Review*, **39**, no. 3, 9–21.

Feeny, D. and Willcocks, L. (1998). Redesigning the IS Function Around Core Capabilities. *Long Range Planning*, **32**, no 3, June, 354–367.

Hirschheim, R. and Lacity, M. (2000). Four Stories of Information Technology Insourcing. *Communications of the ACM*, February.

Kern, T. and Willcocks, L. (2000a). Contracts, Control and 'Presentation' in IT Outsourcing: Research in Thirteen UK Organizations. *Journal of Global Information Management* (forthcoming).

Lacity, M. and Hirschheim, R. (1993a). The Information Systems Outsourcing Bandwagon. *Sloan Management Review*, **35**, no. 1, 73–86.

Lacity, M., and Hirschheim, R. (1993b), Implementing Information Systems Outsourcing: Key Issues and Experiences of an Early Adopter. *Journal of General Management*, **19**, no. 1, Autumn, 17–31.

Lacity, M., Hirschheim, R. and Willcocks, L. (1994) Realizing Outsourcing Expectations: Incredible Expectations, Credible Outcomes. *Information Systems Management*, Fall, 7–18.

Lacity, M., Willcocks, L. and Feeny, D. (1995). IT Outsourcing: Maximise Flexibility and Control. *Harvard Business Review*, May–June, 84–93.

Lacity, M. and Hirschheim, R. (1995b). Benchmarking as a Strategy for Managing Conflicting Stakeholder Perceptions of Information Systems. *Journal of Strategic Information Systems*, **4**, no. 2, June, 165–185.

Lacity, M. and Willcocks, L. (1996). Interpreting Information Technology Sourcing Decisions from a Transaction Cost Perspective: Findings and Critique. *Accounting, Management and Information Technology*, **5**, no. 3/4, 203–244.

Lacity, M., Willcocks, L. and Feeny, D. (1996). The Value of Selective IT Sourcing. *Sloan Management Review*, **37**, no. 3, 13–25.

Lacity, M. and Willcocks, L. (1997). IT Outsourcing—Examining the Privatization Option in US Public Administration. *Information Systems Journal*, **7**, no. 2, June.

Lacity, M. and Willcocks, L. (1998). An Empirical Investigation of Information Technology Sourcing Practices: Lessons From Experience. *MIS Quarterly*, **22**, no. 3, 363–408.

Lacity, M. and Willcocks, L. (2000) A Survey of IT Outsourcing Experiences in USA and UK. *Journal of Global Information Management*, **8**, no. 2, April-June.

Lacity, M., Willcocks, L. and Subramanian, A. (1998). Client Server Implementation: New Technology, Lessons from History. *Journal of Strategic Information Systems*, March.

Subramanian, A. and Lacity, M. (1997). Managing Client Server Implementations: Today's Technology, Yesterday's Lessons. *Journal of Information Technology*, **12**, no. 3, 169–186.

Willcocks, L. (1994). Managing Information Systems in UK Public Administration— Trends and Future Prospects. *Public Administration*, **72**, no. 2, 13–32.

Willcocks, L. and Choi, C. (1995). Cooperative Partnership and 'Total' IT Outsourcing: From Contractual Obligation to Strategic Alliance? *European Management Journal*, **13**, no. 1, 67–78.

Willcocks, L., Fitzgerald, G. and Feeny, D. (1995). IT Outsourcing: The Strategic Implications. *Long Range Planning*, **28**, no. 5, 59–70.

Willcocks, L., Fitzgerald, G. and Lacity, M. (1996). To Outsource IT or Not? Recent Research on Economics and Evaluation Practice. *European Journal of Information Systems*, **5**, no. 3, 143–160.

Willcocks, L., Lacity, M. and Fitzgerald, G. (1996). IT Outsourcing in Europe and the USA: Assessment Issues. *International Journal of Information Management*, **15**, no. 5, 333–351. A less developed version won the **Best Paper Award** at the Third European Conference in Information Systems, Athens, June 1995.

Willcocks, L. and Currie, W. (1997). IT Outsourcing in Public Service Contexts: Towards the Contractual Organization? *British Journal of Management*, **8**, June, S107–120.

Willcocks, L. and Kern, T. (1998). IT Outsourcing as Strategic Partnering: The Case of the Inland Revenue. *European Journal of Information Systems*, **7**, 29–45.

Willcocks, L. and Lacity, M. (1999a). IT Outsourcing in Financial Services: Risk, Creative Contracting and Business Advantage. *Information Systems Journal*, **9**, September, 163–180.

Willcocks, L. and Lacity, M. (1999b). Information Technology Outsourcing: Practices, Lessons and Prospects. *ASX Perspective*, April.

Willcocks, L., Lacity, M. and Kern, T. (2000). Risk in IT Outsourcing Strategy Revisited: Longitudinal Case Research at LISA. *Journal of Strategic Information Systems*, April.

Willcocks, L. and Sykes, R. (2000). The Role of the CIO and IT Function in ERP: Asleep at the Wheel? *Communications of the ACM*, April.

REFEREED PAPERS: CONFERENCE PROCEEDINGS

Currie, W. and Willcocks, L. (1996). The Impact of Compulsive Competitive Tendering of IT Services in Local Government. Refereed Paper in *Proceedings of the Third Financial Information Systems Conference*, September 9–10, Sheffield.

Currie, W. and Willcocks, L. (1997). Analysing IT Outsourcing Decisions in the Context of Size, Interdependency and Risk. Paper at the *Second UK Association for Information Systems Conference*.

Currie, W. and Willcocks, L. (1998). Large-Scale IT Outsourcing: The Case of British Aerospace plc. *Proceedings of the Third UK Association for Information Systems Conference*. Lincoln, April.

Fitzgerald, G. and Willcocks, L. (1993). IT Outsourcing in the United Kingdom and Europe—Recent Research Evidence. Refereed paper in *Proceedings of the Fourteenth International Conference in Information Systems*, Orlando, USA.

Graeser, V. and Willcocks, L. (1998). IT Projects and Benefit Funding: Case Research at the Californian Franchise Tax Board. *Proceedings of the Sixth European Conference in Information Systems*, Aix-en-Provence, France, June.

Kern, T. and Willcocks, L. (1996). The Enabling and Determining Environment: Neglected Issues in IT Outsourcing Strategy. Refereed Paper in Dias Coelho, J., Jelasi, T. et al. (eds) *Proceedings of the Fourth European Conference in Information Systems*, July 2–4, Lisbon.

Kern, T. and Willcocks, L. (1998). Cooperative Relationship Strategy in Global Information Technology Outsourcing: The Case of Xerox Corporation. *Proceedings of the Fifth International Conference on Multi-Organizational Partnerships and Cooperative Strategy*. Balliol College, Oxford, July.

Kern, T. and Willcocks, L. (1999). Presentation in Contracting for IT Outsourcing. A Study of Thirteen Organizations. *Proceedings of the Seventh European Conference In Information Systems*, June 23–25. Copenhagen.

Kumar, K. and Willcocks, L. (1996). Offshore Outsourcing: A Country Too Far? Refereed paper in Dias Coelho, J., Jelasi, T. et al. (eds) *Proceedings of the Fourth European Conference in Information Systems*, July 2–4, Liston.

Willcocks, L., Fitzgerald, G. and Feeny, D. (1994). Information Technology Outsourcing: From Incrementalism to Strategic Intent. Refereed Paper in *Proceedings of the Second SISNET Conference*, September 26–28, Barcelona.

Willcocks, L. and Fitzgerald, G. (1994b). Towards the Residual IS Organization? Research on IT Outsourcing Experiences in the United Kingdom. In the *Refereed Conference Proceedings: IFIP WG8.2 Transactions on Computer Science and Technology*: Baskerville, R. et al. (eds) *Transforming Organizations with Information Technology*. Elsevier, North-Holland, Amsterdam.

Willcocks, L. and Fitzgerald, G. (1994c). To Outsource IT or Not? Recent Research on Economics and Evaluation Practice. Paper in *Proceedings of the Evaluation Of IT Investments Conference*, 13–14 September. Henley Management College. A much developed version appears in *European Journal of Information Systems*, 1996.

Willcocks, L. and Fitzgerald, G. (1994d). The Outsourcing of Information Technology. Paper in the *Proceedings of the British Academy of Management Conference*, September 12–14, University of Lancaster.

Willcocks, L. and Fitzgerald, G. (1994e). Contracting for IT Outsourcing: Recent Research Evidence. Paper in Gross, J. et al. (eds) *The Proceedings of the Fifteenth Annual International Conference in Information Systems*, December 13–16, Vancouver, pp. 91–98.

Willcocks, L. and Fitzgerald, G. (1994f). Relationships in Outsourcing: Contracts and Partnerships. Paper in the *Proceedings of the Second European Conference on Information Systems*, May 30–31, Nijenrode, The Netherlands.

Willcocks, L., Lacity, M. and Fitzgerald, G. (1995). IT Outsourcing in Europe and the USA: Assessment Issues. *Proceedings of the Third European Conference in Information Systems*. **Best Paper Award**. A much developed version appears in *International Journal of Information Management*, **15**, no. 5, 333–351.

Willcocks, L. and Currie, C. (1996). Information Technology in Public Services: Towards the Contractual Organization? Refereed Paper in *Proceedings of the Tenth Annual Conference of the British Academy Of Management*, September 15–18. Aston Business School, Birmingham. A much developed version appears in *British Journal of Management*, June 1997.

Willcocks, L. and Feeny, D. (1996). Reconfiguring the Information Systems Function: A Core Capabilities Approach. Keynote Speech. *Proceedings of the Australiasian Conference in Information Systems*, December 12–14, Hobart. A developed version was accepted for *Long Range Planning*, 1997.

Willcocks, L. and Currie, W. (1997). IT Outsourcing and Risk Mitigation at the Logistic Information System Agency: A Case Research Study. Refereed Paper at the *1997 British Academy of Management Conference*. London, September.

Willcocks, L. and Kern, T. (1997). IT Outsourcing as Strategic Partnering: The Case of the UK Inland Revenue. *Proceedings of the Fifth European Conference in Information Systems*, June. **Winner of Officers' Prize for Excellence**. A much developed version appears in *European Journal of Information Systems*, 1998.

Willcocks, L. and Lacity, M. (1999). IT Sourcing at Polaris: Risk, Creative Contracting and Business Advantage. *Proceedings of the Seventh European Conference*

In Information Systems, June 23–25. Copenhagen. **Winner of Best Case Paper Award**.

Willcocks, L., Lacity, M. and Kern, T. (1999). IT Outsourcing and Risk Mitigation: Recent Case Research. *Proceedings of the Fifth Decision Sciences Conference*, July 5–7, Athens.

REPRINTS AND SHORTER PAPERS

Feeny, D. and Willcocks, L. (1999). Selective Sourcing and Core Capabilities. *Financial Times*, February 15.

Willcocks, L. and Fitzgerald, G. (1993). Assessing IT Outsourcing Options—Recent UK Case Evidence. Refereed Paper in *Proceedings of the IT Outsourcing Conference*, May 29–30, University of Twente, Netherlands. Published in updated form in *Journal of Strategic Information Systems*.

Willcocks, L. and Fitzgerald, G. (1999). Outsourcing in the United Kingdom: Vendor/Client Issues. Refereed paper in *Proceedings of the Information Resources Management Association International Conference: Managing Social and Economic Change with Information Technology*. May 22–25, San Antonio, USA. Published in updated and extended form in *Proceedings of the Fifteenth Annual International Conference in Information Systems*, December 13–16, Vancouver.

Willcocks, L. and Lacity, M. (1999). Strategic Dimensions of IT Outsourcing. *Financial Times*, March.

Willcocks, L., Lacity, M. and Fitzgerald, G. (1995). IT Outsourcing in Europe and the USA: Assessment Issues. *Refereed Paper in the Proceedings of the Third European Conference in Information Systems*, June 3–5, Athens. **Best Paper Award.** A revised version is in the *International Journal of Information Management*.

CONTRIBUTIONS TO BOOKS

Feeny, D. and Willcocks, L. (1999). The Emerging IT Function—Changing Capabilities and Skills. In Currie, W. and Galliers, R. (eds) *Rethinking MIS*. Oxford University Press, Oxford.

Feeny, D. and Willcocks, L. (2000). Selective Sourcing and Core Capabilities. In FT (ed.) *Mastering Information Management*. FT/Prentice Hall, London.

Feeny, D., Willcocks, L. and Fitzgerald, G. (1993). Strategic Management of IT in the Nineties—When Outsourcing Equals Rightsourcing. In Rock, S. (ed.) *Director's Guide to Outsourcing*. Institute of Directors, London.

Kern, T. and Willcocks, L. (2000b). Cooperative Relationship Strategy in Global IT Outsourcing: The Case of Xerox Corporation's Relationship Locally. In Faulkner, D. et al. (eds) *Cooperative Strategies*. Oxford University Press, Oxford. .

Kumar, K. and Willcocks, L. (1999) Holiday Inn's Passage To India. In Karmel, E. (ed.) *Global Software Teams*. Prentice Hall, New Jersey.

Lacity, M., Hirschheim, R. and Willcocks, L. (1997). Realizing Outsourcing Expectations. In Umbaugh, R. (ed.) *Handbook of IS Management*, Reprint, Auerbach, Boston.

Lacity, M. and Willcocks, L. (2000c). Relationships in IT Outsourcing: A Stakeholder Perspective. In Zmud, R. (ed.) *Framing the Domains of IT Management Research. Glimpsing The Future Through the Past* (forthcoming).

Lacity, M., Willcocks, L. and Feeny, D. (1996). Sourcing Information Technology Capability. A Decision-Making Framework. In Earl, M. (ed.). *Information Management: The Organizational Dimension*, Reprint, Oxford University Press, Oxford.

Lacity, M., Willcocks, L. and Feeny, D. (1999). IT Outsourcing: Maximizing Flexibility and Control. In *Business Value From IT*. Harvard Business Press, Cambridge, Mass.

Willcocks, L. and Currie, W. (1998). IT Outsourcing in Public Service Contexts: Towards the Contractual Organization? Reprinted in Mische, M. (ed.) *The High Performance IT Organization*. Auerbach Publications, Oxford.

Willcocks, L. and Fitzgerald, G. (1995). Pilkington PLC: A Major Multinational Outsources its Head Office IT Function. In Turban, E., Mclean, E. and Wetherbe, J. (eds) *Information Technology For Management*, Wiley, New York.

Willcocks, L. and Fitzgerald, G. (1996). The Changing Shape of the Information Systems Function. In Earl, M. (ed.) *Information Management: The Organizational Dimension*, Reprint, Oxford University Press: Oxford.

Willcocks, L., Fitzgerald, G. and Feeny, D. (1993). Effective IT Outsourcing—The Evidence in Europe. In *The Management of Change: Market Testing and Outsourcing of IT Services*. Elite/British Computer Society, London.

Willcocks, L. and Lacity, M. (2000). Strategic Dimensions of IT Outsourcing. In FT (ed.) *Mastering Information Management*. FT/Prentice Hall, London.

Willcocks, L. and Lacity, M. (2000). Experience of Information Technology Outsourcing. In Angel, J. (ed.) *The Outsourcing Practice Manual*. Sweet & Maxwell, London.

Willcocks, L., Lacity, M. and Fitzgerald, G. (1995). Information Technology Outsourcing: Economics, Contracting and Measurement. In Farbey, B., Land F. and Targett, D. (eds) *Hard Money, Soft Outcomes: Evaluating and Managing the IT Investment*. Reprint, Alfred Waller, Henley.

Willcocks, L. and Sauer, C. (2001). Risk and its Management in IT Outsourcing. In Pritchard, J. (ed.) *Mastering Risk*. FT/Prentice Hall, London.

WORKING PAPERS

A range of Working Papers is available from Oxford Institute of Information Management, Contact `Jenny.Peachey@templeton.oxford.ac.uk`. Tel: 0044-(0)1865-422500.

Index